750 Spanish Verbs and Their Uses

Jan R. Zamir, Ph.D.

Edgardo J. Pantigoso, Ph.D.

Eduardo Estevanovich,
Profesor de Español

John Wiley & Sons, Inc.

New York • Chichester • Brisbane • Toronto • Singapore

Published by John Wiley & Sons, Inc.

Library of Congress Cataloging-in-Publication Data

Zamir, Jan Roshan, 1941–
    750 Spanish verbs and their uses / Jan Zamir, Edgardo J.
Pantigoso, Eduardo Estevanovich.
        p.   cm.
    ISBN 0-471-53939-2 (pbk. : alk. paper)
    1. Spanish language—Verb.   I. Pantigoso, Edgardo J.
II. Estevanovich, Eduardo.   III. Title.
PC4271.Z35   1992
468.2'421—dc20   92-8103

Printed in the United States of America

10 9 8

Preface

The main purpose of this book is to give the user a clear picture of the uses of 750 common Spanish verbs, with their prepositions in the proper contexts. A number of illustrative sentences for each entry implicitly reflect the various usages of the verb and its preposition in context.

For the most part, each verb is introduced first without a preposition in order to show the basic and the most common usage of the verb. If the verb is associated with a certain preposition, we provide the preposition within the meaning of the entry; and, under the same entry, we give examples that illustrate the verb with the preposition. If there is a strong collocation between the existing verb and the preposition, we present the verb with its preposition as a subentry (as a phrasal verb)—and herein lies one of the major contributions of this book.

In presenting the verbs with their prepositions, we thus distinguish between two types of verbal expressions. First are the verbs that are predominantly fixed to their prepositions, and often their collocation represents a meaning distinct from that of the main verb. (For example, in English we have such phrasal verbs as "hold up," "hold out," "hold on," "hold back," "hold down," "hold in," "hold off," "hold with,"...). We have presented these types of verbal phrases, following lexicographical convention, together with their objects or complements (e.g., noun, infinitive, gerund,...). Second, we have many common verbs that are not linguistically collocated with the prepositions in a fixed way but are found with given prepositions in certain frequent contexts. For example, we find in English the relationship "to speak up" or "to speak out" as being bound and constituting a phrasal verb; however, we find it useful for the reader to be aware also of the association of "to speak" with commonly used prepositions as in "to speak on (the phone)" or "to speak over (the loudspeaker)," "to speak under (his breath)," "to speak in (a whisper)," etc. For pedagogical reasons we found it useful to include both types.

We have made several critical decisions in the format of this book which make it uniquely valuable. First, we have varied the number of examples for each entry based on the level of difficulty posed by a particular verb to an English-speaking person. Hence, the more unusual expressions are treated more extensively. Second, the examples attempt to give as wide a range as possible for the semantic domain of each entry and include a wide range of phrasal and nominal collocations. Third, where appropriate, we attempt to present the examples in a structurally diversified manner so as to show various tenses. Finally, we have frequently attempted to elucidate the object/verb relationship. Most noticeably, whenever the forms of the direct and indirect object pronouns coalesce (*me, te, nos, os*), in our example, we often provide third-person forms (*lo/le, la/le*) instead in at least one of our Spanish sentences. Since the distinction between the direct and the indirect object pronoun is often more clear in the third person in Spanish, we believe this will help to illustrate this rather difficult aspect of the Spanish language for English speakers. However, the reader must note that this distinction in certain structures may be regionally determined and, thus, can vary in different parts of the Spanish-speaking world. At this juncture we should note that on rare occasions, where other word orders were possible, we have intentionally placed the prepositional objects in the proximity of the verb so as not to confuse the reader. We would also like to add here that our examples in this book are based on a current, everyday usage of the language; hence, we have avoided pedantic and unusual prescriptive structures.

This illustrative usage guide to Spanish verbs and their respective prepositions can be used at all levels of competency—both as an independent source and as a supplementary aid for developing writing skills, providing grammatical practice, etc.

Contents

Abbreviations Used in This Book

English	Abb.	Spanish
adjective	adj	adjectivo
adverb	adv	adverbio
something	algo	algo
for example	e.g.	por ejemplo
et cetera	etc	etcétera
figurative	fig	figurado
gerund	ger	gerundio
humorous	hum	humorístico
idiomatic	idiomatic	idiomático
that is	i.e.	esto es, es decir
infinitive	inf	infinitivo
informal	informal	informal
ironic	ironic	irónico
Latin America	LAm	latinoamericano
literally	lit	literalmente
literary	liter	literario
noun	noun	nombre
oneself	oneself	(a) sí mismo
or	or	o
past participle	ptp	participio pasado
poetic	poetic	poético
preposition	prep	preposición
proverb	prov	proverbio
reflexive	se	reflexivo
somebody	sb	alguien
something	sth	algo
subjunctive	subj	modo subjuntivo
somebody, someone	uno	uno, alguien

A

abalanzarse (hacia, sobre)   to spring (at, upon); to rush (toward, forward)

- El público se abalanzó hacia las salidas (/la entrada).
  The crowd rushed toward the exits (/entrance).

- El perro (/hombre) se abalanzó sobre los ladrones.
  The dog (/man) sprang at the thieves.

- La policía se abalanzó sobre los manifestantes.
  The police hurled themselves upon the demonstrators.

abandonar   to leave, abandon

- El hombre abandonó todo lo que tenía y se fue.
  The man abandoned everything he had and went away.

- El padre ha abandonado a su familia (/su esposa/sus amigos).
  The father has abandoned his family (/wife/friends).

- Abandonamos la idea de visitar a la abuelita (/de esperar en el parque).
  We abandoned the idea of visiting grandma (/waiting in the park).

abandonarse   to abandon *or* surrender oneself to

- Patricia se ha abandonado a su destino.
  Patricia has surrendered to her fate.

- No hay que abandonarse a la suerte.
  Don't leave everything to chance.

abatir   to shoot down, knock down; to destroy

- La artillería abatió tres aviones.
  The artillery shot down three planes.

- El cazador abatió tres pájaros.
  The hunter shot down three birds.

- Los obreros abatieron un árbol detrás de mi casa.
  The workers knocked (or cut) down a tree behind my house.

- Los ciudadanos decidieron abatir las casas viejas y abandonadas.
  The citizens decided to demolish the old and abandoned houses.

abatirse (sobre)   to swoop, pounce (on); (*fig*) to be depressed, get discouraged

- El águila se abatió sobre la liebre.
  The eagle swooped down on the hare.

- Los soldados se abatieron sobre la ciudad indefensa.
  The soldiers pounced on the defenseless city.

- No te vas a abatir por lo que te dijo. (*fig*)
  You will not get discouraged (or be depressed) because of what he told you.

abdicar a   to abdicate, give up

- El rey abdicó a la corona en 1789.
  The king gave up the crown in 1789.

- La reina abdicó al trono.
  The queen abdicated the throne.

abochornar   to heat up

- Al mediodía el sol abochorna en los trópicos.
  The sun heats up at noon in the tropics.

abochornarse (de)   to be ashamed, feel embarrassed (at, about)

- Él se abochornó cuando le dijeron que había fracasado en el examen.
  He felt ashamed when they told him that he had failed the exam.

- Ellos se abochornaron de su ropa porque era vieja.
  They were embarrassed about their old clothing.

- La madre se abochornó de la conducta de su hijo.
  The mother felt ashamed of her son's behavior.

aborrecer   to hate; to loathe

- Luis aborrece a María (/a su hermana).
  Luis hates María (/his sister).

- Aborrecemos el mal tiempo en la playa.
  We hate bad weather on the beach.

- Aborrece desvestirse cuando hace frío.
  She hates to undress when it's cold.

abrasar   to burn, burn up; to dry up

- El fuego abrasó todas las barracas.
  The fire burned all the barracks.

- Las llamas abrasaron el edificio (/la ciudad/toda la familia).
  The flames consumed the building (/city/entire family).

■   El sol abrasará la tierra algún día.
The sun will some day burn (or dry) up the earth.

abrasarse   to burn (up); to catch fire; to be parched

■   La carne (/comida) se abrasó en la parrilla.
The meat (/food) caught on fire on the grill.

■   Los condenados se abrasan en el infierno.
The condemned burn in hell.

■   Nuestros jardines (/nuestras flores/nuestras plantas) se abrasaron porque hacía mucho calor.
Our gardens (/flowers/plants) were parched because it was very warm.

abrasarse de algo   to burn with sth; (*fig*) to be dying of sth

■   María se abrasaba de calor (/de sed/de amor).
Mary was dying from the heat (/had a raging thirst/was burning with love or was violently in love).

abrazar   to embrace, hug

■   Juan abrazó a su hermano (/a su novia/a su esposa).
John hugged his brother(/his sweetheart/his wife).

■   El hombre abrazó una causa noble (/otra religión/una filosofía interesante).
The man embraced (or adopted) a noble cause (/another religion/an interesting philosophy).

abrazarse de algo   to cling to sth, clutch sth; to hug sth

■   La niña se abrazó de las piernas de su madre.
The child clung to her mother's legs.

■   El leñador se abrazó del árbol para no caerse.
The lumberjack clutched the tree so as not to fall.

■   Yo me abracé del pasamanos porque hacía mucho viento.
I hugged the railing because it was so windy.

abreviar   to abbreviate; to shorten

■   Hay que abreviar esta conversación; no tenemos bastante tiempo.
This conversation must be shortened; we don't have enough time.

■   Vamos a abreviar su nombre porque no cabe en el renglón.
We are going to abbreviate your name because it doesn't fit into the line.

■   Yo abrevié mi estancia en Londres para poder visitar Stratford.
I shortened my stay in London in order to be able to visit Stratford.

■   Bueno, para abreviar les contaré el final del cuento.
Well, in order to make it short, I'll tell you the end of the story.

abrigar (de)   to protect, shelter (from); to keep warm; to wrap up; to harbor (*fig*)

- Las montañas abrigan el valle de los vientos.
  The mountains protect the valley from the winds.

- Este saco de lana lo abriga mucho.
  This woolen coat keeps him very warm.

- ¡Abriga bien al niño porque hace frío afuera!
  Button up the child because it's cold outside!

- Creo que ese hombre abriga malas intenciones.
  I think that man harbors bad intentions.

abrigarse   to bundle up, wrap up

- Me abrigo los pies (/la cabeza) cuando paleo nieve.
  I bundle up my feet (/head) when I shovel snow.

abrigarse de algo   to protect against/from sth

- Me abrigué del viento detrás de esa pared.
  I protected myself from the wind behind that wall.

- Los pájaros se abrigan de la lluvia debajo de las ramas de los árboles.
  Birds protect themselves from rain under branches of trees.

abrir   to open; to open up

- Yo abro las ventanas del dormitorio para dormir.
  I open the bedroom windows to sleep.

- Abrió la tienda (/el libro/la camisa/la mano/los ojos).
  He opened the store (/the book/the shirt/his hand/his eyes).

- ¿Quieres abrir el regalo (/el cofre/la caja)? —Sí, lo (/la) abro ahora.
  Do you want to open the gift (/case/box)? —Yes, I'm opening it now.

abrirse   to open; to open out, unfold, spread out

- Ella se abrió la blusa (/el abrigo).
  She opened up her blouse (/coat).

- El chico se cayó de la bicicleta y se abrió la cabeza.
  The boy fell from the bicycle and split open his head.

- Un paisaje maravilloso se abría ante nosotros.
  A beautiful countryside was unfolding before us.

- La ventana (/puerta) se abre hacia el patio.
  The window (/door) opens out to a patio.

absolver (de)   to absolve (from), acquit, clear

- El cura lo absolvió de todos sus pecados.
  The priest absolved him of all his sins.

- El juez absolvió a los acusados.
  The judge acquitted the accused.
- Fue absuelto de todos los cargos.
  He was cleared of all charges.

absorber   to absorb; to soak up
- La esponja absorbe el agua.
  The sponge absorbs water.

abstenerse   to abstain; to refrain
- ¡Absténganse cuando duden!
  When in doubt, abstain!

abstenerse de algo   to abstain from sth; to refrain from sth
- Tengo que abstenerme del tabaco (/del alcohol/del vino).
  I have to abstain from smoking (/alcohol/wine).

abstenerse de + *inf*   to abstain from + *ger*, to refrain from + *ger*
- Los invitados se abstienen de fumar en nuestra casa.
  The guests refrain from smoking in our house.
- ¡Abstente de intervenir en mis negocios (/en mis asuntos)!
  Refrain from meddling in my business (/in my affairs)!
- Me abstuve de intervenir por no ofenderle.
  I refrained from intervening so as not to offend him.
- Los electores se abstuvieron de votar.
  The electorates refrained from voting.

aburrir (con)   to bore (with), weary
- Me aburre este trabajo.
  This job bores me.
- Le aburren las discusiones.
  Discussions bore her.
- La película los aburrió (/La película aburrió a mis padres).
  The movie bored them (/my parents).
- Él nos aburre con sus cuentos (/quejas).
  He bores us with his stories (/complaints).
- Yo aburrí a los alumnos con mi lección.
  I bored the students with my lesson.
- Sus lecciones aburren hasta las moscas.
  His lessons would bore one to death (i.e., would bore even flies).

aburrirse   to be bored, get bored

- Yo me aburro mucho porque no tengo nada que hacer.
  I am so bored because I have nothing to do.
- Se aburrió enseñándole la lección al chico.
  He got bored teaching the lesson to the boy.

aburrirse con/de uno/algo, por algo   to get *or* be bored with/because of sb/sth

- Ellas se aburren con los sermones largos.
  They get bored with long sermons.
- Marta dice que se aburre con su novio.
  Martha says that she gets bored with her boyfriend.
- Los amigos de Roberto se aburrieron de las vacaciones.
  Robert's friends became bored with the vacation.
- Mi madre se aburre por la soledad.
  My mother is bored because of loneliness.
- No creo que usted se haya aburrido por mí.
  I do not think that you got bored because of me.

aburrise de + *inf*   to be bored with, be tired of + *ger*

- Los niños no se aburren de jugar.
  The children are not bored with playing.
- Mi hermano se aburre de no hacer nada.
  My brother is bored of (or bored with) doing nothing.

abusar de uno/algo   to abuse sb/sth, take advantage of sb/sth

- Oscar abusó de la bebida (/del tabaco/de la comida).
  Oscar drank (/smoked/ate) too much.
- Él abusó de la cortesía que le brindaron.
  He abused the courtesy he was given.
- El jefe abusa de sus empleados.
  The boss takes advantage of his employees.
- Ese hombre abusó de una mujer.
  That man abused a woman.

acabar   to finish, end up, come to an end

- Por fin he acabado este trabajo.
  Finally, I've finished this job.
- ¿Acabaste el libro (/la lección/el cuento)?
  Did you finish the book (/the lesson/the short story)?
- Cuando acabes, ¡avísame!
  When you are done, let me know.

■ Si no se cuida, acabará enfermándose (/cogiendo un resfriado).
If he does not take care of himself, he will end up getting sick (/catching a cold).

acabar con uno/algo   to end with sb/sth, put an end to sb/sth, destroy sb/sth, finish
off sb/sth

■ Su nombre (/La palabra) acaba con P.
His name (/The word) ends in P.

■ La novela acaba con un diálogo triste.
The novel ends with a sad dialogue.

■ El nuevo gobierno acabó con la influencia extranjera.
The new government put an end to foreign influence.

■ La peste acabó con las cosechas de trigo.
The pest destroyed the wheat harvest.

■ Vas a acabar con mi paciencia.
You are going to wear my patience thin.

■ Este frío va a acabar con nosotros.
This cold weather is going to do us in.

acabar de + *inf*   to have just + *ptp*; to finish + *ger*

■ Ella acaba de escribir una carta a su tía.
She has just written a letter to her aunt.

■ Acabábamos de salir cuando llegaron los invitados.
We had just left when the guests arrived.

■ Tendremos más dinero cuando acabemos de pagar la deuda.
We'll have more money when we finish paying the debt.

acabar en algo   to end up (in) sth

■ Después de mucho caminar ellos acabaron en el pueblo.
After much walking, they ended up in the town.

■ Tomó tanto licor que acabó en alcohólico.
He drank so much liquor that he ended up an alcoholic.

acabar por + *inf*   to end up + *ger*

■ La mujer acabó por volverlo loco.
The woman ended up driving him crazy.

■ Con tanto tiempo sin dinero ni trabajo, acabó por robar a la gente.
Without a job or money for so long, he ended up robbing people.

■ Si seguimos presionándolo, acabará por ceder.
If we continue pressuring him, he will end up yielding.

■ Jaime acabó por casarse con Sonia.
Jaime finally ended up marrying Sonia.

acabarse   to run out of

- No se les acabaron las provisiones.
  They didn't run out of groceries.

- La película (/conferencia/clase) se acabó a las ocho.
  The film (/lecture/class) finished at eight o'clock.

- A Juan se le acabó el tabaco (/la gasolina/la paciencia).
  John ran out of cigarettes (/gas/patience).

- Se le (/Se nos/Se me) acabó el dinero.
  His (/Our/My) money ran out or He (/We/I) ran out of money.

acalorarse   (*fig*) to get hot, warm up; (*fig*) to get worked up, upset

- Los hombres se acaloraron con el vino.
  The men warmed up because of the wine.

- Se acaloraron discutiendo de política.
  They got worked up discussing politics.

- Ella se acaloró por las burlas del público.
  She became upset because of the heckling of the public.

acampar   to camp

- Acamparon a las orillas del lago.
  They camped by the lake shore.

- Durante el verano, acampamos en la playa (/en el bosque/en las montañas).
  During the summer we camp on the beach (/in the forest/in the mountains).

acceder   to accede, agree

- El Presidente accedió a recibir a los delegados.
  The President agreed to receive the delegates.

- Accedo a tu pedido.
  I agree to your request.

acelerar   to accelerate; to speed up

- El chofer aceleró el coche.
  The driver accelerated the car.

- Las fábricas van a acelerar la producción de latas.
  The factories are going to speed up the production of cans.

- Las emociones aceleran las palpitaciones del corazón.
  Emotions accelerate heart palpitations.

acelerarse   to hurry, hasten

- Se aceleró el ritmo de la marcha.
  The walking pace was accelerated.

■   Con el miedo se acelera el pulso.
    Fear accelerates the heartbeat.

aceptar   to accept; to approve

■   Aceptaron a Juan en el club.
    They accepted John in the club.

■   El gobierno aceptó el tratado de la república del norte.
    The government approved the treaty of the northern republic.

aceptar + *inf*   to agree to + *inf*

■   Aceptaron comer con nosotros.
    They agreed to eat with us.

■   ¿Aceptaste manejar a Limón?
    Did you agree to drive to Limon?

acercar algo   to bring sth near/over/closer

■   Su presencia acercó a las dos familias.
    His presence brought the two families closer (to one another).

■   Ella acercó la luz al espejo.
    She brought the light over to the mirror.

■   ¡Acerca tu silla a la mesa!
    Bring your chair near the table.

■   ¡Acércame la sal (/la pimienta/ese libro)!
    Pass me the salt (/pepper/that book).

acercarse a algo   to draw near sth, approach sth

■   El cometa se acercará a la tierra.
    The comet will draw near the earth.

■   Me acercaba a la edad de la jubilación, cuando mi esposa murió.
    I was approaching retirement age when my wife died.

■   Su sugerencia nos acerca a la solución. (*fig*)
    His suggestion brings us closer to the solution.

acercarse a uno   to approach sb, come up to sb, go up to sb

■   Ella se acercó a él para besarlo.
    She approached (or came up to) him in order to kiss him.

■   Se me acercó en la calle (/en la escuela/en la clase).
    He came up to (or approached) me in the street (in school/in class).

■   María se acercó a su madre para oírla mejor.
    Mary went up to her mother in order to hear her better.

acertar   to get right; to hit (the mark)

- Esta vez sí lo acertaste.
  This time you got it right.

acertar a + *inf*   to manage to + *inf*, succeed in + *ger*

- Me doy cuenta de que no aciertas a entender la tesis.
  I realize you don't (or aren't managing to) understand the thesis.

- El niño no acierta a escribir las letras correctamente.
  The child does not succeed in writing the letters correctly.

acertar con algo   to hit on/upon sth; to get sth

- Has acertado con el color (/vestido/coche) que yo quería.
  You have hit on the color (/dress/car) I wanted.

- Acerté con el camino (/esta idea) por casualidad.
  I hit upon the way (/this idea) by accident.

- He trabajado en este problema por horas y no acierto con la solución.
  I've worked on this problem for hours, and I can't get the answer.

- Acertó con los números de la lotería.
  He got the lottery numbers right.

aclamar   to acclaim, applaud, hail

- Lo aclamaron jefe (/rey).
  He was acclaimed as a leader (/king).

- Aclamaron al rey (/jefe)
  They hailed (or applauded) the king (/leader).

aclarar   to rinse; to thin, thin down; to clear; (*fig*) to clarify, cast light on, explain

- El color de tu camisa está muy oscuro, tenemos que aclararlo un poquito.
  The color of your shirt is too dark; we have to rinse it a little.

- Esta pintura está muy oscura, tendremos que aclararla con agua.
  This paint is too dark; we'll have to thin it down with water.

- Ellos tuvieron que aclarar un trecho de selva para poder levantar sus tiendas.
  They had to clear a patch of jungle in order to set up camp.

- Todo el día estuvo muy nublado, pero a las cinco de la tarde aclaró.
  It was cloudy all day, but at five in the afternoon it cleared up.

- ¡Aclárame lo que has dicho!
  Explain to me what you have said!

- No entendía las ideas de ese filósofo, pero tú me las has aclarado.
  I did not understand the ideas of that philosopher, but you have clarified them for me.

aclararse   to catch on, get it

- Después de esa explicación, se le aclararon las cosas al estudiante.
  After that explanation, the student caught on to things.

- Se nos aclaró el contrato una vez que lo releímos.
  We understood the contract once we reread it.

acoger   to receive, greet, shelter, take in

- A su llegada a esa ciudad, Pedro fue acogido calurosamente.
  Upon his arrival to that city, Peter was received (or greeted) warmly.

- Cuando llegó a su casa, la acogieron con cariño.
  When she arrived at their house, they greeted her affectionately.

- Estéfano fue desterrado por la dictadura, pero lo acogieron en tu país.
  Stephan was exiled by the dictatorship, but he was received in your country.

acogerse   to take refuge; (*fig*) to come under

- Llovía fuertemente y se acogió debajo de un árbol.
  It was raining hard, and he took refuge under a tree.

- Se acogieron a la ley de amnistía general. (*fig*)
  They came (or took refuge) under the general amnesty law.

- Como jubilados se acogen al reglamento del seguro social. (*fig*)
  As retirees they come under social security regulations.

acometer   to attack; to overcome

- Acometieron el trabajo con entusiasmo.
  They attacked the job with enthusiasm.

- Acometieron al enemigo (/invasores extranjeros).
  They attacked (or overcame) the enemy (/foreign invaders).

- El ladrón lo acometió a cuchillazos.
  The thief attacked him with a knife.

- Le acometió la tristeza (/las ganas de llorar/las dudas).
  He was overcome with sadness (/a desire to cry/doubts).

- Fue acometido por el miedo.
  He was filled (or overcome) with fear.

- Me acometió la idea de marcharme.
  The idea of going away came to me.

acomodar   to accommodate, place; to arrange; to lodge

- Acomodaron el mueble en un rincón de la sala.
  They placed (or arranged) the piece of furniture in a corner of the room.

- Acomodamos la sala porque los invitados la habían dejado muy desordenada.
  We arranged the room because the guests had left it in a mess.

■   El hotel estaba lleno, pero el administrador los acomodó en una pequeña habitación.
The hotel was full but the manager lodged them in a small room.

acomodarse a algo   to adapt oneself to sth, comply with sth

■   Tuvieron que acomodarse a las circunstancias.
They had to adapt to the circumstances.

■   Ellos se acomodaron al horario de trabajo.
They adapted to (or complied with) the work schedule.

acompañar   to go with, accompany

■   Este vino acompaña bien la comida.
This wine goes well with the meal.

■   Ella cantaba y él la acompañaba al piano.
She sang, and he accompanied her on the piano.

■   María acompañó a su amiga al cine.
Mary went to the movies with her friend.

■   Lo acompañaré a su casa (/hasta la puerta) porque es tarde.
I'll take you home (/see you to the door) because it's late.

■   Lo acompaño en su dolor.
I share in your sorrow.

aconsejar   to advise, counsel

■   Le aconsejó no viajar a ese país.
He advised her not to travel to that country.

■   Le aconsejo que renuncie.
I advise (or counsel) you to resign.

aconsejarse con/de uno   to consult sb

■   Me aconsejé con mi abogado (/médico).
I consulted my lawyer (/doctor).

■   Tengo que aconsejarme de un buen especialista.
I have to consult a good specialist.

acordar   to agree on, decide

■   Acordaron la fecha de la próxima reunión.
They decided on the date for the next meeting.

■   Los dos no acuerdan un precio.
The two don't agree on a price.

acordar + *inf*   to agree to + *inf*, decide to + *inf*

■   Ambos países (/líderes) han acordado estrechar relaciones culturales.
Both countries (/leaders) have agreed to tighten their cultural relations.

■   Acordaron trabajar por la paz.
They agree (or decided) to work for peace.

■   Nosotros acordamos no discutir de política.
We agreed not to discuss political issues.

acordarse de uno/algo   to remember, recall sb/sth

■   No me acuerdo de aquella mujer (/María/la guerra).
I don't remember or recall that woman (/Mary/the war).

■   ¿Te acuerdas de esta fotografía (/mí/este cuento)?
Do you remember this picture (/me/this story)?

■   No me acuerdo del nombre del libro (/de usted).
I don't remember the name of the book (/your name).

acordarse de + *inf*   to remember to + *inf*

■   ¿Te acordaste de comprar leche?
Did you remember to buy milk?

■   No me acordé de mandarle un regalo.
I did not remember to send him a gift.

■   Julio se acuerda de visitarnos sólo cuando necesita dinero.
Julio remembers to visit us only when he needs money.

acostar   to put to bed

■   La madre acostó al niño en la cama.
The mother put the child to bed.

■   La niñita acuesta a la muñeca en la cunita.
The little girl puts the doll to bed in her little crib.

■   El enfermero acostó al herido en la camilla.
The nurse put the injured person on the stretcher.

acostarse (en)   to go to bed; to lie down (on)

■   ¿A qué hora te acuestas? —Normalmente, me acuesto a las once.
At what time do you go to bed? —Usually I go to bed at eleven.

■   Nos acostamos ahora. Es hora de acostarse.
We're going to bed. It is bedtime.

■   Los chicos se acuestan en la nieve (/playa).
The children are lying down in the snow (/on the beach).

■   Buscó un lugar cerca del río y se acostó en la hierba.
He looked for a place near the river, and he lay down on the grass.

acostumbrar + *inf*   to be used to + *ger*, be in the habit of + *ger*

■   Acostumbran celebrar su cumpleaños en la playa.
They are in the habit of celebrating his birthday on the beach.

- Acostumbramos pintar la casa cada primavera.
  We are used to painting the house each spring.
- Acostumbro levantarme temprano.
  I'm used to (or in the habit of) getting up early.

acostumbrar a uno a algo   to get sb used to sth; to accustom sb to doing sth

- Nos costó mucho acostumbrar a los niños a lavarse los dientes después de comer.
  It was difficult to accustom the children to brushing their teeth after eating.
- No lo han acostumbrado al trabajo (/a la vida de cado).
  They have not gotten him used to working (/married life).

acostumbrarse a + algo   to become used to sth, become accustomed to sth

- No se puede acostumbrar a los zapatos nuevos (/a la vida rural).
  He cannot get used to his new shoes (/to life in the country).
- Nosotros no nos acostumbramos a la contaminación de la ciudad.
  We can't (or don't) get used to the city's pollution.

acostumbrarse a + *inf*   to get used to + *ger*

- Se acostumbró a beber café después de comer.
  He got used to drinking coffee after a meal.
- Se acostumbró a trabajar de noche.
  He got used to working at night.
- Me he acostumbrado a leer caminando.
  I've gotten used to reading while walking.

acudir a uno/algo   to come *or* go to sb/sth; to turn to sb/sth; to respond to sb/sth

- Don Pedro acude al parque todos los domingos por la tarde.
  Don Pedro goes to the park every Sunday afternoon.
- Él acude siempre a sus citas puntualmente.
  He always comes to his appointment punctually.
- Ana acudió a su compañero de colegio para conseguir trabajo.
  Ana turned (or went) to her high school classmate in order to get a job.
- Siempre acude a su madre para salir de los problemas.
  He always turns to his mother in order to get out of his problems.
- Acudieron a los gritos de la víctima.
  They responded to the cries of the victim.
- La idea de un préstamo acudió a su mente.
  The idea of a loan came to his mind.

acudir a + *inf*   to come to + *inf*, respond to + *inf*, turn up to + *inf*

- La madre acudió a ayudar a su hijo que estaba enfermo.
  The mother came (or turned up) to help her son who was ill.

■   Mucha gente acudió a oír al presidente.
    Many people turned up (or responded) to hear the president.

acusar   to show, reveal, register

■   El rostro de Juan acusó sorpresa.
    John's face showed (or registered) surprise.

■   Su silencio acusa mala educación.
    His silence betrays bad manners.

acusar a uno de algo   to accuse sb of sth, blame sb for sth

■   Luis acusó a su mejor amigo.
    Luis accused his best friend.

■   Acusaron al presidente de debilidad.
    The president was accused of weakness.

■   Los acusé del accidente (/de todas nuestras desdichas).
    I blamed them for the accident (/for all our misfortunes).

acusar de + *inf*   to accuse of + *ger*, charge with + *ger*

■   Ha sido acusado de robar el banco.
    He has been charged with robbing the bank.

■   Lo acusan de ser negligente (*or* Lo acusan por negligencia).
    He is accused of negligence.

■   Ella lo acusa de ser el causante de sus problemas.
    She accuses him of being the cause of her problems.

acusarse de algo   to confess sth

■   Me acuso de un pecado (ante el sacerdote/ante mi esposa).
    I confess a sin (to the priest/to my wife).

■   Se acusaron de su crimen a la policía.
    They confessed their crime to the police.

acusarse de + *inf*   to confess to + *ger*

■   Se ha acusado de haberlo hecho.
    He has confessed to having done it.

■   Se acusó de robar el banco.
    He confessed to robbing the bank.

adaptar (a, para)   to adapt, adjust (to); to make suitable

■   Ha adaptado su radio para escuchar emisoras extranjeras.
    He has adjusted his radio in order to listen to foreign radio stations.

■   El país ha adaptado su red telefónica al sistema internacional.
    The country has adapted its telephone network to the international system.

adaptarse a algo   to adapt oneself to sth

■   El muchacho se ha adaptado muy bien a la nueva situación.
The boy has adapted himself very well to his new situation.

■   Los elefantes se adaptan fácilmente al trabajo de circo.
Elephants adapt well to circus work.

adelantar   to move forward, move on, advance

■   La tecnología ha adelantado mucho.
Technology has advanced a great deal.

■   En primavera adelantan los relojes.
In spring clocks are moved forward.

■   El estudiante ha adelantado en sus estudios.
The student has advanced (or moved on) in his studies.

adelantarse   to go forward, move ahead, get ahead

■   La columna de tanques se adelantó a la infantería.
The column of tanks moved ahead of the infantry.

■   Para evitar el accidente tuvo que adelantarse.
In order to avoid the accident she had to go forward.

■   Te has adelantado a los acontecimientos.
You've gotten ahead of events.

adeudar(se)   to owe

■   Se adeudan dos millones.
Two million are owed.

■   Ahora no puedo pagarle, así que le voy a adeudar ese dinero.
Right now I cannot pay you, so I'll owe you that money.

adherir(se) (a)   to adhere, stick (to)

■   Esta goma se adhiere a la madera con facilidad.
This glue sticks to wood easily.

■   ¡Adhiera sello al sobre!
Stick the stamp on the envelope.

adivinar   to guess; to foretell, prophesy

■   ¿Puedes adivinar quién lo hizo?
Can you guess who did it?

■   Ella adivinó el resultado del partido.
She guessed the score of the game.

■   ¿Adivina con quién hablas?
Can you guess who(m) you are talking to?

admirar   to admire

- Admiro su valor (/talento/capacidad de trabajo).
  I admire his courage (/talent/capacity for work).

- Luisa admira el arte de Picasso.
  Luisa admires Picasso's art.

- Ellos siempre han admirado a Juan.
  They have always admired John.

- A ese jugador lo admiran por su velocidad.
  That player is admired because of his speed.

- Me admira su franqueza.
  I am amazed at his frankness.

admirarse   to be amazed, be astonished; to admire

- Te admirarás cuando veas el espectáculo.
  You will be amazed (or astonished) when you see the show.

- No debe admirarse lo malo.
  One should not admire what is bad.

admitir   to admit; to accept

- Admito que no he dicho la verdad.
  I admit that I have not told the truth.

- Me han admitido en la universidad.
  I've been admitted (or accepted) to the university.

- Lo admitieron en la escuela de oficiales.
  He was admitted (or accepted) to officer's school.

admitir + *inf*   to admit to + *ger*

- Admitió decir la verdad (/tener tres novias).
  He admitted to telling the truth (/to having three girlfriends).

- Admitió haber estado en la cárcel.
  He admitted to having been in jail.

adoptar   to adopt

- Adoptaron a un niño pobre.
  They adopted a poor child.

- Desafortunadamente, ellos adoptaron una actitud negativa.
  Unfortunately, they adopted a negative attitude.

- El comité adoptó la resolución de condena.
  The committee adopted the resolution of condemnation.

- Ella ha adoptado la moda francesa en sus creaciones.
  She has adopted the French fashion in her creations.

adorar   to adore, worship

■ Ese muchacho adora a su mamá (/a su novia).
That boy adores (or *worships*) *his mom* (/*girlfriend*).

■ La gente adoraba a los dioses en el templo.
People worshipped the gods in the temple.

■ Luisa adora la playa.
Luisa adores the beach.

adormecer   to make sleepy, put to sleep

■ El licor adormece.
Liquor makes you sleepy.

■ El ruido del tren adormeció al niño.
The noise of the train made the child sleepy.

■ Lo adormecieron antes de operarlo.
They put him to sleep before the operation.

adormecerse   to get sleepy, fall asleep

■ Ella se adormeció esperando al médico.
She got sleepy (or *fell asleep*) *waiting for the doctor.*

■ El niño se adormece con el arrullo de la madre.
The child falls asleep to the mother's lullaby.

■ Tú te adormeces cuando miras televisión.
You get sleepy when you watch television.

adornar   to decorate, adorn

■ María adorna siempre la mesa con flores.
Mary decorates the table with flowers.

■ Las chicas adornaron el coche con cintas.
The girls adorned the car with ribbons.

adornar de/con algo   to decorate with sth

■ El altar estaba adornado de (*or* con) flores frescas.
The altar was decorated with fresh flowers.

■ La corona adornada de (*or* con) diamantes vale diez millones de dólares.
The crown, decorated with diamonds, is worth ten million dollars.

■ La montaña estaba adornada de (*or* con) nubes rojas.
Red clouds adorned the mountain.

adueñarse de algo   to take possession of, appropriate

■ Se adueñaron de la casa por la fuerza.
They took possession of the house by force.

■ El gobierno va a adueñarse de los yacimientos petrolíferos.
The government is going to take possession of (or appropriate) the oilfields.

■ Esa chica se ha adueñado de su corazón.
That girl has taken possession of his heart.

advertir   to warn, alert, notice, observe

■ Les advertimos que no debían arrojar la basura allí.
We warned them not to throw the garbage there.

■ La policía advirtió al público sobre el peligro.
The police warned (or alerted) the public about the danger.

■ La madre advierte que los niños están jugando.
The mother notices (or observes) that the children are playing.

afanarse en algo   to apply oneself to sth

■ Él se afanaba en los estudios.
He applied himself to his studies.

■ La cocinera se afanó en la preparación de la comida.
The cook applied herself to the preparation of the meal.

afanarse por + *inf*   to strive to + *inf*

■ Se afana por conseguir un trabajo en la ciudad.
He is striving to get a job in the city.

■ Ellos se afanan por terminar temprano.
They are trying to finish early.

■ El bebé se afana por tomar su biberón.
The baby is eager to have his bottle.

afectar   to affect, have an effect on

■ Su accidente (/su muerte) lo afectó mucho.
His accident (/his death) affected him very much.

■ El huracán afectó la economía de la costa.
The hurricane affected (or had an effect on) the economy of the coast.

■ Esa enfermedad afecta el sistema nervioso.
That illness affects the nervous system.

afeitar   to shave

■ El barbero lo afeita todos los sábados.
The barber shaves him every Saturday.

■ Le afeitaron el bigote.
They shaved off his moustache.

afeitarse   to shave

■ El se afeita antes de bañarse.
He shaves before bathing.

- Se cortó cuando se afeitaba.
  He cut himself while shaving.

aficionarse a algo   to become fond of sth, to take to sth

- Él se aficiona a los chocolates (/a los helados/a la música clásica/a la numismática).
  He is fond of chocolate (/ice cream/classical music/numismatics).
- ¡No te aficiones a la buena vida!
  Don't get too used to (or fond of) the good life!

aficionarse a + *inf*   to get used to + *ger*

- Te estás aficionando a beber mucho.
  You are getting used to drinking a lot!
- En el ejército él se aficionó a levantarse muy temperano.
  In the army he got used to getting up very early.

agarrar (de, a)   to grasp, grab (from); to hold (on, by), catch

- Yo agarro mi maletín.
  I am holding my briefcase.
- ¡Agarra el libro!, por favor. —Bueno, lo agarraré.
  Hold this book, please. —Okay, I'll hold it.
- Él agarra al niño porque llora (/para que no se caiga).
  He holds the baby because he is crying (/so that he will not fall).
- Lo agarraron cuando robaba otro banco.
  They caught him when he was robbing another bank.
- Anoche hizo mucho frío y agarré un resfriado.
  Last night it was very cold, and I caught a cold.
- Lo agarró de (*or* por) la camisa (/de los pelos/de los pies).
  She held (or grasped) him by the shirt (/hair/feet).
- Agarré a Juan de (*or* por) la camisa (/manga).
  I grasped (or grabbed or held) John by the shirt (/sleeve).

agarrarse (de)   to hold on, grasp (from)

- Me agarré de la ventana.
  I held on from (or grasped) the window.
- Se agarró de la rama para poder subir.
  She held on to the branch in order to climb.

agitar   to wave, shake up, stir; (*fig*) to agitate

- Agito el café para que se disuelva el azúcar.
  I stir the coffee so that the sugar will dissolve.
- El marinero agitaba hábilmente las banderas para transmitir el mensaje.
  The sailor waved the flags skillfully to transmit the message.

- Ese hombre está agitando a los obreros de las fábricas.
  That man is agitating the factory workers.

- Esas palabras han agitado a Juan.
  Those words have agitated (or shaken up) John.

agitarse   to become agitated *or* nervous

- Cuando le hablan de dinero siempre se agita.
  When they talk to him about money, he always gets agitated (or nervous).

- Se agitó mucho por la presión del trabajo.
  He became agitated due to the pressure of the job.

agradar   to please, be pleasing to

- No le agrada este libro (/la comida/su actitud/la música popular).
  This book (/The food/Her attitude/Popular music) doesn't please him.

- Nos agradó mucho verlo nuevamente (/hablar con el director).
  We were pleased to see him again (/to speak to the director).

agradecer   to thank (for), be thankful for

- Agradecemos siempre que nos invitan a comer.
  We always say (or give) thanks when they invite us to eat.

- Le agradecí la tarjeta (/el regalo).
  I thanked him for the card (/gift).

agravar   to aggravate, make worse

- El resfriado agravó su enfermedad.
  The cold aggravated his illness.

- Las huelgas (/Esos incidentes) han agravado la situación económica.
  The strikes (/Those incidents) have aggravated (or made . . . worse) the economic situation.

agregar (a)   to add, join (to)

- Hemos agregado otra sección.
  We have added another section.

- Ahora, agregue tres cucharadas de azúcar a la mezcla.
  Now add three tablespoons of sugar to the mixture.

- Agregaron un nuevo submarino a la flota.
  They added a new submarine to the fleet.

- Dos nuevos profesores han sido agregados a la universidad.
  Two new professors have been added to (or have joined) the university.

aguardar   to expect; to wait for

- Estoy aguardando su llamada.
  I'm waiting for (or expecting) his call.

- ¡Aguarda aquí hasta que yo llegue!
  Wait here until I arrive.

- Aguardamos a que llegara el director para informarnos sobre el incidente.
  We're waiting for (or expecting) the director to come to inform us about the incident.

ahogar (en)   to drown (in), soak

- Ahogaron la cebolla en el aceite.
  They soaked the onion in the oil.

- Sus acciones han ahogado las esperanzas del país. (*fig*)
  His actions have drowned the country's hopes.

ahogarse (en)   to drown (in)

- Él se ahogó en el mar (/la piscina/el río).
  He drowned in the ocean (/pool/river).

- Ellos se ahogaron en agua poco profunda.
  They drowned in shallow water.

ahorrar   to save, economize

- Ella ahorra cien pesos cada mes.
  She saves a hundred pesos each month.

- Esta gente no ahorra mucho.
  These people do not save (or economize) much.

ahorrarse   to save, avoid

- Si lo hago ahora, me ahorraré trabajo más tarde.
  If I do it now, I'll save myself (or avoid) work later.

- Esto les ahorrará un dolor de cabeza más tarde.
  This will save them a headache later.

- Nos ahorramos el pasaje porque el vecino nos llevó en su coche.
  We saved the fare because our neighbor took us in his car.

ajustar (a)   to adjust (to, into)

- Hay que ajustar el presupuesto a la nueva realidad económica.
  The budget must be adjusted to the new economic reality.

- Ajusté el tornillo porque estaba suelto.
  I tightened (or adjusted) the screw because it was loose.

ajustarse   to adjust, tighten

- Él se está ajustando a la cultura hispanoamericana.
  He's adjusting to Spanish American culture.

- Se ajustó la corbata (/la correa/el pantalón/los cordones de los zapatos).
  He tightened his tie (/belt/pants/shoe laces).
- El padre ajustó sus pasos a los del niño.
  The father adjusted his steps to those of the child.

alcanzar (a)   to reach, overtake, catch up; to be enough

- No puedo alcanzar esa fruta. La rama está muy alta.
  I can't reach that fruit. The branch is too high.
- ¡Alcánzame la pimienta (/las papas/el destornillador/esos zapatos)!, por favor.
  Pass me the pepper (/the potatoes/the screwdriver/those shoes), please.
- Lo que usted les paga no les alcanza.
  What you pay them is not enough.
- Lo alcancé cuando iba a abordar el tren.
  I caught up with (or overtook) him when he was boarding the train.
- El corredor español pudo alcanzar al francés.
  The Spanish runner was able to catch up to the French runner.
- El sueldo no me alcanza (para vivir).
  The salary is not enough for me (to live on).
- La harina no nos va a alcanzar (para hacer el pastel).
  The flour is not going to be enough (in order to make the cake).

alcanzar a + *inf*   to succeed in + *ger*, manage to + *inf*

- ¿Alcanzaste a llamar a mamá?
  Did you manage to call (or succeed in calling) Mom?
- Por fin alcanzó a hacer el trabajo (/a escribir su tarea/a ver al director).
  Finally, he managed to do the work (/do his homework/see the director).
- El profesor (/Su padre) no alcanza a comprenderle.
  The teacher (/His father) just can't understand him.
- Alcanzó a comer antes de salir.
  He managed to eat before leaving.

alegrar   to cheer (up), make happy

- Su visita (/premio/llamada/triunfo) la alegró mucho.
  His visit (/award/call/victory) cheered her up a lot (or made her very happy).
- Los payasos alegran a los niños.
  Clowns cheer children up (or make children happy).
- Las palabras del hijo alegraron a la madre.
  The words of the son cheered up the mother.

alegrarse (con, de, por)   to be glad, be happy (about)

- Me alegro mucho de que no estés enfermo ya.
  I am happy that you are no longer sick.

- Se alegraron con la llegada de la familia.
  They were happy about the family's arrival.

- Me alegré mucho de que Juan decidiera no venir.
  I was glad that John decided not to come.

- Te alegraste por haber recibido una carta.
  You were happy at having received a letter.

- Nos alegramos por su llegada.
  We are happy about (or because of) his arrival.

alegrarse de + *inf*   to be glad to + *inf*

- Se alegró de verlo (/de conocer el autor famoso).
  She was glad to see him (/to get to know the famous author).

- Nos alegramos de poder celebrar esta fiesta juntos.
  We are glad (or happy) to be able to celebrate this holiday together.

alejar (de)   to remove, move away (from)

- ¡Aleja la cama! Te puedes caer.
  Move the bed away. You can fall.

- Sus acciones alejaron toda sospecha.
  Her actions removed all suspicions.

- La madre aleja los vasos (/pasteles) del niño.
  The mother moves the glasses (/cakes) away from the child.

alejarse de algo   to move *or* get away from sth

- El automóvil se alejaba de la ciudad (/del camino).
  The car was moving away from the city (/road).

- Ella se ha alejado de sus amigos.
  She has gotten away from her friends.

- ¿No puedes alejarte de los vicios?
  Can't you get away from vices?

aliviar   to ease, relieve

- La aspirina alivia el dolor de cabeza.
  Aspirin relieves (or eases the pain of) a headache.

- Esta decisión va a aliviar a María.
  This decision is going to relieve Mary.

aliviarse de algo   be relieved of sth; to get better, recover

- Se ha aliviado de sus deudas (/su enfermedad).
  He has been relieved of his debts (/has recovered from his illness).

- Nos hemos aliviado de tener que hacerlo todos los días.
  We have been relieved from having to do it everyday.

almorzar   to have *or* eat lunch

- Almorzamos a la una (/al mediodía).
  We have lunch at one o'clock (/at noon).

- ¿A qué hora almuerzas? —Almuerzo a la una de la tarde.
  At what time do you eat lunch? —I have lunch at one o'clock in the afternoon.

alquilar   to rent

- Alquilaremos un coche para viajar.
  We'll rent a car to travel.

- Ellos alquilan un apartamento (/cuarto) en la calle central.
  They are renting an apartment (/room) on the main street.

alternar (con)   to alternate (with); to mix

- Yo alterno mis camisas; un día me pongo la azul, otro la blanca.
  I alternate my shirts; one day I wear the blue one, and, on the next day, the white one.

- Ella alterna su residencia entre Santiago y San Juan.
  She alternates her residence between Santiago and San Juan.

- Ellos alternan con políticos de la capital.
  They mix with politicians from the capital.

- Será mejor que él no alterne con esos chicos (/ese grupo).
  It will be better if he doesn't mix with those boys (/that group).

aludir a uno/a algo   allude to sb/sth, mention sb/sth

- Aludió al problema económico en ese discurso.
  He alluded to (or mentioned) the economic problem in that speech.

- En la carta ellos aludían a su propuesta anterior.
  In the letter they alluded to (or mentioned) their previous offer.

alumbrar   to shed light on, illuminate

- Él me (/le) alumbró el camino.
  He illuminated the way for me (/him).

- La vela alumbraba el cuarto.
  The candle illuminated the room.

- Tu sugerencia alumbró el problema.
  Your suggestion shed light on the problem.

alzar   to lift (up), pick up, raise (prices)

- Yo alcé los zapatos del suelo.
  I picked up the shoes from the floor.

- Alzamos al niño para que viera el desfile.
  We lifted up the child so he could see the parade.

- Han alzado el precio del arroz (/coche).
  They have raised the price of rice (/the car).

alzarse (contra)   to pick up; to raise up (against)

- El pueblo se alzó contra el tirano.
  The people rebelled (or rose up) against the tyrant.

- Se alzó el dinero que estaba en la mesa.
  He picked up the money that was on the table.

amar   to love

- Ella ama a su patria (/ama a su hija/ama sus libros).
  She loves her country (/daughter).

- Lo amaba con pasión (/ternura/cariño).
  She loved him passionately (/tenderly/affectionately).

amenazar (con, de)   to threaten (with)

- Amenazó a todo el mundo (/a mi hermano).
  He threatened everyone (/my brother).

- Me amenazó con un cuchillo.
  She threatened me with a knife.

- Lo amenazaron de muerte.
  They threatened him with death.

amenazar con + *inf*   to threaten to + *inf*

- Me amenazó con quitarme la vida.
  She threatened to kill me.

- Luis amenaza con dejar la universidad.
  Luis is threatening to leave the university.

amparar (de)   to protect (from)

- La iglesia ampara a los ancianos (/pobres/niños).
  The church protects the elderly (/poor/young).

- La ley ampara a los jubilados.
  The law protects the retired.

- Le amparó el presidente (del escándalo).
  The president protected him (from the scandal).

ampararse a algo   to have recourse to sth, seek protection under sth

- Él se amparó a los derecho humanos.
  He sought protection under human rights.

- Él se amparó a la ley y salió libre.
  He sought protection under (or had recourse to) the law and was released.

ampararse con/de algo   to protect with/from sth

■ El guerrero se amparó con su escudo.
The warrior protected himself with his shield.

■ Me amparé de la lluvia (/del frío) en una choza.
. *I protected myself from the rain (/cold) in a hut.*

amueblar (con, de)   to furnish (with)

■ Él amuebló la casa la semana pasada.
He furnished his house last week.

■ Amueblaron el apartamento con (*or* de) muebles metálicos.
They furnished the apartment with metal furniture.

andar   to go, go along, walk; to be

■ Él anda muy rápidamente.
He walks fast.

■ Luis anda a pie (/a caballo/en bicicleta).
Luis goes on foot (/on horseback/by bicycle).

■ Él anda tras un trabajo (/ladrón/una chica/un libro).
He is going after a job (/thief/a girl/a book).

■ Mi libro anda por aquí.
My book is around here.

■ Juan anda en los 25.
John is about 25.

andar en algo   to run into sth; to be engaged in sth

■ Él anda en problemas (/líos/amores/enredos).
He's running into problems (/difficulties or *He's in a muddle/He's in love/He's in a mess).*

■ Él anda de mensajero (/futbolista/vendedor).
He is engaged (or works) as a messenger (/soccer player/salesman).

animar   to enliven, liven up; to comfort, cheer up

■ El animó la fiesta con su canción.
He enlivened the party with his song.

■ Cuando estuve triste me animaron mucho.
When I was sad, they comforted me (or cheered me up) a lot.

animar a uno a + *inf*   to encourage sb to + *inf*

■ Me animaron a viajar (/cantar/trabajar/correr).
They encouraged me to travel (/sing/work/run).

animarse a + *inf*   to make up one's mind to + *inf*, resolve to + *inf*

- Me animé a cruzar el río (/a pilotear un avión/a aprender a nadar).
  I decided to cross the river (/pilot a plane/learn how to swim).
- Se animaron a hablarle a Rosita.
  They resolved to speak to Rosita.

anticipar   to anticipate; to cause to bring forward *or* in advance

- Anticipamos la llegada del presidente (/el mal acontecimiento).
  We anticipated the president's arrival (/bad turn).
- Anticipé el pago de la casa.
  I made the payment for the house ahead of time (or I made an advance payment for the house).

anticiparse   to take place *or* act before

- El gobierno se anticipó a los huelguistas y cerró las calles.
  The government acted ahead of the strikers and closed down the streets.
- Yo me anticipé a mis amigos y pagué la cuenta.
  I acted ahead of my friends and paid the bill.

anticiparse a + *inf*   to be *or* go *or* do sth ahead

- Nos anticipamos a pintar la casa antes de que lloviera.
  We went ahead with painting the house before it rained.
- Ella se anticipa a estudiar lo que el profesor explica al día siguiente.
  She studies ahead of time what the professor explains the following day.

anunciar   to announce; to foretell; to proclaim

- Anunciaron la llegada del vuelo 720.
  They announced the arrival of Flight 720.
- El periódico anuncia las próximas elecciones.
  The newspaper announces the upcoming elections.
- Algunos anuncian el fin del mundo.
  Some people foretell the end of the world.
- Anunciaron el reinado de Juan Carlos.
  They proclaimed the reign of Juan Carlos.

añadir (a)   to add (to)

- ¡Añade otro plato porque tenemos visitas!
  Add another place setting because we have visitors.
- Añadí cien dólares más al presupuesto mensual.
  I added a hundred more dollars to the monthly budget.

- Le añadí a la casa más habitaciones.
  I added more rooms to the house.
- La costurera añadió un encaje al vestido.
  The seamstress added lace to the dress.
- El profesor añadió tres páginas.
  The professor added three pages.

apagar   to put out (flame, fire), to extinguish; to turn off (light)

- El viento apagó la fogata.
  The wind put out the bonfire.
- Los bomberos apagaron el fuego (/los incendios).
  The firemen put out the fire (/flames).
- Apagaron la luz a las tres.
  They turned off the light at three.

apagarse   to quench, (*fig*) kill

- Sé apagó la luz por la tormenta.
  The lights went out because of the storm.
- Él se apagó la sed con vino.
  He quenched his thirst with wine.

aparecer (en, por)   to appear, show (*or* turn) up (in, on)

- Todas las mañanas aparece el sol. El sol aparece en el horizonte.
  The sun appears every morning. The sun appears on the horizon.
- Aparecieron langostas en los campos.
  Locusts appeared in the fields.
- Ya aparecieron las llaves.
  The keys showed (or turned) up already.

aparecerse (a, en)   to appear (to, in)

- El fantasma se apareció a los niños.
  The ghost appeared to the children.
- Después de dos años él se apareció en el pueblo.
  After two years he showed up (or appeared) in town.

apartar (de)   to separate, set aside, divide up, take away (from)

- Ella lo apartó de sus amigos.
  She separated him (or took him away) from his friends.
- ¡Aparta comida para el perrito!
  Set aside food for the puppy.
- Apartemos el dinero para la fiesta.
  Let's divide up (or set aside) the money for the party.

■   Apartaron tres asientos en el teatro.
   They set aside three seats in the theater.

apartarse de algo   to keep away from sth

■   Le dije que se apartara de la droga.
   I told him to keep away from drugs.

■   Hace muchos años que me aparté de ese grupo.
   I separated myself from that group a long time ago.

■   Él se apartó del camino.
   He kept away (or went off or deviated away) from the road.

apegarse a uno/algo   to become attached to sb/sth, grow fond of sb/sth

■   Él se apegó más a su padre que a su madre.
   He was more attached to his father than to his mother.

■   Me apego mucho a los lugares que visito.
   I become very attached to (or fond of) the places I visit.

■   Los niños se apegan mucho a los animales.
   Children are very fond of animals.

apelar a uno/algo   to appeal to sb/sth

■   Él apeló a sus vecinos para que lo ayudasen.
   He appealed to his neighbors for help.

■   El abogado apeló a un tribunal superior para que revocara la sentencia.
   The lawyer appealed to a higher court to revoke the sentence.

apenar   to grieve, trouble; to cause pain

■   La muerte apena.
   Death causes sadness (or grief).

apenarse de/por algo   to grieve sth, be distressed on acount of sth

■   No se apene por lo que le voy a decir.
   Don't be distressed by what I will tell you.

■   Ellos se apenaron de la muerte del abuelo.
   They grieved the death of their grandfather.

aplaudir   to applaud

■   Aplaudí al cantante.
   I applauded the singer.

■   Nosotros aplaudimos su actuación.
   We applauded her performance.

aplicar algo (a)   to apply sth (to)

- Aplicaron un criterio muy importante a este problema (/esa cuestión).
  They applied an important criterion to this problem (/that question).

- Necesitamos aplicar más pintura a esa pared.
  We need to apply more paint to that wall.

- Los médicos aplicaron electrochoque a mi abuelo enfermo.
  The doctors applied electro-shock to my sick grandfather.

aplicarse (a, en)   to work hard; to devote *or* dedicate *or* apply oneself (to)

- El alumno se aplica más este año.
  The student is applying himself more this year.

- Juan se aplicaba en el estudio.
  John worked hard at his studies.

- El profesor se aplica en escribir un libro.
  The professor is devoting (or dedicating) himself to writing a book.

- Esta ley se aplica a todos.
  This law applies to everyone.

apoderarse de algo   to take possession of sth

- Se apoderó del tesoro (/de las propiedades de su familia).
  He took possession of the treasure (/properties of his family).

- Nos apoderamos de la finca.
  We took possession of the farm.

apostar (a)   to bet, stake (on)

- No me gusta apostar.
  I don't like to bet.

- A él le gusta apostar a los caballos.
  He likes to bet on horses.

- Ella apostó tres pesos (/al ganador).
  She bet three pesos (/on the winner).

- Apostamos al corredor etíope.
  We bet on the Ethiopian runner.

- El teniente apostó tres vigías en la colina.
  The lieutenant staked (or placed) three watchmen on the hill.

apoyar (en)   to support; to lean, rest (on)

- Apoyamos la candidatura del senador Pérez.
  We support the candidacy of Senator Perez.

- Yo apoyo a María Pérez para presidenta del club.
  I support Mary Perez for the presidency of the club.

- La apoyó en la pared.
  He leaned it on the wall.

- Apoyaron las columnas en un suelo firme.
  They rested the columns on solid ground.

- Apoyé la silla (/escalera) en la pared.
  I leaned the chair (/ladder) against the wall.

apoyarse en algo   to lean on/against sth; to rest on sth

- Me apoyo en una silla para pararme.
  I lean on a chair in order to get up.

- Nos apoyamos en la familia cuando hay problemas. (*fig*)
  We lean on the family when there are problems.

- El edificio se apoya en cimientos sólidos.
  The building rests on a solid foundation.

aprender (de)   to learn (from)

- Él aprende la lección (/el poema/la historia).
  He is learning the lesson (/poem/history).

- Hay que aprender de los sabios (/mayores).
  One has to learn from the wise (/elders).

- Dice que aprendió de mí muchas cosas.
  He says that he learned many things from me.

aprender a +*inf*   to learn how to + *inf*

- Elena aprende a manejar (/hablar francés/cocinar).
  Elena is learning how to drive (/speak French/cook).

- Juana y María aprendieron a jugar tenis.
  Juana and Mary learned to play tennis.

aprestarse (para)   to get ready (for)

- Se aprestaban para un largo viaje.
  They were getting ready for a long trip.

- Nos aprestamos para salir a la calle.
  We are getting ready to go out.

aprestarse a + *inf*   to get ready to + *inf*

- Se aprestan a comer con la familia.
  They get ready to eat with the family.

- Te aprestabas a realizar un larga jornada.
  You were getting ready to take (or carry out) a long journey.

apresurar   to hurry, rush, hasten, quicken

- Apresuro a María para que no llegue tarde.
  I am hurrying (or rushing) Mary so that she doesn't arrive late.
- Ella apresuró el paso.
  She hastened (or quickened) her pace.

apresurar(se) a +*inf*   to hasten to + *inf,* hurry to + *inf*

- El profesor nos apresuró a terminar el examen.
  The professor hurried us to finish the exam.
- Me apresuro a concluir el trabajo.
  I hasten to finish the job.

apresurarse por + *inf*   to hurry in order to + *inf*

- Nos apresuramos por llegar a tiempo.
  We are hurrying in order to arrive on time.
- Te apresuraste por comprar los juguetes.
  You hurried in order to buy the toys.

apropiarse de algo   to appropriate sth

- Se apropió de nuestras ideas.
  He appropriated our ideas.
- Es un delito apropiarse de lo ajeno.
  It is a crime to appropriate what is not yours.

aprovechar   to make good use of, use, utilize

- Aprovecho la comida (/las lecciones/el dinero).
  I make good use of the food (/lessons/money).
- Él aprovecha en el estudio.
  He makes progress in his studies.
- Yo aproveché en matemáticas.
  I made progress in math.

aprovechar + *inf*   to take advantage of sth

- Aprovecho comer mucho cuando visito a mi mamá.
  When I visit my mother, I take advantage (of the situation) and eat a lot.
- Aprovechamos visitar la caverna.
  We took advantage of the visit to the cave.

aprovecharse de uno/algo   to take advantage of sb/sth

- Me aproveché de la oferta y compré un auto.
  I took advantage of the offer and bought a car.

- Se aprovechó de que yo estaba fuera del país para robarme.
  He took advantage of my being out of the country to rob me.

aprovecharse de + *inf*   to take advantage of + *ger*

- Nos aprovecharemos de visitarla cuando lleguemos a la ciudad.
  We'll take advantage of visiting her when we arrive in the city.

apuntar (a)   to aim, point (at); to jot (down)

- Ella apunta el fusil.
  She aims the rifle.

- Juan apuntó a la botella.
  John aimed (or pointed) at the bottle.

- El cañón del barco apuntó al fuerte.
  The ship's cannon aimed at the fort.

- Yo apunté unas notas.
  I jotted down some notes.

apurar   to drink up; to hurry, quicken

- El apura un vaso de vino (/cerveza).
  He drinks up a glass of wine (/beer).

- Él apura el paso cuando camina de noche.
  He hurries his pace when he walks at night.

apurarse   to worry, fret; to rush, hurry up

- Mi mamá se apura siempre por poca cosa.
  My mother always worries (or frets) about little things.

- ¡Apúrate!
  Hurry up!

apurarse a/en + *inf*   to rush to, hurry to + *inf;* to worry about + *ger*

- Me apuro a terminar la tarea.
  I am rushing to finish my homework.

- Se apuró a conseguir dinero.
  He rushed to get money.

- ¡No te apures en pagarme!
  Don't rush to pay (or worry about paying) me.

- ¡Apúrate en servirnos el café!
  Hurry up serving us the coffee!

arrancar (a, de)   to pull up (out), tear off (away); to snatch away (from)

- El jardinero arrancó la mala hierba.
  The gardener pulled out the weed.

■ Arranca la naranja del árbol.
   He tears off the orange from the tree.

■ El niño arrancó la hoja del cuaderno.
   The child tore out a sheet from his notebook.

■ El motor no arranca en el invierno.
   The motor does not start in winter.

■ El ladrón le arrancó la cartera.
   The thief snatched the purse from her.

arrancar a uno (de algo)   to drag *or* pull sb away (from sth), uproot sb (from sth)

■ Lo arrancaron de su terruño.
   They uprooted him from his homeland.

■ Le arrancaron los pelos en la pelea.
   *He pulled (or *tore out*) his hair in the fight.*

■ Te arrancó un botón de la camisa.
   He tore off a button from your shirt.

arrancar de algo   to come from sth, originate in sth

■ Estos problemas financieros (/Estas influencias) arrancaron de la revolución.
   These financial problems (/influences) originated in the revolution.

■ Esta corriente literaria arranca del siglo XVIII.
   This literary current comes from the XVIII century.

arreglar   to settle; to arrange; to fix, repair

■ Arreglaron el problema de dinero.
   They settled the problem of money.

■ Arreglaron el motor del auto.
   *They fixed (or *repaired*) the car's motor.*

■ Tienes que arreglar tu cuarto.
   You have to straighten out your room.

arreglarse   to fix, settle

■ Ella se arregló el pelo.
   She fixed her hair.

■ Ella se arregló para salir.
   She fixed herself up to go out.

■ El ministro de trabajo se arregló con los huelguistas.
   The Minister of Labor settled with the strikers.

■ Ella se arregló con el novio.
   She came to an agreement with her boyfriend.

arrepentirse de algo   to regret sth, repent of sth

- Yo me arrepiento de mis errores.
  I regret my errors (or I am repenting of my sins).
- Ella se arrepintió de su mala conducta.
  She regretted her bad behavior.

arrepentirse de + *inf*   to regret + *ger*

- Se arrepintió de pagar tanto.
  She regretted paying so much.
- Nosotros nos vamos a arrepentir de ver esa película.
  We are going to regret seeing that movie.

arrojar (de)   to throw, fling, hurl, throw up (out)

- El niño arrojó la comida que había ingerido.
  The child threw up the meal he had ingested.
- El niño arrojó una piedra con fuerza.
  The child threw (or flung) a stone forcefully.
- Lo arrojaron del edificio porque no pagaba el alquiler.
  They threw him out of the building because he did not pay his rent.

arrojarse a/en algo   to throw oneself into *or* on sth

- Él se arrojó al (*or* en el) río (/a la piscina/al mar).
  He threw himself into the river (/into the swimming pool/into the sea).
- El hombre se arrojó al (*or* en el) pavimento.
  The man threw himself down on the pavement.

arrojarse de/por algo   to throw oneself from/out of sth

- El hombre se arrojó de (*or* por) la ventana.
  The man threw himself from (or out of) the window.

ascender a uno/a algo   to promote sb; to ascend *or* climb sth

- Ha sido ascendido a coronel del ejército (/a vicepresidente).
  He has been promoted to colonel of the army (/to vice president).
- El andinista ascendió a la cima de la montaña.
  The mountain climber ascended (or climbed) to the top of the mountain.
- El globo asciende a las nubes.
  The balloon went up to the clouds.

asegurar   to assure, affirm; to insure; to secure

- Le aseguró que limpiaría la habitación.
  He assured her that he would clean the room.

■   Aseguró las ventanas y las puertas.
    He secured the windows and doors.

■   ¿Contra qué vas a asegurar la casa?
    What kind of insurance are you getting for the house?

■   Voy a asegurar la casa contra incendios.
    I am going to insure the house against fire.

asegurarse de algo   to make sure of sth

■   Yo me voy a asegurar de que la puerta está cerrada.
    I am going to make sure that the door is locked.

■   ¡Asegúrate de que es verdad lo que ha dicho tu amigo!
    Make sure that what your friend has said is true.

asemejarse   to be alike, be similar

■   Los gemelos (/autos) se asemejan muchísimo.
    The twins (/cars) are very much alike (or very similar).

asemejarse a algo   to be like sth, resemble sth

■   El niño se asemeja a su mamá.
    The child resembles his mother.

■   Nuestra casa se asemeja a la de mi tío.
    Our house is like my uncle's.

asistir a uno/a algo   to assist

■   Las enfermeras asisten a los pacientes.
    The nurses are helping (or assisting) the patients.

■   El médico español asistió en la operación de mi papá.
    The Spanish doctor assisted in my dad's operation.

asistir a   to attend, be present

■   Irene va a asistir a la conferencia.
    Irene is going to attend (or be present at) the conference.

■   Hoy no asistió a la escuela.
    He did not go to school today.

■   Ella asistió a la inauguración presidencial.
    She attended (or was present at) the presidential inauguration.

asociar   to associate, put together

■   Para memorizar hay que asociar ideas.
    In order to memorize one should associate ideas.

■   La policía asoció los hechos del accidente.
    The police put together the facts of the accident.

asociar(se) a/con uno/algo   to associate with sb/sth, join sb/sth

- Nuestro matrimonio he asociado mi familia a (*or* con) la tuya.
  Our marriage has joined my family with yours.

- Nos asociamos a (*or* con) los hermanos Rodríguez.
  We joined (or *became associates of) the Rodriguez brothers.*

- Se han asociado a (*or* con) una cooperativa.
  They have joined a co-op.

asomar (a, por)   to appear, show (at, through)

- El sol asoma en las mañanas.
  The sun appears in the morning.

asomar algo a/por   to show sth on/from

- Ana asoma el vestido a (*or* por) la ventana.
  Ana shows her dress from the window.

- Los soldados asomaron los rifles al (*or* por el) balcón.
  The soldiers showed their rifles on the balcony.

asomarse a/por algo   to appear on sth; to show oneself from sth

- La chica se asomó al (*i.e.,* por el) balcón.
  The girl appeared on (i.e., *showed herself from) the balcony.*

- Julia se asomaba a (*or* por) su ventana.
  Julia used to appear in the window.

asombrarse de algo   to be amazed at sth, be astonished by sth

- La chica se asombró de la velocidad del auto.
  The girl was amazed at the speed of the car.

- Ellos se asombran de la habilidad musical de su hermano.
  They are amazed at (or *astonished by) his brother's musical ability.*

aspirar   to breathe (in), inhale

- Aspiramos aire puro (/mucho polvo).
  We breathe in (or *inhale) pure air (/a lot of dust).*

aspirar a algo   to aspire to sth

- Aspiran a una vida mejor.
  They aspire to a better life.

- Aspiramos a una buena posición económica.
  We aspire to a good economic situation.

aspirar a + *inf*   to aspire to + *inf*

- Aspiran a ser escritores.
  They aspire to be writers.

■   Aspiraron a hacerlo.
    They aspired to do it.

asustar   to frighten, scare, startle

■   Los pájaros me asustaron.
    The birds scared me.

■   El despertador lo asustó.
    The alarm clock startled him.

asustarse de (*or* por) algo   to be frightened by sth, afraid of sth

■   Las niñas se asustaron de (*or* por) los perros.
    The girls were afraid of the dogs.

■   Yo me asustaba de (*or* por) los malos sueños.
    I used to be frightenend by bad dreams.

asustarse de + *inf*   to be afraid to + *inf/ger*

■   Se asustaron de viajar en avión.
    They were afraid to travel by plane.

■   Me asusté de ver a mi padre tan delgado.
    I was afraid seeing my dad so thin.

atacar   to attack

■   Las tropas (/soldados) atacaron al enemigo (/el país/el castillo).
    The troops (/soldiers) attacked the enemy (/country/castle).

■   Lo atacó una rara enfermedad.
    A rare disease attacked him.

atender a uno/algo   to attend to sb/sth, take care of sb/sth

■   Él atendió el teléfono.
    He answered the phone.

■   Ella atendió las quejas del cliente.
    She attended to the client's complaints.

■   Atendemos a los invitados (/la familia).
    We are attending to (or taking care of) the guests (/the family).

atenerse a uno/algo   to rely on sb/sth; to depend on sb/sth

■   Yo me atengo a los hechos.
    I rely on the facts.

■   Ella se atiene a su hermano para conseguir empleo.
    She is depending on her brother to get employment.

■   No tengo a qué atenerme.
    I do not have anything to rely on.

atentar a/contra algo   to commit an outrage against sth, endanger sth

- Echar basura en la calle es atentar a (*or* contra) la salud pública.
  Throwing garbage on the street endangers public health.

- No hay que atentar a (*or* contra) las buenas costumbres.
  One must not violate (or endanger) good habits.

atravesar   to cross; to go through, go across

- Los niños no deben atravesar en esta esquina (/calle).
  The children shouldn't cross at this corner (/street).

- Los soldados atravesaron la frontera.
  The soldiers crossed the border.

- Lo atravesé con una espada.
  He pierced him with a sword.

atravesarse en   to come (in) between; to interfere

- El gato se me atravesó en el camino.
  The cat got in my way.

- Un hueso de pollo se le atravesó en la garganta.
  A chicken bone got stuck in his throat.

- La competencia se atravesó en nuestro negocio.
  The competition interfered with our business.

atreverse a + *inf*   to dare to + *inf*

- Yo no me atrevo a torear.
  I do not dare to fight bulls.

- Se atrevió a cruzar el canal de la Mancha.
  He dared to cross the English Channel.

- Él se atreve a pelear con el campeón.
  He dares to fight the champion.

avanzar (en, hacia)   to advance (in, towards)

- Avanzó en su trabajo.
  He made progress in his work.

- Avanzaron hacia la capital (/ciudad/plaza).
  They advanced towards the capital (/city/square).

avenirse   to come to an agreement, be reconciled

- Él se aviene a esta situación.
  He is reconciled to this situation.

avenirse con uno/algo   to be in agreement with sb/sth, get on well with sb, go well with sth

- Cecilia se aviene con Pedro muy bien.
  Cecilia agrees (or gets on well) with Peter.

■ Esta corbata se aviene con mi saco muy bien.
   This tie goes well with my coat.

avenirse a + *inf*   to agree to + *inf*

■ Roberto se aviene a trabajar.
   Robert agrees to work.

avergonzarse de/por algo   to be ashamed about/of sth; to be embarrassed by/about sth

■ Él se avergüenza de (*or* por) su origen humilde.
   He is ashamed of his humble origin.

■ Nosotros nos hemos avergonzado de (*or* por) la conducta de nuestro hijo.
   We have been ashamed of (or *embarrassed by*) *our children's behavior.*

avergonzarse de/por + *inf*   to be ashamed to + *inf*, be ashamed of + *ger*

■ Cecilia se avergonzaría de (*or* por) cantar en público.
   Cecilia would be ashamed of singing (or to sing) in public.

■ Él se avergonzó de no haberla reconocido.
   He was ashamed of not having recognized her.

averiguar   to find out, inquire

■ ¡Averigua la causa del problema!
   Find (out) the cause of the problem.

■ Queremos averiguar dónde está la playa (/a qué hora sale el avión).
   We want to find out where the beach is located (/at what time the plane leaves).

avisar   to inform, notify

■ Nos avisaron que Luis había llegado.
   They informed us that Luis had arrived.

■ Le avisamos a María que Luis había llegado.
   We advised Mary of Luis' arrival.

ayudar (con, en)   to help, aid, assist (with, in)

■ Nos ayudan con (*or* en) las labores de campo.
   They help us with the farm work.

■ Me ayudaste con (*or* en) el tejido del suéter.
   You helped me with the knitting of the sweater.

ayudar a uno a + *inf*   to help sb + *inf*

■ Me ayudó a aprender inglés.
   He helped me learn English.

■ Le ayudamos a construir su casa.
   We helped him build his house.

B

bailar   to dance

- ¿Quieres bailar conmigo (/con el chico)?
  Do you want to dance with me (/the boy)?

- Los muchachos bailaron hasta que se cansaron.
  The boys and girls danced until they got tired.

- Me gustaría bailar bajo el cielo del Caribe.
  I'd like to dance under the Caribbean sky.

- Mis pies bailan en los zapatos. *(fig)*
  My feet swim in these shoes.

bajar (desde, por)   to go down, descend (from), lower, sink

- La temperatura baja mucho después de medianoche.
  The temperature goes down a lot after midnight.

- Para ir al sótano hay que bajar la escalera (/por el ascensor).
  To get to the basement, you have to go down the stairs (/in the elevator).

- Él baja la cabeza para poder entrar.
  He lowers his head to be able to enter.

- ¡Bajen la cortina (/la voz/los precios/el radio)!, por favor.
  Please lower the curtain (/your voice/prices/or turn down the radio).

- Sus pedidos han bajado mucho últimamente.
  Their orders have fallen off a lot lately.

- Bajaron desde la cima (/por el lado abrupto) de la colina.
  They descended from the top (/the steep side) of the hill.

- El hombre ha bajado en mi estima. *(fig)*
  My opinion of the man has gone down.

bajar a algo   to go down to sth

- Las aguas bajaron a su nivel normal (/al mar/al desierto).
  The water went down to its normal level (/to the sea/to the desert).

bajar a + *inf*   to go down to + *inf*

- Bajamos a comer (/hablar/trabajar) con nuestros amigos.
  We went down to eat (/talk/work) with our friends.

bajar de algo   to get off sth, get out of sth *(vehicle, etc.)*

- Bajó del auto con mucha prisa (/con dificultad).
  He got out of the car in a hurry (/with difficulty).

- Bajamos de la montaña después de la tormenta.
  We came down from the mountain after the storm.

bajar por algo   to come down (by, in) sth

- Siempre bajamos por el ascensor.
  We always come down in the (or by) elevator.

- El conejo bajó por la ladera, dejando atrás a los perros.
  The rabbit came down the hillside leaving the dogs behind.

bajarse a + *inf*   to lower oneself to + *inf*

- No quiero bajarme a hacer eso (/discutir este tema con él). *(fig)*
  I don't want to lower myself to do that (/to discuss this subject with him).

balbucear   to stammer, hesitate *(in speech)*

- No podía hablar por el dolor que le causaba la herida; apenas pudo balbucear algunas palabras antes de morir.
  He was not able to speak because of the pain caused by the wound; he could only stammer a few words before he died.

- El balbucea cuando habla.
  He stammers when he speaks.

bañar a uno/algo   to bathe sb/sth, wash sb/sth

- La mamá baña al niño en la tina.
  The mother bathes the child in the bathtub.

- Las costas del Peru están bañadas por el océano Pacífico. El mar baña las costas.
  The Peruvian coast is washed by the Pacific Ocean. The sea washes the shores.

- El sol baña de luz las montañas a esa hora.
  The mountains are bathed in the light of the sun at that hour.

bañarse   to bathe, have a swim, go swimming; to take *or* to have a bath

- ¿Adónde vas a bañarte? —Me gusta bañarme en la playa (/piscina).
  Where are you going to swim? —I like to swim at the beach (/swimming pool).

- La pobre mujer se bañó en llanto por la muerte de su hijo. *(fig)*
  The poor lady bathed herself in tears over the death of her son.

- El se bañó porque estaba muy sucio.
  He took a bath because he was very dirty.

barrer   to sweep

- Mi padre está barriendo el piso (/el baño/la casa/el dormitorio).
  My father is sweeping the floor (/bathroom/house/bedroom).

- Por favor, barre los rincones.
  Please sweep the corners.

bastar to be enough, be sufficient

- Me bastan mil pesos para viajar.
  One thousand pesos is enough for me to travel on.

- ¿Te basta esa botella de agua?
  Is that bottle of water enough for you (or sufficient)?

bastar a uno con algo sth to be enough for sb

- Me basta con tu palabra.
  Your word is enough for me.

bastar con + *inf* to be enough to + *inf,* be enough + *ger*

- Basta (con) comer una vez al día para vivir.
  It's enough to eat once a day (or Eating once a day is enough) in order to survive.

- Basta (con) decir que llegué tarde.
  It's enough to say (or Suffice it to say) that I arrived late.

- Para entender matemáticas basta (con) practicarlas.
  In order to understand mathematics, all one needs is to practice it.

bastar de + *inf* to be enough + *ger*

- ¡Basta de jugar con el perro!
  Enough playing with the dog!

- ¡Basta de beber licor!
  Enough drinking liquor!

batallar (con, por) to fight, struggle (with, about, *or* over)

- El hombre siempre batalla con su esposa por dinero.
  The man always quarrels with his wife over (or about) money.

- Ese muchacho ha tenido que batallar desde que nació.
  That boy has had to struggle since birth.

- Desde hace un siglo los dos países batallan por ese territorio.
  The two countries have been fighting over that territory for a century.

- Las mujeres han tenido que batallar por su emancipación.
  The women have had to struggle for their emancipation.

- Mucho ha tenido que batallar mi hermano para salir adelante en su trabajo.
  My brother had to struggle a lot to get ahead in his job.

batir (con) to beat, mix; to stir, churn (with)

- Bata solo las claras.
  Beat the egg whites only.

- Voy a batir la sopa.
  I'm going to stir the soup.

- Ella bate el chocolate caliente con un tenedor (/una cuchara de palo/con un molinillo/con una espátula).
  She mixes the hot chocolate with a fork (/wooden spoon/mixer/spatula).

batirse   to fight, have a fight

- Él se batió dignamente.
  He fought a duel with dignity.

- Los soldados se batieron constantemente (/ferozmente).
  The soldiers fought constantly (/ferociously).

bautizar   to baptize, christen; to name

- Ese sacerdote bautizó a todos los niños (/a mis hijos).
  That priest baptized all of the children (/my children).

- La bautizaron con el nombre de Rosa.
  She was baptized Rose.

- Los bautizan para hacerlos miembros de la iglesia.
  They baptize them to make them church members.

beber (a, por)   to drink (to)

- Luis bebe agua del vaso (/de la botella/de la fuente).
  Louis is drinking water from the glass (/bottle/fountain).

- Ella lo bebió con mucha sed.
  She drank it with much thirst.

- ¡Bebamos por (*or* a) la salud de nuestro invitado (/nuestra victoria)!
  Let's drink to our guest's health (/our victory).

bendecir a uno/algo   to bless sb/sth

- Mi familia (/padre) bendice los alimentos.
  My family (/father) always says grace.

- El sacerdote bendice al niño.
  The priest blesses the child.

- ¡Dios le bendiga, señor López!
  May God bless you, Mr. López!

besar   to kiss

- Él besó a su novia con delicadeza.
  He kissed his girlfriend delicately.

- Yo la besé en las mejillas (/en los ojos/en la frente/en los labios).
  I kissed her on the cheeks (/eyes/forehead/lips).

besarse   to kiss each other

- Las muchachas se besaron en las mejillas al conocerse.
  The girls kissed each other on the cheek when they met.

- Los novios se besaron (en los labios) después de la ceremonia.
  The bride and groom kissed each other (on the lips) after the ceremony.

borrar (de)   to erase (from); to cross out (from)

- Yo borré las palabras mal escritas.
  I erased (or crossed out) the incorrect words.

- El profesor borró la frase de la pizarra (con un borrador).
  The professor erased the sentence on the board (with an eraser).

- Él ha borrado a María de la lista. Él quiere borrarla de su memoria para siempre.
  He has erased Mary from the list. He wants to erase her from his memory forever.

borrarse (de)   to fade, disappear, be erased (from)

- Las líneas de este dibujo se han borrado por la acción del tiempo.
  The lines of this drawing have faded with the passing of time.

- Se borró su nombre (/el hecho) de la memoria colectiva.
  His name (/This event) was erased from collective memory.

- Se le borraron los malos recuerdos y volvió a ser feliz.
  Her bad memories disappeared, and she became happy again.

bostezar (de, en)   to yawn (of, at)

- Bostezamos cuando estamos aburridos.
  We yawn when we are bored.

- Él bosteza de sueño (/de hambre/de aburrimiento).
  He yawns because he's sleepy (/of hunger/of boredom).

- Ese hombre bostezó en mi cara.
  That man yawned in my face.

botar algo (de)   to throw sth away, (*fig*) throw sth (out of), fling sth, hurl sth; to launch sth

- Disgustado con su fracaso, el escritor botó todos los papeles escritos.
  Disgusted with his failure, the writer threw away all his writings.

- Bótame ese suéter (/la pelota), por favor.
  Throw me that sweater (/the ball), please!

- Por favor, bota a la basura estos papeles.
  Please, throw these papers in the garbage.

- El nuevo acorazado fue botado al agua ayer a las tres.
  The new battleship was launched yesterday at three o'clock.

- Lo botaron de su trabajo (/de la escuela). (*fig*)
  They threw him out of his job (/the school).

bregar (con)   to contend (with), struggle (with)

- Para cultivar esta tierra hay que bregar con el clima.
  To work (or cultivate) this land, one has to contend with the weather.

- Con frecuencia bregamos con el destino.
  Frequently, we struggle with destiny.

brincar (a, de)   to jump, hop (to); to jump up and down (for *or* because of)

- Brincaron al otro lado de la cerca.
  They jumped to the other side of the fence.

- Las chicas brincaron de alegría.
  The girls jumped (up and down) for joy.

brindar (por)   to drink (a toast to), to toast

- ¡Brindemos por la salud de tu esposa!
  Let us toast (or drink (a toast) to) your wife's health!

- Ellos brindaron por la victoria del equipo.
  They toasted the team's victory.

- Brindaron al por el cumpleaños de Jorge.
  They toasted George's birthday.

bromear (con)   to joke, kid; to make fun (with, about)

- Miguel bromea.
  Michael is joking.

- Los chicos siempre bromean con él.
  The boys are always kidding (around with) him.

- Uno no debe bromear con la muerte.
  One should not joke about death.

broncearse   to tan, sunbathe

- Ellos se broncearon (durante tres horas).
  They sunbathed (for three hours).

- Se broncean para tener aspecto saludable.
  They are sunbathing for a healthier appearance.

bucear   to dive; to swim under water, skin-dive

- Bucearon a tres millas de la costa.
  They were skin-diving three miles from shore.

- Buceaban en un lago (/en una piscina pública).
  They were diving in a lake (/in a public swimming pool).

bullir   to move about, boil, bubble (up)

- El agua (/La leche) bullía ligeramente.
  The water (/milk) was boiling slightly.

- Las moscas bullían (en el pastel).
  Flies were moving about (the cake).

bullir de/en algo   to teem with sth, swarm (*or* swarming) with sth, seethe with sth

- Pedro bullía de cólera.
  Peter was livid (or seething) with anger.

- La plaza (/El mercado) bullía de gente (/de actividad).
  The square (/market) was swarming with people (/activity).

- Los mares tropicales bullen de peces.
  The tropical seas are teeming with fish.

- Estaba tan enojado que me bullía la sangre en las venas. (*fig*)
  I was so angry that my blood was boiling.

- Las hormigas bullían en el jardin. (*fig*)
  The garden was full of ants.

burlar   to deceive by avoiding, trick

- El ladrón burló al guardia y entró en la tienda.
  The thief tricked the guard and entered the store.

- El jugador de fútbol burló a dos adversarios y metió el gol.
  The soccer player avoided two opponents and scored.

- ¡Burlemos los obstáculos!
  Let's avoid the obstacles!

burlarse de uno   to mock sb, ridicule sb, scoff at sb; to make fun of sb

- ¡No se burle de mí (/del profesor/de José)!
  Don't make fun of (or ridicule or mock) me (/the teacher/Joseph)!

- ¡Nunca se burle de los ancianos!
  Never make fun of (or scoff at) the elderly!

buscar   to look for

- Busco una casa que tenga piscina.
  I'm looking for a house with a swimming pool.

- Buscaba el libro rojo que tú habías leído.
  He was looking for the red book that you had read.

- Hace mucho tiempo que busca esposa.
  He has been looking for a wife for a long time.

- Busqué a Pedro toda la noche.
  I looked for Peter all night.

C

cabalgar (en)   to ride (on), go riding

- Cabalgamos todo el día.
  We rode (or went riding) all day.
- Nos gusta cabalgar durante el verano.
  We like to ride during the summer.
- Cabalgó en un camello (/una mula).
  He rode on a camel (/mule).

cabecear   to nod (off), fall asleep; to head (*in soccer*)

- Hay un estudiante que siempre cabecea durante mis lecciones.
  There is a student who always nods off during my lessons.
- Mi abuelita cabecea y ronca cuando los programas de la televisión son aburridos.
  My grandmother falls asleep and snores when the TV programs are boring.
- El jugador cabeceó y anotó el primer gol.
  The player headed the ball and scored first.

caber   to fit, go in

- El anillo no le cabe.
  The ring doesn't fit her.
- No creo que esto quepa ahí.
  I don't think this will fit (or go in) here.

caber de algo   to be filled with sth

- Rosita no cabe de contenta (/felicidad/gozo) con la noticia.
  Rosita is filled with content (/happiness/joy) at the news.

caber en algo   to fit in/into sth

- El mueble (/sofá) no cupo en la sala.
  The piece of furniture (/sofa) did not fit in the living room.
- En este frasco cabe un litro.
  A liter fits in this flask (or bottle).

- Mario es tan bueno que el corazón no le cabe en el pecho. *(fig)*
  Mario is so good that his heart does not fit in his chest. (i.e., Mario is big-hearted).

- Tú no cabes en este sitio.
  You don't fit in this place.

caber + *inf*   to be worth + *ger,* be appropriate + *inf*

- Cabe manifestar que los políticos son astutos.
  *It is appropriate to say (*or *worth saying) that politicians are astute.*

cacarear   to cackle; to boast *(fig)*

- Todas las gallinas cacarean.
  All chickens cackle.

- Usted cacarea de lo que tiene. *(fig)*
  You are boasting about what you have.

caer   to fall; to fail

- Algo cayó afuera.
  Something fell outside.

- El avión cayó a las 4 de la mañana.
  The airplane crashed at four in the morning.

caer a/en algo   to fall in/into/on sth

- La piedra ha caído al (*or* en el) río.
  *The stone fell in (*or *into) the river.*

- Las gotas caen al (*or* en el) césped.
  The drops are falling on the grass.

- Todos caímos a la (*or* en) la cama.
  We all fell into bed.

caer de algo   to fall from/on sth

- La maceta cayó del edificio.
  The flower pot fell from the building.

- El dinero no cae del cielo. *(fig)*
  Money does not fall from heaven.

- El boxeador cayó de lado (/de espalda).
  The boxer fell sideways (/on his back).

caerse   to fall; to fall down; to drop; to collapse

- Mi hijo tiene los pies planos, por eso se cae mucho.
  My son falls down often because he has flat feet.

- Mi tía se cayó y se golpeó la cabeza.
  My aunt fell and hit her head.

- A mi abuela se le cayó la taza.
  My grandmother dropped the cup.

- ¡Cuidado, se cae!
  Be careful! It is falling (or collapsing).

caerse a algo   to fall on/into sth

- Rolando se cayó al agua (/al pozo/al piso).
  Roland fell into the water (/the well/on the floor).

caerse de algo   to fall from/off sth

- Se cayó del caballo cuando iba a bajarse.
  He fell from (or off) the horse when he was going to get off.

- El mono se cayó de la rama.
  The monkey fell from (or off) the branch.

- Todo se me cae de las manos.
  Everything falls from my hands.

calentar   to heat

- Calentamos el café (/el agua/la leche).
  We heated the coffee (/water/milk).

- El sol calienta la tierra.
  The sun heats the earth.

calentarse   to get angry *(fig)*

- Se calentó cuando oyó las noticias.
  He got angry when he heard the news.

- Me calenté porque no me llamaste.
  I got angry because you didn't call me.

calzar   to wear *(on feet)*

- ¡Qué lindos zapatos calza usted hoy!
  You are wearing very pretty shoes today!

- ¿Qué número de zapato calza usted? —Yo calzo un 45.
  What size shoe do you wear? —I wear size 12.

calzar algo   to wedge sth, put a wedge under sth

- Hay que calzar la mesa porque se tambalea.
  We have to put table cups under the legs (or wedge the table) because it wobbles.

calzar a uno   to shoe sb, put on shoes for sb; to make shoes for sb

- Mi zapatero calza a los reyes.
  My shoemaker makes shoes for kings.

- La enfermera calzó al enfermo.
  The nurse put the shoes on the patient.

calzarse con algo   to wear sth (*on feet*)

- Me calzo con botas altas cuando voy de cacería.
  I wear high boots when I go hunting.

- Ella se calza con sandalias cuando va a la playa.
  She wears sandals when she goes to the beach.

callar   to be quiet

- El maestro les dijo que deberían callar.
  The teacher told them that they should be quiet.

callarse   to be silent, keep quiet; to shut up (*idiomatic*)

- ¡Calla (/Cállate/Cállese)!
  Be (or Keep) quiet! or Shut up!

- El público se calló durante el funeral.
  The public was silent during the funeral.

- Ellos se callaron cuando vieron al maestro.
  They got quiet when they saw the teacher.

cambiar   to change, alter, convert

- La situación de mi país cambiará el próximo año.
  The situation in my country will change next year.

- No cambies tu dinero todavía.
  Don't convert (or exchange) your money yet.

cambiar(se) de algo   to change sth

- Oscar cambia de auto cada año.
  Oscar changes cars every year.

- La mujer cambió de peinado.
  The woman changed her hairdo.

- Cambié de opinión después de leer su artículo.
  I changed my mind after reading your article.

- Mi amigo se cambió de clase.
  My friend changed classes.

- Usted se cambia de casa como cambiarse de camisa.
  You change homes like (you are) changing shirts.

cambiar algo por algo   to exchange sth for sth

- Cambié una vaca por un caballo.
  I exchanged a cow for a horse.

- Elena cambiará la guitarra por una mandolina.
  Elena will exchange her guitar for a mandolin.

cambiarse   to change (*clothes*)

- Me cambié en un minuto.
  I changed clothes in a minute.

- ¡Cámbiate que vamos a salir!
  Change (clothes) because we are going to leave.

cambiarse en algo   to change to sth, be changed to sth

- Mi dolor se cambió en alegría.
  My sorrow (was) changed to happiness.

- ¡Cambia tu negativismo en optimismo!
  Change your pessimism to optimism!

caminar   to walk, to go

- Si usted camina todos los días, se sentirá como nuevo.
  If you walk every day, you will feel like new.

- ¡Camine directo y en la esquina doble a la izquierda!
  Walk (or Go) straight ahead and, at the corner, turn left.

caminar a/hacia algo   to walk to/towards sth

- Caminamos al trabajo todos los días para hacer ejercicio.
  I walk to work every day in order to exercise.

- Caminaremos a la cima de la montaña.
  We shall walk to the top of the mountain.

- Ellas caminan hacia el norte.
  They walk towards the north.

caminar en/por algo   to walk in/on/through sth

- Caminaremos en (*or* por) el bosque antes de que salga la luna.
  We will walk in (or through) the forest before the moon rises.

- Me gusta caminar en (*or* por) la playa durante la noche.
  I like to walk on the beach at night.

caminar hasta algo   to walk (up) to *or* as far as sth

- Quieren caminar hasta mi ciudad.
  They want to walk (up) to (or as far as) my city.

■ Camino hasta aquel pueblito que se ve a lo lejos.
I walk (up) to that little town in the distance.

canjear   to exchange, swap

■ Canjeamos las cosas que teníamos.
We exchanged (or swapped) the things we used to have.

canjear algo por algo   to exchange sth for sth

■ Debemos canjear esto por algo mejor.
We must exchange this for something better.

■ Canjeé un saco de arroz por un quintal de azúcar.
I exchanged a sack of rice for a hundred kilos of sugar.

cansar   to tire (out), be tiring

■ El ciclismo cansa mucho.
Cycling is very tiring.

■ Este trabajo me cansa mucho.
This work tires me out.

■ Tus palabras cansan.
Your words are tiring.

cansarse   to get *or* become tired

■ Voy a dormir porque ya me cansé.
I am going to sleep because I've become (or gotten) tired.

cansarse de algo   to get tired of sth, grow weary of sth

■ Me he cansado de su actitud (/comportamiento).
I've gotten tired (or grown weary) of your attitude (/behavior).

cansarse de + *inf*   to get tired of + *ger*

■ Se cansaron de esperar la pensión.
They got tired of waiting for their pension.

■ Los músicos se cansaron de tocar y ellos se cansaron de bailar.
The musicians got tired of playing, and they got tired of dancing.

cantar   to sing

■ Juan siempre canta esta melodía cuando se ducha.
John always sings this tune when he showers.

■ Ellas cantaban en el coro de la iglesia.
They used to sing in the church choir.

carecer de algo   to lack sth, be in need of sth, be without sth

■ Muchos países carecen de recursos naturales.
Many countries lack (or are in need of) natural resources.

- Usted carece de habilidad para aprender idiomas.
  You lack the ability to learn languages.
- En estos momentos carezco de dinero (/coche).
  Right now, I am without money (/a car).

cargar   to load

- Cargaron todo el maíz que se había recogido.
  They loaded all the corn that had been gathered.
- Cargaron el camión.
  They loaded the truck.
- Cargó la escopeta y disparó.
  He loaded the shotgun and fired.

cargar a/en algo   to load on sth, carry on sth

- Los peones cargan a (*or* en) hombros grandes racimos de bananas.
  The workers carry large bundles of bananas on their backs.
- Cargaré a (*or* en) la espalda al niño porque no puede caminar más.
  I'll carry the child on my back because he can't walk anymore.

cargar con algo   to load with sth, assume sth

- El cazador cargó con municiones el fusil.
  The hunter loaded the gun with munitions.
- Yo cargué con toda la responsabilidad (/culpa/vergüenza).
  I assumed all responsibility (/the blame/the shame).

cargar de algo   to load (down) with sth

- Cargaremos de troncos los camiones.
  We'll load the trucks with logs.
- Vamos a cargar de arroz la carreta.
  We are going to load the cart with rice.
- El gobierno cargó de impuestos al pueblo.
  The government loaded the people down with taxes.

cargar sobre uno/algo   to load on sb/sth, burden sb/sth

- Yo cargo sobre mis espaldas una gran responsabilidad. (*fig*)
  I carry a heavy load of responsibility on my back.
- Él ha cargado sobre nosotros la culpa.
  He has burdened us with guilt.

cargarse de algo   to be loaded with sth

- El arbolito se carga de mangos todos los años.
  Every year the little tree is loaded with mangoes.

■ Las nubes se cargaron de electricidad.
The clouds were charged with electricity.

■ Los esposos se cargaron de hijos en muy pocos años. (*fig*)
The couple loaded itself down with children in a few years.

casar a uno   to marry sb, join sb in marriage

■ Antes los padres casaban a sus hijos, aunque estos no lo quisieran.
In the past parents married off their children even if they did not desire it.

■ El sacerdote los casó el sábado.
The priest married them on Saturday.

casarse   to marry, get married

■ Nos casaremos por la iglesia.
We will get married by the church.

■ El actor se casó en segundas nupcias.
The actor got married for a second time.

■ Se casaron y partieron para Europa.
They got married and left for Europe.

casarse con uno   to marry sb, get married with sb

■ El viejo se casó con una joven.
The old man married a young woman.

■ Quiero casarme con la mujer (/el hombre) ideal.
I want to marry the ideal woman (/man).

ceder   to hand over, give up, part with; to yield

■ Hay un letrero que dice: "ceda el paso."
There is a sign that reads: "Yield the right of way."

ceder a uno/algo   to yield to sb/sth, give way to, submit to sb/sth

■ Este país cedió parte de su territorio a su vecino.
This country ceded (or gave up) part of its territory to its neighbor.

■ La columna del edificio cedió al peso y se quebró.
The building's column gave way under the weight and collapsed.

■ El enemigo cedió a las fuerzas del gobierno.
The enemy yielded (or submitted) to government forces.

■ Mientras viva, no quiero ceder a mis hijos todos los bienes que poseo.
I do not want to give to my children all my estate while I am still living.

cegar   to blind, make blind

■ Lo cegó la luz del faro.
The headlights blinded him.

- Una luz intensa puede cegar a una persona.
  Bright light can blind a person (or make a person blind).

cegarse de algo   to become blinded by sth

- El boxeador se cegó de cólera y golpeó al rival hasta derribarlo.
  The boxer was blinded by anger and kept hitting his opponent until he knocked him down.

- Cuando se cegó de amor, no sabía lo que hacía.
  When he was blinded by love, he did not know what he was doing.

cerrar   to close, shut; to block (up), obstruct

- Por favor, cierre la puerta después de salir.
  Please close (or shut) the door after leaving.

- Los niños cerraron los ojos y saltaron.
  The children closed their eyes and jumped.

- ¡Cierre el hoyo con cemento!
  Fill (or Block up) the hole with cement.

- ¿Quién cerró la llave del agua (/gas)? —Yo la cerré.
  Who shut the water (/gas) off? —I shut it off.

cerrar con algo   to lock with sth

- ¡Cierre la puerta de su casa con llave!
  Lock the door of the house (with a key).

- Cerramos el portón con una aldaba.
  We locked the gate with a latch (or bolt).

cerrarse   to close oneself to sth, shut oneself off from sth

- ¡No se cierre a los cambios de la vida moderna! *(fig)*
  Do not shut yourself off from (close yourself to) the changes of modern life!

- Se cerraron a todas las sugerencias.
  They closed themselves to all suggestions.

cesar   to cease, stop, suspend; to fire, dismiss

- La lluvia ya cesó.
  It stopped raining already.

- Cesaron a mi padre por edad.
  They fired (or retired) my dad because of age.

cesar de + *inf*   to stop + *ger*

- El niño cesaba de llorar cuando su madre lo acariciaba.
  The child would stop crying when his mother caressed him.

- El viento cesó de soplar.
  The wind died down (or stopped blowing).

cesar en algo   to stop (in) sth

- Mi padre cesó en sus funciones (/en el trabajo) en 1980.
  My dad stopped performing duties (/stopped working) in 1980.

cocer   to cook; to bake

- Ya cocieron las verduras.
  They cooked the vegetables already.
- Coció la zanahoria a fuego lento.
  He cooked the carrots on a slow fire.
- Cocimos la carne primero, luego cocimos las papas.
  We cooked (or baked) the meat first; then we cooked (or baked) the potatoes.

cocinar   to cook, prepare

- ¿Quién cocina en tu casa? —Mi mamá cocina.
  Who cooks in your house? —My mother cooks.
- Voy a cocinar un platillo especial.
  I am going to cook (or prepare) a special dish.

coger a/uno/algo   to take hold of sth; to seize, grasp sb/sth to catch

- El tiene que coger el avión (/tren) a las 5 en punto.
  He has to catch the plane (/train) at five o'clock sharp.
- ¡No coja ese pedazo de pan porque está caliente!
  Don't touch (or take) that piece of bread because it's hot.
- A Marcos lo cogió la lluvia.
  Marcos got caught in the rain.
- La policía cogió al delincuente.
  The police caught (or seized) the criminal.
- El toro cogió al torero y lo hirió gravemente.
  The bull caught the bullfighter and gravely wounded him.

coger de algo   to take hold of by sth

- El mago cogió de las orejas al conejo.
  The magician grasped the rabbit by the ears (or took hold of the rabbit's ears).
- Al ver el toro, cogí de la mano a Cecilia y la metí en la casa.
  On seeing the bull, I took Cecilia by the hand and got her in the house.
- ¡Coja la sartén del mango!
  Take (hold of) the frying-pan by the handle.

colaborar   to collaborate, cooperate

- Yo siempre colaboro.
  I always cooperate.

colaborar con/en algo   to collaborate with/in sth; to help with sth

- Debemos colaborar con las causas nobles.
  We must help with noble causes.

- Colaboraremos en todo lo que nos diga.
  We'll collaborate in (or cooperate with) whatever you say.

colar   to strain (off); to filter

- Tienes que colar la bebida.
  The beverage has to be strained (or They have to filter the beverage).

- Voy a colar el café para eliminarle la broza.
  I am going to strain the coffee to get rid of the sediment.

colarse en algo   to sneak in

- Gabriel siempre se cuela en el estadio.
  Gabriel always sneaks in the stadium.

- Se coló en el teatro porque no tenía dinero.
  He sneaked in the theater because he did not have money.

colegir   to infer; to gather

- Tienes que colegir del texto la intención del autor.
  You have to infer the author's intention from the text.

- Colegimos todas las ideas del autor.
  We gathered all the author's ideas.

colgar   to hang (up)

- ¡Cuelguen los abrigos aquí!
  Hang your coats (up) here.

- Para decorar el lugar, colgaremos muchas plantas.
  To decorate the place, we will hang many plants.

- ¡No cuelge el teléfono!
  Don't hang up the phone!

colgar de/en algo   to hang from/on sth

- Tomás colgó la camisa de (*or* en) un clavo.
  Thomas hung his shirt from (or on) a nail.

- Los mangos cuelgan de (*or* en) las ramas.
  Mangoes hang from the branches.

- Su trabajo cuelga de un hilo. (*fig*)
  His work hangs from a thread.

colgarse   to hang oneself

- El delincuente se colgó antes de que la policía lo capturara.
  The criminal hung himself before the police could catch him.

colindar   to be adjacent, be adjoining

- Nuestras propiedades colindan.
  Our properties are adjacent (or adjoining).

colindar con algo   to adjoin with sth, be adjacent to sth

- Mi finca colinda con la tuya.
  My farm adjoins yours.

- Tu propiedad colinda con cuatro propiedades más.
  Your property adjoins (or is adjacent to) four other properties.

colmar   to fill to the brim, fill up

- Colmó el vaso y se desbordó el vino.
  He filled the glass to the brim, and the wine overflowed.

- Colmó todas las cajas que empacó.
  He filled to the top all the boxes that he packed.

colmar de algo   to fill to the brim with sth

- Colmó el basurero de libros viejos.
  He filled the trash can to the brim with old books.

- La viejecita me colmó de bendiciones. (*fig*)
  The little old lady gave me many blessings.

- !No colmes la jarra de cerveza!
  Don't overfill the pitcher with beer!

colocar   to place, put, position (in); to arrange

- Coloqué todos los muebles como estaban antes.
  I put (or arranged) the furniture as it was before.

- Nuestra empresa va a colocar un producto nuevo.
  Our company is going to put out a new product.

- He colocado los zapatos en el ropero (/la vitrina/el estante).
  I've placed the shoes in the closet (/glass case/on the shelf).

colocarse   to place oneself, station oneself

- Nos hemos colocado en el hospital porque pagan bien.
  We have found a job in the hospital because it pays well.

- El candidato se ha colocado en primer lugar según las encuestas.
  According to the polls, the candidate is in first place.

colocarse de uno   to place oneself as sb

- Antonio se colocó de conserje (/botones/cajero) en un hotel.
  Anthony found a job as a porter (/bellhop/cashier) in a hotel.

combatir to fight, struggle

- A los soldados se les llama a combatir cuando hay conflictos.
Soldiers are called to fight when there is conflict.

- Los guerrilleros combatieron durante cuarenta y ocho horas.
The guerrillas fought for 48 hours.

- Debemos combatir las enfermedades.
We must combat sickness.

combatir con algo to fight with sth

- Los primeros seres humanos combatían con palos y piedras.
Primitive man fought with stone and sticks.

- Voy a combatir con buenos argumentos tus ideas.
I am going to fight your ideas with good arguments.

combatir contra uno to fight against sb

- Los guerreros combatieron contra un enemigo muy peligroso.
The warriors fought against a very dangerous enemy.

combinar to combine, mix; to join, unite, put together; to match

- Combinaremos dos substancias para observar las reacciones.
We shall mix two substances (or put two substances together) in order to observe the reaction.

- Elena siempre combina las prendas que va a vestir.
Elena always matches her outfits.

- Si combinas los colores mejor, pintarás un cuadro excelente.
If you combine (or mix) the colors better, you will paint an excellent picture.

combinar con algo to combine with sth, mix with sth; to match sth, go with sth

- Combinó la pintura amarilla con la azul y obtuvo un verde precioso.
He mixed the yellow paint with the blue, and he obtained a beautiful green.

- Armando combinó sus ideas con las de Susana y escribió un ensayo contra el gobierno.
Armando combined his ideas with Susan's and wrote an essay against the government.

- Tu pantalón no combina con la camisa que compraste.
Your trousers do not match the shirt you bought.

comentar sobre/acerca de algo to comment on/about sth to expound on sth

- Rogelio comentó acerca de lo que estaba pasando en su país.
Roger commented on what was happening in his country.

- No me gusta comentar sobre asuntos sin importancia.
I do not like to comment on (or make comments about) unimportant matters.

■ El astrónomo comentó extensamente (sobre) la teoría de la relatividad.
   The astronomer expounded extensively on the theory of relativity.

comenzar   to begin, start

■ Mañana vamos a comenzar muy temprano.
   Tomorrow we will start very early.

■ Comenzó el libro y nunca lo terminó.
   He began the book and never finished it.

comenzar con algo   to begin with sth

■ Comenzaron con una copita de vino y terminaron con una botella.
   They began with a little glass of wine and finished with a bottle.

■ No comiences con tus mentiras de siempre.
   Don't start with your lies like always.

comenzar a + *inf*   to start to + *inf/ger*

■ Comencé a preparar las maletas para el viaje.
   I began to pack for the trip.

■ He comenzado a envejecer.
   I've begun (or started) to age.

■ Comenzamos a comer a las diez.
   We started to eat at ten.

comenzar por + *inf*   to start by + *ger*

■ Si quieres discutir conmigo, comencemos por ser sinceros.
   If you want to argue with me, let's begin by being sincere.

■ El director comenzó por decirnos que . . . .
   The director started by telling us that . . . .

comer   to eat

■ El panadero de mi barrio nunca come pan.
   The baker in my neighborhood never eats bread.

■ Tengo tanta hambre que me comería una vaca entera.
   I'm so hungry I could eat a whole cow.

comer con/de algo   to eat with/from sth

■ Siempre como con mucho apetito.
   I always eat with relish.

■ El pájaro come de su mano.
   The bird is eating from her hand.

■ Ella come con las manos.
   She eats with her hands.

comerse   to eat up, chew

- Él se come las uñas cuando está nervioso.
  He chews his fingernails when he's nervous.

- Nos comimos todo el arroz que quedaba.
  We ate up all the rice that was left.

comerciar   to trade, do business

- Los Estados Unidos y Japón van a comerciar más intensamente.
  The United States and Japan are going to trade more intensely.

- Los indios comerciaban productos agrícolas.
  Indians traded agricultural products.

comerciar con uno/algo   to trade with sb/sth, deal in sth

- Nuestro país comerciará con los países del sur.
  Our country will trade with the countries of the south.

- Un verdadero comerciante comercia con todo.
  A good merchant deals in everything.

cometer   to commit, make

- Tres hombres cometieron una estafa millonaria.
  Three men committed a multimillion dollar swindle.

- Tú cometes muy pocos errores porque hablas despacio.
  You commit (or make) very few errors because you speak slowly.

- En su ensayo cometió diez faltas de ortografía.
  He made ten spelling errors in his essay.

compadecer   to pity, be sorry for, sympathize with

- Compadecemos a todos aquellos que sufren.
  We feel sorry for (or sympathize with) all those who suffer.

- Compadecí al pobre hombre que asaltaron en la calle.
  I felt sorry for (or pitied) the poor man who was mugged on the street.

compadecerse de uno   to pity sb, be sorry for sb, sympathize with sb

- Ella se compadece de los damnificados del terremoto.
  She feels sorry for the victims of the earthquake.

- Me compadezco de las madres que perdieron a sus hijos en la guerra.
  I feel sorry for (or pity) the mothers who lost their children in the war.

comparar (con)   to compare (to)

- Comparamos las cifras y ninguna coincidió.
  We compared the numbers, and they did not match.

- Yo comparé la calidad de los dos productos.
  I compared the quality of the two products.

- El pueblo comparó el gobierno actual con el anterior.
  The people compared the current administration with the preceding one.

- ¡No me compares con mi padre!
  Don't compare me to my father!

compartir   to share

- Los hermanos compartieron la habitación.
  The brothers shared the room.

- Ningún gobernante quiere compartir el poder.
  No ruler wants to share power.

compartir algo con uno   to share sth with sb

- La niña no quiere compartir sus juguetes con su hermanito.
  The girl does not want to share her toys with her little brother.

- Me gusta compartir la comida con mis compañeros.
  I like to share food with my friends.

compartir algo en/entre uno/algo   to divide sth between sb/sth, share (out) sth between sb/sth

- Compartieron los bienes del difunto entre seis parientes.
  The estate of the deceased was divided among (or shared between) six relatives.

- Hay que compartir las frutas en estas dos cajas.
  The fruit should be divided between these two boxes.

compensar   to compensate for

- Hay que compensar el peso, poniendo más carga de ese lado.
  You have to compensate for the weight by loading more on the other side.

- El juez le dijo que tenía que compensar el daño cometido.
  The judge told him that he had to compensate for the damage he had done.

compensar con algo   to compensate with sth

- Compensaron los perjuicios ocasionados con una cantidad de dinero.
  They compensated for the damages with a sum of money.

- El compensa con esfuerzo su falta de talento.
  He compensates with effort for his lack of talent.

competir   to compete

- Los dos mejores atletas competirán esta noche.
  The two best athletes will compete tonight.

- No podrá competir el domingo.
  He won't be able to compete on Sunday.

competir con uno/algo   to compete with *or* against sb/sth

- Ana va a competir con una atleta panameña.
  Ann is going to compete with (or against) a Panamanian athlete.
- Nuestra compañía competirá con la empresa más grande.
  Our company will compete with the biggest company.

competir por/en algo   to compete for/in sth

- Están compitiendo por el primer premio.
  They are competing for the first prize.
- Compiten por dinero.
  They compete for money.
- Las modelos compiten en elegancia (/belleza/gracia/simpatía).
  The models compete in elegance (/beauty/grace/charm).

complacer   to please, be pleasant to

- Me complació su visita.
  Your visit pleased me.
- Me complace la presencia de nuestro presidente en mi casa.
  I am pleased by the presence of our president in my house.
- Le complace que usted haya ganado la beca.
  He is pleased that you've won the scholarship.
- Intentamos complacer al cliente.
  We try to please (or be pleasant to) the customer.

complacerse en + *inf*   to be pleased to + *inf*, take pleasure in + *inf*

- Nos complacemos en anunciar la boda de nuestro hijo.
  We are pleased to announce the wedding of our son.
- Me complazco en presentarles al señor Ramírez.
  I am pleased to introduce (or take pleasure in introducing) Mr. Ramirez to you.
- Nuestra institución se complace en invitarle a la fiesta de aniversario.
  Our institution is pleased to invite you to the anniversary party (or celebration).

componer   to compose; to make up; to fix, put together

- Mozart compuso sinfonías bellísimas.
  Mozart composed beautiful symphonies.
- ¿Quién va a componer el televisor?
  Who is going to fix (or put together) the television set?
- Seis diplomáticos componen la directiva (/el comité/el grupo).
  Six diplomats make up the board of directors (/the committee/the group).

componerse de algo   to consist of sth, be composed of sth

- El comité se compone de nueve miembros.
  The committee is composed (or consists) of nine members.

- La célula se compone de varias partes.
  The cell is comprised of several parts.

comprar   to buy, purchase

- Hoy compraré todo lo que necesito para la comida.
  Today I'll buy everything I need for the dinner.
- La muchacha compró un abrigo de lana.
  The girl bought a woolen coat.
- La compañía ha comprado tres aviones nuevos.
  The company has bought (or purchased) three new planes.
- Le compraré un regalito a mi hija menor.
  I'll buy a small gift for my youngest daughter.

comprar algo de uno   to buy sth from sb

- Lo compré de Luis.
  I bought it from Louis.
- Compramos de los mercaderes esta manta.
  We bought this blanket from the merchants.
- Hemos comprado la casa de mi tía.
  We've bought the house from my aunt.

comprometer   to compromise, implicate

- Sus declaraciones a la policía comprometieron a su amigo.
  His statements to the police compromised (or implicated) his friend.

comprometerse   to get involved, make a commitment

- Antonio y Rosa se han comprometido. Se casarán el próximo mes.
  Anthony and Rose got involved (or made a commitment). They will marry next month.

comprometerse a + *inf*   to agree to + *inf*, commit (oneself) to + *ger*

- Se comprometieron a llegar temprano.
  They agreed to arrive (or have committed themselves to arriving) early.
- Nos comprometemos a cuidar los caballos.
  We agree to watch the horses.
- Te has comprometido a jugar el domingo.
  You have agreed to play on Sunday.

comunicar   to communicate; to connect, link

- Yo te comunicaré las noticias cuando lleguen.
  I'll communicate the news to you when it arrives.
- Este puente comunica las dos ciudades.
  This bridge links the two cities.

- Esta carretera comunica la capital con las provincias.
  This highway connects (or links) the capital with the provinces.

comunicarse con uno/algo   to get in touch with sb/sth, communicate with sb

- Me comuniqué con Juan (/mi amigo).
  I got in touch (or communicated) with John (/with my friend).

- Nos pudimos comunicar con Santiago (/ese teléfono).
  We were able to get in touch (or communicate) with Santiago.

concentrar   to concentrate

- Por favor, concentra la atención.
  Please, concentrate (or give me your attention).

concentrar(se) en algo   to concentrate on sth

- La policía concentró a la multitud en el parque.
  The police confined the crowd to the park.

- Nos concentramos en un solo tema.
  We will concentrate on one theme only.

- Esta industria se ha concentrado en la producción de substancias químicas.
  This industry has concentrated on the production of chemical substances.

concluir   to conclude, finish, end

- La novela concluye tristemente.
  The novel ends sadly.

- Han concluido el trabajo.
  They have concluded the work.

concluir con/en algo   to conclude with sth, end with/in sth

- La ópera concluye con la muerte de la heroína.
  The opera ends (or concludes) with the death of the heroine.

- Los obreros concluyeron con la construcción del edificio.
  The workers finished the construction of the building.

- El profesor concluyó con la explicación de la lección.
  The professor concluded by explaining the lesson.

conluir en algo   to conclude in/with sth

- Mi apellido concluye en la letra "O."
  My last name ends with (or in) the letter "O."

- Esa revolución concluyó en el siglo XVIII.
  That revolution ended in the 18th century.

- No creo que la procesión haya concludido en la iglesia.
  I don't believe that the procession has ended in the church.

■ La fiesta concluyó en la madrugada.
The party ended at dawn.

concluir por + *inf* to end up + *ger*

■ Ella ha concluido por no ponerme atención.
She ended up not paying attention to me.

■ Si voy así, concluiré por tirarme de los pelos.
If I go on like this, I will end up pulling out my hair.

■ Tanto la quiere que ella concluirá por casarse con él.
He loves her so that she'll end up marrying him.

concurrir (a)   to meet (at), attend

■ La gente concurre a la playa para ver el desfile.
The people are meeting (or gathering) at the beach to see the parade.

■ Los socios concurren a la sesión del club.
The members are attending the club meeting.

concurrir en + *inf* to concur in + *ger*

■ Los estudios concurren en culpar al gobierno.
The studies concur in blaming the government.

■ Los testigos concurren en acusarlo.
The witnesses agree in accusing him.

■ Los estudios sobre el cáncer concurren en señalar al tabaco como causante de los tumores.
Studies about cancer concur in pointing out tobacco as the cause of tumors.

condenar (a)   to condemn, sentence (to)

■ El pueblo condenó la actitud del presidente (/las acciones bélicas).
The people condemned the president's attitude (/warlike actions).

■ Condenaron el edificio (/la ventana/la puerta).
They condemned the building (/the window/the door).

■ Lo condenaron a trabajos forzados (/10 años de prisión/exilio/muerte).
They sentenced him to forced labor (/ten years in prison/exile/death).

condenar a + *inf* to sentence + *inf*

■ La condenaron a pagar 10 mil pesos (/a morir en la horca).
She was sentenced to pay 10,000 pesos (/to death by hanging).

condenarse   to be damned, indict oneself

■ Para muchas religiones los pecadores se condenan.
In many religions sinners will be damned.

■ El acusado se condenó solo cuando respondió a la pregunta del fiscal.
The accused damned (or indicted) himself when he answered the public prosecutor's question.

- El delincuente se condenó solo.
  The criminal indicted himself.

conducir (a)   to drive (to)

- Usted conduce muy bien el auto.
  You drive the car very well.
- Los conducimos al aeropuerto (/al circo/al teatro/a su casa/al colegio).
  We'll drive you to the airport (/circus/theater/your house/school).

conducir a algo   to lead to

- Esta decisión ha de conducir a la ruina (/al desastre).
  This decision is bound to lead to ruin (/disaster).

conducirse   to behave, conduct

- Se condujo en el juego (/la fiesta/el gobierno/la escuela) muy bien.
  He conducted himself (or behaved) well in the game (/party/government/school).

confesar (a)   to confess (to)

- Confesó todos sus errores (/los pecados/las culpas).
  He confessed all his errors (/sins/faults).
- Confesó a la policía (/al juez/al sacerdote/al maestro).
  He confessed to the police (/judge/priest/teacher).

confesarse (a, con, de)   to confess, make one's confession (to)

- Se confesó con el sacerdote (/Dios).
  He confessed to the priest (/to God).
- Se confesó de sus culpas (/errores/pecados).
  He confessed his faults (/errors/sins).

confiar(se) de/en uno/algo   to trust sb/sth, entrust (oneself) to sb/sth

- Ella (se) confiaba de (*or* en) la voluntad divina.
  She trusted (or entrusted herself to) divine will.
- Miguel no (se) confía de (*or* en) nadie (/nada).
  Michael does not trust anyone (/anything).
- No confíes de (*or* en) lo que te dicen.
  Don't trust what they tell you.
- ¡Confía(te) de (*or* en) lo que te dicen tus padres!
  Trust what your parents tell you.
- ¡No (te) confíes de (*or* en) nadie!
  Do not trust (or entrust yourself to) anyone!
- No (nos) confiamos de (*or* en) su opinión.
  We do not trust his opinión.

conformar   to make agree, agree in; to shape, to form

- Debemos conformar nuestros criterios.
  We must make our judgements (or points of view) agree.

- Los casados deben conformar su manera de ser.
  Married couples must agree in their way of life.

- Van a conformar la selección nacional de fútbol.
  They are going to put together (or form) the national soccer team.

conformarse   to conform

- Se conformó cuando le dije que tendría un asiento.
  He conformed (or was agreeable) when I told him that he would have a seat.

conformarse con algo   to agree to sth; to settle for sth

- Yo me conformo con un sueldo razonable.
  I resign myself to a reasonable salary.

- Se conformó con poco (/un chocolate/diez pesos).
  She settled for (or agreed to) a little (/a chocolate/ten pesos).

confundir   to confuse

- Luis confundió las calles y se perdió.
  Luis confused the streets (or got the streets mixed up) and got lost.

- Yo siempre confundo a estos dos autores.
  I always confuse these two authors.

- Tú vas a confundir al niño hablándole tantas lenguas a la vez.
  You are going to confuse the child speaking to him in so many languages at the same time.

- Él confundió a las dos hermanas.
  He confused the two sisters.

confundir uno/algo con uno/algo   to confuse sb/sth with sb/sth, mistake sb/sth for sb/sth

- Los turistas confundieron un hipopótamo con un rinoceronte.
  The tourists confused a hippopotamus with a rhinoceros.

- ¡No confundas la gordura con la hinchazón!
  Do not confuse fatness with swelling.

- Confundieron las peras con las manzanas.
  They mistook pears for apples.

confundirse   to get confused

- Me confundo cuando te escucho hablar alemán.
  I get confused when I hear you speak German.

confundirse con/en algo   to get confused with/by/in sth

- Me confundí con sus instrucciones.
  I got confused with (or by) his directions.

- Nos confundíamos con el dinero de ese país.
  We got confused by that country's money.

- Ella no quería confundirse en sus respuestas.
  She did not want to get mixed up (or confused) with (or by) the answers.

- Es posible que se haya confundido en sus percepciones (/apreciaciones).
  It is possible that she has gotten confused in her perceptions (/estimates).

conocer   to know; to meet

- ¿Conoces al nuevo empleado? —No, no lo conozco.
  Do you know the employee? —No, I don't know him.

- Ella conoce a tu abuelita.
  She knows your grandma.

- Conocemos el restaurante que se incendió.
  We know the restaurant that burned down.

- Conocí a Lola en la playa.
  I met Lola at the beach.

- Ayer conocimos a los pintores franceses.
  Yesterday we met the French painters.

conocer de uno/algo   to know about sb/sth, know of sb/sth

- El profesor conocía algo de nuestros problemas.
  The professor knew something of our problems.

- Como usted conoce de fontanería, podría reparar la bañera.
  As you know about plumbing, you could repair the tub.

- Nunca le he hablado, sólo la conozco de vista.
  I've never talked to her; I only know (of) her by sight.

conocer por algo   to know for/by sth, be known for/by sth

- Lo conocemos por su inmensa fortuna.
  We know him for his huge fortune.

- La conocen (*or* es conocida) por su voz melodiosa.
  She is known for her melodious voice.

conseguir   to obtain, come by, get

- Conseguí una silla antiquísima (/dos billetes para el partido).
  I got (or came by) a very old chair (/two tickets for the game).

- Todos consiguieron aumentos de sueldo.
  Everybody obtained a salary increase.

- Consiga un poco de azúcar, por favor.
  Get some sugar, please.

consentir (a)   to consent (to); to permit, allow; to spoil, pamper

- Yo no consentiría lo que hacen tus empleados.
  I would not allow what your workers do.

- Él consintió esa situación.
  He allowed for (or permitted) that situation.

- La madre lo consiente tanto que va a convertirlo en un niño mimado.
  The mother pampers him so much that she is going to make him a spoiled child.

consentir en uno/algo   to agree with sb/sth

- El jefe consiente en lo que proponen (/en mi decisión).
  The boss agrees with what is proposed (/with my decision).

- El novio consintió en todo a la novia.
  The bridegroom agreed with the bride in everything.

consentir en + *inf*   to agree to + *inf*, to agree in + *ger*

- Todos consienten en comer a las tres.
  All agree in eating at three.

- Consintió en escribir un artículo, si se le pagaba doscientos dólares.
  He agreed to write an article if he was paid $200.

- Consintió en hablar por nosotros, si se lo pedíamos.
  He agreed to talk for us if we asked him.

consistir en algo   to consist of sth, be made of sth

- El infinitivo consiste en la raíz y el sufijo.
  The infinitive consits of the stem and the suffix.

- La historia consiste en el estudio de los hechos pasados.
  History consists of the study of past events.

- Mi oferta consiste en lo siguiente: . . .
  My offer consists of the following: . . .

consistir en + *inf*   to consist in + *ger*

- El secreto de la salud consiste en comer bien.
  The secret to health consists in eating well.

- El truco consiste en hacerlo rápidamente.
  The trick is to do it quickly.

constar   to be clear, be listed, be included

- Conste que el señor Pérez no trabajó para mí.
  Let it be clear that Mr. Perez did not work for me.

- ¿Por qué aquí no consta su testimonio?
  Why is his testimony not listed (or included) here?

■ En la licencia para manejar (/el documento) no consta su edad.
His age is not included on the driver's license (/document).

constar de algo   to consist of sth

■ El examen consta de diez preguntas.
The exam consists of ten questions.

■ El poema consta de cuatro estrofas, cada una de cuatro versos.
The poem consists of four stanzas, each with four verses.

constar en algo   to be clear from sth, stated clearly in sth

■ Como consta en el documento, yo quedo liberado de toda responsabilidad.
As is clearly stated in the document, I am absolved of any responsibility.

■ En el acta consta que no hubo quórum.
It is clear from (or stated clearly in) the minutes that there was no quorum.

■ Es necesario que conste en la carta de venta que el artículo tiene garantía.
It's necessary that it be clear in the letter of sale that the product does have a guarantee.

constituir   to establish, form, set up

■ Vamos a constituir una sociedad.
We are going to form (or set up) a society.

■ En 1980, varios estudiantes constituyeron un grupo de poetas.
In 1980 several students established a group of poets.

construir   to construct, build, erect, put up

■ Ellas construyen una casa muy bonita.
They are building a very pretty house.

■ Por favor, construya una oración pasiva.
Please, construct (or form) a passive sentence.

construir con algo   to build with sth

■ En ese pueblo construyen las casas con cañas de bambú.
In that town houses are built with bamboo.

■ Construímos una columna con ladrillos y concreto.
We're building a column with brick and concrete.

consultar   to consult, discuss

■ He consultado mis dudas gramaticales (con el maestro).
I've discussed my grammatical doubts (with the teacher).

■ Consultemos el diccionario, así saldremos de duda.
Let's consult the dictionary; we'll be sure that way.

consultar a/con uno (acerca de, sobre)   to consult (with) sb (about)

- No quiero consultar a (*or* con) mis amigos sobre el problema.
  I don't want to consult my friends about the problem.

- Está consultando con un abogado del asunto.
  He's consulting with a laywer about the matter.

- Voy a consultar a (*or* con) un ingeniero (/arquitecto) antes de comenzar la obra.
  I am going to consult with an engineer (/architect) before beginning.

contar (acerca de, de)   to tell (about); to count (to); (*fig*) to count, matter

- Te contaré un cuento de hadas.
  I'll tell you a fairy tale.

- Les contó la historia de su vida.
  He told them the story of his life.

- ¡Cuéntele a él acerca de tu matrimonio!
  Tell him about your marriage.

- Ellos contaban el dinero cuando los visité.
  They were counting the money when I visited them.

- El niño puede contar de uno a cien (/puede contar hasta cien).
  The child can count from one to one hundred (/can count up to one hundred).

- Esos puntos no cuentan.
  Those points don't count.

contar con uno/algo   to count on sb/sth, rely on sb/sth

- Carmen contaba con nuestra presencia (/ayuda) en la reunión.
  Carmen was counting on our presence (/help) at the meeting.

- Cuento con su testimonio en el tribunal.
  I am counting on your testimony in court.

- ¡Cuenta conmigo (/con ello)!
  You can rely (or count) on me (/it)!

contender   to contend, compete, fight

- Los dos contendían acaloradamente.
  The two contended (or competed or fought) heatedly.

contender con uno   to compete with sb, contend with sb; to fight with sb

- Miguel contendía con Juan por el amor de una mujer.
  Michael competed (or was contending) with John for the love of a woman.

- No vale la pena contender con ese individuo.
  It's not worthwhile to compete (or contend) with that individual.

- El contendía con los ladrones.
  He fought with the thieves.

contender en algo   to compete in sth

- Las concursantes han contendido en elegancia (/simpatía).
  The participants have competed in elegance (/charm).

contender sobre algo   to argue over sth

- Los ministros contendieron sobre la economía.
  The ministers argued over the economy.

- Siempre contendían sobre temas controversiales.
  They would always argue over controversial topics.

contentar   to satisfy, make content; to please, make happy

- Hay que contentar a Rosita.
  Rosita must be pleased (or *made happy).*

- Aquí tienes este regalo para que te contentes.
  Here, you have this present so that you'll be content (or *satisfied).*

contentar a una con algo   to please sb with sth

- Lo contentamos con un juguete.
  We pleased him with a toy.

- El gobierno cree que nos contenta con fiestas.
  The government thinks that holidays make us happy.

contentarse con algo   to be pleased with sth, be satisfied with sth

- Nos contentamos con un regalito.
  We were satisfied with a small gift.

- Se han contentado con mi decisión.
  They have been pleased with my decision.

- No me contento con un solo plato.
  I am not satisfied with only one dish.

contestar   to answer, reply

- El estudiante no le pudo contestar a la profesora.
  The student couldn't answer the teacher.

- ¿Puedes contestar esta pregunta? —No, no puedo contestarla.
  Can you answer this question? —No, I can't answer it.

- Mi mamá me ha escrito dos cartas y yo no las he contestado.
  My mother has written two letters to me and I haven't answered them (or *replied).*

- Juan te llamó dos veces. —¿Le contestaste?
  John called you twice. —Did you answer him?

- ¿Has contestado la llamada de tu mamá? —Sí, ya la contesté.
  Have your answered your mom's call? —Yes, I have already answered.

continuar   to continue, go on with

■ Debo continuar el trabajo.
   I must continue (or go on with) the work.

■ Continuaremos la construcción de la escuela.
   We will continue building the school.

continuar + *ger*   to continue + *inf/ger*, go on + *ger*

■ Continuaremos eschuchando la conferencia.
   We'll continue listening (or to listen) to the conference.

■ Continuó trabajando (/pintando la casa/hablando a su esposa).
   He continued working (/painting the house/talking to his wife).

continuar con/en algo   to continue with sth, go on with sth

■ La maestra continuó con el cuento.
   The teacher continued with the story.

■ Ha continuado con la lectura del libro.
   He has gone on with (or continued) reading the book.

■ Todavía continúo con este trabajo.
   I am still going on with (or continuing) this work.

■ Mi hermana continúa en Costa Rica.
   My sister is still in Costa Rica.

■ Continuaremos en huelga hasta que el gobierno ceda.
   We shall go on with the strike until the government yields.

contraponer   to compare; to oppose

■ El siempre contrapone sus ideas.
   He's always comparing his ideas.

■ No me gusta que contrapongan mis decisiones.
   I don't like my decisions opposed.

contraponer algo a algo   to oppose sth with sth, contradict sth with sth

■ ¡No contrapongas tus opiniones a las mías!
   Don't contradict my opinions with yours!

■ Contrapondremos a esta fuerza otra mayor.
   We shall meet this force with a greater force.

■ Ellos contrapusieron a un argumento falso otro verdadero.
   They opposed a true argument over a false one.

contrastar   to contrast, be in contrast

■ En el mundo todo contrasta.
   In the world everything is in contrast.

■ Es necesario que los colores contrasten.
   It's necessary for the colors to (be in) contrast.

contravenir (a)   to contravene, act counter to, violate

■ ¡No contravengas (*less frequently:* a) las leyes!
   Do not violate (or act counter to) the law!

■ Fueron expulsados por contravenir (*less frequently:* a) las disposiciones del colegio.
   They were expelled for violating the school's regulation.

■ Contravino el (*less frequently*: al) reglamento de nuestra institución.
   He violated the rules of our institution.

contribuir   to contribute

■ No puedo contribuir. No tengo dinero.
   I can't contribute. I don't have money.

contribuir a/para algo   to contribute to/towards sth

■ Contribuiremos a (*or* para) la construcción de la escuela.
   We'll contribute to (or towards) the construction of the school.

■ He contribuido a (*or* para) una buena causa (/al éxito del proyecto).
   I have contributed to (or towards) a good cause (/to the success of the project).

contribuir con algo   to contribute with sth

■ Contribuí con libros para la biblioteca.
   I contributed with books for the library.

■ Estéfano ha contribuido con mano de obra a la construcción de la escuela.
   Stephen has contributed his labor to the school's construction.

convalecer (de)   to recuperate, recover (from), get better (after)

■ Mi amigo está convaleciendo.
   My friend is recuperating.

■ Él convalece de una enfermedad grave (/operación).
   He is recovering from a serious illness (/an operation).

■ Me dijo que Miguel no convalecía del accidente.
   He told me that Michael was not getting better after (or recovering from) the accident.

convencer (con)   to convince (with), pursuade

■ Tus palabras no podrán convencerla.
   Your words will not be able to convince her.

■ Lo convencí con una oferta excelente.
   I persuaded him with an excellent offer.

■ No lo vas a convencer sólo con palabras.
   You are not going to convince him only with words.

convencerse (de)   to be convinced (of/about)

- Me convencí de tu deslealtad.
  I was convinced of your disloyalty.

- Quiero que se convenza de lo que ha pasado en realidad.
  I want him to be convinced about what actually happened.

- Finalmente se convenció.
  Finally, he was convinced.

convenir   to suit, be suitable

- Conviene que el niño tome mucha leche.
  It's suitable for the child to drink a lot of milk.

convenir a uno   to be convenient for sb; to suit sb; to be good for sb

- Conviene al enfermo no levantarse.
  It is good for the patient not to get up.

- Este negocio me conviene, por lo tanto lo haré.
  This business suits me; therefore, I'll do it.

- ¿Qué les conviene a ustedes: un coche o una camioneta?
  What is convenient for you—a car or a station wagon?

convenir con uno/en algo   to agree with sb/sth, agree on sb/sth

- Convine con Andrés en el precio del piano.
  I agreed with Andrew on the price of the piano.

- Convinimos con los vecinos sobre las obligaciones de cada uno.
  We agreed with the neighbors about each other's obligations.

- No pensamos que hayan convenido en la liberación de los rehenes.
  We do not think they have agreed on the release of the hostages.

- El director y el profesor convinieron en la expulsión de dos estudiantes.
  The principal and the teacher agreed on the expulsion of two students.

convenir en + *inf*   to agree on + *ger*

- Pedro y yo convenimos en comprar una nueva máquina de escribir.
  Peter and I agree on buying a new typewriter.

- Todos convinimos en trabajar los sábados.
  Everybody agreed on working on Saturday.

converger   to converge

- Los dos ríos convergen antes de llegar al mar.
  The two rivers converge before reaching the sea.

converger en algo   to converge on sth

- Las dos líneas convergen en este punto.
  The two lines converge on this spot.

■ Las ideas convergen en algunos aspectos. (*fig*)
*The ideas converge (*or *concur) on some aspects.*

conversar   to talk, converse

■ A mis amigas les encanta conversar.
*My friends love to talk (*or *converse).*

■ Está bien, conversaremos, si es lo más conveniente para resolver el problema.
Fine, we'll talk, if that is the most convenient way to resolve the problem.

conversar con uno   to talk to sb

■ Ojalá que Margarita haya conversado con tu hermano.
I hope Margaret has talked to your brother.

■ Quiero conversar con tu padre.
I want to talk to the engineer.

■ Deseo que Gabriel converse con el ingeniero.
I want Gabriel to talk to the engineer.

conversar de/sobre uno/algo   to talk about sb/sth

■ ¡Conversemos de (*or* sobre) el accidente!
Let's talk about the accident.

■ Ellos conversaban sobre (*or* de) Lucía (/el actor famoso).
They were talking about Lucy (/the famous actor).

convertir   to convert, turn, change

■ Por fin lo convertimos, ahora está con nosotros.
Finally, we converted him; now he's with us.

convertir algo en algo   to convert sth to sth, turn sth into sth, transform sth into sth

■ Convertiremos nuestras ideas en hechos.
We will convert our ideas into deeds.

■ Ha convertido su garaje en oficina.
He has turned his garage into an office.

■ Cristo convirtió el agua en vino.
Christ transformed water into wine.

convertirse a algo   to convert to sth

■ Roberto se convirtió al cristianismo (/judaísmo/islam).
Robert converted to Christianity (/Judaism/Islam).

convertirse en uno/algo   to change into sb/sth, become sb/sth

■ En la película el hombre se convirtió en vampiro.
In the film the man transformed himself into a vampire.

■ Me he convertido en una persona responsable.
I've changed into a responsible person.

- Ellos se convirtieron en alcohólicos.
  They became alcoholics.
- El pueblo se convirtió en un infierno después de la guerra.
  The town became an inferno after the war.

convidar   to invite

- Iremos a la fiesta porque Luis nos ha convidado.
  We'll go to the party because Luis has invited us.

convidar a algo   to invite to sth

- El jefe nos convidó a sus fiestas.
  The boss invited us to his parties.
- Te convidaré al cine cuando me paguen.
  I'll invite you to the movies when they pay me.

convidar a + *inf*   to invite to + *inf*

- Le convidó a cenar en el mejor restaurante de la capital.
  She invited him to the best restaurant in the capital.
- Te convidaré a ver una magnífica película.
  I'll invite you to see a great movie.

convocar   to summon, call (together)

- Los médicos han sido convocados urgentemente.
  The doctors have been urgently summoned (or *called together*).
- ¿Te han convocado a tí?
  Have they summoned (or *called for*) *you?*

convocar a algo   to call for/to sth

- Convocaremos a una reunión a todos los miembros del club.
  We'll call for a meeting of all the members of the club.
- Nos convocaron al congreso anual de filología.
  We were called to the Annual Conference of Philology.

corregir   to correct

- He corregido todas las frases (/equivocaciones).
  I've corrected all the sentences (/errors).
- La maestra corrigió las pruebas (/al muchacho).
  The teacher corrected the tests (/student).

correr   to run; to race

- El atleta correrá 40 km mañana.
  The athlete will run 40 km tomorrow.

■ Corrió al mercado (en el parque/hacia su novia).
He ran to the market (/through the park/to his sweetheart).

■ La electricidad corre por los cables.
The electricity runs through (the) cables.

■ El agua corre al norte (/en esta dirección).
The water runs north (/in this direction).

corresponder a/con algo   to correspond with sth

■ Lo escrito no corresponde a (*or* con) lo dicho.
What is written does not correspond with what was said.

■ La factura no corresponde con el cheque.
The bill does not correspond with the check.

corresponder con algo   to reciprocate with sth

■ Correspondimos con nuestro agradecimiento(/nuestra visita).
We reciprocated with our gratitude (/visit).

cortar   to cut, (up, off, through, etc.)

■ ¡Cortemos la tabla!
Let's cut the board (or plank).

■ Cortaré el pantalón para ir a la playa.
I'll cut off the pants to wear to the beach.

■ Corté el papel por la mitad con las tijeras.
I cut the paper down the middle with scissors.

costar   to cost

■ ¿Cuánto cuesta la entrada al teatro?
How much does the ticket to the theater cost?

■ Eso le costó su vida (/mucho tiempo).
That cost him his life (/a lot of time).

costar (a uno) + *inf*   to cost sb to + *inf*

■ ¿Cuánto me cuesta viajar a España (/quedarme en un hotel)?
How much will it cost me to travel to Spain (/to stay a day in a hotel)?

■ ¿Cuánto cuesta reparar (/comprar) el coche?
How much does it cost to repair (/to buy) the car?

■ ¡Me cuesta estudiar!
It's hard for me to study.

crecer   to grow; to increase; to rise

■ Nuestro hijo crece demasiado rápidamente.
Our son is growing up too quickly.

- El río creció demasiado.
  The river rose too much.
- El maíz ha crecido.
  The corn has grown.
- Ha crecido la intensidad del viento.
  The intensity of the wind has increased.

creer   to think, believe; to deem, consider

- Muchas personas creen que hay vida en otros planetas.
  Many people believe that there is life on other planets.
- No creemos que Lola venga hoy.
  We don't think Lola will come today.
- Lo creen un cobarde.
  They consider him (a) coward.
- Creemos que es necesario.
  We deem it necessary.

creer en uno/algo   to believe in sb/sth

- Creo en la justicia y en la libertad.
  I believe in justice and liberty.
- Siempre hemos creído en su sinceridad.
  We have always believed in her sincerity.

creerse   to believe oneself to be

- Rolando se cree superior a sus amigos.
  Roland believes he's better than his friends.
- José se cree muy guapo.
  Joseph thinks he is quite handsome.

cruzar   to cross; to cut across

- El ciego pudo cruzar la calle.
  The blind man managed to cross the street.
- Cruzaremos el puente.
  We'll cut across (or cross) the bridge.

cubrir   to cover

- El escultor cubrió la estatua.
  The sculptor covered the statue.
- Este dinero cubre todos los gastos.
  This money will cover all expenses.

cubrir(se) con algo   to cover (oneself) with sth

- Ella cubrió el maniquí con ropas finísimas.
  He covered the mannequin with very fine clothes.

- En algunos países las mujeres se cubren con un velo la cara.
  In some countries women cover their faces with a veil.

- Se cubrió con un poncho.
  He covered himself with a poncho.

cuidar   to take care of, look after

- Te aconsejo que cuides tus pertenencias.
  I advise you to take care of (or look after) your property.

- Él cuida la escuela cuando está cerrada.
  He takes care of the school when it's closed.

cuidar de uno/algo   to take care of sb/sth

- Tú cuidas muy bien de tu familia.
  You take good care of your family.

- ¡No bebas más, cuida de tu vida!
  Don't drink anymore. Take care of your life!

- ¡Cuidaremos de tu salud, no te preocupes!
  We'll take care of your health; don't worry!

cuidarse   to take care of oneself

- Me cuido mucho, por eso tengo buena salud.
  I take good care of myself; that is why I enjoy good health.

- Tienes que cuidarte, recuerda que has estado muy enferma.
  You have to take care of yourself; remember that you've been very sick.

cuidarse de uno   to protect oneself from sb, be careful of sb

- Nos hemos cuidado de nuestros enemigos.
  We've protected ourselves from our enemies.

- Se cuidaron de que nadie los perturbara.
  They took pains so nobody would disturb them.

- Me cuidaré de los conductores imprudentes.
  I'll watch out for (or protect myself from) reckless drivers.

- ¡Cuídate de las malas compañías!
  Protect yourself from (or against) bad company.

culpar   to blame, accuse

- No quiero culpar a nadie.
  I do not want to blame anyone.

- El jurado lo culpó.
  The jury found him guilty.

culpar a uno por/de algo   to blame sb for sth, accuse sb of sth

- Me culpó por los daños causados en el accidente.
  He blamed me for the damages caused by the accident.

- Él siempre me culpa a mí de su fracaso.
  He always blames me for his failure.

- Vamos a culparlo por robo.
  We are going to accuse him of robbery.

- Lo culpan de negligencia.
  They accuse him of negligence.

cumplir   to carry out, fulfill; to turn (*age*)

- He cumplido el tratado.
  I've carried out the treaty.

- Ella cumplió su palabra.
  She fulfilled (or kept) her word.

- Mi abuela cumple hoy ochenta años.
  My grandmother turns eighty years old today.

cumplir con algo   to fulfil sth, comply with sth

- Me voy porque he cumplido con todas las obligaciones.
  I am leaving because I've fulfilled all my obligations.

- Cumplió con lo que le prometió a Irene.
  He fulfilled his promise to Irene.

- Te aconsejo que cumplas con todos los requisitos de migración.
  I advise you to comply with all immigration requirements.

curar (con)   to cure; to treat (with)

- No creo que esa medicina cure.
  I don't think that medicine will work.

- Te curaré la herida (con alcohol).
  I'll treat your wound with alcohol.

curarse (con)   to cure oneself (with), recover

- Me curaré con plantas medicinales.
  I'll cure myself with medicinal plants.

- Margarita se curará pronto.
  Margaret will recover soon.

- Su enfermdedad se cura con penicilina.
  His disease is treated with penicillin.

curarse de algo   to recover from sth

- Me alegro de que te hayas curado de tu dolencia.
  I am glad that you've recovered from your illness.

- La niña se ha curado de la gripe (/tos).
  The girl has recovered from a cold (/cough).

Ch

charlar   to talk, chat; to chatter

- Charlemos mientras viene mamá.
  Let's talk (or chat) while we are waiting for mom.

- A ti te encanta charlar.
  You love to talk.

charlar de/sobre algo   to talk about sth

- El profesor charlará de (*or* sobre) los aztecas.
  The professor will talk about the Aztecs.

- Es agradable charlar de (*or* sobre) tiempos pasados con los amigos.
  It's pleasant to talk about old times with friends.

chocar   to collide, crash; to shock

- Anoche dos carros chocaron en esta esquina.
  Last night two cars collided (or crashed) on this corner.

- Su comentarios chocaron a los presentes.
  His comments shocked those present.

chocar con uno/contra algo   contra to collide with sb/sth, crash into sb/sth; to clash with sb, fight with sb

- Él choca con todos sus compañeros.
  He clashes (or fights) with all his friends.

- El tren chocó con (*or* contra) un autobús.
  The train collided with a bus.

D

dar (a) to give, hand, pass (to); to yield, produce; to work, function

- Le doy mi libro (/dinero/agua/un beso).
  I give you my book (/money/water/a kiss).

- Por favor, dame el martillo (/ese libro/la azucarera).
  Please, hand (or pass) me the hammer (/that book/the sugar bowl).

- Ese valle da muchas manzanas.
  That valley produces (or yields) a lot of apples.

- Esa lámpara da mucha luz.
  That lamp gives out (or produces) a lot of light.

- La batería no da energía.
  The battery doesn't work.

- Me dio un beso en la mejilla.
  She kissed me on the cheek.

dar (con, en) to hit, strike (with); to hit, land (on)

- Le dio con un palo (/un azote/una piedra).
  She hit (or struck) him with a stick (/whip/rock).

- Le dieron un golpe muy duro.
  They hit her very hard.

- Me dieron un pelotazo cuando jugaba.
  They hit me with the ball when I was playing.

- El reloj de la iglesia dio las tres.
  The clock of the church struck three.

- Ese viento me daba en la cabeza.
  That wind was hitting (or blowing in) my head.

- La pelota le dio en la cara.
  The ball hit her in the face.

dar a to look (out) on, overlook; to face (towards)

- Mi ventana da al jardín (/a la calle principal).
  My window overlooks (or faces) the garden (/the main street).

dar con uno/algo   to meet sb/sth, find sb/sth; to hit on/upon sth

- Después de mucho trabajo dieron con la solución.
  After a lot of work, they hit upon the solution.

- Finalmente dio con la persona que buscaba.
  Finally he found (or *met*) *the person he was looking for.*

- La busqué por todo el pueblo y no pude dar con ella.
  I looked for her all over town, and I could not find her.

dar de algo   to hit, kick, strike

- Los chicos le dieron de patadas (/de puñetazos/de palos/de manazos).
  The boys kicked him (/*hit him with their fists*/*hit him with sticks*/*hit him with their hands* or *slapped him*).

dar en algo   to shine in/on/through, *etc.* sth

- El sol de la mañana daba en su ventana.
  The morning sun shone in (or *through*) *her window.*

- El sol le daba en los ojos.
  The sun was shining in her eyes.

dar en (*or* por) + *inf*   to take to + *ger,* get into the habit of + *ger*

- Le dio en (*or* por) comer sólo carne de pollo.
  He took to eating only chicken.

- A esa chica le ha dado en (*or* por) dormir de día.
  That girl has taken to sleeping in the daytime.

- En el colegio han dado en (*or* por) llamarle el Gordo.
  In this school they've taken to (or *they're in the habit of*) *calling him the "fat one."*

dar algo por + *adj*   to consider sth + *adj*

- ¿El contrato? ¡Dalo por hecho!
  The contract? Consider it done.

- Mi jefe lo dio por cierto (/por terminado).
  My boss considered it certain (/finished).

- Lo vieron en el suelo y lo dieron por muerto.
  They saw him on the ground, and they thought (or *figured*) *he was dead.*

darse con algo   to hit oneself with sth

- Pedro se dio con el libro en la cabeza.
  Peter hit his head with the book.

- Me di con la pluma en el ojo.
  I hit myself in my eye with the pen.

darse uno a algo   to give oneself to sb/sth, dedicate oneself to sb/sth, surrender to sb/sth

- Se dio a la bebida.
  He took to drink.

- Se dieron al estudio (/a las matemáticas).
  They applied (or dedicated) themselves to studying (/mathematics).

- Se dio al deporte con todo su ser.
  He gave himself to sports with all his being.

darse + *inf* por algo   to make oneself + *ptp* by sth

- Se dio a conocer por una novela de suspenso.
  He made himself known by a mystery novel.

- El mudo se da a entender por señas.
  The deaf mute makes himself understood by signs.

datar   to date, put a date on

- ¡Data la carta antes de cerrarla!
  Date the letter before closing it!

datar de algo   to date from sth, date back to sth

- Los documentos que han encontrado datan del siglo XV (/de muy atrás).
  The documents they have found date from (or back to) the 15th century (/go a long way back).

deber   to owe

- Me debes diez pesos.
  You owe me ten pesos.

- Le debíamos mucho dinero al banco.
  We used to owe a lot of money to the bank.

- Nosotros le debemos este favor (/una visita).
  We owe you this favor (/a visit).

deber + *inf*   to have to + *inf* (*must = obligation*)

- Debo ir (/dormir tarde/lavarme/hacerlo).
  I have to (or must) go (/to sleep late/wash up/do it).

- Debes pagar los impuestos a tiempo.
  You must pay your taxes on time.

- Debieras llamarla porque ella llamó tres veces.
  You ought to (or should) call her because she called three times.

deber de + *inf*   to be supposed to + *inf* (*must = supposition*)

- El avión debe de llegar temprano hoy.
  The plane is supposed to (or should) arrive early today.

■ Debió de estar viajando por Europa.
   He was supposed to be traveling through Europe.

■ Si malgasta así el dinero, debe de ser muy rico.
   If he wastes his money like that, he must be very rich.

■ No la encuentro en casa, debe de estar en el parque.
   I can't find her here; she must be in the park.

decidir algo   to decide sth

■ ¡Piénsalo bien, pero decide esta situación pronto!
   Think about it, but decide what to do about this situation soon.

decidir(se) a + *inf*   to decide to + *inf*, make up one's mind to + *inf*

■ Finalmente decidimos comprar la casa.
   Finally, we decided to buy the house.

■ Después de mucha discusión decidimos hacerlo.
   After much discussion we decided to do it.

■ Decidiste vender los muebles.
   You decided to sell the furniture.

■ Decidí (*or* Me decidí a) hablar en público.
   I made up my mind to speak in public.

■ Decidió (*or* Se decidió a) trabajar con su padre.
   He decided to work with his father.

decidirse por algo   to decide (on) sth, choose sth

■ Ella se decidió por el coche rojo.
   She chose (or decided on) the red car.

■ Los jueces se decidirán por la legalidad de la ley.
   The judges will decide (on) the legality of the law.

decir   to say; to tell

■ Yo le digo siempre la verdad.
   I always tell him the truth.

■ ¿Quién te dijo que yo no vendría?
   Who told you I was not coming?

■ ¿Qué le dijiste a María?
   What did you say to Mary?

■ Yo le dije al jefe: "buenos días."
   I said good morning to the boss.

decir de/sobre uno/algo   to say about sb/sth, tell about sb/sth

■ ¿Qué dices de este libro (/de esto)?
   What do you say about this book (/that)?

■ ¿Qué tenía que decir sobre (*or* de) ese asunto (/este profesor)?
What did he have to say about that business (/this professor)?

■ En su carta no dice nada sobre (*or* de) la situación política.
In his letter he does not say anything about the political situation.

decir algo por + *inf*   to say sth to + *inf*

■ Sólo lo digo por jugar.
*I only say it to joke (*or *as a joke).*

■ Yo sé que lo dice por fastidiarme.
I know he says it to bother me.

decir por uno   to tell for/about sb

■ Eso lo dije por él, no lo dije por ti.
I said that referring to him, not about you.

dedicar algo a uno/algo   to dedicate sth to sb/sth

■ Yo le dediqué el poema.
I dedicated the poem to her.

■ Ella le dedica a su hijo todas las horas del día.
She dedicates all hours of the day to her son.

■ Juan dedicaba a sus estudios tres horas diarias.
John would dedicate three hours to his studies daily.

dedicar a + *inf*   to dedicate to + *inf*, devote to + *inf*

■ Todo su tiempo lo dedica a escribir.
*He devotes (*or *dedicates) all his time to writing.*

■ Dedica media hora a trabajar en su jardín (/a ejercitarse).
He devotes half an hour to working in his garden (/exercise).

dedicarse a + *inf*   to devote oneself to + *ger*, dedicate oneself to + *ger*

■ Ahora sólo me dedico a escribir.
*Now I devote (*or *dedicate) myself to writing only.*

■ Es tiempo de dedicarse a estudiar para los exámenes.
It's time to devote ourselves to studying for the exams.

dedicarse uno a algo   to devote oneself to sb/sth

■ Se ha dedicado toda su vida a Dios (/su familia/a la política).
He has dedicated his whole life to God (/his family/to politics).

defender   to defend

■ Los soldados defendieron el fuerte (/su posición/su país) hasta la muerte.
The soldiers defended the fort (/their position/their country) until death.

- El abogado defendió al acusado.
  The lawyer defended the accused.

- El ministro defendió la política exterior de su país.
  The minister defended his country's foreign policy.

defender(se) contra/de uno/algo to defend (oneself) against/from sb/sth, protect (oneself) from/against sb/sth

- Las vitaminas defienden al cuerpo contra (*or* de) las enfermedades.
  Vitamins protect the body from disease.

- Su familia lo defendió contra (*or* de) los ataques del partido.
  His family defended him from the attacks of the party.

- Con un buen abrigo me defiendo contra (*or* de) este frío.
  I protect myself from this cold with a warm coat.

- Nadie defendió a la anciana contra el (*or* del) ladrón.
  No one defended the old lady from the thief.

dejar to leave, forget; to abandon, desert; to lend; to give up, stop, set down; to let, allow to

- Dejé la casa a las siete (/mi país cuando era muy joven).
  I left the house at seven o'clock (/my country when I was very young).

- Dejó su libro (/bolsa) en tu casa.
  She left (or forgot) her book (/purse) in your house.

- Mi papá (/El taxi) me va a dejar en la estación del tren.
  My dad (/The taxi) will leave me at (or take me to) the train station.

- Lo dejaron en medio del desierto.
  They left (or abandoned) him in the middle of the desert.

- Ya estoy cansado, dejemos esto para mañana (/para después).
  I'm tired; let's leave the work for tomorrow (/later).

- Yo lo dejé para que lo hiciera Luis.
  I left it for Louis to do.

- ¿Dónde dejo el paquete? —¡Déjalo sobre la mesa!
  Where do I leave (or set) the package (down)? —Leave it on the table.

- Dejaron a María sin dinero.
  They left Mary without money.

- ¡Dejemos esta discusión (/cuestión ahora)!
  Let's stop (or give up or drop) this argument (/question now)!

- ¿Me dejas el auto (/5 dólares)?
  Can you lend me your car (/5 dollars)?

- Mi mamá no me deja ir al baile con mi novio.
  My mom won't let me go to the dance with my boyfriend.

- Quiero hacerlo, pero no me dejan.
  I want to do it, but they won't let me.

- La policía no deja que se acerquen.
  The police don't allow them to get near.

dejar de + *inf*   to stop + *ger,* quit + *ger*

- Ya ha dejado de llover.
  It has stopped raining already.
- Dejé de comer (/trabajar) en ese restaurante.
  I stopped eating (/working) in that restaurant.
- No puede dejar de fumar.
  He can't quit smoking.

dejarse + *inf*   to let oneself be + *ptp*

- !No te dejes dominar por la pereza!
  Do not let yourself be dominated by laziness.
- Yo me he dejado llenar la cabeza de mentiras.
  I have let my head be filled with lies.
- El se dejó ganar por un jugador sin experiencia.
  He let himself be beaten by a player without experience.

demostrar   to demonstrate, show; to prove

- El alumno demostró que sabía la lección.
  The student demonstrated (or proved) that he knew the lesson.
- Él demuestra inteligencia en sus acciones.
  He shows intelligence through his actions.
- El abogado demostró habilidad en los tribunales.
  The lawyer demonstrated skill in the courts.

depender de uno/algo   to depend on sb/sth

- Nuestro viaje depende de que consigamos reservaciones.
  Our trip depends on whether we get reservations.
- El turismo depende de la situación política.
  Tourism depends on the political situation.
- Depende de lo que hagan los García.
  It depends on what the Garcias will do.
- No depende de mí (/ti/Juan/sus padres).
  It does not depend on (or rest with) me (/you/John/his parents).

derivar(se) de algo   to derive from sth, be derived from sth

- ¿De qué lengua (se) deriva la palabra "pampa?" —Del quechua.
  From what language is the word "pampa" derived? —From Quechua.
- El ron se deriva de la caña de azúcar.
  Rum is derived from sugar cane.

- Los productos plásticos se derivan del petróleo.
  Plastic products are derived from oil.

derivar hacia algo   to divert to/towards sth; to drift towards

- Ella deriva siempre la conversación hacia la política (/otro asunto).
  She always diverts the conversation to politics (/another topic).

- Ese barco derivó hacia las rocas.
  That ship drifted towards the rocks.

desayunar(se) (con)   to breakfast, have breakfast (with)

- ¿A qué hora desayunaste esta mañana?
  At what time did you have breakfast this morning?

- Durante el verano me desayuno muy temprano.
  During the summer I have a very early breakfast.

- Esta mañana me he desayunado con frutas (/café caliente).
  This morning I had breakfast with fruits (/hot coffee).

descansar (sobre, en)   to rest; to support, be supported (on, upon, by)

- Posiblemente ha descansado mucho porque se ve muy bien.
  She has possibly rested (or slept) well because she looks good.

- Yo descanso en mi casa (/la playa/las vacaciones).
  I rest at my home (/on the beach/on vacations).

- La economía del país descansa en la exportación de minerales. (*fig*)
  The country's economy rests on mineral exports.

- La torre descansa sobre cuatro enormes bloques de cemento.
  The tower rests on (or is supported by) four huge cement blocks.

- Ella descansa sobre la arena (/en *or* sobre el césped).
  She rests on the beach (/on the grass).

descender a algo   to descend to sth, go down to

- Descendieron al cráter del volcán (/a las profundidades de la caverna).
  They descended into (or went down into) the volcano's crater (/depths of the cavern).

- Descendimos al sótano del banco.
  We descended to the bank's basement.

descender de algo   to descend from sth; to be derived from sth

- Esa familia desciende de antigua nobleza.
  That family descends from old nobility.

- Hay muchas palabras en español que descienden del árabe.
  There are many words in Spanish that are derived from Arabic.

descender sobre uno/algo   to descend upon/on sb/sth

- Descendió sobre el valle (/ellos) una terrible tormenta.
  A terrible storm descended upon the valley (/them).

describir   to describe, sketch

- Pepita, ¿me puedes describir a tu maestro? —No, no lo puedo describir.
  Pepita, can you describe your teacher to me? —No, I can't describe him.
- El testigo describió al ladrón.
  The witness described the thief.
- Por favor, descríbale (al juez) lo que pasó.
  Please, describe to him (the judge) what happened.
- El artículo describe la situación política del país.
  The article describes the country's political situation.

desear (de)   to wish (for), desire, want (from)

- El chico desea una bicicleta.
  The boy wants to have (or desires) a bicycle.
- Le deseamos a María buena suerte (/toda clase de éxito).
  We wish Mary good luck (/every success).
- Le deseo a usted mucha felicidad.
  I wish you lots of happiness.
- Deseo que la guerra termine (/que llegue el buen tiempo).
  I wish the war would end (/that the good weather would arrive).
- Deseo de todos mucho esfuerzo en esta empresa.
  I want a lot of effort from everyone in this enterprise.

desear + *inf*   to want to + *inf*

- Deseo comer un buen pastel de manzana.
  I want to eat a good apple pie.
- Deseaba viajar este verano.
  He wanted to travel this summer.

desertar (de)   to desert (from), abandon

- Desertaron del ejército tres soldados.
  Three soldiers deserted from the army.
- El desertó de la empresa que habían comenzado.
  He deserted (or abandoned) the enterprise they had started.

desesperar   to despair, lose hope

- ¡No desesperes, ten paciencia, habrá solución!
  Don't despair (or lose hope); be patient. There will be a solution.
- Lo desesperaba no poder correr.
  He despaired because he could not run.

desesperar(se) de + *inf* to lose hope of + *ger*

- Desesperaron de encontrarlo vivo, ya había pasado mucho tiempo.
  They gave up (or lost) hope of finding him alive; too much time had elapsed.
- Se desesperaba de ver que no mejoraba.
  She despaired (or lost hope) upon seeing that she did not improve.
- Nos desesperábamos de no poder ayudarte.
  We despaired of not being able to help you.

desesperar de + *subj* to give up on

- Desesperó de que llegara a tiempo.
  He gave up on his arriving on time (or They lost hope that he'd come on time).

deshacer to undo, unmake; to spoil, ruin

- Los niños deshicieron lo que habían hecho.
  The children undid what they had made.
- Deshizo todos los planes de viaje.
  She spoiled (or ruined) all her travel plans.
- La chica deshizo el peinado de su hermana.
  The girl undid her sister's hairdo.

deshacerse de algo to get rid of sth

- Tú te has deshecho de esos documentos.
  You have gotten rid of those documents.
- Quiero deshacerme de los servicios de esa compañía.
  I want to get rid of that company's services.
- Antes de morir se deshizo de sus propiedades.
  Before he died he got rid of his properties.

deshacerse por algo (*fig*) to die for sth

- Me deshago por un helado de chocolate.
  I'm dying for a chocolate ice cream.
- Se deshacía por su amor.
  He was dying for her love.

desistir to stop, desist

- Ya desistió.
  He already stopped (or desisted).

desistir de algo to desist from sth

- Finalmente él desistió de su posición intransigente (/de su proyecto).
  Finally, he desisted from his uncompromising position (/gave up his project).

desistir de + *inf*   to desist from + *ger,* stop + *ger*

- Desistimos de trabajar con esa compañía.
  We stopped working with that company.

- Las tropas desistieron de atacar la ciudad.
  The troops stopped attacking the city.

deslizar (en/por/sobre)   to slide (on/over/along/*etc.*)

- La madre desliza la mano por (*or* en, sobre) la mejilla de su hijo.
  The mother caresses (or slides her hand across (or over)) her child's cheek.

- Deslizó la mano sobre (*or* en, por) la superficie de la mesa.
  He slid his hand over (or on, along) the surface of the table.

deslizarse (en/entre)   to slide (on/into, between)

- Se deliza en la cama suavemente.
  He slides into the bed softly.

- El pez se deslizó entre mis manos.
  The fish slipped through my hands.

- La serpiente se deslizó sobre (*or* en, por) la arena del desierto.
  The snake slid over (or on, through) the desert sand.

desnudar a uno/algo   (*fig*) to strip sb/sth, bare sth; to undress sb

- La madre desnudó al bebé para bañarlo.
  The mother undressed the baby to bathe him.

- El poeta desnuda su alma en ese poema. (*fig*)
  The poet bares his soul in that poem.

desnudarse   to undress, strip

- Se desnudó cuando llegó al río.
  He stripped when he arrived at the river.

- El médico le dijo que se desnudara hasta la cintura.
  The doctor told him to undress up to his (or strip to the) waist.

despedir   to see off, say goodbye; to give off

- Sus ojos despedían centellas de cólera.
  Her eyes were giving off sparks of anger.

- La flor despedía un olor penetrante.
  The flower gave off a penetrating smell.

- Está despidiendo a los invitados.
  He is off seeing (or saying goodbye) to the guests.

- Fuimos a despedirlo.
  We went to see him off.

despedir de algo   to be expelled from sth, fired from sth

- Lo despidieron de su trabajo.
  They fired him from his job.

- La fuerza centrífuga lo despidió de su asiento.
  The centrifugal force threw him from his seat.

despedirse de uno/algo   to say goodbye to sb/sth

- Me voy a despedir de mis amigos (/de mi trabajo en esta compañía).
  I'm going to say goodbye to my friends (/my job in this company).

- Siempre se despide de su mamá con un beso.
  He always says goodbye to his mom with a kiss.

despertar(se)   to wake (up), awaken

- ¡Despierta a Juan! Ya es tarde.
  Wake John up. It's already late.

- Las campanas de la iglesia despiertan al pueblo.
  The bells of the church awaken the town.

- Por favor, despiértame cuando te levantes.
  Please, wake me up when you get up.

despertar(se) de algo   to wake (up) from sth, awaken from sth

- La explosión lo despertó de su profundo sueño.
  The explosion awakened him from a deep sleep.

- Se despertó de sus fantasías muy tarde.
  He woke up too late from his fantasies.

despojar de algo   to strip of sth, clear of sth

- El nuevo gobierno lo ha despojado de sus títulos (/su autoridad).
  The new government has stripped him of all his titles (/authority).

- La han despojado de todas sus propiedades.
  She has been stripped of all her properties.

- Los ladrones lo despojaron de sus ropas.
  Thieves stripped him of his clothes.

despojarse de algo   to undress, take off sth

- Se despojó de sus ropas y se metió al agua.
  He took off his clothes (or undressed) and got in the water.

- Me despojé de mi pesada chaqueta.
  I took off my heavy jacket.

desprender   to separate, part with

- El terremoto desprendió las cornisas.
  The earthquake separated the cornices.

- El golpe desprendió la llanta del aro.
  The blow separated the tire from the rim.

desprenderse de algo   to give off/up sth, part with sth; to get rid of sth

- Él se desprendió de todos sus libros.
  He got rid of (or parted with) all his books.

- Ella se ha desprendido de toda la ropa de su abuela.
  She has gotten rid of all her grandmother's clothes.

- Un olor muy agradable se desprende de esa flor.
  That flower gives off a very pleasant smell.

destinar (a, para)   to set aside (for, to); to assign (to)

- Vamos a destinar este dinero para comprar un coche.
  We are going to set aside this money to buy a car.

- Ha sido destinado a (*or* para) la embajada en Washington.
  He has been assigned to (or destined for) the embassy in Washington.

destinarse (a, para)   to set aside (to, for)

- Ya se han destinado los fondos a (*or* para) la universidad.
  Funds have already been set aside for the university.

- Se ha destinado el dinero a (*or* para) la región sur.
  The money has been assigned to the southern region.

destruir   to destroy

- Los manifestantes destruyeron los documentos (/edificios).
  The demonstrators destroyed the documents (/buildings).

- El ácido ha destruido mi camisa.
  The acid has ruined my shirt.

desvelar   to keep awake; to unveil, reveal

- El ruido del mar lo desveló toda la noche.
  The sounds of the sea kept him awake all night.

- Finalmente desvelaron el secreto.
  Finally, they unveiled (or revealed) the secret.

- El alcalde desveló el monumento en la ceremonia.
  The mayor unveiled the statue at the ceremony.

desvelarse por   to care very much for, be very concerned about sth

- Ella se desvela por la educación de sus hijos.
  She is very concerned about her children's education.

- Ella se develaba por hacer bien las cosas.
  She would take great care to do things well.

desviar   to divert, deviate

- El avión ha desviado su vuelo.
  The plane has rerouted its flight.

- Han desviado el tránsito a otra calle.
  They have diverted the traffic to another street.

desviar(se) de algo   to deviate from sth, turn (aside) from sth

- Los últimos incidentes lo han desviado de su objetivo.
  The last incidents have diverted (or turned) him from his objective.

- Sus padres le desviaron de su propósito.
  His parents dissuaded him from his plans.

- Se ha desviado del tema de conversación.
  He has deviated from the topic of conversation.

- Me he desviado de mi camino.
  I have deviated from my path.

detener a uno/algo   to stop sb/sth; to detain sb/sth

- La policía lo detuvo durante tres horas.
  The police detained (or held) him for three hours.

- El ejército detuvo su marcha en el río (/en la frontera).
  The army stopped its march by the river (/at the border).

- Juan detendrá el autobús en esa esquina.
  John will stop the bus on that corner.

detenerse   to stop

- El tiempo no se detiene.
  Time does not stop.

- Los turistas no se detuvieron.
  The tourists did not stop.

- El tren no se detiene aquí después de las tres.
  The train does not stop here after three.

detenerse a + *inf*   to stop + *inf*

- Las chicas se detuvieron a mirar el mono (/a mirarlo).
  The girls stopped to see the monkey (/to see him).

■ Él se ha detenido a contemplar la puesta de sol.
He has stopped to contemplate (or watch) the sunset.

determinar   to determine, decide, settle, fix

■ Ahora vamos a determinar quién va.
We are now going to determine (or decide) who goes.

■ El tribunal determinó la fecha del interrogatorio.
The court set (or fixed) the date of questioning.

determinarse a + *inf*   to decide to + *inf*, make up one's mind to + *inf*

■ Se determinó a estudiar con más empeño (/a escribirles más a menudo).
He decided to study with more effort (/to write them more often).

■ Me he determinado a no llegar tarde a clase.
I've decided (or made up my mind) not to arrive late to class.

devolver   to return, give back

■ ¡Devuélveme el dinero que te presté!
Give me back the money I lent you.

■ Lo devolví a la biblioteca.
I returned it to the library.

■ He devuelto a la tienda todo lo que compré.
I've returned everything I bought to the store.

diferenciar (entre, por)   to differentiate (between, by)

■ Hay que diferenciar las latas por medio de colores.
It's necessary to differentiate the cans by means of color.

■ Diferenciamos las semillas grandes de las pequeñas.
We differentiate between large and small seeds.

diferenciarse (por)   to be differentiated (by), be different

■ Nos diferenciamos sólo por el color de los ojos.
We are differentiated (or told apart) by the color of our eyes only.

■ Se diferencian en que uno es grande y el otro pequeño.
They are different in that one is large and the other small.

■ Estos peces se diferencian por el tamaño de la aleta dorsal.
These fish are differentiated by the size of the dorsal fin.

dirigir (a, hacia)   to direct (to, towards); to address (to); to conduct

■ Dirija su correspondencia al secretario del colegio.
Direct (or address) your correspondence to the school's secretary.

■ Dirigió a María unas palabras.
He directed a few words to (or at) Mary.

- El director dirige la orquesta sinfónica.
  The director conducts the symphonic orchestra.

dirigirse (a, hacia)   to go, head for (at, to, towards); to address

- Nos dirigimos hacia el parque (/la plaza/el colegio).
  We are headed for (or going to) the park (/square/school).

- Se dirigió al director para solicitar trabajo.
  He addressed the director to request work.

disculpar   to excuse, forgive

- Ella siempre disculpa todos sus errores (*or* los errores de él).
  She always excuses (or forgives) all his faults.

- ¡Disculpa! *or* ¡Discúlpame (por mi retraso/por esta situación)!
  I'm sorry (for my delay/for this situation)!

- Disculpa que no tenga el dinero (/que llegue tarde/que no cocine hoy).
  Forgive me for not having the money (/for being late/for not cooking today).

disculparse por algo   to excuse oneself for sth; to apologize for sth

- Me he disculpado porque no tengo tiempo.
  I've excused myself because I do not have time.

- Mi padre se disculpó por su tardanza (/la tardanza del hijo/su conducta).
  My father apologized for his delay (/the delay of his son/his behavior).

disculparse por + *inf*   to apologize for + *ger*

- Ellos se disculparon por haber llegado tarde (/hacer ruido).
  They apologized for having arrived late (/making noise).

discutir   to argue

- Ellos discuten siempre que se encuentran.
  They always argue when they meet.

- El congreso discute el problema económico.
  Congress is discussing the economic problem.

discutir de algo   to discuss sth; to argue about sth

- Los muchachos discuten de política.
  The boys are discussing politics.

- No discuto de deportes porque no conozco la materia.
  I won't argue about sports because I am not familiar with the subject.

discutir con uno   to discuss with sb; to argue with sb

- No discutas con tu padre.
  Don't argue with your father.

- La mujer siempre discute los problemas diarios con su marido.
  The woman always discusses her daily problems with her husband.

disfrutar (con)   to enjoy (with)

- Los niños disfrutaron jugando en la arena.
  The children enjoyed playing in the sand.

disfrutar con/de algo   to enjoy sth

- Disfruto con esta música (/con la música clásica/con la música salsa).
  I enjoy listening to this music (/classical music/salsa).

- El niño disfrutó con la pelota (/el juguete/el refresco).
  The child enjoyed the ball (/toy/drink).

- ¿Disfrutaste de tus vacaciones?
  Did you enjoy your vacation?

- Mis padres disfrutan de buena salud (/de sus visitas).
  My parents enjoy good health (/their visitors).

- La empleada disfruta del favor del director (/de su posición de poder).
  The employee enjoys the favor of the director (/her position of power).

- La gente disfruta del clima de este país (/de buenos sueldos).
  The people enjoy the good climate of this country (/good salaries).

disgustar a uno   to annoy sb, upset sb; to offend sb

- Le disgusta que duermas todo el tiempo.
  It annoys (or upsets) her that you sleep all the time.

- Me disgustan los malos modales.
  I'm offended by bad manners.

- Me disgusta tener que lavarlo (/repertirlo).
  It annoys me to have to wash it (/to repeat it).

- Mi voz (/Su presencia) le disgustó al director del coro.
  My voice (/His presence) displeased the choir director.

disgustarse con uno   to get upset with sb

- Me disgusté con María (/sus amigos).
  I was (or got) upset with Mary (/his friends).

- Nos disgustamos con todos los empleados de la compañía.
  We got upset with all the company employees.

disgustarse de/por algo   to get upset about/by sth

- Me disgusté de lo que se dijo de la familia.
  What was said about the family upset me.

- Se disgustaron por el mal tiempo.
  They got upset about the bad weather.

- Se disgustaron por su mala conducta.
  They were upset by his bad behavior.

disgustarse por + *inf*   to get upset for + *ger*

- Se disgustaron por no ganar el partido.
  They got upset for not winning the game.

disparar (a, contra, en)   to shoot, fire (at, into)

- Dispararon 21 cañonazos en honor al rey.
  They fired a 21 gun salute in honor of the king.

- La policía disparó al aire (/contra los manifestantes).
  The police fired into the air (/at the demonstrators).

- El centro delantero disparó un potente tiro contra la valla del rival.
  The center forward fired a powerful shot against the rival's goal.

- Disparamos contra la pared (/al animal que atacaba).
  We shot at the wall (/fired at the animal that was attacking).

dispararse   to dash off, run off

- Los galgos se van a disparar cuando vean la liebre.
  The greyhounds are going to go off when they see the hare.

- Los muchachos se dispararon hacia la playa cuando vieron el mar.
  *The boys dashed (or *ran*) off to the beach when they saw the sea.*

dispensar (de)   to excuse (from)

- Hay que dispensarlo porque no sabe lo que hace.
  He must be excused because he doesn't know what he's doing.

- Por favor, ¡dispénseme! No sabía que usted estaba aquí.
  *Please, excuse (or *pardon*) me. I did not know you were here.*

- Tienes que dispensar a María porque es nueva en su trabajo.
  You have to excuse Mary because she's new at her job.

- ¡Dispensa mi mala educación!
  Excuse my bad manners!

- Lo han dispensado del servicio militar.
  He's been excused from military service.

disponer   to arrange, set up, to lay out

- Habrá que disponer el menú para la comida de mañana.
  *We'll have to arrange (or *set up*) the menu for tomorrow's meal.*

- Tenemos que disponer la mesa para los invitados.
  We have to arrange (or lay out) the table for the guests.

disponer de algo   to have (available), have at one's disposal

- No dispongo de mucho dinero (/tiempo/equipo).
  I do not have (available) much money (/time/equipment).

- Toda su vida han dispuesto de muchas comodidades.
  All of their lives they have had (or enjoyed) many comforts.

- Dispusieron del dinero como si fuera de ellos.
  They disposed of the money as if it were theirs.

- Podemos disponer de la comida si es necesario.
  We can have the food if it's necessary.

disponerse a/para + *inf*   to prepare to/in order to + *inf*, get ready to/in order to + *inf*

- Se disponía a salir cuando sonó el teléfono.
  He was getting ready to leave when the phone rang.

- Nos disponemos para pintar la casa.
  We are getting ready (or preparing) to paint the house.

- Nos disponemos a viajar (/comer/trabajar).
  We are getting ready to travel (/eat/work).

- Se disponen para correr en la maratón de julio.
  They are getting ready to run in the July marathon.

distinguir (de, entre) algo   to distinguish sth, make sth out (from, between)

- Está muy lejos, no lo distingo bien.
  It is too far; I can't make it out.

- No se puede distinguir a los mellizos.
  The twins cannot be told apart.

- ¿Puede distinguir esa casa de la otra?
  Can you tell (or distinguish) that house from the other?

- No puedo distinguir entre un melón maduro y uno verde.
  I can't distinguish between a ripe and a green melon.

distinguirse de uno/algo   to be distinguished from sb/sth, stand out from

- Esas casas se distinguen de las otras porque son muy viejas.
  Those houses are distinguished from the others because they are very old.

- El estudiante se distingue de sus amigos porque es muy estudioso.
  That student stands out from his friends because he is very studious.

distinguirse por algo   to be distinguished for sth, stand out for sth

- Pedro siempre se distingue por su amor al trabajo.
  Peter always distinguishes himself by his love of work.

- Los soldados se distinguieron por su valor.
  The soldiers were distinguished by (or stand out for) their courage.

- Esas montañas se distinguen por su especial belleza.
  Those mountains are distinguished by their special beauty.

disuadir a uno (de + *inf*)   to dissuade sb (from + *ger*)

- Finalmente pudieron disuadir a Pedro de despedir al portero.
  Finally, they were able to dissuade Peter from firing the janitor.

- La situación política me disuadió de hacer el viaje.
  The political situation dissuaded me from making the trip.

divertir a uno   to amuse sb, entertain sb

- Esa comedia me divirtió.
  That comedy entertained me.

- El perrito (/La película) divirtió a los niños.
  The puppy (/movie) amused the children.

- Los payasos divierten a la gente.
  Clowns entertain people.

divertirse (con)   to have a good time (with), enjoy oneself

- Se divierten jugando (/comiendo) en la playa.
  They're having a good time playing (/eating) on the beach.

- Nos vamos a divertir en la fiesta.
  We are going to enjoy ourselves at the party.

- Se ha divertido mucho con sus amigos.
  She enjoyed herself greatly (or had a great time) with her friends.

divorciar a uno/algo   to divorce sb, separate sth

- El juez divorció a la pareja.
  The judge granted a divorce to the married couple.

- Divorcia en tu mente esas dos ideas.
  Divorce (or separate) in your mind those two ideas.

divorciarse (de)   to get a divorce, separate (from)

- Me divorcié el año pasado.
  I got a divorce last year.

- Él se divorció de su esposa el mes pasado.
  He divorced his wife last month.

- Hace ya mucho tiempo que él se divorció del partido.
  It's been a long time since he divorced himself (or separated) from the party.

doblar   to double; to turn; to fold

- ¡Dobla a la izquierda!
  Turn (to the) left.

- Luis ha doblado sus ganancias (/sus pérdidas/su sueldo) en un año.
  Louis has doubled his profits (/losses/salary) in one year.

- Dobló el papel en dos para ponerlo en el bolsillo.
  He folded the piece of paper in two to put it in his pocket.

- Doblaron el hierro para que quedara bien.
  They bent the piece of iron so that it would look good.

doblarse   to bend down, buckle

- El se dobló para recoger el papel del suelo.
  He bent down in order to pick up the piece of paper from the floor.

- Me doblé la rodilla y me duele mucho.
  I buckled my knee, and it hurts a lot.

doler   to hurt, ache, cause pain

- A María le duelen las muelas.
  Mary's teeth hurt.

- Le duele la cabeza (/el brazo/el estómago).
  His head aches (or He has a headache) (/His arm hurts/His stomach hurts).

- Te duele cuando te ponen una inyección.
  It hurts when they give you a shot.

- Me duele tu actitud.
  Your attitude hurts me.

dolerse de uno/algo   to regret sth; to repent of sth; to show sb sympathy

- Ella se duele de que no haya podido visitarte.
  She regrets that she has not been able to visit you.

- ¡Duélete de mí!
  Show me some sympathy!

- Los criminales se dolieron de sus pecados.
  The criminals repented of their sins.

dormir   to sleep

- Duerme diez horas los domingos.
  He sleeps ten hours on Sundays.

- Dormimos muy bien en esta cama.
  We slept very well on this bed.

dormirse   to fall asleep, go to sleep

- Se durmió mirando televisión.
  He fell asleep watching television.

- Me dormí en la clase de literatura.
  I felt asleep (or went to sleep) in the literature class.

dudar de que...   to doubt that...

- Dudo de mucho que venga (/vaya/coma allí/se mejore).
  I doubt very much that he'll come (/go/eat there/get better).

- Dudamos de que ella pueda llegar sola.
  We doubt that she'll be able to get there alone.

dudar de uno/algo   to doubt sb/sth, mistrust sb/sth

- Él duda de la veracidad de esa información.
  He doubts the veracity of that information.

- El pueblo duda del presidente.
  The people mistrust the president.

dudar en + *inf*   to hesitate to + *inf*

- Dudamos en ir a su casa a visitarlo.
  We hesitated about going to his house to visit him.

- Dudan en comer esa fruta.
  They hesitate to eat that fruit.

E

echar algo   to throw sth; to put forth sth, to give off sth

- ¡No me eches agua porque me mojas!
  Don't throw water at me because you'll get me wet.

- Las niñas le echaban flores a la reina durante el desfile.
  The girls were throwing flowers at the queen during the parade.

- El naranjo del jardín echó flores.
  The orange tree in the garden put forth flowers.

echar a algo   to throw to/in sth

- Echaremos a la basura todo lo que sobre.
  We'll throw all leftovers in the garbage.

- Lo echaron al agua.
  They threw him in the water.

- ¿Quién ha echado carbón a la estufa?
  Who has thrown coal in the stove?

echar a + *inf*   to begin + *inf*, start to + *inf*

- Cuando vimos el toro, echamos a correr como alma en pena.
  When we saw the bull, we began to run like a bat out of hell.

- Al oír el disparo los pájaros echaron a volar.
  Upon hearing the shot, the birds began to fly.

- A las tres echamos a andar hacia la casa.
  At three we began to walk toward the house.

echar de algo   to expel from sth, throw out of sth

- ¿Por qué te han echado del hotel (/de la fiesta)?
  Why have they thrown you out of the hotel (/party)?

- A mi hijo lo echaron del club (/de la escuela/del cine).
  My son was thrown out of (or expelled from) the club (/school/movie theater).

echar en algo   to pour into sth

- Él echó leche (/té) en la taza.
  He poured milk (/tea) in his cup.

■   Ella echa más vino en el vaso.
She is pouring more wine in her glass.

echarse algo   pour oneself sth; to get into sth, have sth

■   Ricardo se echó un trago de ron.
Richard poured himself a shot of rum.

■   Nos echamos una partida de ajedrez.
We got into (or had) a chess game.

echarse (en)   to lie down (on)

■   Me eché en la arena (/cama/hamaca).
I lay down on the sand (/bed/hammock).

echarse a + *inf*   to lie to + *inf*

■   Me eché a dormir (/leer/descansar) como a las once.
I lay down to sleep (/read/rest) about eleven.

■   Se ha echado a descansar en la arena.
He has lain down on the sand to rest.

echarse en algo   to throw oneself in/into/on sth

■   Tan cansado estaba que se echó en la cama con ropa y zapatos.
He was so tired that he threw himself on the bed with his clothes and shoes on.

■   Ella se echó en brazos de su padre.
She threw herself into the arms of her father.

egresar de algo   to graduate from sth

■   Mi prima egresó de la secundaria en 1968.
My cousin graduated from high school in 1968.

■   No creo que tu egreses de una institución tan difícil.
I don't believe you will graduate from such a difficult institution.

■   En 1976 egresamos de la universidad (/de la facultad de medicina).
In 1976 we graduated from the university (/from medical school).

ejercer   to exercise; to exert, use, bring to bear, practice

■   ¡Ejerce tu derecho! ¡Vota por Margarita!
Exercise (or use or exert) your right! Vote for Margaret!

■   Es médico (/abogado), pero ya no ejerce.
He is a doctor, (/lawyer) but no longer practices.

ejercer de uno/algo   to practice sth, work as sb/sth

- Irene ejerce de psiquiatra en un hospital modernísimo.
  Irene practices psychiatry (or works as a pychiatrist) in a very modern hospital.

- Elenita ya ejerce de enfermera (/médica/abogada).
  Elenita is a practicing nurse (/doctor/lawyer) already.

elegir   to choose, select, opt for, elect

- ¡Elija el color que le guste!
  Choose the color you like.

- El pueblo me eligió en los cincuentas.
  The people elected me in the fifties.

- Ha elegido la carrera más difícil.
  He has chosen (or selected or opted for) the most difficult career.

elegir (a uno) de/para algo   to choose (sb) for/as sth, elect (sb) for/as sth

- Elegiremos de (*or* para) presidente a una persona capaz.
  We'll elect a capable person for president.

- Es posible que lo hayan elegido de (*or* para) consejero.
  It's possible he's been chosen as counselor.

- No te elegirán de (*or* para) director este año.
  You will not be elected director this year (or They will not elect you director this year).

elegir entre unos/algo   to choose between some people/sth

- Elija entre estos dos perfumes franceses.
  Choose between these two French perfumes.

- Eligieron a Gloria entre muchas candidatas.
  They chose Gloria among many candidates.

- Hay que elegir entre dos coches (/tres tipos).
  One has to chose between two cars (/three types).

elegir por algo   to choose for/because of sth

- No elegiremos por la figura, sino por la inteligencia.
  We'll not choose based on appearance but based on intelligence.

- Lo han elegido por su dedicación al trabajo.
  He has been chosen because of his dedication to work.

- Nos eligieron por nuestra habilidad.
  They chose us for our ability.

elevar   to raise, uplift, elevate, make fly

- Por fin los muchachos elevaron el avión de juguete.
  Finally, the boys were able to lift (or make fly) the toy airplane (off the ground).

■   Mis nietos elevan la cometa muy alto (en el parque).
My grandchildren made the kite rise very high (in the park).

elevar a uno/algo   to raise to sb/sth; to promote sb/sth

■   Te han elevado a director general de bancos.
You have been promoted to Director General of the Bank.

■   Lo elevaron a presidente del congreso.
They raised (or promoted) him to (the position of) president of the congress.

■   Lo elevaron a juez de la Corte Suprema.
He was promoted to judge of the Supreme Court.

elevarse   to rise (up)

■   El volcán más alto se eleva a 6 mil metros.
The highest volcano rises to (or reaches) six thousand meters.

■   El avión se elevó y se perdió de vista.
The airplane rose (or gained) altitude and was lost from sight.

■   Dicen que el santo se elevó y permaneció en el aire algunos minutos.
It is said that the saint rose (or floated) up and remained in the air a few minutes.

elevarse a algo   go up to sth, rise to sth

■   El globo se elevó a una altura sorprendente.
The balloon rose to a surprising height.

■   El cohete se elevó a las nubes.
The rocket rose into the clouds.

embarcar   to embark, put on board, load; to ship

■   Tienes que embarcar todas tus pertenencias.
You have to load all your belongings.

■   Embarcamos la mercancía hacia Guatemala.
We loaded the merchandise for Guatemala (or We shipped the merchandise to Guatemala).

embarcarse   to board sth

■   Nos embarcaremos en el "Crucero del Amor" mañana.
We'll board the "Love Boat" tomorrow.

■   Se han embarcado en este puerto.
They've boarded at this port.

> **embarcarse en algo**   to embark on sth; (*fig*) to get involved in sth
>
> ■   Te embarcaste en una empresa que no da ganancias.
> *You embarked upon a business that is not profitable.*
>
> ■   No deseo embarcarme en tu compañía.
> *I do not wish to get involved in your company.*

embarcarse de uno   to board as sb

- Se ha embarcado de tripulante.
  He got on board as a crew member.
- No creo que se haya embarcado de grumete.
  I do not think he boarded as a cabin boy.

embarcarse para algo   to sail for sth

- Te embarcaste para Africa y no me lo comunicaste.
  You sailed for Africa and did not tell me about it.
- Nos embarcaremos para tierras desconocidas (/para las islas del Caribe).
  We'll sail for unknown lands (/for the Caribbean Islands).

empapar   to soak, saturate, drench

- La lluvia empapó los muebles que estaban afuera.
  The rain soaked (or drenched) the furniture that was outside.
- ¡Empape un trapo y limpie la mesa!
  Soak a rag and clean the table.

empaparse de algo   to soak up sth, soak in sth

- Se empaparon de aceite al arreglar la máquina.
  They got soaked in oil while fixing the machine.
- Mi hermana se ha empapado de política. (*fig*)
  My sister has learned (or soaked up) a lot about politics.
- Te aconsejo que te empapes de repelente para que no te piquen los mosquitos.
  I suggest you drench yourself with mosquito repellent so that the mosquitoes won't bite you.

empeñar   to pawn, pledge

- Tuve que empeñar el televisor, por la necesidad económica que tenía.
  I had to pawn the TV set due to economic necessity.
- Empeñé mi palabra. Sólo así creyeron que terminaría la obra.
  I gave (or pledged) my word. Only then did they believe I would finish the job.

empeñar en algo   to pawn for sth

- Empeñé el reloj en una cantidad de dinero muy baja.
  I pawned the watch for a very small sum.
- Armando va a empeñar los muebles en 1400 pesos (/dólares).
  Armand is going to pawn the furniture for 1400 pesos (/dollars).

empeñarse en que *subj*   to be determined to + *inf*, to persist to until

- Se ha empeñado en que ellos obtengan las mejores localidades.
  He is determined to get them the best accommodations.

■ Me empeñaré en que la situación mejore para todos.
I'll persist until the situation improves for everybody.

empeñarse en + *inf*   be determined to + *inf*, be set on + *ger*

■ Tomás se ha empeñado en bajar de peso y lo está logrando.
Thomas is determined to lose weight, and he is succeeding.

■ Max se ha empeñado en ser el mejor estudiante de medicina de toda la universidad.
Max is determined to be the best medical student in the university.

■ Nosotros nos empeñaremos en terminar la obra que habíamos dejado inconclusa.
We are determined to finish (or set on finishing) the work that we had left undone.

empezar   to begin, start

■ Empezaron muy temprano.
They began very early.

■ ¿A qué hora empieza la función (/película)?
At what time does the program (/movie) start?

empezar a + *inf*   to start to + *inf*

■ Empezaron a correr antes de oír el disparo de salida.
They began to run before hearing the starter.

■ Julia no ha empezado a estudiar todavía.
Julia has not started to study yet.

■ Empezamos a comer antes de su llegada.
We began to eat before his arrival.

empujar   to push, shove

■ Empuje la puerta, por favor.
Push (or shove) the door open, please.

■ Vamos a empujar el piano lentamente.
We are going to push the piano slowly.

empujar a/hacia algo   to push to/towards sth

■ Empujemos los muebles a (*or* hacia) esa pared.
Let's push the furniture to that wall.

■ Nos empujaron a (*or* hacia) un rincón muy reducido.
They pushed toward a very narrow corner.

■ ¡Qué lástima!, te han empujado a (/hacia) la droga.
What a pity! They've pushed you into (or towards) drugs.

enamorar a uno   to court sb, inspire love in sb, win the love of sb

■ Mario enamora a todas las chicas que conoce.
Mario courts every girl he meets.

- Don Juan enamoraba a cuanta doncella conocía.
  Don Juan courted (or *won the love of*) *every maiden he met.*

enamorarse de uno/algo   to fall in love with sb/sth

- Cecilia se ha enamorado de Alberto (/de un profesor/de un muchacho muy guapo).
  Cecilia has fallen in love with Albert (/a professor/a very handsome boy).

- Mi madre se enamoró del anillo de Rosa (/de mi auto).
  My mother fell in love with Rosa's ring (/my new car).

- Me enamoré de Flor cuando tenía 15 años.
  I fell in love with Flor when I was 15 years old.

encargar   to entrust; to charge; to urge, request

- Le encargaremos tres kilos de café de Costa Rica.
  We urge (or *request* or *charge*) *you to bring three kilos of Costa Rican coffee.*

- Te encargo la casa. ¡Cuídamela!
  I am entrusting the house to you. Take care of it for me.

encargarse de algo   to take charge of sth; to take sth over; to look after sth

- Alfonso se encargará del mantenimiento del hotel.
  Alfonso will be in charge of (or *take over* or *look after*) *the maintenance of the hotel.*

- Yo me encargaré de que no te falte nada.
  I'll see to it that nothing is missing.

- Te encargas de las compras del almacen.
  You are in charge of buying supplies (from the store).

encargarse de + *inf*   to take charge of + *ger*, undertake + *inf*

- Ojalá que el actual presidente se encargue de arreglar la situación.
  I hope that the current president will take charge of rectifying (or *undertake to rectify*) *the situation.*

- Me encargo de recibir a los turistas.
  I'm in charge of receiving (or *greeting*) *the tourists.*

encender   to light, ignite; to set fire to; to turn on

- Encenderé el reflector, así veremos mejor.
  I'll turn on the spotlight so we can see better.

- El amor enciende pasiones incontrolables.
  Love sets fire to (or *ignites*) *uncontrollable passions.*

- Encendimos la estufa y comenzamos a preparar la cena.
  We lit (or *turned on*) *the stove and began to prepare dinner.*

encenderse   to catch fire, ignite; to light up, flare up

- Cuando Ana escuchó el piropo, se le encendió la cara. (*fig*)
  When Anna heard the compliment, her face lit up.

- Al escuchar el insulto, se encendió tanto que me golpeó en la cara. (fig)
  Upon hearing the insult, he flared up so much that he hit me in the face.

encerrar   to enclose, shut in, to lock in, lock up (*with a key*)

- La policía nos encerró durante dos horas.
  The police locked us up for two hours.

- La cerca encierra un bello jardín.
  The fence encloses (or surrounds) a beautiful garden.

- A menudo lo encierran porque muerde y ladra.
  They often lock (or shut) it up because it barks and bites.

encerrarse en algo   to lock oneself in sth

- José se encerró en su habitación durante una semana.
  Joseph shut himself up in his room for a week.

- ¡Enciérrese en su cuarto y no salga hasta que le avise!
  Lock yourself in your room, and don't come out until I tell you!

encoger(se)   to shrink, to contract; to shorten, shrivel up

- Hay telas que no se pueden lavar porque encogen.
  There are fabrics that can't be washed because they shrink.

- Cuando seamos viejos, nos encogeremos.
  When we get old, we will shrink (or be shorter).

- Estudiamos acerca de un insecto que se encoge cuando se toca.
  We studied an insect that contracts when you touch it.

- ¡Qué voy a hacer!, se me encogió el pantalón.
  What am I going to do! My pants shrunk.

encogerse de algo   to cringe from/in sth; to shrug (*one's shoulders*)

- El niño se encogió de hombros y salió corriendo.
  The child shrugged his shoulders and ran out.

- Me encogía de la vergüenza cada vez que una chica me miraba.
  I cringed from embarassment every time a girl looked at me.

- Me encogí de miedo cuando vi el fantasma.
  I cringed in fear when I saw the ghost.

encontrar a uno/algo   to find sb/sth

- No puedo encontrar la dirección que me diste.
  I can't find the address that you gave me.

- Encontró las llaves por casualidad.
  He found the keys by accident.

- No puedo encontrarlas en ninguna parte.
  I can't find them anywhere.

encontrarse (en)   to be, be situated, be located (in); to find oneself

- La tienda se encuentra en la plaza principal.
  The store is located in the main square.

- ¿Cómo te encuentras ahora? —Hoy me encuentro enfermo (/desorientado).
  How are you now (or How do you feel now)? —I am ill (/disoriented) today.

- ¿Dónde se encuentra usted ahora? —Me encuentro muy lejos de la ciudad.
  Where are you now? —I find myself far from the city (or I'm far from the city).

- El parque se encuentra en una zona boscosa.
  The park is (situated) in a wooded zone.

- En estos momentos me encuentro en el avión.
  Right now, I'm (or I find myself) on the plane.

   encontrarse con uno/algo   to meet sb/sth, to run across sb/sth

   - María se encontró con Andrea en el parque.
     Mary met Andrea in the park.

   - Tus opiniones se encuentran con las mías sólo en dos puntos.
     Your opinions concur with (or meet) mine on only two points.

   - Nos hemos encontrado con varios problemas, por esa razón no hemos cumplido a tiempo con lo acordado.
     We have run across several problems; therefore, we haven't fulfilled our agreement on time.

enderezar   to straighten, unbend; to rectify

- Enderezamos la barra de aluminio muy fácilmente.
  We straightened the aluminum bar easily.

- El ministro de economía enderezó la situación financiera del país.
  The Minister of Finance rectified (or straightened out) the financial situation of the country.

enderezarse   to straighten up

- El paralítico se enderezó y comenzó a llorar.
  The paralytic straightened up and began to cry.

- ¡Enderézate, que pareces el jorobado de Notre Dame!
  Stand up straight (or Straighten up)! You look like the hunchback of Notre Dame.

- El jugador se enderezó, tomó la pelota y la pateó con toda su fuerza.
  The player straightened up, took the ball, and kicked it with all his might.

enemistar a uno   to make an enemy of sb

- Los chismes de la vieja enemistaron a Oscar y a Max.
  The old woman's gossip made enemies of Oscar and Max.

enemistarse con uno/algo   to make an enemy sb/sth; become an enemy sb/sth

- No puedo creer que te hayas enemistado con tus parientes (/vecinos).
  I can't believe that you've made enemies of your relatives (/neighbors).

■   En el futuro no voy a enemistarme con nadie.
In the future I am not going to make enemies of anyone.

enfadar a uno   to anger, irritate, annoy sb; to offend sb/sb

■   No me enfades porque no sé como puedo reaccionar.
Don't anger me because I don't know how I'll react.

■   La acción del niño enfadó mucho a su padre.
What the child did irritated (or offended) his father greatly.

enfadarse (con)   to get angry, get cross, get annoyed (with)

■   Mi esposa se enfada cuando escucha mentiras.
My wife gets angry when she hears lies.

■   Yo casi nunca me he enfadado.
I have almost never gotten angry (or annoyed) with him.

■   Se enfadó porque no le compré un dulce.
He got angry because I did not buy him candy.

■   La maestra se enfada con los estudiantes todos los días.
The teacher gets annoyed with the students every day.

■   Espero que no se haya enfadado con tu madre.
I hope he has not gotten angry with your mother.

enfadarse por algo   to get angry for/because of sth

■   Se enfadó por los insultos que le proferiste.
She got angry because of the insults you uttered.

■   No me enfadaré por pequeñeces.
I won't get angry because of small matters.

■   Espero que no te enfades por mi decisión.
I hope you do not get angry about my decision.

enfatizar   to emphasize, stress

■   Voy a enfatizar este capítulo.
I am going to stress this chapter.

■   Hay que enfatizar el término "justicia" para que se comprenda mejor.
The term "Justice" should be emphasized so it can be better understood.

■   Por favor, no enfatice los conceptos confusos.
Please, do not stress the confusing concepts.

enfermar   to make ill; to fall ill, be taken ill

■   El viejo enfermó y murió tres días después.
The old man fell (or was taken) ill and died three days later.

■   Hay ciertas situaciones que enferman.
There are certain situations that make you ill.

enfermar(se) de algo   to get ill *or* sick with/form sth

- Después del viaje, todos (nos) enfermamos de gripe (/del estómago).
  After the trip we all got sick with a cold (/to our stomach).

- Había una vez una princesa que (se) enfermó de tristeza.
  Once there was a princess who became sick with sadness.

enfrentar   to face

- Hay que enfrentar la vida valerosamente.
  One has to face life courageously.

- Enfrenta toda situación adversa que se te presente.
  Face the adverse situations that may come up.

enfrentarse con uno/algo   to face (up to) sb/sth, confront sb/sth

- Hay que enfrentarse con· el peligro (/mil obstáculos).
  One must face up to (or confront) the danger (/a thousand obstacles).

- El héroe de la película se enfrentó con su enemigo mortal.
  The hero of the film faced (up to) his mortal enemy.

engañar   to deceive, be deceitful, trick; to cheat

- ¡No engañes!, así la gente siempre te creerá.
  Do not deceive (or be deceitful); this way people will always believe you.

- No engañemos a nadie, mucho menos a nuestros padres.
  Let's not deceive anyone, much less our parents.

- Esta pregunta engaña a cualquiera.
  This question will deceive (or fool) anyone.

- El vendedor de libros engañó a su cliente.
  The bookseller cheated his client.

engañar (a uno) con algo   to deceive (sb) with sth

- Hay personas que engañan con artimañas.
  There are people who deceive with cunning.

- Usted no me engaña con ese argumento.
  You do not fool me with that argument.

engañarse   to fool oneself, deceive oneself, make a mistake

- No te engañes. Ya no te quiero.
  Do not fool (or deceive) yourself. I do not love you anymore.

- Él se engañó cuando lo compró.
  He deceived himself when he bought it.

> **engañarse con algo**   to make a mistake with sth, be fooled by sth; to deceive oneself with sth
>
> - Roberto se engañó con el negocio.
>   *Robert made a mistake with the business.*

- No hay que engañarse con las apariencias.
  One must not be fooled by appearances.
- Se engaña con falsas esperanzas.
  They delude themselves with false hopes.

engañarse por algo   to be fooled by sth

- Con frecuencia los humanos nos engañamos por (*or* con) las apariencias (/el dinero).
  People are often fooled by appearances (/money).

enojar   to anger; upset, annoy

- Su actitud intransigente enoja.
  His intransigent attitude is upsetting.

- Me enoja que los empleados lleguen tarde.
  It annoys me that the employees arrive late.

- ¡No enoje a su padre!
  Do not upset your father!

- Enojé al toro para que atacara.
  I made the bull angry so that it would charge.

enojarse   to get angry, get upset

- Te daré un regalo, si no te enojas.
  I'll give you a gift if you do not get upset.

- Mis hijos se enojan si no salimos los domingos.
  My children get upset if we do not go out on Sundays.

enojarse con/contra uno/algo   to get angry with/at sb/sth

- La gente se enojó con el opresor y se lanzó a las calles.
  The people became angered at the oppressor and rushed out to the streets.

- Me enojaré con ustedes, si no recogen la basura.
  I'll get angry at you if you don't pick up the garbage.

- El entrenador siempre se enoja con los jugadores.
  The coach always gets mad at his players.

enojarse de/por algo   to get angry at sth

- No me gusta la gente que se enoja de (*or* por) todo.
  I don't like people who get angry at just anything.

- Nos enojamos del (*or* por el) servicio del restaurante.
  We got mad at the restaurant's service.

- Alejandro se enojó de (*or* por) lo que dijo la gente de él.
  Alexander got angry at what people said about him.

enredar   to net, catch in a net, confuse (*fig*); to entangle, tangle (up), confound

- Los gatos enredaron la lana de la abuela.
  The kitten tangled up the grandmother's wool.

- Los pescadores enredan delfines en lugar de atunes.
  The fishermen netted dolphins instead of tunas.

- El enredó más este asunto. (*fig*)
  He confused (or tangled up) this matter even further.

enredarse   to become entangled, become mixed up

- Se me han enredado las ideas.
  My ideas have gotten mixed up.

- A Jorge se le enreda la lengua cuando habla alemán.
  George's tongue becomes entangled when he speaks German.

enredarse con uno   to get involved with sb

- La joven se enredó con un hombre de edad.
  The young woman got involved with an older man.

- Se enredaron con delicuentes.
  They got mixed up with delinquents.

enredarse en algo   to get caught in sth, get involved in sth, get mixed up in sth

- El delincuente se enredó en su misma trampa.
  The criminal got caught in his own trap.

- Me enredé en un asunto oscuro y tuve problemas con la justicia.
  I got involved (or mixed up) in a shady deal, and I had problems with the law.

- La red de los pescadores de atún se enredó en los arrecifes.
  The net of the tuna fishermen got caught in the coral reefs.

- Con frecuencia enredaba a su padre en sus mentiras.
  Frequently, he'd involve his father in his lies.

enredarse entre algo   to get tangled up among sth, get mixed up between sth

- Los turistas se enredaron entre los carrizos del bosque tropical.
  The tourists got entangled among the reeds of the tropical forest.

- Los sabelotodos se enredan entre verdades y suposiciones.
  The know-it-alls get mixed up between truth and supposition.

- El niño se ha enredado entre las zarzas y se ha llenado de espinas.
  The child got entangled among the bramble, and he has gotten full of thorns.

enseñar   to teach, instruct; to show

- El próximo año enseñaré español en una escuela pública.
  Next year I'll teach Spanish in a public school.

■ Me enseñó la cicatriz que le quedó de la operación.
  He showed the scar left from the operation.

■ Te voy a enseñar mi coche (/radio/libro).
  I am going to show you my car (/radio/book).

enseñar a + *inf*   to teach (how) to + *inf*; to show how to + *inf*

■ El carpintero me ha enseñado a construir muebles.
  The carpenter has shown me how to make furniture.

■ Le enseñaremos a jugar a las cartas.
  We'll show (or teach) you how to play cards.

■ Deseo que usted le enseñe (a él) a respetar a los mayores.
  I want you to teach him to respect his elders.

■ La escuela me enseñó a ser una persona responsable.
  School taught me to be a responsible person.

entender   to understand, comprehend; to realize

■ No entiendo nada. ¡Repítelo otra vez!
  I don't understand anything. Repeat it again.

■ Roxana no entendía el problema de álgebra.
  Roxanne did not understand the algebra problem.

■ No hemos entendido algunos capítulos de este libro.
  We have not understood some chapters from this book.

entender de algo   to be an expert on sth, be good at sth, know all about sth

■ Lo contrataré porque entiende de fontanería.
  I'll hire him because he's good at (or an expert on) plumbing.

■ Recurro a usted porque no entiendo nada de leyes.
  I come to you because I don't know anything about the law.

entenderse (por)   to be understood, understand oneself; to be meant by

■ Yo me conozco muy bien, por eso me entiendo.
  I know myself very well; that's why I understand myself.

■ ¿Qué se entiende por estos símbolos?
  What is meant by these symbols?

■ Se entiende que se interrumpe la comunicación, si se aprieta este botón.
  It is understood that communication gets cut off if you press this button.

> **entenderse con uno**   to come to an understanding *or* agreement with sb, make an agreement with sb
>
> ■ Si quiere resolver su problema, entiéndase con el vendedor.
>   *If you want to solve your problem, come to an agreement (or make an arrangement) with the salesman.*

- Yo no tengo que ver en ese asunto, es mejor que usted se entienda con mi esposa.
  I do not have anything to do with that matter; it is better that you deal (or come to an understanding) with my wife.
- Ellos van a entenderse con su jefe.
  They are going to make an agreement with their boss.

enterar   to inform, tell, make one aware

- El gerente me enteró de la situación de la compañía.
  The manager made me aware (or told me) of the company's situation.
- Los periódicos nos enteran diariamente.
  Newspapers inform us daily.

enterarse   to find out, learn

- Nadie sabe cómo se enteró Susana.
  No one knows how Susan found out.
- Dudamos de que el jefe se haya enterado.
  We doubt the boss has found out.

enterarse uno/algo   to find out about sb/sth, learn of sb/sth

- Las muchachas se han enterado de que Juan es un verdadero Don Juan.
  The girls have learned that John is a true Don Juan.
- Creo que nunca voy a enterarme de la verdad.
  I think I will never find out (or learn) the truth.
- Lo sentimos mucho. Nos hemos enterado de la tragedia.
  We are sorry. We have heard of the tragedy.
- Me enteré de lo que pasó ayer.
  I found out what happened yesterday.
- Acabo de enterarme de que Juan llegó ayer.
  I just found out that John arrived yesterday.

entrar   to enter

- Por favor, entre y tome asiento.
  Please come in and have a seat.
- La señora entró acompañada de su hija.
  The lady entered accompanied by her daughter.
- ¡Qué felicidad!, ya entró la primavera.
  How wonderful! Spring has arrived.

entrar a uno/algo   to introduce sth, bring *or* get sb/sth in, show sb/sth in

- ¡Entra el coche en el garaje!
  Bring (or Get) the car in the garage.
- No me entran las matemáticas.
  I don't get mathematics.

- Entra al bebé en el auto.
  Get the baby into the car.

entrar en algo   to enter in/into sth, fits in/into sth

- Entraron en la escuela (/el cuarto/el dormitorio/la cocina).
  They entered the school (/the room/the bedroom/the kitchen).
- Tobías ha entrado en los cuarentas.
  Tobias has entered his forties.
- Lola ha entrado en la adolescencia.
  Lola has entered adolescence.
- Me alegro de que hayan entrado en una sociedad de prestigio.
  I'm glad you've been admitted to a prestigious society.
- El abrigo (/paquete) no entró en la maleta.
  The coat (/the parcel) didn't fit in the suitcase.

entregar   to deliver, hand in *or* over, give

- El cartero entregó toda la correspondencia.
  The mailman delivered all the mail.
- No puedo entregarte el documento sin autorización.
  I cannot give (or deliver) the document without permission.
- Nos entregaron la llave del apartamento.
  They handed (over) to us the key to the apartment.

entregarse a uno/algo   to devote oneself to sth; to give oneself up to sb, surrender to sb

- El ratero se ha entregado a la policía.
  The thief has given himself up to the police.
- Carlos se entregó a la medicina.
  Carl devoted himself to medicine.
- La jovencita se entregaba a la droga.
  The young lady was turning to (or indulging in) drugs.

entregarse a + *inf*   to devote oneself to + *inf*

- Él se entregó a trabajar (/estudiar/practicar).
  He devoted himself to his work (/study/practice).

entretener   to entertain, amuse; to delay, detain

- Entretuvimos a los invitados (/a nuestros parientes) por ocho horas.
  We entertained the guests (/our relatives) for eight hours.
- El payaso nos entretuvo durante dos horas.
  The clown entertained us for two hours.
- Mi hermano las entretuvo, mientras yo compraba unos refrescos.
  My brother entertained (or amused) them while I bought refreshments.

- Hemos llegado tarde porque el director nos entretuvo.
  We've arrived late because the principal delayed us.

entretenerse (con algo)   to amuse oneself (with sth)

- Yo me entretengo viendo televisión (/pintando/viendo fotografías viejas).
  I amuse myself watching television (/painting/looking at old photos).
- Ellos se entretienen con las historias del abuelo.
  They entertain themselves listening to grandfather's stories.
- El chico se entretiene con su bola de fútbol (/con juegos divertidos).
  The boy amuses himself with his soccer ball (/enjoyable games).

entrevistar   to have an interview

- El periodista va a entrevistar esta tarde.
  The journalist is going to have an interview this afternoon.

entrevistar a uno   to interview sb

- Entrevistamos a un juez de la Corte Suprema.
  We interviewed a justice of the Supreme Court.
- Los reporteros han entrevistado a un guerrillero herido (/a nuestro jefe).
  The reporters have interviewed a wounded guerrilla (fighter) (/our boss).

entrevistarse con uno   to have an interview with sb, meet with sb

- `Ella va a entrevistarse esta tarde con un congresista.
  She is going to meet (or have an interview) with a congressman this afternoon.
- Me entrevistaré con nuestro presidente.
  I'll meet with our president.
- María se entrevistará con los suegros.
  Mary will meet with her in-laws.

enviar (con)   to send (with)

- Hoy enviaremos la mercadería (/un mensaje al director).
  We'll send the merchandise today (/a message to the director or principal).
- Te envío mil besos y abrazos.
  I send you a thousand (or lots of) hugs and kisses.
- La empresa me envió con un regalo para usted.
  The company sent me with a gift for you.
- Me han enviado con una maleta equivocada.
  They've sent me with the wrong suitcase.

enviar a algo   to send to sth

- La policía lo envió a los tribunales.
  The police sent him to the courts.

- Esta carta será enviada a un país muy lejano.
  This letter will be sent to a country far away.

- Ojalá que pueda enviarte a una buena universidad.
  I hope I am able to send you to a good university.

enviar a uno de   to send as sb

- Me enviaron de reportera para que entrevistara al rey.
  They sent me as a reporter (in order) to interview the king.

- ¿A quién enviaron de embajadora? —Enviaron de embajadora a Elena.
  Who was sent as ambassador? —They sent Helen as ambassador.

- Le enviaron de cónsul a un país oriental.
  They sent him as a consul to an oriental country.

envolver   to wrap (up), pack (up)

- Por favor, envuelva bien el regalo.
  Please wrap the gift well.

- El vendedor envolvió los zapatos y me los dio.
  The salesman wrapped (up) the shoes and gave them to me.

- Envolvieron todo porque se van a mudar de casa.
  They packed up everything because they are going to move.

envolver a uno en algo   to get sb involved in sth

- Envolvieron a José en negocios de dudosa reputación.
  They got Joseph involved in business deals of a dubious nature.

envolver con/en algo   to wrap with/in sth

- Envolvimos el anillo con (*or* en) papel de regalo.
  We wrapped the ring in wrapping paper.

- La madre lo envolvió en (*or* con) una manta gruesa.
  The mother wrapped him in a heavy blanket.

envolverse con/en algo   to wrap oneself (up) in sth; to get involved in sth

- Tenía tanto frío que tuvo que envolverse con (*or* en) una manta de lana.
  He was so cold he had to wrap himself in a woolen blanket.

- Ellas se envolvieron en un asunto que las perjudicó.
  They got involved in a matter that hurt them.

equivocar algo (con algo)   to misinterpret sth, understand sth incorrectly, mistake sth (for sth)

- ¡Discúlpeme!, equivoqué las palabras.
  Excuse me. I misunderstood the words.

- Él ha equivocado los postulados de nuestro partido.
  He has mistaken the principles of our party.

- Equivocamos el camino a la capital.
  We've taken the wrong road to the capital.
- Equivoqué A con B en el alfabeto griego.
  I mistook A for B in the Greek alphabet.

equivocarse   to be wrong, be mistaken; to make a mistake

- Usted se equivoca, yo no lo hice.
  You are wrong (or mistaken). I did not do it.
- ¡Perdón!, me equivoqué.
  Excuse me. I made a mistake.

> **equivocarse de uno/algo**   to get sb/sth wrong, make a mistake about/with sb/sth, have the wrong sb/sth
> - ¡Otra vez me he equivocado de nombre!
>   *Again I've made a mistake with the name (or gotten the name wrong).*
> - Creo que te has equivocado de persona.
>   *I think you've gotten the person wrong (or have the wrong person).*
> - Te equivocaste de día. La cita es para mañana.
>   *You have the wrong day. The appointment is for tomorrow.*

> **equivocarse en algo**   to make a mistake in sth
> - La cajera del restaurante se equivocó en la cuenta.
>   *The cashier of the restaurant made a mistake on the bill.*
> - Es problable que Carlos se haya equivocado en sus palabras.
>   *It's probable that Carl made a mistake with his (choice of) words.*
> - Se equivocaba en la ortografía.
>   *She used to make mistakes in spelling.*

escalar   to climb, scale

- El señor Barquero escalará el monte más alto de Ecuador.
  Mr. Barquero will climb the highest mountain in Ecuador.
- Roxana quiere escalar la torre de una televisora (/el acantilado).
  Roxanne wants to climb a television tower (/the cliff).
- Pedro escaló una posición muy alta en el congreso. (*fig*)
  Peter climbed to a high position in the congress.

escapar (con)   to escape (with)

- El conejo escapó mientras el zorro dormía.
  The rabbit escaped while the fox slept.
- Los prisioneros que escaparon el sábado, fueron capturados el domingo.
  The prisoners that escaped on Saturday were captured on Sunday.

- Los ladrones escaparon con el dinero.
  The thieves escaped with the money.

- La madre escapó con el niño.
  The mother escaped with the child.

escapar de algo   to escape from sth

- Los perros guardianes escaparon de la jaula.
  The watch dogs escaped from the cage.

- Ha escapado un león del zoológico.
  A lion has escaped from the zoo.

- Es posible que escape gas de estas rocas.
  It's possible that gas may escape from these rocks.

escaparse   to escape, run away, get away

- El niño del cuento se escapará durante la noche.
  The child in the story will get away during the night.

- Se te ha escapado una palabrota.
  You let a bad word slip out.

- El expía (/canario) se escapó.
  The spy (/canary) got away.

escaparse de uno/algo   to get away from sb/sth

- Las gallinas se escaparon del gallinero.
  The chickens got out of the chicken coop.

- Nosotros nos escaparemos de este país.
  We'll get away from this country.

- Las ideas se me escapan del cerebro. (*fig*)
  The ideas escape my comprehension.

escoger   to choose, select, pick (out)

- ¡Escoge el anillo que más te guste!
  Choose (or pick) the ring that you like the best.

- Espero que sepas escoger el camino que seguirás en tu vida.
  I hope you'll know how to choose (correctly) your life's path.

escoger de algo   to choose from

- Escogeré sólo una banana del racimo.
  I'll choose only one banana from the bunch.

- El sargento escogió un rifle del armario.
  The sergeant chose a rifle from the gun rack.

escoger entre uno/algo   to choose among *or* between sb/sth

- Es difícil escoger entre tantas cosas bonitas.
  It's hard to choose among so many pretty things.
- Tendrá que escoger entre dos universidades del este.
  He will have to choose between two eastern universities.
- ¡Escoje entre quedarte en casa o ir conmigo!
  Choose between staying home or going with me.

escribir   to write; to spell

- ¿Quién escribió la carta? —Yo la escribí.
  Who wrote the letter? —I wrote it.
- ¿Quién le escribió? —Mi novia me escribió.
  Who wrote to you? —My girlfriend wrote to me.
- ¿Cómo se escribe tu nombre?
  How do you spell your name?
- Esta palabra se escribe sin hache.
  This word is spelled without an "H."
- Cuando mi hija escribe, no entiendo nada.
  When my daughter writes, I don't understand anything.

escribir de/sobre uno/algo   to write about sb/sth

- Elena ha escrito un libro de (*or* sobre) historia.
  Helen has written a book about history.
- Espero que escribas de (*or* sobre) mí.
  I hope you'll write about me.
- ¿Qué han escrito de (*or* sobre) nuestros presidentes?
  What have they written about our presidents?

escribirse   to write to each other

- La madre y la hija se escriben a menudo (/seis veces por año).
  The mother and daughter write to each other often (/six times a year).
- Generalmente los buenos amigos no dejan de escribirse.
  Generally, good friends do not stop writing each other.

escuchar algo   to listen to, hear sth (in)

- ¡Escuchen ese ruido extraño!
  Listen to that strange sound!
- Algunos adolescentes no escuchan razones.
  Some adolescents or teenagers do not listen to reason.
- A mi padre le gusta escuchar la radio (/las noticias) antes de dormir.
  My father likes to listen to the radio (/news) before going to sleep.

■ Escucha en silencio el consejo de tu papá.
    Listen silently to the advice of your father!

escuchar a uno   to listen to sb, hear sb

■ Esta noche iremos a escuchar a una cantante famosa.
    Tonight we'll go to listen to (or hear) a famous singer.

■ Escucha a tu abuelo; él ha vivido más que tú.
    Listen to your grandfather; he has lived longer than you have.

■ Yo escuché a los congresistas discutir de economía.
    I heard the congressmen discuss economics.

escuchar con algo   to listen + adv

■ Quiero que escuches con atención la poesía que voy a leer.
    I want you to listen attentively to the poem I'm going to read (or I want you to
    pay attention to the poem I'm going to read).

■ ¡Escuchemos con cuidado las recomendaciones del científico!
    Let's listen carefully to the recommendation of the scientist.

escurrir   to drain; to wring out

■ Escurriré la camisa, así se secará más rápido.
    I'll wring out the shirt; it'll dry faster that way.

■ ¡Cuelga el pantalón en el cordel para que escurra el agua!
    Hang your pants on the line so they will drip dry.

■ Rodolfo escurrió la botella de ron (/el ron de la botella).
    Rudolph drained the bottle of rum (/the rum from the bottle).

escurrirse de/entre   to slip; to drip, trickle

■ El jabón se me escurrió de (/entre) las manos.
    The bar of soap slipped from (/between) my hands.

■ Las ideas se nos escurren de la mente cuando no las escribimos.
    Ideas slip away from the mind when we don't write them down.

esforzar   to strengthen, invigorate; to strain

■ ¡No esfuerces tu vista, leyendo a oscuras!
    Do not strain your eyes (or sight) reading in the dark.

■ Ella esforzó los músculos y ahora le duelen.
    She strained her muscles, and they hurt her now.

■ Esfuerza tus piernas para que llegues a la cima de la montaña.
    Strengthen your legs so that you'll arrive at the mountain top.

esforzarse en/por algo   make an effort in/for, try hard in sth

■ Deseo que te esfuerces en (*or* por) tus estudios.
    I want you to try hard in your studies.

■ Ella se esforzó tanto en (*or* por) su trabajo que el jefe la premió.
She made such an effort in her work that the boss rewarded her.

esforzarse en/por + *inf*   to make an effort + *inf*, try to + *inf*

■ Nosotros nos esforzaremos en (*or* por) terminar este trabajo.
We'll make an effort to finish this work.

■ Linda se esfuerza en (*or* por) obtener las mejores notas de la universidad.
Linda is making an effort to get the best grades in the university.

■ Voy a esforzarme en (*or* por) bajar algunos kilos.
I am going to try to lose a few kilos.

espantar a uno   to frighten sb, scare sb

■ El aullido nos espantó.
The howl frightened us.

■ La novela (/película/historia de terror) las espantó.
The novel (/film/horror story) frightened them.

espantarse   to become frightened, get scared

■ Voy a decirte el precio, pero no te espantes.
I am going to tell you the price, but don't get scared.

■ Él no se espanta fácilmente.
He does not get frightened easily.

   espantarse con uno/algo   to get frightened by sb/sth

   ■ Las jóvenes se espantaron con la historia que el viejo les contó.
   The young women got frightened by the story the old man told them.

   ■ No creo que él se espante con ese monstruo de papel.
   I don't think that paper monster will scare him.

esparcir   to spread, scatter

■ Cuando tú barres, esparces el polvo.
When you sweep, you spread the dust.

■ No esparza lo que te he contado.
Do not spread what I've told you.

esparcir en/por algo   to spread on sth, scatter over sth

■ La policía esparció a la gente en (*or* por) todo el parque.
The police scattered the people throughout the park.

■ El azúcar fue esparcido en (*or* por) toda la mesa.
Sugar was spilled all over the table.

■ Las abejas esparcen el polen en (*or* por) el bosque.
Bees scatter (or spread) pollen all over the forest.

esperar (de)   to hope for; to wait for, await; to expect (of)

- El pueblo espera que el presidente cumpla su palabra.
  The people hope that the president will live up to his word.

- Teresa está esperando su llegada (/llamada).
  Teresa is expecting (or waiting for) his arrival (/call).

- Espero que sí (/que no/que todo te salga bien).
  I hope so (/not/everything will be fine with you).

- Mi padre no esperaba menos de ti.
  My father expected (or hoped for) nothing less from you.

- Esperé tres horas y no llegaste.
  I waited three hours, and you didn't arrive.

- ¡Espera un momento!
  Wait a moment!

- Esperamos el taxi (/avión) ¿Lo espera también?
  We are waiting for the taxi (/plane). Are you waiting for it too?

- Mal día (/Una mala noticia) le espera.
  A bad day (/Bad news) is in store for you (or awaits you).

- ¿Dónde espera usted el tren? —Lo espero en la estación.
  Where do you wait for the train? —I wait for it at the station.

- No te (/lo) espero después de medianoche.
  I won't wait for you (/him) after midnight.

esperar a que... + *subj*   wait for... + *inf*

- Ellas esperan a que las llamen a comer.
  They are waiting to be called (or for you to call them) to eat.

- Siempre esperábamos a que el profesor saliera del auto.
  We always waited for the professor to get out of the car.

- Esperaremos a que mi madre salga y después iremos a tomar té.
  We'll wait for my mother to come out, and then we'll go for tea.

esperar en uno/algo   to trust in sb/sth

- Espero en mi capacidad para poder salir adelante.
  I trust in my ability to go forward.

- Espero en Dios que podamos resolver los problemas.
  I trust in God to be able to resolve the problems.

esperar + *inf*   hope to + *inf*, to expect to + *inf*

- Sandra espera ganar la lotería (/cantar en la fiesta).
  Sandra hopes to win the lottery (/to sing at the party).

- Esperamos comer puntualmente esta noche.
  We hope (or expect) to eat on time tonight.

- Esperamos ganar en el partido de baloncesto.
  We hope (or expect) to win the basketball game.

esperarse   to be expected

- Como podía esperarse, el gobierno aumentó los impuestos otra vez.
  As might have been expected, the government raised the taxes again.

- La obra no fue tan buena como se esperaba.
  The play wasn't as good as was expected.

estar   to be

- El actor está enfermo (/triste/indispuesto).
  The actor is sick (/sad/indisposed).

- La ventana estaba cerrada.
  The window was closed.

- ¿Cómo has estado? —He estado bien (/enfermo).
  How have you been? —I've been fine (/sick).

- Mi maleta (/casa) está ahí.
  My luggage (/home) is there.

- La caja (/El regalo) está envuelto en papel.
  The box (/gift) is wrapped in paper.

estar + *ger*   to be + *ger*

- Estaba corriendo (/caminando) a la casa.
  He was running (/walking) home.

- Los atletas están corriendo.
  The athletes are running.

estar a algo (de)   to be (priced) at sth, sell at sth; to be sth (*times, distance*) (from)

- Las naranjas están a buen precio.
  Oranges are (selling) at a good price.

- Los mangos están a cuarenta pesos cada uno.
  Mangoes are (priced) at 40 pesos each.

- Ellas están a diez millas de su casa.
  They are ten miles from home.

- Estamos a un minuto de la medianoche.
  We are at a minute away from midnight.

estar de algo   to be out (*or* because of sth; to be only + *ger*)

- En la oficina no hay nadie, todos están de vacaciones.
  There is no one at the office; everyone is (away) on a holiday.

- Él no vive aquí, solo está de visita.
  He does not live here; he is only visiting.

- No vamos a quedarnos aquí, solo estamos de paso.
  We are not going to stay here; we are just passing through.

estar de uno   to act as sb, work as sb

- Yo soy profesor, pero hoy estoy de director de la escuela.
  I am a teacher, but today I am the acting school principal.
- Gloria está de periodista. Vamos a ver si logra una buena entrevista.
  Gloria is working as a journalist. Let's see if she gets a good interview.
- El estudiante estuvo de obrero (/de camarero/cartero).
  He was working as a workman (/waiter/postman).

estar en uno/algo   to be in *or* like sb; to be busy with sth; to be involved in sth

- No está en Cecilia, ofender a nadie.
  It's not in Cecilia to offend anyone (or It's not like Cecilia to offend anybody).
- No está en él, infringir la ley.
  It's not in him to violate the law (or It's not like him to violate the law).
- ¿Ya obtuvo la visa su hermano? —Está en eso.
  Did your brother already get the visa? —He's doing (or busy with) it.
- Usted tiene que estar en la música para ser buen músico.
  You have to be (very) involved in music in order to be a good musician.
- Ser actor no está en hablar bien.
  To be a good actor means more (or more involved) than speaking well.

estar en que   to lie in sth, be (found) in sth

- El problema está en que ustedes no trabajan con interés.
  The problem is that you lack interest in your work.
- El problema está en que llueve todos los días (/no llega temprano).
  The problem is that it rains every day (/you are not coming early).
- La solución está en que ustedes lo hagan juntos.
  The solution is that you do it together.

estar para + *inf*   to be about to + *inf*, be on the verge of + *ger*

- Está fruta está para comer.
  This fruit is ready to be eaten.
- El barco está para hundirse.
  The ship is about to sink (or on the verge of sinking).
- ¡Mira que oscuridad!, está para llover.
  Look how dark it is! It is about to rain.

estar por algo   to be in favor of; to back support, side with

- Estamos por la liberación femenina (/por los derechos del niño).
  We support women's liberation (/the rights of the children).

■ Jorge está por el partido demócrata.
George is in favor of the democratic party.

■ Estoy por las buenas comidas.
I am all for good food.

estar por + *inf* (*LAm*) to be about + *inf*

■ Ella está por dejar el trabajo (/por vender su casa). (*LAm*)
She is about to leave her job (/about to sell her house).

■ Está por llover. (*LAm*)
It's about to rain.

■ Estoy por confesarte la verdad. (*LAm*)
I am about to tell the truth (or *confess*).

estar por + *inf* to be still undone, be yet to be done

■ La historia de la revolución está por escribirse.
The history of the revolution is still to be written.

■ La casa está por pintarse.
The house is yet (or *still*) *to be painted.*

■ La ley está por aprobarse.
The bill is about (or *yet/still*) *to be passed.*

estar sin + *inf* to remain + *ptp*

■ Mi casa todavía está sin venderse.
My home still remains unsold.

■ El carro (/La máquina de escribir) estaba sin arreglarse.
The car (/typewriter) was still unrepaired.

estimar (alrededor de) to estimate; to appraise (about); to appreciatep

■ Estimo la vida.
I appreciate life.

■ Estimo que tu casa cuesta alrededor de tres millones.
I estimate your house to cost about three million.

estimar a uno to have regard for sb

■ Jorge estimaba a tu familia (/a sus estudiantes/a sus amigos/a Laura).
George holds your family (/his students/his friends/Laura) in high regard.

■ Ella te estimaba a ti, no a mí.
She held you in high esteem, not me.

estimarse to be expected, be thought; to respect oneself

■ Se estimaba que los precios subirían de nuevo.
It was expected (or *thought*) *that prices would go up again.*

- Se estima que la tempertura será de más de cuarenta grados centígrados.
  It's thought (or expected) that the temperature will reach above 40 degrees centigrade.
- Si se estimara no propondría este plan.
  If he had any self-respect, he would not propose this plan.

estrechar   to narrow; to make smaller

- Hemos tenido que estrechar la habitación.
  We have had to make the room smaller.
- Estrecharon la calle principal.
  The main road was made narrower.

estrecharse en algo   to squeeze into sth; to reduce sth

- Nos estrechamos en el presupuesto (/en las gastos del hogar).
  We have reduced the budget (/domestic expenditures).
- No me gusta estrecharme en lo monetario.
  I don't like to reduce my monetary expenses.
- Las aterias se estrecharon en luz.
  The openings of the arteries have been reduced.

estudiar (para)   to study (for)

- Ellos estudian español (/filología/el plano del edificio/una lengua indígena).
  They study Spanish (/philology/the building's blueprint/an Indian language).
- Me dijo que estudiaría cualquier cosa.
  She told me she'd study anything.
- Estoy estudiando (para el examen).
  I'm studying (for the exam).
- He estudiado ocho horas en la biblioteca.
  I've studied eight hours in the library.
- Su propuesta (/sugerencia) es interesante, la estudiaré.
  Your proposal (/suggestion) is interesting; I'll think about (or study) it.

estudiar para algo   to study to become sth

- Gabriel estudió para dentista (/médico/maestro/cura/abogado).
  Gabriel studied to become a dentist (/doctor/teacher/priest/lawyer).

estudiar   **para** + *inf* to study to + *inf*

- Laura estudia para superarse.
  Laura studies to get ahead.
- Estudiará para llegar a ser una buena antropóloga.
  She'll study to become a good anthropologist.
- Estudiará para ser médico.
  He'll study to be a doctor.

excitar   to excite; to arouse, stir up

- El ruido me excita los nervios.
  The noise bothers (or gets on) my nerves.

- El orador excitó al populacho a levantarse en armas (/a rebelarse).
  The speaker excited (or aroused) the populace (or mob) to rise up in arms (/rebel).

excitarse   to get excited; to get worked up

- El niño se excitó con los medicamentos y comenzó a llorar.
  The child got worked up (or excited) because of the medicine and began to cry.

- Los caballos se excitaron por los cohetes y escaparon del corral.
  The horses got excited because of the fireworks and ran away from the corral.

excluir de algo   to exclude from sth

- El director me excluyó de la orquesta.
  The director excluded me from the orchestra.

- La censura excluyó dos líneas del texto.
  The censors office excluded two lines of the text.

- Lo excluyeron del viaje.
  They excluded him from the trip.

excusar a uno   to excuse sb, pardon

- ¡Excúseme! por favor.
  Excuse (or Pardon) me, please!

- Mi madre me (/la) excusó.
  My mother excused me (/her).

- Hablaré por tí y te excusaré.
  I'll speak for you, and I'll excuse you.

excusarse con uno (de algo)   to apologize to sb (for sth)

- Excúseme con su esposa (/familia/oficina).
  Apologize for me to your wife (/family/office).

- Me excusé con Roberto (/con la hermana de Ana).
  I apologized to Roberto (/Ana's sister).

- Pablo se ha excusado de su comportamiento (/de lo que dijo).
  Paul has apologized for his behavior (/for what he said).

- Nos excusamos de nuestras malas acciones (/de todo).
  We apologize for our bad behavior (/for everything).

excusarse de + *inf*   to apologize for + *ger*

- Me excuso de hablar mal del prójimo (/de haber llegado tarde).
  I apologize for speaking ill of my neighbor (/for arriving late).

■   Se excusó de haber hecho eso (/de haber mentido).
He apologized for having done that (/having lied).

exigir   to demand

■   Exigimos que nos devuelva el dinero.
We demand that he return the money.

■   La joven exigió protección.
The young woman demanded protection.

explicar   to explain

■   El profesor explica su materia (/la teoría) muy claramente.
The professor explains his subject (/expounds the theory) very clearly.

■   Todo lo que usted explica está en este libro.
Everything that you're explaining is in this book.

explicarse   to explain (oneself), clarify

■   Jorge no se explicaba por qué lo habían expulsado del club.
George can't explain (or didn't clarify) why he was expelled from the club.

■   No nos explicamos cómo pudo suceder el accidente.
We can't explain how the accident could have happened.

exponer (a)   to expose (to), show, display

■   ¡No exponga la película al sol!
Don't expose the film to the sun!

■   Las editoriales expusieron nuevos libros.
The publishing houses displayed the new books.

■   Los editoriales expusieron a los políticos corrompidos.
The newspaper editorials exposed the corrupt politicians.

exponerse a algo   to expose oneself to sth, run the risk of sth

■   ¡Nos expusimos al peligro (/al ridículo/a un fracaso)!
We exposed ourself to danger (/ridicule/ran the risk of a failure).

■   Todo político se expone a la crítica.
Every politician is exposed to criticism (or Every politician is a target for criticism).

exponerse a + *inf*   to run the risk of + *ger*

■   Con su actitud se expone a sufrir castigo.
With his atitude he runs the risk of suffering the punishment.

■   Si come en la calle, se expondrá a contraer enfermedades.
If he eats (from the stands) in the street, he runs the risk of contracting disease.

■   Usted se expone a perder el oído con esa música caótica.
You run the risk of losing your hearing listening to that chaotic music.

exportar (a)   to export (to)

- Es mejor exportar que importar.
  It is better to export than import.

- Mi país exporta frutas a los Estados Unidos (/a España).
  My country exports fruits to the United States (/Spain).

expresar   to express; to voice

- Creo que usted no ha expresado su opinión.
  I believe you haven't expressed (or voiced) your opinion.

- De vez en cuando es conveniente expresar los sentimientos.
  From time to time it is useful to express feelings.

- Expresó una opinión muy interestante.
  He expressed a very interesting opinion.

expresarse   to express oneself

- A veces no me expreso bien.
  At times I don't express myself well.

- Los artistas se expresan por medio de las artes.
  Artists express themselves through the arts.

expulsar   to expel, eject

- ¡No dé motivos para que lo expulsemos!
  Don't give us a reason to expel you!

- Margarita no visitará este año el club porque fue expulsada.
  Margaret won't visit the club this year because she was expelled.

- Nos expulsaron a golpes.
  They physically ejected us.

expulsar de algo   to expel from sth

- Lo expulsaron del colegio (/club).
  They expelled him from school (/the club).

- Es lamentable que la expulsen de este país.
  It's too bad that she was expelled from this country.

extender algo   to extend sth, spread sth (out)

- La dama extendió el abanico.
  The lady opened up (or spread out) her fan.

- Extiende la masa antes de enrollarla.
  She spreads (out) the dough before rolling it.

extenderse (a, de)   to extend, spread, range (to, from)

- Nuestro país se extiende de océano a océano.
  Our country extends from ocean to ocean.

- El gas tóxico se extendió rápidamente.
  The toxic gas spread quickly.

- El examen se extendió por dos días.
  The exam was spread over two days.

extenderse por algo   to extend over *or* through sth, spread over *or* throughout sth

- La noticia se extendió por todo el país.
  The news traveled (or spread) throughout the whole country.

- Los artículos (/Los ensayos/Las reglas) se extienden por cuatro páginas.
  The articles (/essays/regulations) extend (or run) to four pages.

- Sus fincas (/propiedades) se extienden por una milla.
  His farms (/properties) spread over a mile.

- La epidemia se extendió por todo el estado.
  The epidemic was everywhere.

- El conferencista se extendió por más de dos horas.
  The lectures went on for more than two hours.

- El agua se extendió por toda la mesa.
  The water ran all over the table.

extrañar a uno/algo   to miss sb/sth; yearn for sb/sth; to find sth strange, find sth surprising

- Extraño el colegio (/mi país/mi casa).
  I miss (or yearn for) school (/my country/my home).

- Extrañaba su juventud.
  He used to miss his youth.

- Nos extraña que usted no quiera ir con nosotros.
  We find it odd (or surprising) that you don't want to go with us.

- Extraña a sus padres (/a su novia/a sus amigos).
  He misses his parents (/girlfriend/friends).

- Les extrañó esa idea suya tan loca.
  Your crazy idea surprised them (or They are surprised by your crazy idea).

extrañarse de que...   + *subj*   to be surprised that..., be amazed that...

- Él se extraña de que el niño haya crecido tanto.
  He is amazed that the child has grown so much.

- Nos extrañamos de que haya llovido en pleno invierno.
  We are surprised that it has rained in the middle of winter.

- No se extrañe de que aquí le digan Pepe y no José.
  Don't be surprised if they call you Pepe instead of José here.

F

fabricar   to manufacture, build, make

- La compañía fabrica un nuevo producto cada año.
  The company manufactures a new product every year.

- ¿Dónde se fabricaban los mejores perfumes?
  Where were the best perfumes made?

faltar a uno algo/algo de   be lacking sth; to need sth; to be missing sth (from)

- ¿Le falta dinero a Juan? —No, no le falta dinero.
  Does he lack money (or Does he need money)? —No, he doesn't need money.

- Me falta tiempo para estudiar.
  I lack the time to study (or I am short of time to study).

- Me falta el libro (de la biblioteca) que me prestaste.
  I'm missing the (library) book you lent me.

- ¿Faltaba algo? —No, no faltaba nada.
  Was anything missing? —No, nothing was missing.

- Nos (/Les) falta la sal y la pimienta.
  We (/They) are missing the salt and pepper.

- Faltan cinco estudiantes de la clase.
  Five students from class are missing.

- Nos faltan tres libros de la biblioteca.
  We are missing three library books.

- Le falta un plato de la cocina.
  You are missing a kitchen plate.

faltar a algo   to miss sth

- Te recomiendo que no faltes a las reuniones (/a las citas).
  I suggest that you don't miss meetings (/the appointments).

- Ojalá que no faltes a la fiesta de esta noche.
  I hope you don't miss the party tonight.

- Él faltó a clase tres días.
  He missed class three days.

faltar en algo   to fall short in sth

- Tratará de no faltar en lo moral.
  He will try not to fall short in regard to morals.

- Fue amonestado porque faltó en su ética.
  He was admonished because he fell short in his ethical behavior.

faltar algo para + *inf*   to be lacking sth to + *inf,* need sth to + *inf*

- Falta un clavo para terminar la mesa.
  A nail is needed in order to finish the table.

- Nos faltan cinco kilómetros para llegar a nuestro destino.
  We need to go five kilometers to get to our destination.

- Me faltan palabras para expresarle mi pena (/agradecimiento).
  I lack the words to express my sorrow (/gratitude) to you.

faltar por + *inf*   to still need to + *inf*

- Falta por pintar el frente del edificio.
  The front of the building still needs to be painted.

- Nos faltaba por estudiar los huesos de la cara.
  We still needed to study the bones of the face.

familiarizar(se) con algo   to familiarize (oneself) with sth, acquaint (oneself) with sth, become accustomed to sth

- Él familiariza al piloto con los instrumentos de vuelo.
  He acquaints (or familiarizes) the pilot with the flight instruments.

- Los extranjeros se han familiarizado con nuestras costumbres.
  The foreigners have gotten acquainted (or become familiar) with our customs.

- Patricia se familiarizó con la pronunciación inglesa.
  Patricia became accustomed to English pronunciation.

- Andrés se familiariza con la guitarra poco a poco.
  Andres is becoming accustomed to the guitar little by little.

fatigar   to tire (out), be tiring

- Me fatigó la caminata.
  The walk tired me (out).

- El ruido de los aviones nos (/les) fatiga.
  The noise of the airplanes is tiring to us (/them).

- La pena fatiga.
  Sadness is tiring.

fatigar a uno   to make sb tired, tire sb out

- Fatigaron a los niños para que se durmieran.
  They made the children tired so they would go to sleep.

■   El sargento fatigó a los soldados.
The sergeant made the soldiers weary.

fatigarse de + *inf*   to get tired of + *ger*

■   Se fatigaron de trabajar al sol.
They got tired of working under the sun.

■   Es posible que se haya fatigado de correr.
It's possible that he has gotten tired of running.

felicitar a uno por algo   to congratulate sb on/for sth

■   Pedro felicita a Lola por su cumpleaños (/por el cumpleaños de su hijo).
Peter is congratulating Lola for (or on) her birthday (/for her son's birthday).

■   Le felicité por sus buenas notas.
I congratulated her for her good grades.

■   Te felicito por el interés con que has hecho el trabajo.
I congratulate you for the interest you have shown in your job.

fiar   to entrust; to sell on credit

■   Yo vendo al contado, no fío.
I sell for (or deal with) cash, not on credit (or I do not give credit).

■   Te voy a fiar mi problema, por favor, ¡guárdalo como un secreto!
I'm going to entrust my problem to you (or trust you with my problem); please keep it a secret!

fiarse de uno/algo   to trust sb/sth; to confide in sb

■   ¿Te fías de Pedro? —No, no me fío de él—No me fío de nadie.
Do you trust Peter? —No, I don't trust him—I do not trust anyone.

■   No hay que fiarse de algunas noticias periodísticas.
One should not trust some media news.

■   No me fío de ti.
I don't trust you (or I won't confide in you).

fijar (en)   to fix, set; to secure, fasten (on); to focus, fix (on)

■   Ellos fijaron la fecha de la boda.
They fixed (or set) their wedding date.

■   Fijaremos el precio lo más pronto posible.
We'll fix (or set) the price as soon as possible.

■   Te voy a hipnotizar. ¡Fija la vista en este punto y escúchame!
I'm going to hypnotize you. Fix your eyes (or focus) on this spot, and listen to me.

■   Hemos fijado el televisor en la mesa para que no se caiga con los temblores.
We have fastened the TV set on the table so it wouldn't fall during the earthquakes.

- Fijó la mirada en los ojos de la chica.
  He fixed his eyes (or sight) on the girl's eyes.

fijarse en algo   to notice sth; pay attention to sth; to settle in sth, lodge in sth

- No me había fijado en su pelo.
  I had not noticed her hair.

- ¡Fíjate en los detalles de la pintura (/en los precios)!
  Notice the painting's details (/Just look at these prices)!

- Muchos turistas no se fijan en los aspectos culturales de un país.
  Many tourists do not pay attention to the cultural aspects of a country.

- El intenso dolor se le ha fijado en la espalda (/pierna).
  The intense pain has settled in his back (/leg).

- La bala (/flecha) se fijó en la pared.
  The bullet (/arrow) got lodged in the wall.

filtrar   to filter

- Si el agua no es potable, debes filtrarla.
  If the water is not potable, you should filter it.

- Hay rocas que filtran los líquidos.
  There are rocks that filter liquids.

filtrarse por algo   to filter through sth, leak through sth

- Tendremos que impermeabilizar la pared porque el agua se filtra por ella.
  We'll have to seal the wall because water is leaking through it.

- La lluvia se filtraba por el techo.
  Rain was leaking through the roof.

fingir   to pretend, feign

- Raúl fingió tan bien un dolor que el médico le creyó.
  Raul feigned a pain so well that the doctor believed him.

- Fingieron sorpresa (/alegría) cuando recibieron la carta.
  They feigned surprise (/happiness) when they received the letter.

fingir + *inf*   to pretend to + *inf*

- La mujer fingía ser millonaria.
  The woman pretended to be a millionaire.

- El niño fingía dormir cuando su madre entró en el cuarto.
  The child pretended to be asleep when his mother entered his room.

firmar   to sign

- Los dos firmaron el contrato (/cheque/recibo) ante un abogado.
  The two signed the contract (/check/receipt) before a lawyer.

- Siempre lea los documentos antes de firmar.
  Always read documents before signing them.

formar   to form, shape, establish

- Todos los niños formaron un círculo.
  All the children formed a circle.

- Formaremos una fraternidad diferente.
  We'll form (or establish) a different fraternity.

formarse   to form; to be trained

- Mi madre se formó en una magnífica universidad.
  My mother was trained at a great university.

- Una pequeña tormenta se ha formado en el Caribe.
  A small storm has formed in the Caribbean.

forrar   to line, cover; to upholster

- La costurera forraba los botones para que hicieran juego con la tela.
  The seamstress covered the buttons so they would match the material.

- Vamos a forrar los muebles de la sala.
  We are going to upholster the living room furniture.

forrar con algo   to line with sth, cover with sth; to upholster with sth

- Forraremos con pana el estuche del violín.
  We'll line the violin case with corduroy.

- Gloria ha forrado las paredes con papel pintado.
  Gloria has covered the walls with wallpaper.

- ¡Forra la caja con terciopelo antes de introducir el regalo!
  Line the box with velvet before placing the gift in it.

fortalecer   to encourage, strengthen

- El presidente dijo que iba a fortalecer la agricultura.
  The president said he was going to boost agriculture.

- Debemos fortalecer la moral de la gente joven.
  We should strengthen (or encourage) the morality of young people.

- Las buenas costumbres fortalecen el cuerpo y el espíritu.
  Good habits strengthen body and spirit.

forzar a uno/algo   to force sth open; to break into sth; to rape sb

- El ladrón forzó la puerta.
  The thief broke in (or forced open) the door.

- Fue juzgado y condenado porque forzó a una mujer.
  He was judged and found guilty because he raped a woman.

forzar a uno/algo a + *inf*   to force sb to + *inf*

- Nadie puede forzarme a hacer lo que no quiero.
  No one can force me to do what I do not want to do.

- Lo forzaron a comer porque estaba en huelga de hambre.
  They forced him to eat because he was on a hunger strike.

- El gobierno forzó al sindicato a suspender la huelga.
  The government forced the union to call off the strike.

fregar   to mop; to wash (dishes); (*fig*) to bother

- Hoy tienen que fregar los pisos.
  They have to mop the floors today.

- ¿A quién le toca fregar los platos?
  Whose turn is it to wash the dishes?

- ¡Ya no me friegues! (*fig*)
  Don't bother me!

freír   to fry

- El cocinero va a freír la carne.
  The cook is going to fry the meat.

- Cuando Roberto vivía solo, freía todos los alimentos.
  When Robert lived alone, he fried all his food.

freírse   (*fig*) to fry, burn

- En esa playa ustedes se van a freír de calor. (*fig*)
  You are going to get fried (or burned) on that beach.

- ¡Qué calor! Me voy a freír. (*fig*)
  What heat! I am going to fry (or get fried).

fumar   to smoke

- No he fumado durante un mes.
  I haven't smoked in a month.

- Usted fuma como una chimenea.
  You smoke like a chimney.

- ¿Se permite fumar?
  May I smoke? (or Is smoking allowed)?

fumarse   to smoke; (*fig*) to waste

- Pedro se fuma un paquete de cigarrillos diariamente.
  Peter smokes a pack of cigarettes daily.

- Te has fumado las ganancias de la empresa. (*fig*)
  You've wasted the profits of the company.

funcionar   to function, work, run; to be operating

- Mi coche no funciona.
  My car won't run (or broke down).

- No sé por qué el televisor (/la cámara) no funciona.
  I don't know why the TV (/camera) doesn't function (or work).

- Los riñones no le funcionan eficientemente.
  His kidneys don't work efficiently.

- Los bancos no funcionan hoy.
  The banks are not open (or operating) today.

fundamentar en algo   to set up on sth, base on sth

- Fundamentaremos el edificio en roca muy sólida.
  We'll set this building up on very solid rock.

- Ellos fundamentarán su opinión en la evidencia.
  They'll base their opinion on the evidence.

fundamentarse en algo   to base oneself on sth; to be based on sth

- Mis argumentos se fundamentan en la razón (/en los hechos).
  My arguments are based on reason (/on facts).

- No creemos que sus opiniones se fundamenten en la verdad.
  We don't believe his opinions are based on the truth.

fundar   to found, set up, establish

- La junta directiva decidió fundar un asilo para ancianos.
  The board of directors decided to found an old people's home.

- El gobierno fundará un nuevo banco.
  The government will set up a new bank.

fundarse en algo   to be founded on sth, be based on sth

- La decisión del juez se fundó en la evidencia.
  The judge's decision was founded (or based) on the evidence.

- No creía que tus palabras se fundaron en la verdad.
  I did not think your words were based on the truth.

- ¿En qué año se fundó la ciudad de Lima?
  In what year was the city of Lima founded?

fundir   to fuse (together), join, unite; to melt

- Fundieron una campana gigantesca.
  They cast a huge bell.

- Han fundido sus compañías (en una).
  They united (or joined) their companies.

■ Los partidos políticos de izquierda fundieron sus puntos de vista.
   The political parties of the left fused their viewpoints.

■ El platero funde la plata en un crisol muy pequeño.
   The silversmith is melting the silver in a very small crucible.

fundirse   to fuse together

■ El oro y la plata se han fundido.
   Gold and silver have fused together.

■ El motor del auto se fundió (al recalentarse).
   The engine of the car became overheated.

G

ganar   to gain; to win; to defeat; to get, acquire; to earn (*money*), win

■ Nuestro equipo ganó el partido de fútbol.
   Our team won the soccer game.

■ El estudiante ganará suficiente dinero para pagar su matrícula universitaria.
   The student will earn enough money to pay for his university registration.

■ Las tropas del rey ganaron la entrada del castillo sin dificultad.
   The king's troops gained (or won) the entrance to the castle without difficulty.

■ ¿Quién ganó? —Yo gané seis a cero.
   Who won? —I won six to nothing.

■ Le gané a Luis por dos puntos.
   I defeated Luis by two points.

■ Le ganaron al ajedrez (/al tenis/al golf).
   They beat him in chess (/tennis/golf).

■ La ciudad ganó nuevas tierras del estado.
   The city acquired new lands from the state.

ganarse   to gain, win for oneself; to earn for oneself

■ Se ganó un premio en la rifa.
   He won (himself) a prize in the raffle.

■ Por sus acciones se ganó el odio de María.
   By his actions he earned Mary's hatred.

■ Nos ganamos el pan con el sudor de la frente.
   We earn our daily bread with the sweat of our brow.

gastar (en)   to spend (on)

■   Gasté mucho dinero (/tiempo) en el proyecto.
   I spent a lot of money (/time) on the project.

■   He gastado en María mucho dinero.
   I've spent a lot of money on Mary.

■   Gastó en comer y nada más.
   He spent (money) on eating and nothing else.

■   Gastamos en banquetes (/fiestas/ropa/zapatos).
   We spent (money) on banquets (/parties/clothing/shoes).

gemir (de)   to groan, moan (from)

■   El enfermo gimió toda la noche porque tenía dolor.
   The sick man moaned all night because he was in pain.

■   Cuando el profesor les dijo que tendrían un examen, los estudiantes gimieron.
   When the teacher told them that they would have a test, the students groaned.

■   Gimió de dolor (/de hambre/de pena).
   He groaned from pain (/hunger/sadness).

girar (a/en/sobre/alrededor de)   to turn (to/on/about), revolve around; to spin

■   La rueda gira sobre su eje rápidamente.
   The wheel is spinning on its axis quickly.

■   Cuando oyó el ruido, el animal giró la cabeza.
   When it heard the sound, the animal turned its head.

■   Ella gira a la izquierda. Pero tiene que girar a la derecha.
   She turns (to the) left. But she has to turn (to the) right.

■   Júpiter gira alrededor de una estrella.
   Jupiter revolves around a star.

■   La conversación giraba en torno al matrimonio de María.
   The conversation revolved (or centered) around Mary's wedding.

■   El oficial saludó y giró sobre sus talones.
   The officer saluted and turned on his heels.

girar alrededor de algo   to approximate sth, be about sth

■   El número de alumnos de esta escuela gira alrededor de mil.
   The number of students in this school approximated one thousand.

■   El presupuesto nacional gira alrededor de los mil millones.
   The national budget is about one billion.

glorificar   to glorify, praise

■   La historia glorificó su valentía.
   History glorified his courage.

■ Glorificaban a Dios.
   They glorified (or praised) God.

gobernar   to govern, rule

■ Ese virrey gobernó México y Perú.
   That viceroy governed Mexico and Peru.

■ Los ancianos gobiernan la tribu.
   The elders govern (or rule) the tribe.

■ El rey Alfonso gobernó a los castellanos con sabiduría.
   King Alfonso ruled the Castilians wisely.

gozar   to enjoy

■ Los niños gozan jugando en el jardín.
   The children enjoy playing in the garden.

gozar de algo   to enjoy sth

■ Gozamos mucho de la visita de mi hermano (/de la comida/del juego de tenis).
   We enjoyed my brother's visit (/the food/the tennis game) very much.

■ El sacerdote goza del respeto de su pueblo.
   The priest enjoys the respect of his people.

■ Tiene 85 años y ha gozado siempre de buena salud.
   He is 85 years old, and he has always enjoyed good health.

gravitar (hacia)   to gravitate (towards)

■ Los planetas gravitan hacia las estrellas.
   The planets gravitate toward the stars.

■ La posición de ese senador gravitó hacia la izquierda.
   The position of that senator gravitated toward the left.

gritar   to shout, yell; to scream, cry out

■ La mujer lloraba y gritaba.
   The woman was crying and screaming.

■ Le gritaron y lo insultaron.
   They shouted at him and insulted him.

■ El maestro le gritó al estudiante (/a la chica).
   The teacher shouted (or yelled) at the student (/the girl).

guardar   to keep; to watch over, protect

■ Ella guarda la ropa en el ropero.
   She keeps the clothes in the closet.

■ Dios guarda a sus hijos.
   God protects his children.

■ El pastor guarda los rebaños.
   The shepherd watches his flocks.

guardarse de algo   to look out for sth, protect oneself from sth

■ Se guarda de los insectos con un mosquitero.
   He protects himself from the insects with a mosquito net.

■ En este bosque hay que guardarse de las fieras.
   In this forest one has to look out for wild animals.

guardarse de + *inf*   to be careful not to + *inf*; refrain from + *ger*

■ ¡Guárdate de no decirle nada sobre esta conversación!
   Be careful not to tell him about this conversation!

guiar (en, a, hacia)   to guide (in, through); to lead, direct (to)

■ El general guió a sus tropas en la batalla.
   The general guided (or lead) his troops in battle.

■ Los perros pueden guiar a los ciegos.
   Dogs can guide (or lead) blind people.

■ Dios (/Su instinto) le guía en las dificultades.
   God (/His instinct) guides him through difficulties.

■ Él me guió hacia la salida del pueblo.
   He led me toward the edge of of town.

guiarse por algo   to be guided by sth, be ruled by sth; to go by sth

■ Él se guía por la ley antigua (/por sólidos principios morales).
   He was guided (or went) by ancient law (/by solid moral principles).

■ Para hacer funcionar esa máquina hay que guiarse por el manual de indicaciones.
   In order to operate that machine, one has to go by the instruction manual.

■ Él siempre se guiaba por el amor a la patria (/por las estrellas).
   He was always guided by the love of his country (/by the stars).

guiñar   to wink

■ Me guiñó el ojo.
   She winked at me.

■ Le guiñó el ojo a Sonia.
   He winked at Sonia.

gustar   to please, be pleasing, like

■ Me gusta el libro (/el café/la chica).
   The book (/coffee/girl) pleases me. (or I like the book (coffee/girl)).

■ ¿Le gustaron las manzanas?
Did the apples please him? (or Did he like the apples?)

gustar + *inf*   to like to + *inf*

■ No me gustaría hablar con él.
I wouldn't like to talk to him.

■ ¿Les gusta viajar (/comerlas)? —Sí, nos gusta viajar (/comerlas).
Do you like to travel (/eat them)? —Yes, we like to travel (/eat them).

H

haber + *ptp*   to have (*auxiliary*) + *ptp*

■ He comido (/llegado/vuelto).
I have eaten (/arrived/returned).

■ Lo habría hecho, si hubiera tenido tiempo.
I would have done it if I had had the time.

■ Después de haberlo escrito, decidí no enviarlo al ministro.
After writing it (or After having written it), I decided not to send it to the minister.

hay/había/ha habido/ . . .   there is, there are/there was, there were/there has been, there have been/ . . .

■ Hay un árbol(/tres árboles) en el jardín.
There is a tree (/There are three trees) in the garden.

■ Había un estudiante (/Había tres estudiantes) en el salón de clase.
There was one student (/There were three students) in the classroom.

■ Hubo un accidente (/tres accidentes) en la esquina.
There was an accident (/There were three accidents) on the corner.

■ Habrá una fiesta (/tres fiestas) este fin de semana.
There will be a party (/There will be three parties) this weekend.

■ Ha habido un accidente (/tres accidentes) en esa esquina.
There has been an accident (/There have been three accidents) on the corner.

haber de + *inf*   to be supposed to + *inf*, have to + *inf*; to be probably

■ Hemos de salir mañana temprano.
We are (supposed) to leave early tomorrow.

- Como todos los días, el sol ha de salir mañana.
  Like every day, the sun has to (or *will*) *rise tomorrow.*

- ¿Por qué hemos de comprar algo que no necesitamos?
  Why do we have to buy something we do not need?

- Ha de ser muy rico porque se viste muy bien.
  He must be very rich because he dresses very well.

- La criada ha de limpiar la casa esta tarde.
  The maid is supposed to clean the house this afternoon.

- ¿Qué hora es? —Han de ser las tres (/Ha de ser la una).
  What time is it? —It must be about three (/one) o'clock.

- No tengo dinero. ¿Qué he de hacer?
  I don't have money. What am I to do?

haber que + *inf*   to be necessary to + *inf*

- Hay que trabajar para comer.
  It's necessary to work in order to eat.

- Había que estudiar mucho para aprobar el curso.
  One had to study a lot in order to pass the course.

- Habrá que pintar la casa.
  The house will have to be painted (or *It will be necessary to paint the house*).

habitar en algo   to inhabit sth, live in sth

- Los osos habitan en el bosque.
  Bears inhabit (or *live in*) *the forest.*

- Los beduinos habitaban en el desierto.
  Bedouins used to live in the desert.

hablar   to speak, talk

- ¿Hablas alemán? —No lo hablo.
  Do you speak German? —I don't speak it.

- Habla una lengua que no conozco.
  He is speaking a language I do not know.

- Ella hablaba un español elegante.
  She used to speak an elegant Spanish.

hablar a/con uno/algo   to speak to sb/sth, talk to/with sb/sth

- Juan habla a (*or* con) María por teléfono.
  John talks to Mary by telephone.

■ El presidente habló a (*or* con) los ministros.
The president spoke to the ministers.

■ Hemos hablado a (*or* con) María esta noche.
We have spoken (or talked) to Mary tonight.

■ Fue necesario hablar al (*or* con el) director del colegio.
It was necessary to talk to the school principal.

hablar de uno/algo   to speak about sb/sth, talk about/of sb/sth

■ Hablé de mis amigas.
I talked about my friends.

■ Hablamos de historia y política.
We talked about history and politics.

hacer   to make, build, prepare, create; to do

■ Él hace pasteles para vender.
He makes pastries to sell.

■ Nosotros hicimos esta mesa.
We made (or built) this table.

■ Mi hermana hará la cena (/ensalada/cama) esta vez.
My sister will make (or prepare) the supper (/salad/bed) this time.

■ Yo hice lo que me dijiste (/mandaste/pediste).
I did what you told (/ordered/asked) me.

■ Dios hizo al hombre (/el universo/la luz).
God made (or created) man (/the universe/light).

■ La madre le hizo un peinado my bonito a María.
Mary's mother styled her hair very attractively.

■ El gallo hace quiquiriquí. (*idiomatic*)
The rooster goes cock-a-doodle-doo.

■ La mamá hará que los chicos se acuesten temprano.
The mother will make the boys go to bed early.

hacer a uno + *inf*   to make sb + *inf*

■ Me haces reír (/llorar) mucho.
You make me laugh (/cry) so much.

■ Ella no pudo entender por qué Héctor nos hizo visitar ese museo tan malo.
She couldn't understand why Hector made us visit that terrible museum.

■ Les hice venir.
I made them come.

hacer   to be (*meteorology*)

■ Mañana hará buen tiempo.
It will be good weather tomorrow.

■ Hace (/Hizo) viento (/frío/calor) hoy.
It is (/was) windy (/cold/warm) today.

hacer ...   ... ago (*time*)

■ Hace 3 años (/Hace poco). . . .
Three years ago (/A short while ago). . . .

■ Hace dos semanas que se fue.
He left two weeks ago.

hacer de uno   to work as sb, act as sb

■ Hace de maestro (/mecánico/americano/portero) aunque no lo es.
*He works as a teacher (/mechanic/acts as if he's American/works as a caretaker)
even though he is not one.*

■ Su tía hizo de madre cuando se les murió su verdadera madre.
Their aunt acted as their mother when their real mother died.

■ Siempre hace de tonto en todas las fiestas.
He always plays the fool at all the parties.

hacerse   to become

■ Eduardo se hizo médico después de que salió del colegio.
Eduardo became a doctor after he graduated from high school.

■ Se hicieron ricos.
They became rich.

hacerse a algo   to get used to sth, become accustomed to sth

■ Se hizo a la idea (/a sus costumbres/al modo de ser/a la vida del campo).
He became accustomed to the idea (/her habits/the way of life/life in the country).

hallar   to find; to discover

■ Hallé una moneda en la vereda.
I found a coin on the sidewalk (or *path*).

■ Los médicos han hallado la causa de su enfermedad.
The doctors have found (or discovered) the cause of his illness.

■ Hallaron a sus amigos en el restaurante.
They found their friends in the restaurant.

hallarse (en)   to be; to find oneself (in, with)

■ Se halla en Madrid esta semana.
He is in Madrid this week.

- El doctor se halla ocupado.
  The doctor is occupied.

- Me hallo completamente desorientado.
  I find myself completely disoriented.

- Me hallé en serios problemas.
  I found myself with serious problems.

hallarse con uno/algo   to find oneself with sb/sth; to get used to sb/sth

- Ellos se pudieron hallar con Carolina.
  They were able to get used to Carolyn.

- Al final de la vida se halló con muchos hijos y vieja.
  She found herself old and with many children at the end of her life.

- Nunca nos hallamos con esa gente.
  We never got used to those people.

- Si no tienes más cuidado, te puedes hallar con un problema muy serio.
  If you are not more careful, you can find yourself with a very serious problem.

hartar (con)   to satiate, tire (with)

- El frío en esa ciudad lo hartó y se fue.
  He got tired of the cold in that city and went away.

- Él simplemente la harta con sus quejas (/problemas/estupidez).
  He simply tires her with his complaints (/problems/stupidity).

hartarse de algo   to get tired of sb; to eat one's fill of sth

- Ella se hartó de él.
  She got tired of him.

- Me harté de tanta fruta (/de pasteles/de la cerveza).
  I ate my fill of much fruit (/of cakes/drank my fill of beer).

hartarse de + *inf*   to get one's fill + *ger*; to get tired of + *ger*

- Se hartaron de comer y beber tanto.
  They got their fill of eating and drinking.

- Nos hartamos de ir a la playa.
  We got our fill of (or tired of going to) the beach.

- Nos hartamos de esperar.
  We got tired of waiting.

hastiar   to bore; to sicken, disgust

- El invierno hastía.
  Winter bores (or wearies) one.

- Ese alimento lo hastió.
  That food sickened him.

hastiarse de uno/algo   to tire of sb/sth, get fed up with sb/sth
- Se hastió de la manera cómo la trataban (/de su novio). (*fig*)
  She got tired of the way she was treated (/tired of her boyfriend).

hastiarse de + *inf*   to tire of + *ger*
- Ella se hastió de trabajar en el campo.
  She got tired of working in the fields.
- Me hastío de hacer lo mismo todos los días.
  I get tired of doing the same thing every day.

helar(se)   to freeze
- Este frío me hiela.
  This cold makes me freeze.
- El agua se está helando en la calle.
  The water on the street is freezing.
- Ellos se helaron en la montaña.
  They froze on the mountain.
- Se me heló el corazón cuando lo vi. (*fig*)
  My heart froze when I saw him.

heredar (de)   to inherit (from)
- Los dos muchachos heredaron la inteligencia de su padre.
  The two boys inherited their intelligence from their father.
- Ellos heredarán de sus abuelos mucha riqueza (/la casa/una hacienda).
  They will inherit great wealth (/the house/a farm) from their grandparents.

herir   to injure, hurt, wound
- La trampa le hirió la pata al oso.
  The trap wounded the bear's paw.
- Ese chillido me hiere los oídos.
  That screeching hurts my ears.
- Sus palabras hirieron al mejor amigo.
  His words hurt his best friend.
- El jinete hirió al caballo con las espuelas.
  The rider injured the horse with the spurs.

hervir   to boil; to cook
- El agua hierve a 100 grados centígrados.
  Water boils at 100 degrees centigrade.
- ¿Has hervido ya la carne (/comida)?
  Have you cooked the meat (/food) yet?
- Los enfermeros hierven los intrumentos para desinfectarlos.
  The nurses boil the equipment to disinfect it.

hervir de uno/algo   to seethe with sth, swarm with sb/sth

■   Ella hervía de cólera.
She was seething with anger.

■   La plaza hierve de gente.
The square is swarming (or teeming) with people.

■   Encontraron la jalea hirviendo de hormigas.
They found the jam swarming with ants.

honrar   to honor, revere, respect

■   El pueblo honra la memoria de los caídos en la guerra.
The people honor the memory of those fallen in the war.

■   ¡Honra a tus padres!
Honor (or Respect) your parents!

■   Sus triunfos honran a su país.
Her triumphs honor her country.

honrar con algo   to honor with sth, be honored with sth

■   Usted me honra con su amistad (/presencia).
You honor me with your friendship (/presence).

■   Usted nos ha honrado con su visita.
You have honored us with your visit.

honrarse de + *inf*   to be honored to + *inf*

■   Me honro de haber trabajado con ese gran maestro.
I am honored to have worked with that great maestro.

■   Se honra de representar a su país en las olimpiadas.
He is honored to represent his country in the Olympic games.

■   Nos honramos de conocerlo (/de complacerlo).
We are honored to have met you (/pleased you).

huir (a/de)   to flee, escape, run (away) (to/from)

■   —¿Piensan huir mañana? —Sí, huirán mañana.
Do they intend to escape (or flee) tomorrow? —Yes, they will escape tomorrow.

■   Ese estudiante me huye (*or* huye de mí).
That student avoids (or runs from) me.

■   Ellos nos deben mucho dinero y cuando nos ven nos huyen (*or* huyen de nosotros).
They owe us a lot of money, and, when they see us, they run from us.

■   Huyó a su pueblo natal.
He fled to his native town.

■   Huyeron de la prisión (/de un campo de concentración).
They fled from prison (/a concentration camp).

- Cuando la ve en la escuela, él huye de ella.
  When he sees her in school, he runs away from her.

- Los asaltantes pudieron huir de la policía.
  The assailants were able to flee from the police.

hundir (en)   to sink; to submerge, engulf (in)

- El submarino hundió el acorazado.
  The submarine sank the battleship.

- El delfín sacaba y hundía la cabeza.
  The dolphin was lifting and submerging its head.

- Él está hundido en problemas (/en la incertidumbre/en la depresión).
  He's engulfed in problems (/uncertainty/depression).

hundirse (en)   to sink, be sunk (in, into)

- El barco chocó contra la mina y se hundió.
  The ship collided with the mine and sank.

- La economía del país se hundió después de la guerra.
  The economy of the country sank (or collapsed) after the war.

- Los edificios se están hundiendo.
  The buildings are sinking.

- El hombre se hundía en sus pensamientos.
  The man sank into (deep) thought.

I

ignorar   to ignore; to not know, be unaware of

- Ignoro todo lo que me dices.
  I ignore everything you tell me.

- Ignoraba que habías llegado.
  I did not know you had arrived.

- Debes ignorar a Carlos (/la presencia de Carlos), porque es muy mal educado.
  You have to ignore Carl (/Carl's presence) because he's very rude.

igualar   to make even, be equal to; to level (off)

- Ese terreno (/camino) está muy desigual, hay que igualarlo.
  That land (/road) is very uneven; it has to be leveled off.

- Es necesario igualar la calidad de los productos.
  *It's necessary to to make the quality of the products equal (*or *consistent).*

- Hay que igualar la carga del camión.
  The truck load has to be made even.

igualarse (a)   to be equal (to), balance out

- La calidad del producto nacional se iguala al producto extranjero.
  The quality of the local product is equal to that of a foreign product.

- Se igualaron las pérdidas y las ganacias.
  *The losses and earnings balanced out (*or *were equal).*

igualarse a/con uno/algo   to be like sb/sth

- Yo no me igualo al (*or* con el) esa gente.
  I am not like those people.

- Este libro no se iguala al (*or* con el) que leí anoche.
  This book is not like the one I read last night.

- Ella no se iguala a (*or* con) su mamá.
  She is not like her mom.

impedir   to impede, obstruct, prevent from

- El accidente impidió el tránsito de vehículos.
  The accident obstructed vehicular traffic.

impedir a uno + *inf*   to prevent sb from + *ger*

- Mi situación me impidió viajar (/comprarla).
  My situation prevented me from traveling (/buying it).

- Ese dolor en la pierna le impide correr rápidamente.
  That pain in his leg prevents him from running quickly.

impedir algo a uno   to block sth from/to sb

- La policía impedía el paso a los peatones.
  The police blocked the passage to pedestrians.

impedir (a uno) que + *subj*   to stop from + *ger,* prevent sb from + *ger*

- Me impidió que entrara en el edificio.
  *He stopped (*or *prevented) me from entering the building.*

- Esto no impide que todos deban participar.
  This does not alter the fact that everyone should participate.

■ El me impide que la vea (/que la visite).
  He prevents me from seeing her (/visiting her).

imponer (a)   to impose (on)

■ El ejército impuso el toque de queda.
  The army imposed a curfew.

■ El maestro impone silencio a los estudiantes.
  The teacher imposes silence on the students.

■ El juez impuso silencio en el tribunal.
  The judge imposed silence in the courtroom.

■ ¡Impón tu autoridad!
  Impose your authority!

imponerse   to prevail, triumph

■ Finalmente los cuerdos se impusieron.
  The sane (people) finally prevailed.

■ Siempre se impondrá la paz.
  Peace will always prevail (or triumph).

importar (de, a)   to import (from); to be important, matter (to)

■ El país tiene que importar carne de Argentina.
  The country has to import meat from Argentina.

■ Importamos directamente de Alemania.
  We import directly from Germany.

■ No importa lo que tú digas.
  It's not important what you say.

■ Me (/Le) importa mucho a mí (/a él) lo que dice el profesor.
  It's very important to me (/to him) what the teacher says.

impregnar (de)   to impregnate (with); to saturate (with)

■ La camisa estaba impregnada de aceite.
  The shirt was saturated with oil.

■ El cuarto se impregnó de mal olor (/de un perfume de rosas).
  The room was impregnated (or filled) with a bad smell (/the smell of roses).

imprimir   to print

■ Esa editorial imprimió tu libro hace tres años.
  That publishing house printed your book a year ago.

■ Vamos a imprimirlo en un papel fino.
  We are going to print it on a high quality paper.

incendiar   to set on fire, set fire to

- Las bombas incendiaron los almacenes.
  The bombs set the warehouses on fire.

- Incendiaron la casa en que vivía.
  They set fire to the house in which he lived.

incendiarse   to catch fire; to burn down

- Ayer se incendió la escuela.
  Yesterday the school caught on fire (or burned down).

- Aquí se incendian los bosques a menudo.
  Here the forests catch on fire often.

incidir en algo   to fall into sth; to affect sth

- Has incidido en el mismo error.
  You have fallen into the same error.

- Ella incide en faltas cuando se pone nerviosa.
  She makes mistakes when she gets nervous.

- Los recortes en el presupuesto van a incidir en la economía.
  The budget cuts are going to affect the economy.

inclinar   to incline; to bend, incline, tilt

- Ella inclinó el torso para recoger la moneda.
  She bent (her body) down in order to pick up the coin.

- Al entrar inclinó ligeramente la cabeza.
  Upon entering he bowed (or tilted) his head slightly.

inclinar a uno a + *inf*   to induce *or* persuade sb to + *inf*

- Tus palabras me inclinan a tomar otra decisión.
  Your words persuade me to make another decision.

- Su conciencia lo inclinó a arrepentirse.
  His conscience induced him to repent.

inclinarse a + *inf*   to be inclined to + *inf*

- Yo me inclino a ir hoy.
  I am inclined to go today.

- Se inclinan a hacerlo de una vez.
  They are inclined to do it right away.

inclinarse ante algo   to bow (down) to/before sth

- Ella se inclinó ante el altar.
  She bowed before the altar.

- Los vasallos se inclinaron ante el rey.
  The vassals bowed to (or before) the king.

- Ellos se inclinaron ante la fuerza de sus argumentos.
  They bowed down before the force of her arguments.

inclinarse por uno   to prefer sb

- Ella se inclina por Luis más que por Juan.
  She prefers Louis to John.

- Naturalmente él se inclina por sus amigos.
  Naturally he prefers his friends.

incluir (en)   to include (in); to comprise, contain

- ¿Incluiste el recibo? —Sí, lo incluí.
  Did you include the receipt? —Yes, I included it.

- Este pago incluye todo lo que te debo.
  This payment includes (or comprises) everything I owe you.

- La lista incluye a todos sus amigos.
  The list includes all of his friends.

- Incluí en el paquete unos periódicos.
  I enclosed in the package some newspapers.

incurrir en algo   to incur sth; to commit sth

- Los hombres incurrieron en la ira de Dios.
  Men incurred the wrath of God.

- Han incurrido en mi desprecio.
  They have incurred my scorn.

- El general incurrió en el error cuando habló de sus adversarios.
  The general committed an error when he spoke of his adversaries.

- Vamos a incurrir en una traición si no le decimos.
  We are going to commit treason if we do not tell him.

- De nuevo has incurrido en una falta.
  Again you have commited an error.

indicar   to indicate

- Todo aquello fue indicado en la carta.
  All that was indicated in the letter.

- El senado lo indicó en su documento.
  The senate indicated it in its document.

- Su conducta me (/le) indicaba que fue mal criado.
  His behavior indicated to me (/to him) that he was not brought up well.

indignar   to anger, make indignant; to provoke, stir up

- Sus palabras lo indignaron mucho.
  His words angered (or provoked) him much.

- Tu conducta indignará a tus padres.
  Your conduct will anger your parents.

- La política del gobierno indignó al pueblo.
  The government's policy provoked the people.

indignarse con uno/algo   to get indignant with sb/sth

- Se indignó con nuestra conducta.
  She got indignant with our behavior.

- Me indigné con Juan.
  I got indignant with John.

indignarse por algo   to get indignant *or* angry about sth

- Ella se indignó por el poco dinero que ganó.
  She got indignant about how little money she earned.

- Nos indignamos por ese comentario.
  We got angry about that comment.

indisponer a uno con uno   to set sb against sb

- Él me indispuso con el profesor.
  He set me against the professor.

- Lo indispusieron con los amigos de Miguel.
  They pitted him against Michael's friends.

indisponerse (con uno)   to fall out (with sb); to become indisposed

- Se indispuso con sus amigos.
  He fell out with his friends.

- Él se indispuso hoy.
  Today he became indisposed (or he became ill or felt bad).

inducir a uno a + *inf*   to induce sb to + *inf*; cause sb to + *inf*

- Ella lo indujo a robar por primera vez.
  She induced him to steal for the first time.

- La pobreza en que vivían los indujo a emigrar de su tierra.
  The poverty in which they lived caused them to emigrate from their homeland.

- La enfermedad de su esposa lo indujo a buscar atención médica especializada.
  The illness of his wife forced him to look for specialized medical attention.

infectar (con)   to infect (with)

- Su hermano lo infectó.
  His brother infected him.

- Los mosquitos infectaron a la población del valle.
  Mosquitos infected the people of the valley.

- Los perros pueden infectar con la rabia al hombre.
  Dogs can infect man with rabies.

infectarse (con, de)   to become infected (with, from/by)

- La herida se infectó.
  The wound became infected.

- La mujer se infectó con SIDA.
  The woman became infected with AIDS.

- Seguramente se infectaron con alimentos contaminados.
  They were probably infected by contaminated food.

- Te has infectado de él.
  You got infected from (or by) him.

influir con uno   to pressure sb, put pressure on sb

- Influyó con amigos poderosos para que lo dejaran libre.
  He put pressure on powerful friends to set him free.

- Influyó con el jefe para que empleara a su hija en la oficina.
  He pressured the boss to employ his daughter in the office.

influir en uno/algo   to have influence on sb/sth

- Estas circunstancias influyeron en el éxito del negocio.
  These circumstances influenced the success of the enterprise.

- El presidente influye en su gabinete.
  The president influences (or has influence on) his cabinet.

- Los padres influyen mucho en la educación de sus hijos.
  The parents have a big influence on their children's education.

informar (de, sobre)   to inform, tell (about); to find out; to report (on)

- Los negociadores informaron que todo iba bien.
  The negotiators reported (or found out) that all was well.

- Los periódicos informan de lo sucedido en Rusia.
  The newspapers are reporting on what happened in Russia.

- Yo te informo del (*or* sobre el) progreso de su salud.
  I will inform (or tell) you about his health progress.

- El científico informó de su proyecto.
  The scientist reported on his project.
- Esa revista nos informa sobre la economía nacional.
  That magazine informs us about the national economy.

informarse (de, sobre)   to find out (about); to gather information (about)

- Los historiadores buenos se informan en las fuentes primarias.
  Good historians gather information from primary sources.
- Nos informamos en la comisaría.
  We found out in the police station.
- ¡Infórmese de lo que él hizo anoche!
  Find out what he did last night.
- Me voy a informar de su secreto.
  I am going to find out her secret.
- El gobierno se informó de las actividades de los espías en el país.
  The govenment found out about the activities of the spies in the country.
- El gobierno se está informando sobre la mejor manera de ayudar a las víctimas.
  The government is gathering information about (or inquiring into) the best way to help the victims.

ingresar a/en algo   to enter sth, join sth; to deposit (*money*)

- Ingresó a la universidad en 1914.
  He entered the university in 1914.
- Ingresó al hospital a las tres.
  She entered the hospital at three.
- Ingresamos en la compañía juntos.
  We joined the company together.
- Han ingresado miles (/doscientos dólares) en su cuenta corriente.
  They have deposited thousands (/two hundred dollars) in their checking account.

insistir (sobre)   to insist (on); to persist

- Él insistió sobre ese punto (/ese problema/ese argumento/esa teoría).
  He insisted on that point (/problem/argument/theory).
- Ella insistió.
  She insisted (or persisted).

insistir en + *inf*   to insist on + *ger*

- Él insistió en permanecer callado (/decir la verdad/pegarle al caballo).
  He insisted on remaining silent (/telling the truth/hitting the horse).

- Ella insiste en visitar a su abuela.
  She insists on visiting her grandmother.

insistir en que...   to insist that...

- El insiste en que ellos se vayan.
  He insists that they leave.

- Mi esposa insistió en que yo sólo tenía la culpa.
  My wife insisted that I alone was at fault.

inspirar a uno   to inspire sb

- La obra de El Greco lo inspiró profundamente.
  The work of El Greco inspired him deeply.

inspirar a uno (algo)   to inspire sb with (sth); to inspire sth

- La conducta de la chica le inspiró celos.
  The girl's behavior inspired jealousy in him.

- Las palabras de su padre inspiraron nuevos deseos de triunfar en el hijo.
  The father's words inspired new desires to succeed in his son.

- Las ideas políticas del presidente inspiraron a sus seguidores.
  The president inspired his followers with new political ideas.

inspirarse en algo   to be inspired by sth, find inspiration in sth

- Ese poeta se inspiró en el mar para escribir el libro.
  That poet found the inspiration in the sea to write the book.

- La novela se inspiraba en el primer amor del autor.
  The novel was inspired by the author's first love.

instruir (en)   to instruct, teach (in, on)

- Leer y viajar instruyen mucho.
  Reading and traveling teach a great deal.

- El maestro instruye a los alumnos.
  The teacher instructs the students.

- El ingeniero los instruyó en las nuevas tecnologías.
  The engineer instructed them on the new technologies.

- El entrenador lo instruye en la forma correcta de agarrar la raqueta.
  The coach instructs him in the proper way to grip the racquet.

instruirse (en, sobre)   to learn, teach oneself (about); to find out

- Nos intruimos en la música.
  We are learning (or teaching ourselves) music.

- ¡Instrúyete sobre dónde y cuándo tendrá lugar la conferencia!
  Find out (about) where and when the conference will take place.

- Te vamos a instruir sobre la vida de esta región.
  We are going to teach you about life in this region.

intentar   to try, attempt; to mean, intend

- ¿Qué intentabas con ese palo (/libro/cuchillo)?
  What were you trying (or intending) (to do) with that stick (/book/knife)?

- Intentó una respuesta, pero no tuvo éxito.
  He tried (or attempted) an answer, but it didn't work.

intentar + *inf*   to try to + *inf*, attempt to + *inf*, intend to + *inf*

- Intentó saltar la valla, pero no pudo.
  He tried (or attempted) to jump the hurdle, but he wasn't able to.

- Intentaron atacar el castillo y fueron rechazados.
  They attempted to attack the castle, and they were repelled.

- El muchacho intentaba hablarle a la chica después del colegio.
  The boy intended to speak to the girl after school.

interesar   to interest, be of interest to; to appeal to; to concern

- No le interesa ni los deportes ni la política.
  He is not interested in sports or politics.

- No me interesa él.
  He is of no interest (or unappealing) to me.

- La venta de los coches interesó a todos.
  The sale of the cars interested everybody.

- Esto (/Mi propuesta/Ese asunto) le interesa a él mucho.
  This (/My proposal/That matter) is of great interest to (or greatly concerns) him.

interesar a uno en algo   to get sb interested in sth

- Ella lo ha interesado en su país (/en mi idea).
  She has gotten him interested in her country (/in my idea).

- El profesor interesa a sus alumnos en la biología.
  The teacher develops an interest in biology in his students.

interesarse en uno/algo   to be interested in sb/sth, take an interest in sb/sth

- El niño se interesa en (*or* por) juguetes y en nada más.
  The child is interested in toys and nothing else.

- Parece que ella se ha interesado en él.
  It appears that she has taken an interest in him.

interesarse en/por + *inf*   be interested in + *ger*

- Se interesa en (*or* por) comerciar con nosotros.
  He is interested in trading with us.

- Nosotros nos interesamos en (*or* por) comprar un piano.
  We are interested in buying a piano.

- Ellos se interesan en (*or* por) conocerla.
  They are interested in knowing (or meeting) her.

interferir (en)   to interfere (in, with); to upset, affect

- El gobierno interfirió en el proceso de publicación.
  The government interfered in (or affected or upset) the publication process.

- Las manchas solares interfieren en las transmisiones radiales.
  The sun spots interfere with radio transmissions.

interferirse (en)   to interfere (in, with)

- Ella se interfirió en mis asuntos personales.
  She interfered in my personal affairs.

- ¡No te interfieras en lo que yo hago!
  Do not interfere with what I do.

internar en algo   to admit to/into sth (*medical*)

- Ayer internaron a David en un manicomio.
  David was admitted yesterday to a psychiatric hospital.

- Él fue internado en el hospital (/la clínica).
  He was admitted to the hospital (/clinic).

internarse en algo   to go into sth, penetrate sth

- Los exploradores se internaron en las montañas.
  The explorers went into the mountains.

- El muchacho se internó en el interior del castillo.
  The boy penetrated the interior of the castle.

- Él se internó en los secretos de la naturaleza.
  He went deeply into the secrets of nature.

intervenir (en)   to intervene (in); to take part, participate (in)

- Él no intervino en esa revolución (/el debate/este asunto familiar).
  He did not take part in that revolution (/the debate/did not intervene in this family matter).

- El jefe no ha intervenido en esta decisión.
  The boss has not had a hand in this decision.

- Finalmente la policía intervino en la pelea.
  Finally, the police intervened in the fighting.

intervenir por uno   to intercede for sb

- El profesor intervino por el alumno.
  The professor interceded for the student.

- La iglesia intervino por el acusado.
  The church interceded for the accused.

- Sus padres intervinieron por el yerno.
  Her parents interceded for their son-in-law.

introducir (en)   to introduce (in, into); to place (in)

- La profesora introdujo una nueva perspectiva (/una opinión diferente).
  The professor introduced a new perspective (/different opinion).

- Me introdujo en el teatro.
  He ushered me into the theater.

- Lo introdujeron en una bolsa (/caja/saco).
  They introduced it in a bag (/box/sack).

introducirse en algo   to get in/into sth

- Ella se introdujo en la cocina (/la casa/el baño).
  She got into the kitchen (/house/bathroom).

invitar a uno (a)   to invite sb (to); to pay for sb

- Él invitó a su amiga.
  He invited (or paid for) his friend.

- Arturo la invitó a su casa.
  Arthur invited her to his house.

invitar a + *inf*   to invite to + *inf*

- Nos invitaron a comer en su casa.
  They invited us to eat in their house.

- El director le invitó a escribir un artículo en la revista.
  The editor invited him to write an article in the magazine.

inyectar (en)   to inject (into)

- Le inyectaron penicilina (en el brazo).
  They gave him shots of penicillin (in the arm).

- Se inyectó cemento en los cimientos del edificio.
  Concrete was injected in the building's foundation.

ir (a, de, hacia)   to go (to, from, toward) travel, walk; to drive, ride; to go (*fig*)

- Voy a mi casa (/a la iglesia/al mercado/a Madrid/al cine).
  I go (or am going) to my house (/to the church/to the store/to Madrid/to the movie).

- El tren va hacia Chicago.
  The train is going towards Chicago.

- El camino va de aquí a la plaza.
  The road goes from here to the plaza (square).

- Él va en coche a la escuela (/a la oficina/al trabajo/al campo).
  He drives to school (/the office/work/the country).

- ¿Cómo va la salud?
  How is your health?

- Fue de mal en peor.
  It went from bad to worse or *It got worse.*

- No le va bien (/al estudiante) en alemán.
  He (/The student) is not doing very well in German.

- No le van bien los zapatos.
  The shoes don't go well (or suit her).

ir a + *inf*   to go to + *inf*

- Ahora vamos a comer (/trabajar/escribirlo/decirle).
  We are going now to eat (/work/write it/to tell him).

- Voy a verlo.
  I'm going to see him.

ir con uno/algo   to agree with sb/sth; to go with sb/sth

- Voy con Isabel y sus amigas a la ciudad.
  I am going with Isabel and her friends to the city.

- El amarillo va bien con el rojo.
  Yellow goes well (or agrees) with red.

- Fueron con miedo al examen.
  They went fearfully to the exam.

ir contra uno/algo   to go against sb/sth

- Su propuesta va contra mis principios (/mis ideas/mi compañía).
  Your proposal goes against my principles (/my ideas/my company).

- La gente iba contra el dictador (/la dictadura).
  The people went against the dictator (/dictatorship).

ir de algo   to go for sth, go as sth

- Voy de compras (/viaje/caza/pesca/vacaciones/paseo).
  I am going shopping (/on a trip/hunting/fishing/on vacation/for a walk).

■ Voy de chofer (/ayudant/guía/profesor/suplente).
   I am going as a driver (/helper/guide/teacher/substitute).

ir en algo   to go by sth (*travel*)

■ Vamos en tren (/coche/avión) todos los días.
   We take the train (/car/plane) every day.

ir para algo   to be almost sth, be pushing sth; to go to/towards sth

■ Carlos va para los cuarenta.
   Carl is pushing forty.

■ Rosita va para vieja.
   Rose is getting old.

■ Voy para la casa (/la oficina/la escuela).
   I am going to (or *towards*) *the house (/the office/the school).*

ir para + *inf*   to go to + *inf*

■ Voy para ver lo que pasó.
   I am going to see what happened.

■ Voy para cumplir con un deber.
   I am going to fulfill an obligation.

■ Va para estar con la familia.
   He's going to be with the family.

ir por algo   to go for sth

■ Fueron por el médico para que la auxiliara.
   They went for the doctor so he could help her.

■ ¿Dónde está Juan? —Él fue por vino.
   Where is John? —He went for wine.

■ Eso no va por ti, lo dije por él.
   I wasn't referring to you; I said it referring to him.

ir sobre algo   to follow sth

■ Voy sobre sus huellas.
   I'm following his track.

■ No se preocupe; voy sobre el asunto.
   Do not worry; I am following (or *on top*) *of the matter.*

ir tras uno/algo   (*fig*) to go after sb/sth

■ Él fue tras ella (/ese negocio).
   He went after her (/that business).

■ Ellos fueron tras el dinero que perdieron.
   They went after the money they lost.

irse   to go away, leave

- Ella se fue y nunca volvió.
  She went away and never returned.

- Ahora tengo que irme. Es hora de irnos.
  Now I have to go away. It's time we left (or went).

- Mi tío se fue hace seis meses.
  My uncle left six months ago.

- La fecha (/Su cumpleaños/La cita) se me fue de la memoria. (*fig*)
  The date (/His birthday/The appointment) slipped my mind.

irse + *inf*   to go away + *inf*

- Me voy a lavar (/a planchar) la ropa.
  I am leaving to wash (/to iron) the clothes.

- Se fue a trabajar esta mañana.
  She went away to work this morning.

irse por algo   to go (away) by sth, leave by sth

- Ellos se fueron por ese camino. Estoy seguro.
  They went (or left) that way. I am sure.

- Por esta calle se va a mi oficina (/casa). ¿Por dónde se va a la tuya?
  This is the street to my office (/house). Which way is yours?

- Me voy por la calle Central.
  I am going by way of Central Street.

J

jugar (con, contra)   to play (with, against)

- ¡No juegues con fuego (/armas de fuego/palos/fósforos)!
  Don't play with fire (/firearms/sticks/matches)!

- Nuestro equipo no juega hoy (/contra el equipo nacional).
  Our team doesn't play today (/against the national team).

- Pedrito juega con Juanita en el patio.
  Peter is playing with Juanita on the patio.

jugar a algo   to play (*a game, sport*)

- No juego al tenis (/al béisbol/al fútbol/a los naipes).
  I don't play tennis (/baseball/soccer/cards).

- Generalmente no juegan a los caballos (/a la ruleta).
  Generally, they do not play the horses (/roulette).

jugar con uno   to play (around) with sb, toy with sb

- El abuelo siempre juega con su nieta.
  The grandfather always plays with his granddaughter.

- ¡No juegues conmigo porque te podría ir mal!
  Don't mess around with me because it'll go badly for you!

jugarse   to gamble (away), risk

- (Se) jugó 100 dólares en Las Vegas.
  He gambled (away) $100 in Las Vegas.

- Me juego la vida cada vez que cruzo ese puente.
  I risk my life every time I cross that bridge.

- Se juega su felicidad si se casa con Carlos.
  She is gambling on (or risking) her happiness if she marries Carl.

juntar   to join, unite

- Junté esas dos tablas.
  I joined those two boards.

- El interés en el dinero nos junta.
  Our common interest in money unites us.

juntar a/con algo   to join to sth, combine with sth; to put close to sth

- ¡Junte su cama a la mía!
  Join your bed to mine.

- ¡Junta estos zapatos a esos!
  Put these shoes next to those.

- Juntemos su capital al mío para fundar una nueva compañía.
  Let's join your capital to mine in order to start a new company.

- Junta tu empresa con la de tu hermano.
  Combine your business with that of your brother.

juntarse   to meet, assemble, come together

- ¿Por qué se juntan ellos? —Se juntan para oírla (/verlo).
  Why are they assembling? —They are assembling to hear her (/to see him).

- Mis colegas se juntaron en la biblioteca.
  My colleagues met in the library.

juntarse con uno   to join sb; to meet (up) with sb

- Carlos se juntó con él para hacer el proyecto.
  Carl joined him to do the project.

- Me junté con ellos en la estación para despedirme.
  I met (or joined) them at the station to say good-bye.

- Juan no quiere casarse, quiere juntarse con su novia.
  John doesn't want to get married; he wants to live with his girlfriend.

jurar (por, sobre)   to swear (by, on)

- Lo juraría.
  I would swear to it.

- Le juro a usted que no miento (/digo la verdad).
  I swear to you that I'm not lying (/I'm telling the truth).

- Juan juró por lo más sagrado que no había cometido el crimen.
  John swore by all that is sacred that he hadn't committed the crime.

- Juró sobre los evangelios (/la constitución) que no lo había visto.
  He swore on the Gospels (/the constitution) that he didn't see him.

- Yo juro por mi madre (/padre/hijo) que he dicho la verdad.
  I swear on my mother's (/grandfather's/son's) honor that I've told you the truth.

- El testigo juró en falso.
  The witness committed perjury.

juzgar   to judge; to consider, deem, think

- Juzgamos solamente lo que has hecho (/lo que él dijo).
  We judge only what you have done (/what he said).

- No juzgamos oportuno invitarlo a nuestra fiesta (/discutir el tema con ella).
  We don't think (or consider) it fitting to invite him to our party (/discuss the issue with her).

juzgar a uno de algo   to think of sb as sth, take sb for sth

- ¡No me juzgues de mala gente!
  Don't think of me as (or judge me to be) a bad person!

- Lo juzgué de borracho.
  I took him for a drunk.

- Fue juzgado de vagabundo.
  He was thought to be a bum (or vagabond).

juzgar (a uno) por algo   to judge (sb) by sth

- Juzgo por su apariencia (/ropa/coche) que es rica.
  I judge by her appearance (/clothes/car) that she is rich.

- Sólo te juzgo por lo que hablas.
  I only judge you by what you say.

L

lacrar   to injure the health of; to seal with wax

- Las epidemias lacran los pueblos.
  Epidemics injure the health of the people.

- El rey lacró el sobre y se lo dio a su ministro.
  The king sealed the envelope with wax and gave it to his minister.

lacrarse con algo   to harm oneself with sth, be harmed by

- El hombre se lacró con su mala vida.
  The man harmed himself with his bad life style.

- Su reputación se lacró con los rumores persistentes. (*fig*)
  His reputation was harmed by the persistent rumors.

ladear (a, hacia)   to tilt (to, toward)

- Hay que ladear el piano para poder meterlo en la sala.
  You have to tilt the piano in order to be able to make it into the living room.

- Si usted ladea la caja, pasa por la puerta.
  If you tilt the box, it'll go through the door.

- ¡Ladee el armario a (*or* hacia) la derecha!
  Tilt the wardrobe to (or toward) the right.

ladearse (a)   to lean, incline (to, towards)

- Se enojó porque nos ladeamos a la oposición (/al otro partido).
  He got mad because we leaned towards the opposition (/other party).

- Sonia se ladeó a la derecha para la fotografía.
  Sonia leaned to the right for the picture.

lamentar   to be sorry about, regret

- Lamento mucho que usted no pueda ir.
  I'm very sorry (or I very much regret) that you cannot go.

- Lamentamos lo que pasó en la conferencia.
  We're sorry about what happened in the conference.

- Lamento mucho la muerte de su padre.
  I am sorry about the death of your father.

lamentarse de/por uno/algo   to lament, moan over sb/sth; to complain about sb/sth

- El hijo se lamentó de las desgracias de su padre.
  The son lamented the misfortunes of his father.
- Se está lamentando de la vida.
  She is complaining about life.
- No te lamentes de (*or* por) todo.
  *Don't complain (*or* moan) about everything.*
- Yo nunca me lamento de nada.
  I never complain about anything.

lanzar   to throw, pitch, hurl; to launch

- Lanzaron el objecto (/el libro/la revista/la pelota/un ataque).
  They threw the object (/book/magazine/ball/They launched an attack).
- Esta arma lanza proyectiles.
  This weapon launches projectiles.
- Me lanzaron comentarios hirientes. (*fig*)
  They hurled insulting comments at me.

lanzarse a algo   to jump into sth, throw oneself into sth, embark upon sth

- Víctor se lanzó a la piscina (/al río/al mar).
  *Victor jumped (*or* threw himself) into the swimming pool (/river/sea).*
- El mono se lanzó a otra rama.
  The monkey leaped onto the other branch.

lanzarse contra/sobre uno/algo   to hurl oneself against/at sb/sth

- Las tropas se lanzaron contra (*or* sobre) el enemigo.
  The troops threw themselves against the enemy.
- La policía se lanzó contra (*or* sobre) los manifestantes (/la puerta).
  The police charged against the demonstrators (/door).
- Los huelguistas se lanzaron contra (*or* sobre) el edificio (/la puerta).
  *The strikers charged (*or* hurled themselves) against the building (/the door).*

lanzarse de algo   to jump from sth

- Me lancé en paracaídas de un avión.
  *I parachuted (*or* jumped) from an airplane.*
- ¡No se lance de ahí!
  Don't jump from there!
- Los niños se lanzan de la plataforma (/de la parte más alta).
  The children jump from a platform (/the highest part or *point).*

lastimar   to hurt, injure

- Le lastimé la mano (/el brazo/los dedos).
  I injured (or hurt) his hand (/arm/fingers).

- El zapato le ha lastimado el pie al chico.
  The shoe has hurt the boy's foot.

- Le has lastimado su amor propio (/su dignidad). (*fig*)
  You've hurt his pride (/dignity).

lastimarse (con, contra, en)   to hurt oneself, injure oneself (with, on)

- Los hombres se lastimaron los brazos (/los dedos/las espaldas).
  The men hurt their arms (/fingers/backs).

- Los chicos se lastiman los oídos al oír música a todo volumen.
  The boys hurt their ears listening to music with the volume all the way up.

- Me lastimé con una sierra.
  I hurt myself with a saw.

- Se ha lastimado en la escalera.
  He has hurt himself on the ladder (or staircase).

lavar algo   to wash

- Lavé los platos (/el auto/el abrigo/las ventanas).
  I washed the dishes (/the car/the coat/the windows).

lavarse (con, de)   to wash oneself (with)

- Juanita se lava la cabeza.
  Juanita is washing her hair.

- Jaime se lavó las manos con un jabón especial.
  James washed his hands with a special soap.

- Antonio dijo: "Yo me lavo las manos de lo que dije." (*fig*)
  Anthony said, "I wash my hands of what I said."

leer   to read

- No he leído este libro todavía.
  I haven't read this book yet.

- Actualmente la gente no lee mucho.
  Nowadays people don't read much.

- ¡Lea la tarea para mañana!
  Read the homework for tomorrow.

- La gitana me (/le) leyó la mano.
  The gypsy woman read my (/his) palm.

- ¿Leíste la novela que te di? —Sí, la leí.
  Did you read the novel I gave you? —Yes, I read it.

levantar algo   to lift sth (up), raise sth

- No puedo levantar esta maleta. Es muy pesada.
  I can't lift this suitcase. It's too heavy.

- Si quiere permiso, ¡levante la mano!
  If you want permission, raise your hand!

- El gobierno no pudo levantar el nivel de vida de la gente pobre.
  The government could not raise the poor people's standard of living.

levantarse   to rise; to get up, stand up

- ¿A qué hora te levantas? —Me levanto (de la cama) temprano (/tarde/a las seis).
  When do you get up? —I get up (out of bed) early (/late/at six).

- Se levantó de la silla (/de la mesa/del suelo).
  He got (or stood) up from the chair (/table/ground).

- El pueblo se levantó en armas contra el tirano.
  The people rose up in arms against the despot.

- Esas montañas se levantan por encima de las demás.
  Those mountains rise up higher than the others.

liberar a uno/algo de uno/algo   to liberate sb/sth from sb/sth, free from sb/sth; to release sb/sth from sb/sth

- Nuestro partido (/líder) liberó al pueblo del tirano.
  Our party (/leader) liberated the people from the despot.

- El gobierno ha liberado a la firma (/al grupo) de la obligación.
  The govenment has freed the company (/the group) from the duty.

- Liberé a mi hermano de la cárcel.
  I freed my brother from prison.

- Los esclavos se han liberado de sus amos.
  The slaves were liberated from their masters.

- El gobierno lo liberó del impuesto.
  The government released (or exempted) him from the tax.

librar a uno/algo (de algo)   to save *or* rescue sb/sth; to release sb (from sth)

- El libró a su país (/a su pueblo).
  He saved (or rescued) his country (/his people).

- La madre trató de librar a su hija de ese peligro.
  The mother tried to save (or rescue) her daughter from that danger.

- Lo libraron del trabajo (/de sus obligaciones/del puesto).
  They released (or exempted) him from the work (/his obligations/the post).

- Los frenos lo libraron de un serio accidente.
  The brakes saved him from a dangerous accident.

librar de + *inf*   to save from + *ger*

- Me libraron de pagar ese impuesto.
  They saved me from paying that tax.
- Él me libró de comprar esas mercancías robadas.
  He saved me from buying those stolen goods.
- Nosotros te libramos de cocinar hoy.
  We saved you from cooking today.

ligar (a, con, por)   to tie, bind (to, with, by); to alloy (with)

- Un profesor talentoso puede ligar un suceso a (*or* con) otro.
  *A talented teacher can tie (*or* relate) one event to another.*
- Estamos ligados por contrato (/este documento) a su compañía.
  We are bound by contract (/this document) to their company.
- El cirujano le ligó los tubos.
  The surgeon tied her tubes.
- Ellos ligan oro con cobre.
  They alloy gold with copper.

ligarse   to unite, be united

- Los habitantes se ligaron para formar un cooperativa.
  The inhabitants united to form a cooperative.
- Ella y yo nos vamos a ligar en matrimonio.
  She and I are going to be united in matrimony.

limitar   to limit, restrict

- Los políticos quisieran limitar el poder del presidente (/sus prerrogativas).
  *The politicians wanted to limit (*or* restrict) the power of the president (/his prerogatives).*

limitar(se) a uno a + *inf*   to restrict sb to + *ger*

- No me limité a decir lo que usted quería oír.
  I didn't limit myself to telling you what you wanted to hear.
- Me limito a comer sólo vegetales.
  I restrict myself to eating only vegetables.
- El profesor me limitó a escribir sobre la guerra civil.
  The professor restricted me to writing about the civil war.
- La madre lo ha limitado a mirar tres horas de televisión por semana.
  His mother has restricted his watching of TV to 3 hours per week.

limitar con algo   to border sth

- Alemania limita con Francia al oeste.
  Germany borders France on the west.

- Los Estados Unidos limitan con México.
  The United States borders Mexico.

limitarse a algo   to limit oneself to sth

- Cada uno se limita a su capacidad.
  Everyone is limited by his capacity.

- Me limité a los gastos que especifica el presupuesto.
  I limited myself to the expenditures that the budget specifies.

- Nos limitamos a las instruccionos que nos dieron.
  We limited ourselves to the instructions that were given to us.

limitarse a + *inf*   to limit oneself to + *inf*, confine oneself to + *inf*

- Nos limitamos a decir lo necesario.
  We limited ourselves to saying (only) what was necessary.

- Yo sólo me limité a cumplir sus órdenes escritas.
  I confined myself to following his written orders.

limpiar   to clean; to wipe, wipe off

- Tengo que limpiar mi habitación (/mis pantalones/mi camisa/las ventanas).
  I have to clean my room (/pants/shirt/the windows).

- La madre limpia la nariz al niño.
  The mother is wiping the child's nose.

- El joven limpió el parabrisas del automóbil.
  The young man cleaned (or wiped off) the car's windshield.

- Tienes que limpiar tus lentes. —Sí, constantemente los limpio.
  You have to clean your glasses. —Yes, I constantly clean them.

limpiarse (con)   to wipe oneself (with)

- Se limpió la nariz con un pañuelo.
  He wiped his nose with a handkerchief.

- El atleta (/El obrero/Roberto) se limpió el sudor de la frente.
  The athlete (/the workman/Robert) wiped the sweat from his forehead.

- El niño siempre se limpia la cara con una toalla.
  The child always wipes his face with a towel.

lindar con algo   to adjoin, be adjacent to sth, border (on) sth

- El estado de Wisconsin linda con Minnesota.
  The state of Wisconsin is adjacent to (or borders) Minnesota.

- Su casa (/finca) linda con la nuestra.
  Their house (/farm) is adjacent to (or adjoins) ours.

- Lo que tú dices (/La idea/Tu propuesta) linda con el ridículo.
  What you say (/The idea/Your proposal) borders on absurdity.

- Mis ideas lindan con las suyas.
  My ideas are close to yours.

lograr   to get, obtain; to achieve, attain

- Logré mis metas.
  I achieved my goals.

- Hemos logrado lo que nos propusimos.
  We have obtained (or achieved) what we proposed.

- Mi equipo logró diez puntos.
  My team got ten points.

lograr + *inf*   to manage to + *inf*

- Logramos aprender chino (/terminar la pintura).
  We managed to learn Chinese (/to finish the painting).

- Juan logró construir su casa (/llegar temprano).
  John managed to construct his house (/to arrive early).

lucir   to shine; to illuminate, (*fig*) show off, display; to look, appear

- Ella lucía hermosa esa mañana de abril.
  She looked beautiful that April morning.

- Usted luce muy bien.
  You appear very nice.

- La modelo lució una ropa preciosa.
  The model displayed expensive clothes.

- A usted le luce la ropa.
  The dress looks very good on you.

lucirse en algo   to excel in sth; to shine in sth

- Este estudiante se ha lucido en sus estudios.
  This student has excelled (or shone) in his studies.

- El jugador se lució en el partido del domingo.
  The player excelled (or shone) in Sunday's game.

luchar   to fight, struggle

- Quien lucha es un luchador.
  Whoever fights is a fighter.

luchar con/contra uno/algo   to fight with/against sb/sth

- Mi país luchó contra el tuyo.
  My country fought against yours.

- Los niños luchan siempre uno contra el otro.
  The children always fight with each other.

- Laura está luchando con (*or* contra) Carlos en el campo de la política.
  Laura is fighting with Carl in the field of politics.

- El león lucha contra el elefante.
  The lion is fighting with the elephant.

- Yo debí luchar contra mis emociones (/pasiones).
  I should have fought against my emotions (/passions).

luchar por algo   to fight for sth

- Lucharon por la libertad (/una vida decente/un sueño).
  They fought for liberty (/a decent life/a dream).

luchar por + *inf*   to struggle for + *infin*

- Luchamos por recuperar nuestras raíces.
  We struggle to recover our roots.

- Ellos luchan por construir una patria mejor.
  They are fighting to build a better country.

- ¡Luchemos por preservar el ambiente!
  Let's fight to preserve the environment!

LL

llamar   to call, name; to call, telephone

- Le llamaban Roberto (/el Gordo/El Greco).
  They called (or named) him Robert (/Fatty/El Greco).

- El presidente llamó a sus ministros al palacio para discutir el acontecimiento.
  The president called his ministers to the palace to discuss the event.

- No sé cómo le van a llamar.
  I don't know what they are going to call (or name) him.

- Le llamé a las siete pero no estaba en casa.
  I called him at seven, but he wasn't home.

- Le dijo que no la llamara muy tarde.
  She told him not to call her too late.

- Juan estaba enfermo y debimos llamar al médico.
  John was sick, and we had to call the doctor.

- ¡No nos llame por señas!
  Do not use gestures to call us.

- Los invitados llaman a la puerta.
  The guests are knocking at the door.

llamar a uno a + *inf*   to call (on) sb to do + *inf*

- Nos llamaba a comer.
  She was calling us to eat.

- Me llamó para que lo ayudara con el coche.
  He called on me to help him with the car.

- La llamó a atestiguar (/declarar).
  He called her to testify (/to be a witness).

llamarse   to be called, be named

- ¿Cómo te llamas? —Me llamo Sonia. —¿Y cómo se llama ella?
  What's your name? —My name is Sonia. —And what is her name?

- Vendré a la hora exacta, como que me llamo Carlos.
  I will come at the exact time, as sure as my name is Carl!

llegar (a)   to arrive (at); to come (to)

- Van a llegar mañana (/el domingo/a la una).
  They're going to arrive (or come) tomorrow (/on Sunday/at one o'clock).

- ¿Puede avisarnos cuando lleguen los alumnos del intercambio (/extranjeros)?
  Can you tell me when the exchange (/foreign) students arrive?

- ¿Cuándo llegan a París (/Costa Rica)? —No llegan allá hasta las seis.
  When will they arrive in Paris (/Costa Rica)? —They don't arrive there until six o'clock.

- Después de discutir, llegamos a la siguiente conclusión (/decisión).
  After discussing it, we arrived at the following conclusion (/decision).

llegar (a)   to reach; to be enough

- Mi cuerda no llega hasta el toro (/la pared).
  My rope won't reach the bull (/wall).

- Las exportaciones de este año llegarán a 20 millones.
  Exports this year will total 20 million.

■ No llego hasta donde está el sombrero.
I can't reach (up to) where the hat is.

■ El camino asfaltado no llega al pueblo.
The paved road doesn't reach the town.

■ El dinero no llega a cubrir los gastos.
The money is not enough to cover the expenses.

llegar a + *inf* to reach the point of + *ger*, manage to + *inf*

■ No llegamos a escribirlo a tiempo.
We didn't manage to write it on time.

■ Llegué a creer que éramos hermanos.
For a while I thought we were brothers (or We reached the point of believing that we were brothers).

■ Si llegas a saberlo, ¡cuéntamelo!
If you (manage to) find out about it, tell me.

llegar a ser uno/algo + *adj* to become sb/sth + *adj*

■ Va a llegar a ser presidente (/un magnífico doctor).
He's going to become president (/a magnificent doctor).

■ Esta decisión (/Su presencia) llegó a ser el éxito del programa.
This decision (/His presence) became the success of the program.

■ Estoy seguro de que mi país llegará a ser eficiente en cuanto a tecnología.
I am sure that my country will become efficient in regard to technology.

■ Rosita llegará a ser vieja (/rica/fuerte).
Rosita will become old (/rich/strong).

llenar (de) to fill (with); to cover (with); to fulfil

■ Salimos después que llenamos el formulario (/cuestionario).
We left after we filled out the form (/questionnaire).

■ Los revolucionarios (/turistas) llenaban la plaza (/el palacio/las calles de la ciudad).
The revolutionaries (/tourists) filled the square (/palace/streets of the city).

■ Mi viaje por Europa llenó mi mayor deseo (/ambición).
My European trip fulfilled my greatest desire (/ambition).

■ Este contrato requiere que se llenen ciertas condiciones.
In this contract they require certain conditions to be fulfilled.

■ Llena el vaso de agua (/vino/leche).
He's filling the glass with water (/wine/milk).

■ Debo llenar el tanque de combustible.
I must fill up the fuel tank (or I must fill the tank with fuel).

■ Lo llenaron de injurias (/elogios) porque consiguió lo que quería.
They showered him with insults (/praise) because he got what he wanted.

- Los obreros de la ciudad llenaron los huecos del pavimento con asfalto.
  The city workers filled the holes on the road with asphalt.

llenarse   to be *or* become filled *or* full

- El barco se llenó de agua.
  The ship was filled with water.

- Su cuarto se llena de humo (/de olor a pescado/juguetes).
  His room is filled with smoke (/the smell of fish/toys).

- Me llené las manos (/la camisa) de barro.
  I filled (or covered) my hands (/shirt) with mud.

llevar (a)   to carry, take, have, bring, lead (to); to wear; to spend (*time*)

- Enrique lleva la maleta (/a la niña/una silla).
  Enrique is carrying (or bringing) the suitcase (/the baby/a chair).

- ¿Qué lleva el avión (/tren)? —Lleva pasajeros (/un cargamento).
  What is the plane (/train) carrying? —It's carrying passengers (/cargo).

- ¿Quién llevará a Juan (/a tu amigo) a casa? —Yo lo llevaré.
  Who will bring (or take) Juan (/your friend) home? —I will bring (or take) him.

- ¿Adónde nos lleva este camino (/autobús)? —A la ciudad (/A Lima).
  Where is this road (/bus) taking us? —To the city (/To Lima).

- La llevé a la escuela (/a la casa/al museo).
  I took her to school (/home/the museum).

- Esa política (/La pobreza) llevó el hambre a muchas familias de este país.
  That policy (/The poverty) brought hunger to many families in this country.

- ¿Cuánto dinero llevas contigo?
  How much money do you have on (or are you bringing with) you?

- El libro lleva el siguiente título.
  The book has the following title.

- El alcohol lo ha llevado a la ruina.
  Alcohol has led (or brought) him to ruin.

- Llevó (a la fiesta) un vestido muy bonito.
  She wore a beautiful dress (to the party).

- Pedro lleva los zapatos desamarrados.
  Peter is wearing his shoes untied.

- Llevamos una semana en California (/en su hacienda).
  We have been in California (/on their farm) for one week.

- Cecilia lleva tres horas en el baño.
  Cecilia has been in the bathroom for three hours.

- ¿Cuánto tiempo llevas en el aeropuerto? —Llevo 30 minutos aquí.
  How long have you been in the airport? —I've been here 30 minutes.

llevar a uno   to exceed sb; to lead sb by, be ahead of sb

- Yo le llevo a mi hermano 5 años.
  I am five years older than my brother.

- ¿Cuántos centímetros (/pulgados) me llevas? —Te (/Le) llevo 8 (/3 pulgados).
  How many centimeters (/inches) taller than me are you? —I'm eight centimeters (/3 inches) taller than you.

- Él me lleva 2 kilómetros de ventaja.
  He is 2 kilometers ahead of me (or leading me by two kilometers).

- El avión lleva más de doce horas de atraso.
  The plane is over twelve hours delayed.

llevar a uno a + *inf*   to lead sb to + *inf*, take sb to + *inf*

- Mi sugerencia (/oposición/propuesta) le llevó a pensar que. . . .
  My suggestion (/opposition/proposal) led him to think that. . . .

- Nuestro progreso (/El problema) me lleva a creer que. . . .
  Our progress (/The problem) leads me to believe that. . . .

- Nuestro padre nos llevó a comer a un buen restaurante.
  Our father took us to a good restaurant to eat.

- No he llevado a bailar a mi novia.
  I haven't taken my girlfriend to dance.

llevar(se) a cabo algo   to carry out sth, accomplish sth

- Vamos a llevar a cabo una empresa peligrosa.
  We're going to carry out a dangerous enterprise.

- La fiesta se llevó a cabo ayer.
  The party was yesterday.

llevarse a uno/algo   to carry sb/sth off, take sb/sth away

- Roberto se llevó todos sus libros.
  Roberto took away (or carried off) all his books.

- ¿Sabes quién se ha llevado mi bicicleta por equivocación?
  Do you know who has taken my bicycle by mistake?

- El fuerte viento se llevó los papeles.
  The strong wind carried off his papers.

- Los ladrones se llevaron todo lo que tenían.
  The thieves made off with everything that they had.

- ¿Dónde está Juan? —Su amigo se lo llevó al cine.
  Where is John? —His friend took him off to the movies.

llorar   to cry, weep

- Lloro al cortar cebollas.
  My eyes tear (or water) when cutting onions.

- Lloramos desesperadamente.
  We cried (or weeped) despairingly.

- Lloraba cuando veía las telenovelas.
  She would cry when she watched soap operas.

llorar de algo   to cry with sth, weep with sth

- Lloré de pena cuando supe que había muerto.
  I cried out of sorrow when I heard he had died.

- Cuando oigo esa canción, lloro de alegría.
  When I hear that song, I cry out of joy.

llorar por uno/algo   to cry *or* weep about/for/over sb/sth

- La madre lloró por la muerte de su hijo.
  The mother weeped about (or over) the death of her son.

- Una canción se titula: "No llores por mí Argentina."
  There is a song entitled, "Don't Cry for Me Argentina."

llover   to rain

- Hoy no llueve, pero mañana lloverá seguramente.
  Today it isn't raining, but tomorrow it surely will.

- En el trópico llueve todos los días.
  In the tropics it rains every day.

M

maldecir   to curse; to detest, hate

- La mujer maldijo al director (/a su marido/su suerte).
  The woman cursed the director (/her husband/her luck).

- Le dijo al hombre: "¡Le maldigo!"
  He told the man, "Curse (or I detest) you!"

- Maldigo el día en que mi hijo se fue de mi casa.
  I curse (or hate) the day my son left home.

maldecir de uno/algo   to speak ill of sb/sth

- Ella maldice de todo (/de sus colegas/su experiencia).
  She speaks ill of everything (/her colleagues/her experience).

manar (de)   to pour out; to run, flow (from)

■ La mano mana sangre (*or* Sangre mana de la mano).
Blood is flowing (or running) from (or pours out of) his hand.

■ El estigma de la imagen del santo manaba un líquido viscoso.
A sticky liquid flowed from the saint's stigmata.

■ La herida manaba pus.
Pus flowed from the wound.

manar de algo   to spring from sth, flow from sth

■ Mucha savia mana de la corteza de ese árbol.
A lot of sap is flowing from the bark of that tree.

■ El agua mana de las rocas (/del suelo).
The water is springing (or flowing) from the rocks (/ground).

■ Las ideas manaban de su cerebro aceleradamente. (*fig*)
*The ideas sprang quickly from him (*i.e., from his brain).*

mandar   to order; to command; to send

■ El general mandó un ejército en la guerra.
The general commanded an army in the war.

■ Mandó que todos se acostaran temprano.
He ordered everyone to go to bed early.

■ El jefe mandó que le obedeciéramos.
The boss ordered that we obey him.

■ Me mandarán el libro por correo.
They'll send me the book by mail.

■ Mis padres le mandan muchos recuerdos.
My parents send you their warmest regards.

mandar (a uno) a + *inf*   to order sb to + *inf*

■ El presidente mandó a los soldados a izar la bandera.
The president ordered the soldiers to hoist the flag.

■ Mandé a hacer un traje de lana.
I'm having a wool suit made.

■ La madre lo mandó a limpiar la sala.
The mother sent him to clean the living room.

mandar a uno a + *inf*   to send sb to + *inf*

■ Lo mandé a comprar tres docenas de huevos.
I sent him to buy three dozen eggs.

■ La madre mandó al niño a dormir.
The mother sent the child to bed.

mandar (a uno) por uno/algo   to send sb for sb/sth

- El jefe mandó (a Pedro) por los refrescos (/por un libro a la biblioteca).
  The boss sent (Pedro) for (cool) drinks (/for a book from the library).

- Ellos lo mandaron por un taxi (/una pizza/María).
  They sent him for a taxi (/a pizza/Mary).

manejar   to drive; to handle; to run, operate, manage

- ¿Puede manejar? —Manejo, pero no muy bien. —Pues, ¡maneje con cuidado!
  Can you drive? —I drive, but not very well. —Well, then, drive carefully!

- Debes manejar la máquina cuidadosamente.
  You have to handle (or run) the machine carefully.

- ¿Quién maneja este taxi (/camión)? —Mi tío lo maneja.
  Who drives this taxicab (/truck)? —My uncle drives it.

- Ese joven no maneja su dinero prudentemente.
  The young man does not manage his money wisely.

- ¡Maneje con cuidado la situación (/el asunto/cuestión)!
  Handle the situation (/matter/issue) with care.

manejarse   to manage; to act, behave

- Me manejo bien en las ciudades grandes (/en situaciones difíciles).
  I manage well in big cities (/in difficult situations).

- Él se maneja muy bien en su nuevo puesto.
  He manages (or behaves) very well in his new job.

manifestar   to show, reveal, manifest

- Estefanía manifestó su frustración (/su interés por el chico).
  Stephany showed her frustration (/her interest in the boy).

- El ministro de comercio manifestó que subiría el costo de la vida.
  The minister of commerce expressed the view that the cost of living would increase.

- No quiero manifestar mi parecer.
  I don't want to reveal (or manifest) my opinion.

manifestarse (en, contra, con)   to show; to demonstrate (in/from, against); to be evident (with/in/from/by)

- La enfermedad se manifiesta con calentura.
  The sickness manifests itself with (or is evident from) a high temperature.

- Nos manifestamos en favor de la paz.
  We demonstrated (or showed) our desire for peace.

- Se manifestó en contra del gobierno.
  He demonstrated against the government.

mantener   to maintain; to hold (up), keep

■ La chica podía mantener el interés de los niños (/la paz entre ellos).
The girl was able to keep (or hold) the interest of the children (/peace between them).

■ La mamá mantuvo la comida caliente (/la leche fresca).
The mother kept the food hot (/milk fresh).

■ Mantengo todavía mi opinión de que ese político no debería haber hecho ese comentario.
I still maintain my opinion that that politician shouldn't have made that remark.

mantenerse (con)   to live, support oneself (with)

■ Se mantiene con poca comida.
He lives on little food.

■ Mi jefe se mantiene con su trabajo.
My boss supports himself through his work.

mantenerse en algo   to maintain sth, keep (onself in) sth

■ Él siempre se mantuvo en buena condición física.
He always kept himself in good physical condition.

■ Mi colega se mantiene en una posición neutral.
My colleague maintains a neutral position.

■ Su esposo quiere mantenerse en su puesto (/situación actual).
Her husband wants to keep his job (/current situation).

■ La torre de control se mantiene en contacto permanente con los aviones.
The control tower keeps (or maintains) constant contact with the airplanes.

marcar (con)   to mark; to brand (with); to score; to guard (*sports*)

■ Este acontecimiento marcó el comienzo de la revolución.
This event marked the beginning of the revolution.

■ Aquí marcan a los animales con un hierro caliente.
They brand the animals here with a hot iron.

■ Maradona marcó un gol.
Maradona scored a goal.

■ El hombre antipático quería marcar un tanto en cada discusión. (*fig*)
The obnoxious man wanted to score a point in every argument.

■ Tuvieron que marcar a Maradona (/a su mejor jugador).
They had to guard Maradona (/with their best player).

marchar   (*fig*) to go, run; to march

■ ¿Cómo marcha su vida (/matrimonio/negocio/escuela)? —Marcha bien.
How is your life (/marriage/business/school) going? —It's going well.

■ Las cosas no marchan bien.
Things are not going well.

■ Esta máquina marcha bien (/mal/demasiado rápido/no marcha).
This machine is running well (/badly/too fast/isn't working).

■ Los marineros marcharon en el desfile.
The sailors marched in the parade.

marcharse   to go away, leave

■ ¿Te marchas ahora? —Sí, con permiso, me marcho ahora.
Are you leaving now? —Yes, if you don't mind, I must go now.

■ Se marchó de su país y nunca volvió.
He left his country and never returned.

■ Este sitio no es bueno; vamos a marcharnos a otro lugar.
This place isn't any good; let's go to another place.

matar (de)   to kill (by); to slay

■ ¿Quién mató a ese hombre? —Un desconocido lo mató.
Who killed that man? —A stranger killed him.

■ El profesor lo mató de aburrimiento (/con detalles/a preguntas). (*fig*)
The professor bored him to death (/killed him with details/bombarded him with questions).

■ ¡No mate a su perro de hambre!
Don't starve your dog to death!

matarse   to kill oneself, commit suicide; to wear oneself out

■ No creo que se haya matado, era un hombre muy centrado.
I don't believe he committed suicide; he was a very well-balanced individual.

■ Se mató trabajando toda la vida. (*fig*)
He wore himself out working all of his life.

matarse por + *inf*   to struggle to + *inf*

■ Me he matado toda la vida por hacer dinero.
I have struggled all of my life to make money.

■ Se mató por alcanzar la presidencia y perdió las elecciones.
He struggled to reach the presidency, and he lost the elections.

mediar (en, entre, por)   to mediate, intervene (in, for); to be in the middle, get halfway (in, between, for)

■ Mi abogado va a mediar en un asunto muy difícil.
My lawyer is going to mediate a very difficult matter.

■ José medió en una transacción económica.
Jose intervened in an economic transaction.

■ Mediaré entre los dos partidos políticos.
I will be halfway between (or in the middle of) the two political parties.

■   Oscar medió entre dos rivales muy peligrosos.
Oscar mediated between two very dangerous rivals.

■   Medié por María para salvarla de un castigo.
I intervened on behalf of Mary to save her from punishment.

medir   to measure; to survey

■   ¿Cuánto mides de estatura (/de cintura)? —Mido 6 pies (/185 centímetros) de alto (/Mido 30 pulgados (/78 centímetros) de cintura).
How tall are you (/What is your waist size)? —I am 6 feet (/185 centimeters) tall (/My waist is 30 inches (/78 centimeters)).

■   ¿Cuánto mide tu mesa? —Ya la medí: mide 120 cms. de largo y 50 cms. de ancho.
What are the measurements of your table? —I just measured it: It measures 120 cms. in length and 50 cms. in width.

■   En los Estados Unidas se mide por millas y galones; no por kilómetros y litros.
In the United States they measure by miles and gallons, and not by kilometers and liters.

■   Midieron el terreno que voy a comprar.
They surveyed the lot I'm going to buy.

medirse con uno   to measure up to sb; to test oneself against sb

■   Me medí con Daniel en historia.
I tested myself against Daniel in history.

■   Roberto se midió con Francisco en cuanto a fuerza.
Robert measured up to Francis in strength.

mejorar   to improve, make better

■   La medicina (/operación/El médico) la mejoró imediatamente.
The medicine (/operation/doctor) made her better immediately.

■   Ojalá que nuestra situación mejore pronto.
I hope our situation improves soon.

mejorar de algo   improve sth, get better from sth

■   Todos hemos mejorado de situación económica.
We have all improved our economic situation.

■   Sara mejoró de vida.
Sarah improved her way of life.

■   Él ha mejorado de las heridas.
He has gotten better from his injuries.

mencionar   to mention

■   El artículo no menciona a los autores del crimen.
The article does not mention the perpetrators of the crime.

■   ¡No menciones su nombre en esta casa!
Don't mention his name in this house!

mentir   to lie, tell a lie

■   No le miento, el animal era grandísimo.
I'm not lying to you; the animal was huge.

■   Ellos mintieron por placer (/por costumbre/sin necesidad).
They lied (or told lies) for pleasure (/for lying's sake/without necessity).

■   Mercedes mintió contra su voluntad.
Mercedes lied against her will.

■   El niño mintió a todo el mundo (/a su madre).
The child lied to everyone (/his mother).

merecer   to deserve, be worth, merit

■   La obra (/El artículo/La alumna) merece un premio.
The play (/article/student) deserves (or merits) a prize.

■   El zoológico (/El museo/La universidad) merece una visita.
The zoo (/art gallery/university) is worth a visit.

■   Pedro merece que se le dé la beca.
Peter deserves to get (or be given) the scholarship.

merecer + *inf*   to deserve to + *inf*

■   Esta noticia (/historia) merece ser publicada.
This news (/story) deserves to be published.

■   Su hija mereció ganar el premio.
His daughter deserved to win the award.

meter a uno en algo   to involve sb in sth; to send sb to sth; to place sb in sth

■   El padre quiere meter a su hijo en el ejército.
The father wants to send his son to (or place his son in) the army.

■   Metí a mis dos hijos en un colegio público (/una universidad privada).
I placed both my sons in a public school (/private university).

■   ¿Quién lo ha metido en este problema (/este lío horrible)?
Who got you into this problem (/horrible mess)?

■   Ricardo me metió en una situación difícil.
Richard got me into a predicament.

meter algo (en)   to put sth, place sth, insert sth (in/into)

■   Metí mi pañuelo en el bolsillo.
I put (or placed or inserted) my handkerchief in my pocket.

■   No puedo encontrar mi libro. ¿Dónde lo metiste?
I can't find my book. Where did you put it?

■   El vendedor metió las manzanas en la caja (/bolsa).
The salesman put the apples into the box (/in the bag).

- Intentó meterle en la cabeza que yo tenía mucho dinero.
  He tried to put (or get) it into his head that I had a lot of money.

- Metió el dedo en un hueco y lo picó una arañã.
  He put his finger into a hole, and a spider bit him.

meterse a + *inf* to start to + *inf*; to take it upon oneself to + *inf*

- Me metí a estudiar derecho (/a vender autos/a aprender a esquiar).
  I started to study law (/to sell cars/to learn to ski).

- Se metió a gobernar un país en crisis.
  He took it upon himself to govern a country in crisis.

- Nos metimos a trabajar en las minas.
  We began to work in the mines.

meterse a uno   to become sb

- Mi primo se metió a fraile (/médico/maestro) hace dos años.
  My cousin became a monk (/doctor/teacher) two years ago.

- Rosa y Miguel se han metido a empresarios (/vendedores).
  Rose and Michael have become businesspeople (/salespeople).

meterse con uno   to provoke sb, pick a quarrel with sb; to tease sb

- ¡No te metas con mi hermanito!
  Don't tease my little brother.

- ¡No se meta conmigo porque tendrá problemas!
  Don't pick a quarrel with (or provoke) me because you'll have problems!

- Antonio se metió con un boxeador y salió morado.
  Antonio picked a quarrel with a boxer and came out bruised.

meterse en algo   to go into sth, get into sth, enter into sth; (*fig*) to interfere in sth, meddle in sth

- Se metieron en el edificio (/la tienda/la escuela).
  They went into (or entered) the building (/shop/school).

- Me estoy metiendo en algo que no puedo hacer.
  I'm getting myself into (or meddling in) something I cannot do.

- Él se ha metido en problemas (/dificultades/peligros/política).
  He has gotten into problems (/difficulties/danger/politics).

- ¿Dónde se meten estas cajas? —¡Mételas en el garaje!
  Where do these boxes go? —Put them in the garage.

- No se puede meter el corcho en la botella.
  The cork can't be squeezed into the bottle.

- Los dos hermanos se metieron en un buen negocio.
  The two brothers entered into a good business.

- ¡No se meta en lo que no le importa (/en mis asuntos)!
  Mind your own business (/Don't meddle (or interfere) in my affairs)!

mezclar(se) (con)   to mix (with), mix up (with)

■ Mezclé el material (la medicina/el polvo/la pintura) con agua caliente.
I mixed the material (medicine/powder/paint) with hot water.

■ Mezcló las dos bebidas (/los colores/los vinos).
He mixed the two drinks (/colors/wines).

■ ¡Mezcla arena y cemento!
Mix sand and cement.

mezclarse con uno   to mix with sb, mingle with sb; to blend with sb

■ Elena no se mezcla con gente que no sea de su clase social.
Elena doesn't mingle (or mix) with people who are not of her social class.

■ Fue una terrible desgracia para la señorita mezclarse con esas chicas.
It was a terrible disgrace for the lady to mingle with those girls.

mezclarse en algo   to get involved in sth; to meddle in sth

■ ¡No nos mezclemos en negocios sucios!
Let's not get involved in dirty deals!

■ Usted se mezcla demasiado en lo que no le importa (/en mis asuntos).
You meddle too often in things that are none of your business (/in my affairs).

mirar   to look

■ No miro bien de noche.
I don't see well at night.

■ ¡Mira por dónde caminas!
Look where you're walking!

■ ¡Mira! Ese hombre no se mueve pero mira intensamente.
Look! That man isn't moving but he's looking intensely.

■ ¡Mira si el cartero ha llegado!
See if the mailman has arrived.

mirar a uno   look at sb, watch sb

■ ¿A quién mirabas? —Miraba a la chica (/a la señora).
Who were you looking at? —I was looking at the girl (/the lady).

■ La miraba cocinar el pollo (/peinarse).
I watched her cook the chicken (/comb her hair).

■ Le miré a la cara (/a los ojos).
I looked her in the face (/in her eyes).

mirar (a) algo   to look at sth, watch sth; to look toward sth

■ ¿Miraste la foto (/el mar/los árboles)? —Sí, la (/lo/los) miré.
Did you look at the picture (/sea/trees)? —Yes, I looked at it (/it/them).

■ Nuestros hijos miran demasiada televisión.
Our children watch too much television.

- Miramos el reloj y era las dos.
  We looked at our watch, and it was two o'clock.

- Miramos con preocupación a Europa Oriental.
  We are watching (or looking toward) Eastern Europe with anxiety.

- Miré mi vida (/experiencia).
  I looked at or thought about my life (/my experience).

- Miramos el (or al) cielo.
  We looked at (or in the direction of or towards) the sky.

- Miré la (or a la) casa (/calle).
  I looked at (or toward) the house (/street).

- Miramos a nuestro alrededor y la gente ya se había ido.
  We looked around us, and the people had left already.

mirar por uno   to look after sb, (*fig*) take care of sb

- Yo miro por mi padre porque está muy viejo.
  I look after (or am taking care of) my father because he is very old.

- Nuestro gobierno siempre ha mirado por los pobres.
  Our government has always looked after (or taken care of) the poor.

- ¡Mira por tu hermanito, que no se vaya a caer!
  Look after your little brother; don't let him fall down.

mirarse   to look at oneself

- ¡Mírese en el espejo! —Ya me miré. Tengo espuma de afeitar en la cara.
  Look at yourself in the mirror! —I already looked at myself. I have shaving cream on my face.

mirarse en uno   to look up to sb; to take after sb, model oneself on sb

- ¡Mírate en tu padre!
  Look up to (or Take after) your father.

- ¡Mirémonos en la gente honrada para mejorar nuestra vida!
  Let's look up to (or model ourselves on) honorable people in order to better our lives.

mojar algo (en, con)   to make sth wet; to dampen sth, moisten sth (in, with)

- El agua mojó la alfombra (/al chico/mi cámara fotográfica).
  The water wet the rug (/soaked the boy/wet my camera).

- Ella tiene que mojar la ropa con este líquido (/esta substancia).
  She has to dampen (or soak) the clothes with this liquid (/substance).

- Para preparar esta receta, ¡moje el pan en vino!
  For this recipe, moisten the bread with wine.

mojarse   to get wet

- Todo se moja en agua.
  Everything gets wet in water.

- Caminó bajo la lluvia y se mojó.
  She walked in the rain, and she got wet.

- La ropa se mojó cuando comenzó a llover.
  The clothes got wet when it began to rain.

molestar   to bother

- El hombre (/Su actitud/El dolor/El olor) le molestó mucho.
  The man (/His attitude/The pain/The odor) bothered him a lot.

- A mi mamá le molesta repetirlo (/hacerlo).
  It bothers mom to repeat (/do) it.

- Le molesta cuando salgo sin permiso.
  It bothers her when I go out without permission.

molestarse con uno/algo   to get annoyed with sb/sth

- Usted se molestó con su sobrino.
  You got annoyed with your nephew.

- Mi tío se molestó contigo porque no lo invitaste a la fiesta.
  My uncle got annoyed at you because you didn't invite him to the party.

- Me molesté con el ruido que hacían.
  I got annoyed at (or with) the noise they were making.

molestarse en + *inf*   to bother + *ger*

- Por favor, no se moleste en hacer mi trabajo.
  Please don't bother doing my work!

- ¡No te molestes en visitarlos! Ya se fueron.
  Don't bother visiting them. They left already.

montar a (en)   to mount, get on (on); to ride

- Mi hermano no monta a caballo muy bien.
  My brother doesn't mount (or ride) a horse very well.

- Monto en mi bicicleta para ir a la escuela.
  I ride my bicycle to go to school.

- Estamos montando una nueva obra de teatro.
  We are setting up a new (theater) play.

- Ya monté la máquina. Póngala a funcionar.
  I already set up the machine. Turn it on.

- El joyero ha montado la perla en el anillo.
  The jeweler has mounted (or set) the pearl in my ring.

morder   to bite (into)

- Mordí el pan (/el plátano/la carne).
  I bit into (or took a bite of) the bread (/banana/piece of meat).
- Lo mordió el perro (/el gato/el león).
  The dog (/cat/lion) bit him.

morir(se)   to die

- ¿Quién se murió? —Su abuela (se) murió.
  Who died? —His grandmother has died.
- Mi hermano (se) murió joven (/ahogado/en un accidente).
  My brother died young (/drowned/in an accident).

morir(se) de algo   to die of sth

- Su tío se murió de un paro cardiaco (/de vejez/de difteria).
  His uncle died of cardiac arrest (/of old age/of diphtheria).
- Me muero de hambre ahora. (*fig*)
  I'm dying of hunger (or starving) now.
- Mi amiga (se) moría de miedo (/de celos/de envidia/de risa). (*fig*)
  My friend was dying of fright (/of jealousy/of envy/from laughing).

morirse por uno/algo   to be dying for sth; to be crazy about sb/sth

- Me muero por la ópera (/la música clásica/el teatro/el tenis/el chocolate/la comida mexicana). (*fig*)
  I'm crazy about (or dying for) opera (/classical music/live theater/tennis/chocolate/Mexican food).
- Elenita se muere por mí (/este chico). (*fig*)
  Elenita is crazy about me (/this boy).
- Él no se muere por ninguna mujer. (*fig*)
  He is not crazy about any woman.

morirse por + *inf*   to be dying to + *inf*

- Me muero por verte (/ver a esta chica) otra vez. (*fig*)
  I'm dying to see you (/this girl) again.
- Ellas se morían por ir a la playa (/viajar a París/probar esta comida). (*fig*)
  They were dying to go to the beach (/to travel to Paris/to try this food).

mostrar   to show, display, exhibit

- Gerardo mostró mucho interés (/paciencia) durante el curso.
  Gerardo showed (or exhibited) a lot of interest (/patience) during the course.
- El político muestra en público sus atributos.
  The politician displays his qualities in public.

mostrarse   to show (oneself); to appear

- Joaquín siempre se ha mostrado ante el público tal como es.
  Joaquin has always appeared in front of the public as he really is.

- Nos mostramos muy agradecidos (con él).
  We showed our appreciation (to him).

- Me mostré ante todos como un hombre sincero.
  I appeared (or showed myself) before everyone as a sincere man.

motivar (con)   motivate (by)

- El profesor nos motiva con muy buenas explicaciones.
  The professor motivates us with good explanations.

- Me motivó con su argumento, por eso acepté el trabajo.
  He motivated me with his argument; that's why I accepted the job.

mover (a, hacia)   to move (to, toward); to shift

- Por favor, mueve la mesa.
  Please move (or shift) the table.

- (*En ajedrez*): Ahora te toca a ti mover tu pieza.
  (In chess): *It's your turn now to move your piece.*

- No pude mover al chico a hacerlo (/limpiar su habitación). (*fig*)
  I couldn't move the boy to do it (/clean his room).

- Ellos movieron la mesa hacia atrás (/hacia adelante/a un lado/hacia el frente).
  They moved (or shifted) the table back (/forward/to the side/up).

- Los hombres de negocios fueron movidos por sus intereses (/por la curiosidad).
  The businessmen were moved by their own interest (/curiosity).

moverse (alrededor de, con, de, en)   to move (around, with, from, on)

- ¡No se muevan cuando tome la fotografía!
  Don't move when I take the picture.

- La tierra se mueve alrededor del sol.
  The earth moves (or revolves) around the sun.

- No quiero moverme de aquí.
  I don't want to move from here.

- ¡Mire allá! El tráfico no se mueve (/Los coches no se están moviendo).
  Look over there! The traffic isn't moving (/The cars aren't moving).

- Mi abuela se mueve con mucha dificultad (/todavía con agilidad).
  My grandmother moves around with a great deal of difficulty (/still moves with agility).

- Los cocodrilos se mueven en tierra con dificultad.
  Crocodiles move about on land with difficulty.

mudar (en)   to change, alter; to change, transform (into)

- Mamá, ¿Cuándo vas a mudar las sábanas?
  Mom, when are you going to change the sheets?

- Al parecer el humor de la fiesta mudó en alegría.
  Apparently, the mood of the party changed to joyfulness.

- Mudaron las uvas en vino.
  The grapes were changed into wine.

mudar de algo   to change sth

- El animal mudó de piel (/de plumas).
  The animal molted (its) skin (/feathers).

- El pelo de mi amigo ha mudado de color.
  My friend's hair has changed color.

- Mudaron la lámpara de lugar.
  They changed the position of the lamp.

- Mi hijo tiene trece años y está mudando de voz.
  My son is thirteen years old, and his voice is changing.

- Mudó de color cuando le dieron la noticia.
  He changed color when he heard the news.

mudarse de algo   to change sth; to move

- Me mudé de falda (/pantalones/camisa/sombrero).
  I changed my skirt (/pants/shirt/hat).

- Ella se ha mudado de ropa (/falda/pantalones/idea/el color de pelo).
  She has changed her clothes (/skirt/pants/mind/hair color).

- Su familia (/La oficina) se ha mudado de barrio.
  His family (/The office) has moved to another quarter.

- Vamos a mudarnos de aquí (/esta casa/este barrio/este piso).
  We are going to move from here (/this house/this neighborhood/this apartment).

murmurar   to murmur, whisper, mutter

- La gente murmura cuando no tiene nada que hacer.
  People mutter when they have nothing to do.

- Cuando hace viento las hojas de los árboles murmuran.
  When it's windy, the leaves of trees rustle.

- El río murmuraba por el bosque.
  The (sound of the) river murmured through the forest.

murmurar de uno   to criticize sb; to grumble about sb, gossip about sb

- ¡No murmure de nosotros!
  Do not grumble (or gossip) about us.

- Fue despedido por murmurar del jefe.
  He was fired for criticizing the boss.

- No debemos murmurar de nadie.
  We should not gossip about (or criticize) anyone.

N

nacer (en)   to be born (in); (*fig*) to be born, begin

- Nací en Colombia (/los Estados Unidos/Turquía).
  I was born in Colombia (/the United States/Turkey).

- Juanita nació en el hospital (/la casa).
  Juanita was born in the hospital (/at home).

- Vamos a tener una gran fiesta cuando nazca mi niño.
  We are going to have a great party when my baby is born.

- Entre los dos hermanos ha nacido un fuerte odio (/una amistad profunda). (*fig*)
  A strong hatred (/A deep friendship) has begun between the two brothers.

- Al nacer, abrió los ojos.
  At birth he opened his eyes.

- Cuando me dijo eso, nació una sospecha en mí. (*fig*)
  When he told me that, a suspicion began (or was born) within me.

nacer de uno/algo   to be born from/of sb/sth; to begin from sb/sth (*fig*)

- Nació de madre soltera.
  He was born of an unmarried mother.

- Jesús nació de una virgen.
  Jesus was born of a virgin.

- Este problema nació de un malentendido (/una mala idea).
  This problem originated from a misunderstanding (/a bad idea).

nacer para algo/uno   to be born to be sth/sb

- Nació para filósofo (/maestro/mecánico).
  He was born to be a philosopher (/teacher/mechanic).

nacer para + *inf*   to be born to + *inf*

- Nacimos para amar (/sufrir/trabajar).
  We were born to love (/suffer/work).

nadar   to swim

- Carlos está nadando en la piscina (/el lago).
  Carl is swimming in the swimming pool (/lake).

- No sé nadar en el mar.
  I don't know how to swim in the sea.

- Ella nada muy bien de espalda (/pecho).
  She swims the backstroke (/breaststroke) very well.

- Mi tío nada en dinero. (*fig*)
  My uncle wallows in money (or My uncle is rolling in money).

navegar (a, con, en, hacia)   to sail (to, with, in, against); to navigate

- Los españoles navegaron a un mundo desconocido (/a las Américas).
  The Spanish sailed to an unknown world (/to the Americas).

- Estamos navegando con buena brisa (/contra corriente).
  We are sailing with a good breeze (/against the current).

- Navegamos en un buque de guerra (/una balsa).
  We sailed in a war vessel (/on a raft).

- El capitán navegó hacia Africa (a 12 nudos).
  The captain navigated (or sailed) toward Africa (at 12 knots).

necesitar   to need, want

- Necesito dinero (un coche/trabajo/tu ayuda/un borrador).
  I need money (/a car/a job/your help/an eraser).

- Necesitaba un poco de café.
  I needed (or wanted) a little coffee.

necesitar + *inf*   to need + *inf*

- Necesité hablar con el médico.
  I needed to speak with the doctor.

- Necesito hacerlo (/hablarle) mañana.
  I must do it (/speak to you) tomorrow.

negar   to deny; to deny, refuse

- ¿Por qué niegas el hecho? —No, no lo niego. No niego que sea cierto.
  Why do you deny the fact? —I don't deny it. I don't deny that it might be true.

- Le negaron el permiso de entrada.
  They denied him permission to enter.

- El político le negó la mano a su adversario.
  The politician refused to shake hands with his opponent.

- El guardia le negó el paso por la frontera.
  The guard refused to let him cross (or denied him passage across) the border.

- Como no podía hablar, negó con la cabeza.
  As he couldn't speak, he shook his head.

negarse a + *inf*   to refuse to + *inf*

- Me niego a trabajar con esos obreros.
  I refuse to work with those laborers.

- ¿Por qué te niegas a cantar en público?
  Why do you refuse to sing in public?

- Se niega a pagar lo que debe.
  He refuses to pay what he owes.

nevar   to snow

- Está nevando todavía.
  It is still snowing.

- Hoy no nieva. ¿Nevó ayer?
  It isn't snowing today. Did it snow yesterday?

O

obedecer   to obey

- Los hijos no le obedecen a su padre.
  The sons do not obey (or are not obedient to) their father.

- Tú debes obedecer las órdenes de tu padre (/del maestro).
  You must obey the orders of your father (/teacher).

- ¡Obedece a tu profesor (/madre/jefe)!
  Obey your teacher (/mother/boss).

- Hay que obedecer a los superiores.
  One has to obey one's superiors.

obligar   to force, compel, oblige

- La ley nueva obliga solamente a los mayores de dieciocho.
  The new law applies only to people older than eighteen.

- Pedro me obliga con sus atenciones.
  I'm obliged to Pedro because of his (kindness and) attention.

obligar a + *inf*   to force to + *inf*, require to + *inf*

- El calor los obligó a salir del edificio.
  The heat forced them to leave the building.

- El guarda lo obligó a desalojar el museo.
  The guard made him (or required him to) leave the museum.

obligarse a + *inf* to bind oneself to + *inf*, commit oneself to + *ger*

- Me obligo a sacar las mejores notas.
  I commit myself to obtaining the best grades.

- Ella se obligó tanto durante los ensayos que no podía bailar el domingo.
  She was so hard on herself during rehearsals that she was unable to dance on Sunday.

- Debemos obligarnos a cumplir nuestras metas.
  We must push ourselves (in order) to meet our objectives.

observar to observe, notice

- He observado que Gloria ha cambiado mucho durante este año.
  I have noticed that Gloria has changed a lot this year.

- Los astrónomos observaron las estrellas.
  The astronomers observed the stars.

obtener to obtain, get

- He obtenido el permiso y ahora puedo viajar.
  I've obtained permission, and now I can travel.

- ¿Dónde obtuviste la licencia de manejar? —La obtuve en esa oficina.
  Where did you get your driver's license? —I got it in that office.

- Ya obtuve mi título de médico (/abogado).
  I already got (or received) my medical (/law) degree.

ocultar a uno/algo (de) to hide sb/sth, conceal sb/sth (from)

- El chico ocultó el juguete de la niña.
  The boy hid the toy from the girl.

- Oculté los libros del maestro.
  I concealed the books from the teacher.

- Ocultaron al prisionero.
  They hid the prisoner.

ocultarse (de, detrás de) to hide (from, behind)

- Nos ocultamos detrás de unos arbustos.
  We hid behind some shrubs.

- ¿Dónde se ha ocultado mi hermanita?
  Where has my sister hidden?

- ¡Ocúltese allí!
  Hide there!

■ Nos ocultaremos de la policía en aquel edificio.
  We'll hide from the police in that building.

ocupar   to occupy, take up; to occupy, seize

■ Nuestro país ha sido ocupado por el enemigo.
  Our country has been occupied (or seized) by the enemy.

■ Los muebles (/Esas cosas) ocupan demasiado espacio.
  This furniture (/These things) occupy (or take up) too much space.

ocuparse con algo   to busy oneself with sth, spend time with sth; to take care of sth

■ Me ocupo con una tienda que tengo en la ciudad.
  I am busy with (or take care of) a store I have in the city.

■ Nos ocupamos con muchos negocios.
  We are busy with many matters.

■ Ella se ocupa con su jardín.
  She takes care of (or busies herself with) her garden.

ocuparse de algo   to be busy with sth, concern oneself with sth, take care of sth

■ Me ocuparé de este proyecto (/problema).
  I will concern myself with (or take care of) this project (/problem).

■ ¿De qué se ocupan estos hombres?
  What do these men do?

■ ¡Pepe, ocúpate de lo tuyo!
  Mind your own business, Pepe!

ocuparse en + *inf*   to attend to + *ger*, take care + *ger*

■ Ella se ocupa en escribir las cartas.
  She is attending to writing the letters.

■ Nadie se ocupa en abrir las ventanas.
  No one is taking care of opening the windows.

■ ¿Quién se ocupa en guardar los libros?
  Who takes care of (or is keeping) the books?

ocurrir   to occur, happen, take place

■ ¿Dónde ocurrió el accidente? —Ocurrió en la esquina.
  Where did the accident happen (or take place)? —It happened on the corner.

ocurrirse a uno   to occur to oneself

■ Nunca se me había ocurrido que en esta obra había influencia de los romanos.
  It had never occurred to me that there was Roman influence in this work.

■ Se me ha ocurrido una buena idea (/un chiste).
  I've got a good idea (/joke).

ocurrirse a uno + *inf*   to occur to sb + *inf*

- Se me ocurrió comer en un restaurante.
  It occurred to me to eat in a restaurant.

- ¿Cuándo se te ocurrió pintar la mesa?
  When did it occur to you to paint the table?

ofrecer (por)   to offer; to offer, bid (for, on)

- Les ofrecimos a los invitados un pastel (/nuestra ayuda).
  We offered the guests a cake (/our help).

- ¿Cuánto ofreció él por el coche? —Ofreció cinco mil pesos por él.
  How much did he offer for (or bid on) the car? —He offered five thousand pesos for it.

- El enemigo ha ofrecido poca resistencia.
  The enemy has offered little resistance.

ofrecerse a/para + *inf*   to offer to + *inf*, volunteer to + *inf*

- Se ofreció a (*or* para) ayudar en todo.
  He offered (or volunteered) to help in everything.

- Se ha ofrecido a (*or* para) llevarla a la playa (/al cine).
  He has offered (or volunteered) to take her to the beach (/cinema).

- Me ofrezco a (*or* para) traducir la carta (/para hacer el proyecto).
  I offer to translate the letter (/to do the project).

oír   to hear; to listen to

- No podía oír el ruido (/la conversación).
  I couldn't hear the noise (/the conversation).

- Todas las mañanas oigo las campanas repicar.
  Every morning I hear (or listen to) the bells ringing.

oír hablar de uno/algo   to hear about/of sb/sth

- No había oído hablar de usted.
  I had not heard about you.

- No habíamos oído hablar del accidente hasta ayer.
  We had not heard of the accident until yesterday.

- Dice que no ha oído hablar de nuestro país.
  She says that she has not heard about our country.

oler   to smell; (*fig*) to sense

- La rosa (/Esa cosa) huele bien (/mal).
  The rose (/That thing) smells nice (/bad).

- Ella huele bien.
  She smells nice (or She has a good sense of smell).

■ Olieron el peligro (/una conspiración/una intriga). (*fig*)
They sensed the danger (/a conspiracy/a plot).

oler a algo   to smell of *or* like sth

■ El salón huele a flores.
The living room smells of (or *like*) *flowers.*

■ Él olía siempre a tabaco porque fumaba mucho.
He always smelled of tobacco because he smoked a lot.

■ Ese informe huele a mentira (/a trampa). (*fig*)
That report sounds like a lie (/a trick).

oler(se)   to feel, (*fig*) sense

■ Me huele que no va a venir (/que algo malo va a pasar).
I feel (or *sense*) *he's not going to come (/that something bad is going to happen).*

■ Nos huele a peligro.
We feel (or *sense*) *danger.*

olvidar algo   to forget sth, leave sth behind; to leave sth out, omit sth

■ He olvidado su nombre (/la fecha/su dirección).
I've forgotten his number (/the date/his address).

olvidar + *inf*   to forget + *inf*

■ Otra vez olvidó traer el libro.
He forgot to bring the book again.

■ Olvidé lavar los platos (/llamarte).
I forgot to wash the dishes (/to call you).

■ Olvidaron incluir su nombre en la lista.
They forgot to include his name on the list.

olvidarse a uno   to forget

■ Se me ha olvidado su nombre (/la dirección/su cumpleaños/la fecha).
I have forgotten his name (/the address/his birthday/its date).

■ A veces se me olvida hasta el número de mi casa.
Sometimes I even forget my house number.

■ Se le ha olvidado que tenía que llamar por teléfono a Roberto.
He has forgotten that he had to phone Robert.

olvidarse   de uno/algo to forget about sb/sth

■ Me he olvidado de su nombre (/la dirección/su cumpleaños/mi cita).
I have forgotten his name (/the address/his birthday/my appointment).

■ No me he olvidado de ustedes (/mis padres), aunque estén lejos.
I have not forgotten you (/my parents), even though you're (/they're) far away.

- Emilia no quiere olvidarse de lo pasado.
  Emilia doesn't want to forget about the past.

olvidarse de + *inf*   to forget to + *inf*

- Ojalá que no te hayas olvidado de cerrar la puerta de casa.
  I hope you haven't forgotten to close the door of the house.

- ¡No se olvide de tomar los remedios!
  Don't forget to take your medicine.

oponerse   to be opposed; to oppose each other, be in opposition

- Yo no me opongo, si ella quiere hacerlo.
  I'm not opposed if she wants to do it.

oponerse a uno/algo   to oppose sb/sth, be opposed to sb/sth

- Me opuse a su propuesta (/sugerencia).
  I was opposed to his proposal (/suggestion).

- Nos opusimos a la moción porque atentaba contra nuestros principios.
  We opposed the motion because it was against our principles.

- Se oponen al candidato (/a ese ministro).
  They are opposed to (or oppose) the candidate (/that minister).

oponerse a + *inf*   to oppose + *ger*, be opposed to + *ger*; to refuse to + *inf*

- Se opusieron a votar en las elecciones (/a hacerlo).
  They were opposed to voting in the election (/to doing it).

- Me opongo a cooperar con el enemigo.
  I refuse to cooperate with the enemy.

optar a algo   to compete for sth, fight for sth

- Optamos a la presidencia.
  We competed for the presidency.

- Es difícil optar a un empleo cuando no se tiene influencias.
  It is difficult to fight for a job when one doesn't have influence.

- Creo que este alumno no puede optar a las becas.
  I believe that this student may not (or does not have the right to) compete for the scholarship.

optar entre   to choose between, decide between

- Optó entre la vida y el cigarrillo (/entre las dos cosas).
  He chose between life and cigarettes (/between two things).

- Me dijo que tenía que optar entre dos cursos.
  He told me he had to choose (or decide) between two courses.

- El héroe optó entre vivir o morir.
  The hero decided between living and dying.

optar por algo   to choose sth, decide on sth, opt for sth

- Voy a optar por la presidencia.
  I am going to choose the presidency.
- Los dos optaron por el mismo empleo.
  The two decided on (or opted for) the same job.
- El chico optó por una profesión que no era lucrativa.
  The boy chose a profession that wasn't lucrative.

optar por + *inf*   to choose to + *inf*, decide to + *inf*

- Siempre optaba por comer tarde.
  She always chose to eat late.
- Opté por quedarme en un hotel (/por comer mariscos).
  I decided (or chose) to stay in a hotel (/to eat seafood).
- Después de mucho pensar, Miguel optó por salir del país.
  After a lot of thinking, Michael decided to leave the country.

orar (a)   to pray (to)

- Siempre debes orar.
  You must always pray.
- Oraré más tarde.
  I will pray later.
- Voy a orar a Dios.
  I am going to pray to God.
- Los paganos oraban a los dioses (/a las piedras/a los volcanes/al sol).
  Pagans prayed to gods (/stones/volcanoes/the sun).

orar por uno/algo   to pray for sb/sth

- Vamos a orar por ti (/por tu salud).
  We will pray for you (/your health).
- Oraré por la patria (/la paz).
  I will pray for the country (/peace).

ordenar a uno/algo   to arrange sth, put sth in order; to order sb

- Ordené el cuaderno por materias.
  I arranged the notebook by subjects.
- Ordenamos los papeles por orden alfabético.
  We arranged (or put) the papers in alphabetical order.
- El general ordena a sus soldados.
  The general orders his soldiers.

orientar (hacia)   to orient (towards); to give directions to

- Orientamos nuestros pasos hacia el norte.
  We directed our walk toward the north.

- ¡Orienta tu pensamiento hacia metas mejores!
  Orient your thoughts toward better goals.

- La orienté para que llegara a tu casa.
  I gave her directions to get to your house.

orientarse (a, hacia)   to be oriented (towards), orient oneself (towards)

- La economía se orienta al neo-liberalismo.
  The economy is oriented towards neo-liberalism.

- Nos orientamos hacia el sol.
  We orient ourselves toward the sun.

- No me oriento bien en esta ciudad.
  I don't find my bearings (or orient myself) well in this city.

osar + *inf*   to dare to + *inf*

- Osé hablarle después de mucho dudar.
  I dared to talk to him after much doubting.

- Osó dirigirme la palabra.
  He dared to speak to me.

P

padecer (de)   to suffer (from); to suffer, endure

- Mi abuela padece mucho.
  My grandmother suffers a great deal.

- En esa región la gente padece artritis.
  In that region people suffer from arthritis.

- Padeció mucho durante la infancia.
  He put up with (or suffered) a lot during his childhood.

- Padezco del corazón (/de los riñones/del hígado)
  I suffer from a heart (/kidney/liver) ailment.

pagar (con)   to pay for (with), pay for

- Sus padres le pagan los estudios (/la comida/el alquiler).
  His parents are paying for his education (/meals/rent).

- La casa cuesta mucho. No la podemos pagar.
  The house costs so much. We can't afford it.
- Pagaron con dinero (/cheques/la vida/tarjeta de crédito).
  They paid with cash (/checks/their life/a credit card).

pagar por algo   to pay for sth

- Pagamos 700 dólares por el apartamento.
  We pay $700 for the apartment.
- Ella pagó 20 dólares por la cena.
  She paid $20 for the meal.
- Ellos pagaron por su crimen con la vida. (*fig*)
  They paid for the crime with their lives.

parar (en, a)   to stop (at, in/on); to stop, halt, end (up)

- ¿Para el autobús en esta calle? —Sí, para en la esquina (/para allá).
  Does the bus stop on this street? —Yes, it stops at the corner (/stops there).
- Los manifestantes (/taxis) pararon en la plaza.
  The demonstrators (/taxis) stopped in the square.
- Ha parado el viento (/la lluvia/la nieve).
  The wind (/rain/snow) has stopped.
- Van a parar la impresión del libro.
  They are going to halt the printing of the book.
- Esta avenida va a parar a la Plaza de las Américas.
  This avenue ends at the Plaza of the Americas.
- Los rifles pararon en las manos de la policía (/los delincuentes).
  The rifles ended up in the hands of the police (/criminals).

parar de + *inf*   to stop + *ger*

- El niño no paró de llorar (/jugar).
  The child didn't stop crying (/playing).
- Quisiera saber si ha parado de nevar (/llover).
  I would like to know if it has stopped snowing (/raining).
- Pararon de comer por el susto.
  They stopped eating out of fright.

parar en algo   to end up (as) sth, result in sth, come down to sth

- Todo esto iba a parar en un desastre.
  All of this was going to result (or end up) in disaster.
- ¿Dónde parará esto (/este movimiento)? —No sé en qué irá a parar todo esto.
  What will this (/this movement) come down to? —I don't know what all of this is going to come down to.

- Él va a parar en la comisaría (/la cárcel/el hospital).
  He is going to end up in the police station (/in jail/in a hospital).

pararse a + *inf*   to stop to + *inf,* pause to + *inf*

- Se pararon a descansar (/comer/ver el paisaje/lavarse las manos).
  They stopped (or paused) to rest (/eat/see the scenery/wash their hands).

pararse (en)   to stand (on), stand up

- Nos paramos en una silla (/un banco/una caja/una grada) para mirar el desfile.
  We stood on a chair (/bench/box/step) in order to see the parade.

pararse en algo   to stop at/on sth, stand on sth

- Me paré en su casa.
  I stopped at his house.

- Nos paramos en la página tres.
  We stopped on page three.

parecer   to seem, look, appear

- Parece que va a nevar (/llover/nublarse/hacer sol).
  It looks (or seems or appears) as though it's going to snow (/rain/cloud up/to be sunny).

- Me parece mal que no vengas (/que no comas).
  It seems bad (or wrong) that you are not coming (/not eating).

parecerse a uno/algo   to resemble sb/sth, look like sb/sth

- Ella se parece a su mamá. Me parezco a mi papá.
  She resembles her mother. I look like my father.

- Un gemelo se parece al otro.
  One twin looks like the other.

- No se parece a la figura del retrato.
  She doesn't look like the figure in the portrait.

partir (para)   to leave, set out (for)

- Ayer partieron para Argentina.
  They left (or set out) for Argentina yesterday.

- ¿Adónde fueron mis amigos? —Partieron con rumbo a la playa.
  Where did my friends go? —They set out in the direction of the beach.

partir algo (en)   to divide (in), split

- La mamá partió la manzana en dos mitades.
  The mother divided (or split or cut) the apple in two.

partirse   to crack, split (in two)

- Durante el terremoto el edificio se partió por la mitad.
  During the earthquake the building split down the middle.

- Me partí la cabeza jugando fútbol americano.
  I cracked my head playing football.

- Nos partimos el pecho trabajando. *(fig)*
  We broke our backs working.

pasar   to pass; to happen

- El río (/camino) pasa muy cerca de la finca.
  The river (/road) passes very close to the farm.

- ¿Qué pasó? —Nada en particular; algo le pasó a mi coche.
  What happened? —Nothing in particular; something happened to my car.

pasar a uno/algo (a)   to pass sb/sth (to), hand sth over

- Él le pasó a otro corredor (/a otro chofer/a mi madre).
  He passed another runner (/another driver/my mother).

- ¿Me pasas la pimienta (/las papas), por favor?
  Would you please pass me the pepper (/the potatoes)?

- El defensa pasó la pelota al delantero.
  The defender passed the ball to his forward.

- Juan no pasó el examen.
  John didn't pass the exam.

pasar a algo   to proceed to sth; to go in/to sth

- Los invitados pasaron a la sala (/al comedor).
  The guests went into the living room (/dining room).

- Quiero pasar de este sitio a tu casa (/a otro).
  I wanted to go from this place to your house (/another).

- Ha pasado de maestro a administrador (/a director).
  He has gone from teacher to administrator (/to principal).

- Pasaron de Canadá a los Estados Unidos (/de África a España).
  They went on from Canada to the United States (/crossed from Africa into Spain).

- Luis pasó a decirle algo al jefe.
  Luis proceeded to tell something to the boss.

pasar con algo   to make do with sth, get by with sth

- Su familia pasa con poco (/con 500 pesos).
  His family gets by with very little (/makes do with 500 pesos).

- Él puede pasar con pocas provisiones.
  He can make do with very few provisions.

pasar de   to be more than (*a number*), be over (*a number*)

■ La candidata no puede pasar de treinta años.
  The candidate can't be more than thirty.

■ El grupo pasa de diez estudiantes.
  The group is more than ten students.

pasar por uno/algo   pass by sb/through sth; to go by sb/through sth

■ Pasamos el papel por debajo de la puerta (/mesa).
  We passed (or slipped) the piece of paper under the door (/table).

■ El tren (/río) pasa por San Juan (/por Suiza/por la ciudad).
  The train (/river) goes through San Juan (/Switzerland/the city).

■ ¿Pasa el autobús por su casa?
  Does the bus go by your house?

■ Mañana paso por ti a las tres.
  I'll pass by (or come) for you tomorrow at three.

■ Me pasó una idea (/una fantasía) por la cabeza.
  An idea (/fantasy) came to my mind.

■ El oftalmólogo le pasó una luz fuerte por los ojos.
  The ophthalmologist shone a bright light at his eyes.

pasar por + *adj/nombre*   to pass for + adj/noun

■ Él habla el inglés tan bien que pasa por inglés.
  He speaks English so well that he passes for an Englishman.

■ Tan joven se ve mi madre que pasa por mi hermana.
  My mother looks so young that she passes for my sister.

■ Él pasó por tonto (/tímido) en la fiesta.
  He was considered a fool (/timid or a coward) at the party.

pasarse   to pass

■ El hombre se pasó la mano por el pelo.
  The man passed (or ran) his fingers through his hair.

pasarse a uno   to miss, (*lit*) go by sb

■ Se me pasó lo que me dijiste que observara.
  I missed what you told me to watch (or observe).

■ No sé en que pensaba, se me pasó el turno sin darme cuenta.
  I don't know what I was thinking; I missed my turn without realizing it.

■ A ese chico no se le pasa nada.
  Nothing escapes that boy (or Nothing gets past that boy).

■ Se me pasó la hora de medicina.
I forgot to take my medicine on time.

pasarse de + *adj*   to be too + *adj,* be excessively + *adj*
■ Cecilia se pasa de buena (/generosa/amable/loca/tonta).
Cecilia is too good (/too generous/too nice/too crazy/too foolish).

pasear (por)   to travel (through); to go for a walk
■ Paseamos por Europa en coche (/en bicicleta/en avión).
We traveled through Europe by car (/on bicycle/by plane).

pasear a uno/algo (en)   to walk sb/sth, take sb/sth for a walk (in, through)
■ El abuelo pasea a sus nietos en el parque.
The grandfather takes his grandchildren for a walk in the park.

■ Voy a pasear a mi perro para que haga ejercicio.
I'm going to walk my dog so it will have exercise.

pasearse (en, por)   to walk (in, through), go for a walk, stroll
■ Todas las tardes nos paseamos en (*or* por) el campo.
Every afternoon we go for a walk (or *stroll) in* (or *through) the countryside.*

■ El perrito se pasea por todas partes.
The dog walks all over.

■ Los ancianos se pasean por el jardín.
The old people stroll through the garden.

pasmar   to chill, freeze
■ El científico pasmó las rosas para investigarlas.
The scientist froze the roses in order to investigate them.

pasmarse   to be chilled, be frozen, freeze (over); to be astonished
■ Mi jardín se pasmó.
My garden froze (over).

■ Nos pasmamos cuando vimos el monstruo. (*fig*)
We froze when we saw the monster.

■ La vieja se pasmó cuando le dijeron que había ganado la lotería. (*fig*)
The old lady was astonished when she was told she had won the lottery.

pedir   to ask (for), request; to order (*food*)
■ Sin pedir permiso, mi hermano salió de la sala.
Without asking (or requesting) permission, my brother left the room.

■ Ella le pidió a su padre dinero (/un libro/la llave).
She asked her father for money (/a book/the key).

- Pedí que saliera (/que trabajara/que la hiciera).
  I asked that he leave (/work/do it).

- Pedimos cerveza (/vino/café).
  We ordered beer (/wine/coffee).

pedir a uno algo   to ask sb for sth

- Le pedía a Jorge un favor.
  I asked George for a favor.

- Le pedimos un aumento de sueldo al jefe.
  We asked the boss for a salary increase.

- El niño le pidió muchos juguetes a su padre.
  The child asked his father for a lot of toys.

pegar (en)   to stick (on, up); to glue, paste; to hit, strike (in, on)

- Pegué dos sellos en el sobre.
  I stuck two stamps on the envelope.

- He pegado los papeles en la pared.
  I have glued the papers to the wall.

- La flecha pegó en el blanco.
  The arrow hit (or stuck in) the target.

- Pedro me pegó en la cara.
  Peter hit me on the face.

- Él le pegó al hombre (/a la chica).
  He hit the man (/girl).

- Él le pegó a su compañero de clase (/a su amigo/a su enemigo).
  He hit (or struck) his classmate (/friend/enemy).

- Los estudiantes me pegaron la gripe. *(fig)*
  The students gave me (or stuck me with) the flu.

pegar con/contra uno   to run into sb

- Roberto pegó con (*or* contra) Rolando y los dos cayeron.
  Robert ran into Roland, and both of them fell.

- El pájaro le pegó contra el parabrisas cuando volaba.
  The bird flew into his windshield.

pegarse a uno   to stick to/with sb

- Ella se me pegó durante toda la fiesta.
  She stuck to me during the entire party.

- El acento del sur se me ha pegado.
  The southern accent has stuck to (or with) me.

■   El perrito se le pegó en la calle.
    The puppy stuck close to him in the street.

peinarse (con)   to comb one's hair (with)

■   Yo me peino con un cepillo.
    I comb my hair with a brush (or I brush my hair).

■   Ellas se peinaron por dos horas.
    They combed their hair for two hours.

■   Me gustaría peinarme a la última moda.
    I'd like to do my hair in the latest fashion.

pensar   to think

■   Pienso que ella no vendrá a la fiesta.
    I think she won't come to the party.

■   El chico lo dijo (/lo compró/lo hizo) sin pensar.
    The boy said it (/bought it/did it) without thinking.

■   Pensó que era hora de acostarse.
    He thought it was time to go to bed.

pensar en uno/algo   to think of sb/sth, think about sb/sth

■   ¿En qué piensa? —Pienso en mi novia (/trabajo).
    What are you thinking about? —I'm thinking about my girlfriend (/work).

■   La mamá piensa en todo (/en Juanita que tiene fiebre).
    The mother thinks of everything (/of Juanita who has a fever).

■   ¡Piense en mi propuesta!
    Think about (or over) my proposal!

■   Siempre piensa en las cosas que no importan.
    He always thinks about things that aren't important.

pensar + *inf*   to plan + *inf*, intend to + *inf*

■   Pienso comprarlo (/escribir una carta/salir mañana/viajar).
    I plan (or intend) to buy it (/to write a letter/to leave tomorrow/to travel).

percatarse   to notice, take note of

■   Ellos se percataron tarde.
    They noticed too late.

percatarse de algo   to notice sth, take note of sth; to heed sth

■   Ayer nos percatamos de la verdadera situación de nuestro país.
    We took note of the real situation in our country yesterday.

■ Nunca me percato de nada.
I never notice anything.

■ No nos habíamos percatado de su presencia (/del peligro/de la importancia del acontecimiento/de la oportunidad de escapar).
We had not noticed (or heeded) his presence (/the danger/the importance of the event/the opportunity to escape).

perder (por)   to lose (by); to waste; to miss

■ ¿Cuánto perdiste en el casino? —Perdí mucho dinero jugando.
How much did you lose (or waste) at the casino? —I lost a lot of money gambling.

■ ¿Dónde perdió la maleta? —La perdió en la estación del tren.
Where did he lose the suitcase? —He lost it in the train station.

■ Perdí la oportunidad (/la ocasión) de hablar con él.
I lost the opportunity (/missed the chance) of talking to him.

■ Hemos perdido el juego por tres puntos.
We've lost the game by three points.

■ Sin perder un momento empezamos a trabajar (/salir/hacerlo).
Without wasting a moment, we began to work (/leave/do it).

■ Perdimos el tren por dos minutos.
We missed the train by two minutes.

perderse (en, entre)   to get lost (in/into; among); to lose; to stray

■ Ellos se perdieron en la ciudad (/el parque de diversiones/el edificio).
They got lost in the city (/amusement park/building).

■ El pájaro se perdió en la niebla (/el bosque/el árbol).
The bird strayed into the fog (/forest/disappeared in the tree).

■ El corredor se perdió entre los participantes.
The runner got lost (or disappeared) among the crowd (of participants).

■ Si no llueve pronto se perderá la mitad de la cosecha.
If it doesn't rain soon, the crop will be lost (or ruined).

perdonar   to pardon, forgive, excuse

■ ¡Perdóneme usted!
I beg your pardon (or Excuse me)!

■ Perdonen, pero yo no puedo visitarlos.
Sorry, but I can't visit you.

■ El padre le perdonó a su hijo el error.
The father forgave his son for his oversight.

■ El juez lo perdonó.
The judge pardoned him.

perecer (de, por)   to die or perish (of, for/because of)

- El explorador pereció de hambre (/de frío).
  The explorer died of hunger (/cold).

- Es fácil perecer en las montañas.
  It's easy to die (or perish) in the mountains.

- Todos perecieron por inanición.
  Everyone died (because) of starvation.

permitir(se)   to permit, allow

- ¡Permítame que le explique lo que sucedió!
  Permit (or Allow) me to explain to you what happened.

- Yo no permito tonterías.
  I do not permit foolishness.

- Mi médico no me permite fumar (/correr/beber vino).
  My doctor doesn't allow me to smoke (/run/drink wine).

- Yo no le permití ir al cine.
  I will not permit (or allow) him to go to movies.

- No nos permitimos esos lujos.
  We don't permit ourselves (or are not permitted) those luxuries.

permitirse + *inf*   to permit (oneself) to + *inf;* to be permitted to + *inf*

- Aquí no se permite fumar.
  Smoking is not permitted here.

- Me permito explicarle (/decirle/mostrarle) que...
  Permit me to explain to you (/tell you/show you) that...

persistir (en)   to persist (in)

- La lluvia (/La nieve/El viento) persistía.
  The rain (/snow/wind) persisted.

- Hay que persistir en esta empresa hasta vencer.
  One must persist in this enterprise until one prevails.

- Debemos persistir en toda obra que nos propongamos realizar.
  We must persist in all works that we propose to realize.

persistir en + *inf*   to persist in + *ger*

- Él persiste en creer que la economía va a mejorar.
  He persists in believing that the economy is going to get better.

- Ella persistió en pensar que su esposo volvería.
  She persisted in thinking that her husband would return.

pertenecer (a)   to belong (to)

- El anillo no me pertenece (a mí).
  The ring doesn't belong to me.

- Esta península le pertenecía a mi país.
  This peninsula used to belong to my country.

- ¡Déme lo que me pertenece (a mí)!
  Give me what belongs to me!

picar (en)   to bite (on); to peck, peck at; (*fig*) to dabble in; to itch

- Los mosquitos (/insectos) me picaron (en la cara).
  The mosquitoes (/insects) bit me (on the face).

- La víbora lo picó (en la pierna).
  The viper bit him (on the leg).

- El gallo picó a los pollitos.
  The rooster pecked the chicks.

- Estuvo mala la pesca, ningún pez picó.
  Fishing was bad—not even a bite (or nibble).

- Pasó la noche picando diversos bocadillos, por eso no tiene apetito.
  He spent the night sampling all sorts of snacks, so he is not hungry.

- Me pican las piernas (/pican los ojos/pica la cabeza).
  My legs itch (/eyes itch/head itches).

picarse   to be vexed, be offended, get mad

- Se picó cuando le dijimos que no bailaba bien.
  He was vexed (or offended) when we told him he did not dance well.

- ¿Verdad que te picaste cuando te llamaron tonto?
  Weren't you offended (or Didn't you get mad) when they called you silly?

picotear   to nibble sth; (*informal*) to chatter about sth

- El pájaro picotea las frutas.
  The bird is nibbling on the fruit.

- Debemos ahondar en los temas, no picotearlos.
  We must delve into the topics, not just chatter about them.

pintar   to paint

- El artista pintó un cuadro muy bonito.
  The artist painted a beautiful picture.

- Pintaré mi habitación de azul (/de amarillo).
  I will paint my room blue (/yellow).

- ¡Pinta el dibujo de una vaca!
  Paint a picture of a cow (or Draw a cow).

■   No debes pintar todo tan oscuro. (*fig*)
    You shouldn't paint everything so dark.

■   Le gusta pintar al óleo (/al fresco).
    She likes to paint in oils (/frescoes).

■   Es mejor si pintamos la casa con pistola.
    It would be better if we spray-paint the house.

pintarse   to make up (one's face); (*lit*) to paint oneself

■   Mi novia se pinta mucho.
    My girlfriend puts on a lot of make-up.

■   Me voy a pintar las uñas.
    I'm going to paint my fingernails.

■   El niño se pintó la cara con la pintura que dejé en el garaje.
    The child painted his face with the paint I left in the garage.

pisar   to step on, tread on

■   El chofer pisó el acelerador.
    The driver stepped on the accelerator.

■   Ella pisó la cucaracha.
    She stepped on the cockroach.

■   ¡Me pisaste la mano!
    You stepped on my hand!

■   No volveré a pisar esta tierra (/ese sitio/esa escuela).
    I will never set foot in this country (/place/that school) again.

■   Mi esposo no se deja pisar por nadie. (*fig*)
    My husband doesn't let anybody walk all over him.

placer   to please, gratify

■   Me placen las naranjas.
    I like oranges.

placer + *inf*   to please to + *inf*, be pleased to + *inf*

■   Me place presentar al Profesor Sánchez.
    It gives me pleasure (or pleases me) to introduce Professor Sanchez.

■   Me place comer en su compañía.
    I am pleased to eat with you.

■   Nos place viajar a esa ciudad.
    We are pleased to travel to that city.

planear   to plan

■   Hemos planeado un viaje a Inglaterra.
    We've planned a trip to England.

planear + *inf*   to plan to + *inf*

■ No planeamos hacerlo (/escribirle/hablarle).
  We don't plan to do it (/write him/talk to her).

plantar a uno/algo   to plant sth; (*fig*) to stand sb up

■ Plantamos un arbolito (/naranjo/rosal).
  We planted a little tree (/an orange tree/a rose bush).

■ El novio plantó a la novia (*or* El novio dejó plantada a la novia). (*fig*)
  The boyfriend stood up his girlfriend.

plantarse   to stand (oneself), stop

■ Me planté en la puerta y no me moví durante horas.
  I stood (myself) in the doorway and didn't move for hours.

■ El burro se plantó antes de llegar a la esquina.
  The donkey stopped before reaching the corner.

plasmar   to mold, shape, form, create

■ El escultor plasmó una estatua magnífica.
  *The sculptor created (*or* formed) a magnificent statue.*

■ Han plasmado todos sus deseos. (*fig*)
  They've realized all their wishes.

plasmarse en algo   to take the form of sth, emerge as sth

■ Su pensamiento se plasmó en un ensayo brillante.
  His thought took shape in a brilliant essay.

■ Sus pensamientos se han plasmado en realidad. (*fig*)
  His thoughts have emerged as reality.

platicar (sobre)   to talk, chat (about)

■ ¡Platiquemos un poco sobre la vida!
  Let's chat a while about life!

■ Me gusta platicar contigo (/con mis amigas).
  *I enjoy talking (*or* chatting) with you (/with my friends).*

poder   can, be able (to handle), be able (to manage)

■ El trabajo es muy difícil. ¿Puedes tú con él?
  The work is very difficult. Can you manage it?

■ No pude con las matemáticas.
  I couldn't handle math.

■ Los que pueden, se hospedan en hoteles muy caros.
  Those who can, stay in expensive hotels.

poder + *inf*   can + *inf*, to be able to + *inf*

- No puede ir (/pagar/trabajar).
  He can't go (/pay/work).

poner (en)   to put, place, set; to put on (*clothes*); to take (care) (in, on); to translate, render (into); to suppose

- ¿Dónde pusiste mi sombrero? ¿En el sofá? —No, lo puse en la silla.
  Where did you put my hat? On the sofa? —No, I set it on the chair.

- Él pone la mesa a las 6.
  He sets the table at 6:00.

- Puse dinero (/300 dólares) en la cuenta corriente (/en la caja fuerte).
  I put money (/$300) in the checking account (/in the safe).

- ¡Ponga cuidado en el trabajo!
  Pay attention to (or Take care in) your work.

- La madre le puso el gorro al niño.
  The mother put the cap on the boy.

- ¿Puede usted poner la frase en alemán?
  Can you translate (or render) the sentence into German?

- Le pusimos un telegrama (/una carta).
  We sent him a telegram (/letter).

- ¿Cuántos kilómetros quedan por recorrer? —¡Pongamos que 90!
  How many kilometers are still left to go? —Let's say 90 (or I put it at 90).

- Pongamos que él no lo compre.
  Let us suppose he won't buy it.

- Pongamos que ella no vaya.
  Let's suppose she does not go.

ponerse   to put on, wear

- Voy a ponerme un traje (/una falda/los pantalones/un sombrero).
  I'm going to put on a suit (/put on a skirt/put on my pants/wear a hat).

- ¿Qué se puso la chica? —Se puso un vestido muy bonito.
  What did the girl wear? —She had a beautiful dress on.

ponerse + *adj*   to become + *adj*

- Me puse rojo (/furioso) cuando el director me dijo que mi hijo se portaba mal.
  I blushed (/got mad) when the principal told me my son behaved badly.

ponerse a/en algo   to reach sth, get to sth; to put oneself

- Se puso a una hora del pueblo.
  He got an hour away from the town.

- Se puso a mi lado para protegerme.
  He got (or positioned himself) next to me to protect me.
- ¡Ponte en mi situación!
  Place (or put) yourself in my situation.

ponerse a + *inf*   to begin to + *inf*, set about + *ger*

- Luisita se puso a llorar (/gritar/comer).
  Luisita began to cry (/shout/eat).
- Cuando Carlos me vio, se puso a abrazarme.
  When Carl saw me, he set about hugging me.

practicar   to practice, exercise

- Practicaba el fútbol (/la natación) todos los días.
  I used to practice soccer (/swimming) every day.
- Practicaba el francés (/mi pronunciación) con mi profesor.
  I used to practice French (/my pronunciation) with my professor.
- El gimnasta practicó toda la tarde.
  The gymnast practiced (or exercised) all afternoon.

predicar   to preach

- El pastor predicaba la palabra de Dios (/la virtud).
  The pastor preached the word of God (/virtue).
- Los padres deben predicar con el ejemplo.
  Parents should teach by example (or practice what they preach).

preferir (a)   to prefer (to)

- Prefiero el té al café (*or* Prefiero té que café).
  I prefer tea to coffee (or I prefer tea, rather than coffee).

preferir + *inf*   to prefer to + *inf*

- Preferí hablar inglés con él (/no discutir el tema/ir a pie).
  I preferred to speak English with him (/not to discuss the subject/to walk).

preguntar a uno   to ask sb, question sb

- El estudiante le preguntó a la maestra quién era Colón.
  The student asked the teacher who Columbus was.
- Yo le pregunté cuántos años tenía.
  I asked him how old he was.
- ¿Qué le preguntaste? —Le pregunté sobre su país.
  What did you ask him? —I asked him about his country.
- ¿Qué quieren preguntarle al candidato? —Le preguntaremos si. . . .
  What do you want to ask the candidate? —We will ask him if. . . .

- ¡Pregúntele si quiere comer ahora!
  Ask him if he wants to eat now.

preguntar por uno/algo   to ask for *or* about sb/sth

- Él llamó y preguntó por ti (/Carlos).
  He called and asked for you (/Carl).

- Tomás preguntó por la salud de usted.
  Thomas asked about your health.

- Pregunta por nuestra madre.
  He is asking about our mother.

- ¡No pregunte por mí porque no estaré aquí!
  Don't ask for me because I won't be here.

prendarse de uno/algo   to fall in love with sb, be enchanted with sth

- Manuel se prendó de una mujer bellísima.
  Manuel fell in love with a beautiful woman.

- Vine prendado de España (/de la universidad).
  I returned in love (or enchanted) with Spain (/with the university).

preocupar a uno   to worry sb, bother sb

- La noticia (/decisión) le preocupó muchísimo.
  The news (/decision) worried (or bothered) him greatly.

- Me preocupa cómo decirle que su abuelo está muy enfermo.
  I am worried about how to tell her that her grandfather is very sick.

- Le preocupó haber sido injusto con el hombre.
  It worried (or bothered) him that he was unjust to the man.

preocuparse   to worry, care

- No me preocupo en lo más mínimo.
  I don't care (or worry) in the least.

- Él no se preocupa cuando no hay noticias.
  He doesn't worry when there is no news.

preocuparse de/por uno/algo   to worry about sb/sth, be concerned about sb/sth; to make sure of sth

- ¡No se preocupe por (*or* de) eso!
  Don't worry about that.

- ¡Preocúpate de (*or* por) tus asuntos!
  Mind your own business!

- Yo me preocuparé de (*or* por) que todo esté listo.
  I'll make sure (or see to it) that everything is ready.

- No te preocupes por (*or* de) lo que pueda pasar.
  Do not worry about what can happen.

- La mamá se preocupa por (*or* de) cualquier cosa (/por eso).
  Mom worries (or is concerned) about everything (/about that).

- ¡Preocúpate de (*or* por) que no falte nada (/que todos coman bien)!
  Make sure that nothing is missing (/that everyone eats well).

preparar (para)   to prepare (for)

- Los estudiantes están preparados (para el examen).
  The students are well-prepared (for the test).

- A los dieciocho años Juan no estaba preparado para la vida.
  At eighteen John wasn't prepared for life.

- Ella preparó una buena cena para sus sobrinos.
  She prepared a good dinner for her nephews.

prepararse para algo   to prepare oneself, get ready (for)

- ¡Preparémonos para la paz!
  Let's get prepared for peace!

- Mis padres se han preparado para las vacaciones.
  My parents have gotten ready for the vacation.

prepararse a/para + *inf*   to prepare to + *inf*, get ready to + *inf*

- No me preparé para decirle la mala noticia (/escalar la montaña).
  I was not prepared to tell him the bad news (/to climb the mountain).

- ¡Prepárate a mudarte mañana!
  Prepare yourself (or Get ready) to move tomorrow.

- Mi familia se preparaba para comer cuando llegué.
  My family was preparing to eat when I arrived.

- Nos prepararemos para combatir el cólera
  We will be prepared to fight against cholera.

prescindir de algo   to do without sth, go without sth; to get rid of sth

- Prescindimos de dinero (/coche).
  We do without money (/a car).

- Nuestra oficina ha prescindido de los servicios del correo.
  Our office has gotten rid of the mail service.

- ¡Prescinda del cigarrillo!
  Do not smoke (or Do without cigarettes)!

presentar a uno/algo (a)   to present sb/sth, show sth (to); to introduce sb/sth (to)

- El presidente (/La política) presenta señales de deterioro.
  The president (/policy) shows signs of wear.

■ Lo presentaron a la escuela militar.
   They introduced him to the military academy.

■ Le presento a mi padre.
   May I introduce my father to you?

presentarse (ante, en)   to present oneself, report; to appear (before, in)

■ Tengo que presentarme ante el director mañana a las ocho.
   I have to present myself (or report) to the director tomorrow at eight.

■ Se presentó ante un público muy amable.
   He appeared before a sympathetic public.

■ Los refugiados se presentaron en un terrible estado de salud.
   The refugees turned up (or appeared) in an awful state of health.

prestar algo a uno   to lend sb sth

■ ¿Puedes prestarme veinte dólares (/un huevo)?
   Can you lend me $20 (/an egg)?

■ Le prestan cinco mil pesos con interés.
   They lent him five thousand pesos with interest.

prestarse a/para algo   to lend oneself to sth, be suited for sth

■ Se prestó a (*or* para) un negocio sucio.
   He made himself available for a dirty deal.

■ Ella se presta muy bien para ese trabajo.
   She is well-suited for that job.

prestarse a + *inf*   to offer to + *inf*, volunteer to + *inf*

■ Nos prestamos a ayudarlo (/hacerlo).
   We offered (or volunteered) to help him (/to do it).

pretender + *inf*   to try to + *inf*, seek to + *inf*

■ Pretendo convencerlo para que vote por mí.
   I'm trying (or I intend) to convince him to vote for me.

■ Mi hermano pretendía llegar a la cima de la montaña.
   My brother tried to reach the top of the mountain.

■ ¿Qué pretendes hacer con eso?
   What are you trying (or do you mean) to do with that?

prevenir (se)   to prevent; to prepare, get ready, make ready

■ Es mejor prevenir que lamentar.
   It is better to prevent than to regret.

■ Se previnieron para el duro invierno.
   They got ready for the hard winter.

prevenir a uno (de)   to warn sb, advise sb (about/of)

■   Previnimos a Rosa del peligro que corría.
We warned Rose of the peril that she was in.

■   Nos previnieron a todos.
They warned us all.

■   Me (/Le) previno de lo que me podía pasar.
He advised me (/him) about what could happen to me.

■   Hay que prevenir a los hijos de los peligros en las calles.
You have to warn your children of the danger on the streets.

prevenir a uno contra algo   to prepare sb for sth

■   Te voy a prevenir contra la adversidad.
I am going to prepare you for adversity.

■   Nos previnieron contra el intenso frío.
They got us ready for the intense cold.

principiar (con)   to begin (with)

■   Ellos lo principiaron a las siete.
They began it at seven.

■   ¡Vamos a principiar la lección con una frase famosa!
Let's begin the lesson with a famous phrase.

■   El presidente principió su discurso con un lamento.
The president began his speech with a lament.

■   La ceremonia principiará con un himno.
The ceremony will begin with a hymn.

principiar a + *inf*   to begin to + *inf/ger*

■   Principiamos a comer (/jugar) muy tarde.
We began to eat (/play) very late.

■   Principiábamos a trabajar de madrugada.
We used to begin working early in the morning.

privar (de)   to forbid, deny, deprive (of)

■   Nos privaron de libertad.
They denied us our liberty.

■   ¿Por qué lo privaron del permiso de conducir?
Why did they deprive him of (or forbid him) his driver's license?

privar a uno de + *inf*   to forbid sb to + *inf*, prevent sb from + *ger*

■   La mujer lo privó de ver a su hijo.
The woman prevented him from seeing (or forbade him to see) his son.

- ¡No me prives de hacerlo (/hablar/de ver a mis niños)!
  Don't prevent me from doing it (/talking/seeing my children).

privarse de algo   to deprive oneself of sth; to give up sth

- Me privaron de lo que más me gustaba.
  They deprived me of what I liked most.

- No nos privamos de ningún alimento.
  We don't deny ourselves (or deprive ourselves of) any food.

probar   to try, taste, test

- Voy a probar la comida.
  I'm going to try (or taste) the food.

- Voy a correr 12 millas para probar mi resistencia.
  I'm going to run 12 miles to test my endurance.

- En la vida hay que probar de todo.
  In life you have to try everything.

- Probaremos abrir la puerta con esta llave.
  We'll try to open the door with this key.

probar a + *inf*   to try to + *inf*

- Probaré a fumar con filtro.
  I'll try to smoke filter cigarettes.

- Probó a caminar sobre piedras calientes.
  He tried to walk on hot rocks.

probarse   to try on *(clothes)*

- Se probó el vestido (/la camisa) y no le quedó.
  She tried on the dress (/shirt), and it didn't fit her.

- ¡Pruébese este sombrero!
  Try on this hat!

proceder de algo   to come from sth, derive from sth

- Estas manzanas proceden de Chile.
  These apples come from Chile.

- ¿De cuál lengua procede esta palabra? —Procede del sánscrito.
  What language is this word derived from? —It comes from Sanskrit.

- El nombre "Miguel" procede del Hebreo.
  The name "Michael" is derived from Hebrew.

- El vino procede de las uvas.
  Wine comes from grapes.

- Este medicamento procede de ciertas hierbas.
  This medicine comes from certain herbs.

prohibir   to prohibit, ban, forbid

■ El gobierno ha prohibido las drogas (/su entrada a este país).
The government has banned the drugs (/forbidden his entrance into this country).

prohibir (a uno) + *inf*   to forbid sb to + *inf*, forbid + *ger*

■ Ha prohibido hablar en voz alta.
He has forbidden talking in a loud voice.

■ El profesor nos prohibió fumar en los pasillos.
The professor forbade us to smoke in the hallways.

■ Le he prohibido a mi hijo salir de casa después de las 12 de la noche.
I have forbidden my son to leave the house after midnight.

prometer   to promise

■ ¿Qué le prometiste a Juan? —Le prometí hacerlo (/escribirlo) mañana.
What did you promise John? —I promised him to do (/write) it tomorrow.

■ Es un estudiante (/médico/violinista) que promete.
He is a promising student (/doctor/violinist).

■ El padre le prometió (a su hijo) una bicicleta para su cumpleaños.
The father promised (his son) a bicycle for his birthday.

■ Esta situación no promete nada de bueno.
This situation does not look at all hopeful.

prometer + *inf*   to promise to + *inf*

■ Él prometió escribirlo (/trabajar más rápido).
He promised to write it (/work faster).

■ Yo le prometí hacer la tarea.
I promised him to do the homework.

pronosticar   to predict, foretell, forecast (*weather*)

■ Un científico pronosticó un terrible terremoto.
A scientist predicted a terrible earthquake.

■ Nadie podrá pronosticar lo que sucederá en el 2020.
No one can foretell (or predict) what will happen in the year 2020.

■ El servicio nacional de meteorología ha pronosticado fuertes lluvias para hoy.
The national weather service has forecasted heavy rains for today.

pronunciar   to pronounce

■ ¿Cómo pronuncia usted esta palabra? —Es muy difícil pronunciarla.
How do you pronounce this word? —It's very difficult to pronounce it.

■ El niño pronuncia mi nombre muy claramente.
The child pronounces my name very clearly.

■ El juez pronunció la sentencia.
The judge pronounced the sentence.

proponer   to propose, put forward; to suggest

- Los profesores han propuesto a Sandra para una beca.
  The teachers have proposed (or put forward) Sandra for a scholarship.

- Le propongo que vayamos juntos.
  I suggest to you that we go together.

proponerse + *inf*   to propose to + *inf*, plan to + *inf*

- Él se propuso construir una casa solo.
  He proposed (or planned) to build a house by himself.

- Me propongo salir para Boston.
  I plan (or propose) to leave for Boston.

proseguir (con, en)   to continue (with, in)

- No quiero proseguir en (*or* con) mis estudios (/con el cuento).
  I don't want to continue (or go on) with my studies (/the story).

- Su hijo ha proseguido en (*or* con) su mala actitud.
  His son has continued with his bad attitude.

- ¡Prosiga con la declaración!
  Go on with your statement.

proteger a uno/algo (contra)   to protect sb/sth (against)

- ¡Protejamos a nuestros hijos contra las drogas!
  Let's protect our children against drugs.

protegerse (contra)   to protect oneself (against)

- Se protegieron contra los ladrones.
  They protected themselves against the thieves.

- Hemos protegido el edificio contra incendios.
  We have protected the building against fire.

protestar (contra)   to protest (against)

- Los manifestantes protestaron contra el gobierno (/la injusticia/los precios altos/el aborto).
  The demonstrators protested against the government (/injustice/high prices /abortion).

- Protesto contra el fallo.
  I protest the decision (or I object to the decision).

proveer (de)   to provide, supply, furnish (with)

- La naturaleza provee todo lo necesario para que el ser humano viva.
  Nature provides (or supplies) everything necessary for a human being to exist.

- ¿Quién nos va a proveer de las cosas necesarias?
  Who is going to furnish us with the necessary things?
- ¿Quién los proveyó de libros?
  Who provided them with books?

proveerse   de/con algo to provide oneself with sth

- Debemos proveernos de (*or* con) lo básico para subsistir.
  We must provide ourselves with the basics in order to survive.
- ¿Dónde vamos a proveernos de (*or* con) agua?
  Where are we going to get our water?

provenir de algo   to come from sth, arise from sth, stem from sth

- Esta agua proviene de las montañas.
  This water comes from the mountains.
- ¿De dónde provienen sus abuelos?
  Where do his grandparents come from?
- El español provino del latín.
  Spanish arose (or came) from Latin.

provocar a uno   to make sb, move sb

- Hay comidas que me provocan vómito.
  There are foods that make me throw up.
- La crisis que sufre el mundo me provoca angustia.
  The world's crisis causes me anguish.
- Le provocó risa.
  He made him laugh.

provocar (a) + *inf*   to provoke to + *inf*, tempt to + *inf*

- El agua caliente me provoca (a) bañarme.
  The warm water tempts me to bathe.
- Me provocó (a) pegarle.
  He provoked me to hit him.
- Escribe tan bien que me provoca (a) leer más.
  He writes so well that he makes me want to read more.

pulsar   to pulsate; to touch, tap; to play (*music*)

- Pulsó las cuerdas de la guitarra con maestría.
  He played the guitar's cords masterfully.
- Vamos a pulsar ese negocio. (*fig*)
  We are going to explore that business.
- Las venas pulsan al ritmo del corazón.
  Veins pulsate in rhythm with the heart.

Q

quebrar   to break, smash; to fail (*business*)

- Quebré el cristal (/la botella/el tubo fluorescente).
  I broke (or smashed) the glass (/bottle/fluorescent tube).

- Nuestra empresa quebró.
  Our enterprise went bankrupt (or out of business).

- Ese hecho me quebró el corazón. (*fig*)
  That action broke my heart.

quebrar con uno   to break (up) with sb

- María quebró con Pedro (/su amigo). (*fig*)
  Mary broke (up) with Peter (/her friend).

- Miguel ha quebrado con Juana. (*fig*)
  Michael has ended his relationship with Jane.

quedar   to remain; to be (left)

- El trabajo ha quedado sin hacer.
  The work has remained undone.

- Los proyectos quedaron sin realizarse.
  The projects were not carried out.

- Este asunto queda fuera del tema.
  This question lies (or falls) outside this subject.

- Quedan pocos días para tu cumpleaños.
  Only a few days remain until your birthday.

quedar en algo   to result in sth; to agree on sth

- Después de mucho hablar, quedamos en lo mismo.
  After much talking, things stayed the same (or nothing changed).

- Las negociaciones han quedado en un estado prometedor.
  The negotiations have resulted in a hopeful state.

- No quedamos en nada.
  We didn't agree on anything.

quedar en + *inf*   to agree to + *inf,* agree on + *ger;* to arrange to + *inf*

- Quedamos en ir (/vernos/visitarlos) mañana.
  We have agreed to go (/to see each other/to visit them) tomorrow.

- Quedé en verme con ella a las seis.
  I agreed on seeing her at six.

- Quedaron en contarme la historia (/en reunirse mañana).
  They agreed (or arranged) to tell me the story (/to get together tomorrow).

quedar en que...   to agree that...

- Quedamos en que usted no iría (/en que la visitaríamos).
  We agreed that you wouldn't go (/that we would visit her).

- ¿En qué quedamos? —En que todos cantaríamos.
  What did we agree on? —That all of us would sing.

quedarse   to remain, stay

- ¿Cuánto tiempo se quedaban allí? —Nos quedábamos una semana.
  How long did you stay there? —We used to stay a week.

- Me estoy quedando atrás.
  I am falling (or remaining) behind.

- Se quedó durante cinco días en una pensión (/un hotel).
  He stayed at a boarding house (/hotel) for five days.

- Él se quedó con los abuelos.
  He stayed with his grandparents.

quedarse con algo   to keep sth, hold on to sth; to acquire sth, get sth

- Mi amigo se quedó con mi libro (/llave/bicicleta/maleta).
  My friend kept (or held on to) my book (/key/bicycle/suitcase).

- Él que gana la apuesta se queda con el dinero.
  Whoever wins the bet takes (or gets) the money.

- Entre nuestro equipo y ése, me quedo con el nuestro.
  If I have to choose between our team and that one, I'll take (or keep) ours.

quejarse (a, de, sobre)   to complain, grumble (at/to, of, about)

- Yo he tenido una buena vida; no puedo quejarme.
  I have had a good life; I can't complain.

- Debemos quejarnos al director (/a la maestra) sobre este asunto.
  We must complain to the principal (/the teacher) about this matter.

- ¿De qué te quejaste? —Me quejé de la mala comida.
  What did you complain about? —I complained about the bad food.

- El chico se queja de fatiga (/de dolor de cabeza).
  The boy complains about being tired (/a headache).

■　La gente se queja del gobierno (/presidente/juez).
　　People grumble about the government (/president/judge).

quemar (con)　to burn (with); to set on fire

■　El incendio (/sol) quemó al niño.
　　The fire (/sun) burned the child.

■　Los manifestantes quemaron los documentos (/el edificio con gasolina).
　　The demonstrators burned the documents (/building with gasoline).

quemarse (con)　to burn oneself (with)

■　Se quemó con ácido (/gasolina/fósforos).
　　He burned himself with acid (/gasoline/matches).

■　Me quemé la lengua con el café (/la sopa).
　　I burned my tongue on the coffee (/soup).

querer　to wish, want; to love

■　¿A quién quieres? —Quiero a Gloria. Te quiero mucho.
　　Who(m) do you love? —I love Gloria. I love you very much.

■　¿Quieres todavía a Sonia? —Sí, la quiero con toda mi alma.
　　Do you still love Sonia? —Yes, I love her with all my soul.

■　¿Qué más quieres? ¿Quieres un café?
　　What more do you want? Would you like some coffee?

■　¿Cuánto quieres por el coche?
　　How much do you want for the car?

■　Quisiera que hablaras con el jefe de policía.
　　I wish you would talk to the police chief.

querer + *inf*　to want to + *inf*

■　No quise hacerlo (/ir contigo/verlo).
　　I didn't want to do it (/go with you/see him).

quitar　to take (away); to take off, remove

■　Debes quitarle el chuchillo al niño.
　　You should take the knife away from the child.

■　El ladrón me quitó las ganas de viajar.
　　The thief took away my desire to travel.

■　El gobierno (/funcionario) le quitó el pasaporte al periodista.
　　The government (/official) took away the passport from the journalist.

■　El caballero me quitó el abrigo.
　　The gentleman took off (or removed) my coat.

quitarse (de)   to remove oneself; to withdraw (from); to take off; to come off

- Me quité el sombrero (/los zapatos) antes de entrar.
  I took off my hat (/shoes) before entering.

- El alumno se quitó de la vista del maestro.
  The student removed himself (or withdrew) from the teacher's sight.

- La mancha de pintura (/de comida) en mi camisa no se quita.
  The paint (/food) stain on my shirt won't come off.

- ¡Quítate de ahí!
  Get out of here (or Off with you)!

R

rebajar   to lower, reduce, lower the level of

- Todos los comerciantes hemos rebajado los precios.
  All of us merchants have lowered (or reduced our) prices.

- Con esa actitud, usted rebaja su reputación. (*fig*)
  You lower your reputation with that attitude!

- ¡Rebaje cien dólares de mi cuenta!
  Lower my bill by a hundred dollars.

rebajarse   to lower oneself

- Yo no me rebajo a ese nivel.
  I do not lower myself to that level.

- Por favor, no te rebajes pidiéndole ese favor.
  Please, do not lower yourself by asking him that favor.

rebasar   to exceed, surpass; to pass, overtake

- El enemigo rebasó los límites establecidos.
  The enemy exceeded the established limits.

- Un corredor rebasó al otro.
  One runner passed (or overtook) the other.

- Ella rebasó los límites de la prudencia.
  She surpassed the limits of prudence.

- El pequeño bote rebasó al buque.
  The small boat overtook the ship.

rebelarse (contra)   to revolt, rebel (against)

- La gente se rebeló contra el reinado de Luis XVI.
  The people rebelled against the reign of Louis XVI.

- Me rebelaba contra mis padres.
  I rebelled against my parents.

recaer en algo   to fall back into sth, relapse into sth; to fall on/to sth

- Carlos recayó en sus viejos hábitos (/vicios/errores).
  Carl relapsed into his old habits (/vices/mistakes).

- Los premios recayeron en la hija de mi vecina.
  The prizes fell to my neighbor's daughter.

- La culpa (/sospecha) recayó en el barredor de calles.
  The blame (/suspicion) fell on the street sweeper.

- Antonio recayó en el alcoholismo.
  Anthony relapsed into alcoholism.

recibir   to receive; to welcome

- No he recibido todavía los documentos que Luis me ha enviado.
  I still haven't received the documents which Louis has sent to me.

- El ministro lo recibió con honores.
  The minister received him with honors.

- Me recibieron con gran alegría.
  They welcomed me happily.

recibirse   to graduate as (*university*)

- Mi hermana se recibió de enfermera (/de médica/de abogada) el año pasado.
  My sister received her nursing (/medical/law) degree last year (or My sister graduated as a nurse (/doctor/lawyer) last year).

reclamar (contra)   to claim, demand, request; to protest (against)

- Después de su muerte, su nieto reclamó la porción de la herencia que le correspondía.
  After his death, his grandson claimed (or protested) his share of the estate.

- Ella reclamó lo que se le debía.
  She claimed (or demanded) what was owed to her.

- Los clientes reclaman un mejor servicio.
  The clients demand (or request) a better service.

reclinar algo (en)   to lean sth (on)

- Reclinó la silla en la mesa.
  He leaned the chair against the table.

- La mujer reclinó la estatua para que no cayera.
  The lady leaned the statue so that it would not fall.

reclinarse (en, sobre)   to lean, recline (on)

- Se reclinó en (*or* sobre) la mesa.
  He leaned on the table.

- Nos reclinamos en la pared.
  We leaned on (or *against*) *the wall.*

- Voy a reclinarme en esto para descansar.
  I'm going to lean (or *recline*) *on this in order to rest.*

recoger   to pick up, gather (up); to collect (*stamps, etc.*), get

- Pedro recoge el dinero (/la basura).
  Peter is collecting the money (/garbage).

- Él recogió las monedas (/las manzanas) que se habían caído.
  He picked up the coins (/apples) which had fallen.

- ¿Quién irá a recogerla en la estación?
  Who is going to pick her up from the station?

- El jugador recogió la pelota del suelo (con la mano).
  The player picked up the ball from the ground (with his hand).

- Para escribir este ensayo necesitamos recoger datos (/información).
  In order to write this essay, we need to collect (or *get*) *some data (/information).*

- Él murió joven y no pudo recoger el fruto de su trabajo.
  He died young and was not able to reap the fruit of his labor.

recomendar   to recommend, advise

- Les recomiendo a ustedes que lo hagan rápidamente.
  I advise you to (or *recommend that you*) *do it right away.*

recomendar + *inf*   to advise to + *inf*

- Le recomiendo hacer ejercicios (/respirar profundamente).
  I advise you to exercise (/to breathe deeply).

- El maestro nos recomendó estudiar más.
  The teacher advised us to study more.

reconocer (por)   to recognize (by)

- Juan me pareció muy alto; no lo reconocí a primera vista.
  John seemed so tall to me; I didn't recognize him at first.

- Yo no lo reconozco como autoridad (/como jefe/como superior).
  I do not recognize such an authority (/a boss/a superior).

- El director ha reconocido el mérito de mi trabajo.
  The director has recognized the merit of my work.

- Yo lo reconocí por la camisa roja (/su pelo rubio/el parecido a su madre).
  I recognized him by his red shirt (/blond hair/resemblance to his mother).

recordar (de)   to remember, recall (about/of)

- No me gusta recordarte tus deberes (/obligaciones).
  I don't like to remind you of your duties (/obligations).

- Por favor, recuérdame lo que tengo que hacer.
  Please, remind me about what I have to do.

- ¿Qué recuerdas de tu niñez? —No recuerdo mucho.
  What do you remember about (or recall from) your childhood? —I don't remember much.

- Yo no recuerdo la fecha de mi graduación.
  I don't remember the date of my graduation.

referir   to tell; to recount, report

- Mi abuelo refería historias divertidas (/hechos espantosos).
  My grandfather told funny stories (/recounted frightening facts).

referirse a uno/algo   to refer to sb/sth, address sth

- No me refiero a mi hermana, sino a mi prima.
  I'm not referring to my sister but to my cousin.

- No se refiera a lo que pasó ayer.
  Do not refer to what happened yesterday.

- No quiere referirse a ese tema (/problema).
  He doesn't want to refer to (or address) that topic (/problem).

reflejar(se) en algo   to reflect on sth

- La luz se refleja en el muro.
  The light reflects on the wall.

- El alma se refleja en los ojos.
  The soul is reflected in one's eyes.

- ¡Refleja en tus acciones lo que predicas!
  Reflect what you preach in your actions.

regalar   to give (*a gift*); to give away

- Le regalaré un libro para su cumpleaños.
  I will give him a book for his birthday.

- Le regalamos una pintura a Carlos cuando se jubiló.
  We gave Carl a painting when he retired.

- No me gusta que me regalen nada.
  I do not like people to give me presents.

regalar(se) con algo   to treat (oneself) to sth

- Me regalé con un platillo exquisito.
  I treated myself to an exquisite dish.

■   Nos regaló con un vino alemán.
    He treated us to a German wine.

regatear(se)   to haggle over, bargain over

■   Me gusta regatear cuando voy de compras.
    I like to haggle over prices when I go shopping.

■   En los supermercados modernos no se regatea.
    Price haggling is not done in modern supermarkets.

■   No regatees las palabras que vas a expresar contra el presidente.
    Do not haggle (or quibble) over the words you choose to use against the president.

regir   to rule, govern; to run, manage

■   ¡Rija su vida de acuerdo con nuestras costumbres!
    Run your life in accordance with our customs.

■   El gobierno liberal rigió el país por diez años.
    The liberal administration ruled the country for ten years.

regirse por algo   to be ruled by sth, be guided by sth; to follow sth

■   Este club se rige por reglas estrictas.
    This club is ruled by strict regulations.

■   Los cristianos se rigen por los diez mandamientos.
    Christians are guided by the Ten Commandments.

■   Nos regimos por nuestra conciencia.
    We are guided by (or follow) our conscience.

regresar   to come back, go back, return

■   Regresamos a la casa (/escuela/finca) a las ocho de la noche.
    We returned home (/to school/to the farm) at 8 P.M.

■   Desgraciadamente esta gente regresó a los procedimientos antiguos.
    Unfortunately, these people returned (or went back) to former ways.

regresar a + *inf*   to return to + *inf*

■   El grupo va a regresar a cantar el próximo año.
    The group is going to return to sing next year.

■   Regresé a ver lo que había pasado.
    I returned to see what had happened.

rehuir   to avoid, shrink from

■   Yo rehúyo el trabajo.
    I avoid the work.

■   Rehuimos las obligaciones.
    We are shrinking from our obligations.

rehuir + *inf*   to avoid + *ger*

- Rehuyeron hablar conmigo (/con los obreros).
  They avoided talking with me (/with the workers).

- Él rehuyó hacerlo.
  He avoided doing it.

rehusar   to refuse

- ¡No rehúse mi oferta!
  Don't refuse my offer.

rehusar + *inf*   to refuse to + *inf*

- Rehúso hablar.
  I refuse to speak.

- El niño rehusó comer (/hacer lo que se le mandó).
  The child refused to eat (/do what he was told).

reír(se)   to laugh

- Reír es bueno para el alma.
  Laughing is good for the soul.

- El que ríe último ríe mejor. (*prov*)
  He who laughs last laughs longest.

- Sólo me río cuando alguien cuenta un buen chiste.
  I only laugh when someone tells a good joke.

- Ellos se ríen demasiado (/con ganas/bulliciosamente).
  They are laughing too much (/heartily/noisily).

reírse de uno/algo   to laugh at sb/sth, make fun of sb/sth

- ¡No se ría de los viejos!
  Don't laugh at (or make fun of) old people!

- El público se reía de los chistes (/de su argumento/del payaso).
  The audience laughed at the jokes (/his argument/the clown).

- ¿Se ríe usted de mí? ¡No se ría en mi cara!
  Are you making fun of me? Don't laugh in my face!

relacionar (con)   to relate (to); to connect (with)

- El estudiante no puede relacionar una idea con otra.
  The student can't relate (or connect) one idea with (or to) another.

- No hay que relacionarlos porque son hechos históricos diferentes.
  One must not relate them since they are different historical facts.

relacionarse con uno   to get to know sb

- No nos hemos relacionado con los artistas del pueblo.
  We haven't gotten to know the town artists.

- Ella se relaciona con las personas ricas.
  She is getting to know wealthy people.

- En lo que se relaciona con los extraterrestres, diré que no creo ni una palabra.
  I tell you, with regard to extraterrestrials, I don't believe a word of it.

relevar (de)   to relieve (of); to replace, substitute for

- Usted debe relevar a su compañero.
  You have to relieve (or replace) your partner.

- ¡Reléveme porque estoy muy cansado de trabajar!
  Relieve me because I'm so tired of working.

- ¿Relevaron al profesor Sánchez de sus obligaciones? —Sí, lo relevaron de ellas.
  Did they relieve Professor Sanchez of his obligations? —Yes, they relieved him of them.

- El juez lo relevó porque no había cometido el crimen.
  The judge exonerated him because he hadn't committed the crime.

- El Presidente relevó al general de su mando (/cargo).
  The President relieved the general of his command (/post).

relevar a uno de + *inf*   to relieve sb from + *ger*

- ¡Reléveme de actuar (/trabajar/cocinar) esta noche!
  Relieve me from performing (/working/cooking) tonight.

- Voy a relevarlo de conducir el autobús.
  I'm going to relieve him from driving the bus.

remitir   to send

- Le remití una carta a mi hermano que vive lejos.
  I sent a letter to my brother who lives far away.

remitirse a uno/algo   to refer to sb/sth

- Voy a remitirme al texto original para entender mejor el asunto.
  I'm going to refer to the original text in order to understand it better.

- El abogado se remitió a los dos testigos (/a los hechos).
  The lawyer referred to the two witnesses (/the facts).

remontarse a algo   to go back to sth

- Mis recuerdos se remontan a la muerte de mi abuelo (/a mi niñez).
  My memories go back to the death of my grandfather (/my childhood).

- Esta literatura (/Biblia/costumbre) se remonta al siglo XIII.
  This literature (/Bible/custom) dates back to the 13th century.

rendirse (a)   to yield (to); to surrender

- El ejército se rindió al enemigo.
  The army surrendered to the enemy.

■ Nos rendimos a la razón (/a la evidencia).
We yielded to reason (/evidence).

rendirse de algo   to yield *or* cave in to sth

■ Ella se rindió de cansancio (/de fatiga).
She caved in to exhaustion (/fatigue).

renunciar a algo   to renounce sth, give up sth, resign from sth

■ Renuncié a la escuela.
I gave up school.

■ Ayer yo renuncié a mi trabajo (/mi posición).
Yesterday I resigned from my job (/position).

■ El señor presidente renunció a su cargo.
The president resigned from his post.

■ Mañana voy a renunciar a todo.
Tomorrow I'm going to renounce everything.

renunciar a + *inf*   to give up + *ger*

■ Renunció a bailar (/tocar) en público.
He gave up dancing (/playing) in public.

reñir (con, por)   to quarrel, argue, fight (with, over)

■ Los dos chicos riñeron por la chica.
The two boys fought over the girl.

■ Ellos siempre reñían por política (/por dinero).
They always quarreled over politics (/money).

■ Paco riñó con su novia (/familia).
Frank quarreled with his girlfriend (/family).

■ El padre riñe con su hijo muy a menudo.
The father very often argues with his son.

reparar   to repair, mend

■ Tengo que reparar el radio (/la bicicleta/el coche).
I have to repair the radio (/bicycle/car).

reparar en algo   to pay attention to sth, observe sth; to consider sth

■ Los políticos no repararon en su mala actuación (/en los errores del ministro).
The politicians didn't pay attention to their bad performance (/the minister's errors).

■ ¡No repares en el aspecto exterior del edificio!
Do not pay attention to the exterior appearance of the building.

■ Debes reparar en lo que vas a hacer (/escribir).
You have to consider what you are going to do (/write).

- No reparé en lo que el profesor decía (/en lo que pasó entre ellas).
  I didn't pay attention to what the professor was saying (/what happened between them).

- El maestro no reparó en la presencia de Anita (/el accidente).
  The teacher didn't notice (or observe) Anita's presence (/the accident).

repartir (a, entre)   to distribute (to, among); to divide (up)

- El padre repartió el dinero (/los regalos) entre los tres hermanos.
  The father distributed the money (/the gifts) among the three brothers.

- Tienes que repartir los libros en cinco grupos.
  You have to divide the books into five groups.

- Repartieron el alimento a los pobres.
  They distributed the food to the poor.

repetir   to repeat

- El maestro repitió la lección (/el alfabeto).
  The teacher repeated the lesson (/alphabet).

- ¿Cuántas veces tengo que repetirlo?
  How many times must I repeat it?

- Repitieron el partido el domingo.
  They repeated the game on Sunday.

resentirse (con)   to be affected, be weakened (by)

- El edificio (/puente) se resintió con la explosión (/el terremeto)
  The building (/bridge) was weakened by the explosion (/earthquake).

- La salud de mi padre se ha resentido con las penalidades (/la enfermedad).
  My father's health has been affected by the hardships (/sickness).

resentirse con uno   *(fig)* to resent sb, be offended by sb

- ¡No se resienta con nosotros (/conmigo)!
  Don't be angry with us (/me).

- Se resintió con ella cuando le cobró lo que le debía.
  He was offended when she charged him what he owed her.

- Ella no se ha resentido con nadie.
  She is not angry (or upset) with anyone.

resentirse de/por algo   *(fig)* to offended by sth

- Se resintió de (*or* por) lo que pasó.
  He got offended (or hurt) by what happened.

- Se resintieron de (*or* por) mis palabras.
  They were offended by my words (or They took offense at what I said).

■ Pepe se resintió de (*or* por) lo que había hecho María.
Pepe was offended by what Mary had done.

resignarse (a, con)   to resign oneself (to)

■ ¡Resígnate!, la vida es así.
Resign yourself; that's life!

■ Se resignó con su destino trágico.
She resigned herself to her tragic destiny.

■ Se resignó a los maltratos que le ocasionaba su padrastro.
He resigned himself to being mistreated by his stepfather.

■ El prisionero se resignó a los trabajos forzados.
The prisoner resigned himself to forced labor.

resignarse a + *inf*   to resign oneself to + *ger*

■ Me he resignado a trabajar largas horas.
I have resigned myself to working long hours.

■ Se resignó a amarla platónicamente (/a no fumar).
He resigned himself to loving her platonically (/to not smoking).

resistir   to resist; to bear

■ No resisto este dolor.
I can't bear (or stand) this pain.

■ La mujer resistió los avances del director.
The woman resisted the advances of the director.

■ No puedo resistir el deseo de comer chuletas de puerco.
I can't resist eating pork chops.

resistirse a + *inf*   to refuse to + *inf*, resist + *ger*

■ No comprendo por qué él se resistió a creerme (/a volver a esa vida).
I don't understand why he refused to believe me (/to go back to that life).

■ Los huelguistas se resistieron a volver a trabajar.
The strikers resisted returning to work.

resolver   to solve, resolve

■ La policía no ha resuelto el crimen (/problema).
The police haven't solved the crime (/problem).

■ La mamá (/El juez) resolvió el conflicto entre los dos a favor de la menor.
The mother (/judge) resolved the conflict in favor of the younger one.

resolver + *inf*   to resolve to + *inf*

■ Han resuelto construir una casa nueva.
They resolved to build a new house.

■ Resolvimos volver a Sudamérica.
We resolved to return to South America.

resolverse   to be resolved; to work out

■ Los conflictos no se resolvieron en un minuto.
The conflicts were not resovled (or worked out) in a minute.

■ Estos problemas complejos no se resuelven fácilmente.
These complex problems are not solved easily.

■ Ojalá que sus disputas se resuelvan pacíficamente.
I hope that their disputes work (themselves) out peacefully.

resolverse a + *inf*   to resolve to + *inf*

■ Mi hijo se resolvió a salir (/abandonar su empleo).
My son is resolved to leave (/to quit his job).

responder a uno/algo   to answer sb/sth, reply to sb/sth, respond to sb/sth

■ No le quiero responder porque es un hombre grosero.
I don't want to answer him because he is a rude man.

■ Yo le respondí que lo haría cuando tuviera tiempo.
I responded that I would do it when I had time.

■ Este señor tiene una pregunta. ¿Por qué no quiere usted responderle? —Ya le he respondido.
This gentleman has a question. Why don't you want to answer him? —I have already answered (or responded to) him.

■ Por favor, responda a esta pregunta específica. —Ya la he respondido.
Please, answer this specific question. —I have already answered it.

■ No pudo responder a mi pregunta (/a la pregunta del maestro).
He couldn't answer my question (/the teacher's question).

■ ¿Has respondido a su carta (/llamada)? —No, no la (/le) he respondido.
Have you responded to his letter (/call)? —No, I haven't answered (or replied to) it.

■ El enfermo no respondió a ningún tratamiento (/a los antibióticos).
The patient didn't respond to any treatment (/antibiotics).

■ Respondieron a nuestra amistad (/hospitalidad/injurias) con amabilidad.
They answered our friendliness (/hospitality/insults) with kindness.

■ El perrito responde al nombre de Fido.
The puppy responds to the name Fido.

responder de/por algo   to be responsible for sth; to answer for sth

■ El padre responde de lo que hagan sus hijos.
The father is responsible for what his sons may do.

■ Yo respondo de que los niños lleguen a tu casa a tiempo.
I am responsible for the children getting to your house on time.

■ El presidente debe responder por el pueblo (/por sus ministros).
The president must be responsible for the people (/his ministers).

■ Yo no puedo responder de lo que digan mis colegas.
I can't answer for what my colleagues say.

responder por uno/algo   to vouch for sb/sth

■ ¿Quién responderá por Jaime? —Su madre (/El jefe/Mi padre) responderá por él.
Who will vouch for James? —His mother (/The boss/My father) will vouch for him.

■ Él responderá por lo que hizo su hermano.
He'll vouch for what his brother did.

resultar   to turn out (to be)

■ Esta inversión resultará buena si trabajamos mucho.
This investment will turn out to be a good one if we work a lot.

■ Resulta que cuando llegué a Nueva York el avión se había ido.
It turned out that when I arrived in New York, the plane had already left.

■ Todo resultó bien a pesar del susto.
Everything turned out well in spite of the scare.

resultar de algo   to result from sth

■ ¿Qué resultó de la discusión? —De ella resultaron las resoluciones siguientes.
What resulted from the discussion? —The following resolutions followed from.

■ De estas manifestaciones (/protestas) resultó una política liberal.
A liberal policy resulted from these demonstrations (/protests).

resultar en algo   to result in sth, prodouce sth

■ Las negociaciones han resultado en la paz.
The negotiations have resulted in (or produced) peace.

retirar algo (de)   to remove sth, withdraw sth (from)

■ Retiraron los platos de la mesa.
They removed the dishes from the table.

■ Retiré todo mi dinero del banco.
I withdrew all my money from the bank.

retirarse (de)   to go away from, leave (from)

■ Nos retiramos de su casa muy temprano.
We left their house very early.

■ Se retiró del servicio militar.
He retired from military service.

retraer   to bring (back) again

- Vamos a retraer el tema que discutíamos ayer.
  We are going to bring up (or treat) again the subject we were discussing yesterday.

retraerse de algo   to withdraw from sth; to give up sth

- Mi padre se retrajo de los negocios.
  My father withdrew from (or gave up) business.
- Me retraje de la vida mundana.
  I withdrew from the mundane life.

reunir algo (con)   to assemble sth, gather sth; to combine (with)

- Los obreros reunieron mil firmas.
  The workers gathered 1,000 signatures.
- El maestro (/padre) reunía la firmeza con la amabilidad.
  The teacher (/father) combined firmness with kindness.
- La convención reunió a tres mil socios.
  The convention assembled (or gathered) together 3,000 members.

reunir a uno/algo para + *inf*   to get sb/sth together to + *inf*, unite sb/sth to + *inf*

- Quiero reunir a mis amigos para cantar (/jugar).
  I want to assemble my friends to sing (/play).
- Este fin de semana reúno a mis amigos para ir a la playa.
  This weekend I will get my friends together (in order) to go to the beach.
- Los dos ejércitos reunieron sus tropas para atacar al enemigo.
  The two armies united their troops in order to attack the enemy.
- Carlos está reuniendo dinero para comprarse uno computadora.
  Carl is gathering (or saving) money in order to buy a computer.

reunirse (con)   to meet *or* get together (with)

- Me reuniré con ustedes esta noche (/a las cinco/por la tarde).
  I'll meet you tonight (/at five/in the afternoon).
- Siempre nos reunimos durante las fiestas de navidad.
  We always get together during the Christmas holidays.

reunirse para + *inf*   to get together to + *inf*

- Nos reunimos con los Sánchez para festejar los cumpleaños.
  We get together with the Sanchez family to celebrate birthdays.
- Los muchachos se reunieron para charlar (/estudiar).
  The boys and girls got together to talk (/study).

revolver (en)   to go *or* rummage through (in); to mix

- Mis niños han revuelto todo en la casa.
  My chidren have rummaged through everything in the house.
- Los ladrones habían revuelto mi maleta (/apartamento).
  The thieves had rummaged (or gone) through my luggage (/apartment).
- ¡Revuelva bien los ingredientes para que el platillo quede bien!
  Mix the ingredients well so that the dish will turn out well.
- Julia revolvió la ensalada (/masa con el agua).
  Julia mixed the salad (/dough with water).
- Esta comida le revuele el estómago.
  This food upsets (or turns) his stomach.

revolverse   to turn about/around/over

- Se revolvió la situación económica del país.
  The economic condition of the country turned around.
- Toda la noche me revolví en la cama.
  All last night I tossed and turned in bed.
- Los niños se revolvían en la alfombra (/el suelo).
  The children were turning (or rolling) about on the rug (/ground).
- Se me revuelve el estómago cuando me entero de las guerras.
  My stomach turns (over) when I learn about wars.

rezar (a, por)   to say; to pray (to, for)

- Este escrito reza lo siguiente.
  This document says the following.
- El cirujano reza siempre antes de operar.
  The surgeon always prays before operating.
- Ella le reza a la Virgen María (/a Dios/a San Marcos/a Jesucristo).
  She prays to the Virgin Mary (/God/St. Mark/Jesus Christ).
- Rezamos por la paz (/por los Santos Difuntos).
  We prayed for peace (/for all souls).

robar (de, a)   to steal (from), rob (from)

- Robaron el banco (/un millón de dólares del banco).
  They robbed the bank (/stole a million dollars from the bank).
- Él le robó la bolsa a Sonia. Le robó todo el dinero que tenía.
  He stole the purse from Sonia. He stole all the money she had.
- Él le robó a Sonia el corazón (/la tranquilidad). (*fig*)
  He stole Sonia's heart (/peace of mind).
- Usted pagó demasiado por el reloj. Le han robado.
  You paid too much for the watch. They cheated (or robbed) you.

rogar   to beg, ask for

- Le ruego un favor (/una gracia) *or* Le ruego que me haga un favor (/una gracia).
  I'm asking (or begging) you for a favor (/a kindness) or I beg you to do me a favor (/a kindness).

rogar a uno que + *subj*   to ask sb to + *inf*; to ask that . . .

- Le rogué que fuera (/lo hiciera) lo más pronto posible.
  I asked him to go (/to do it) as soon as possible.

- ¡Ruega a Dios que el médico lo salve!
  Beg (or Pray to) God that the doctor will save him.

- ¡Ruéguele al director que permita a mi hijo matricularse!
  Please ask the principal to let my son register.

rogar a uno + *inf*   to ask sb to + *inf*, beg sb to + *inf*

- Le ruego hablar en voz baja (/no insultarnos).
  I ask you to speak quietly (/not to insult us).

- Te ruego recapacitar sobre aquel asunto.
  I beg you to reflect on that subject.

romper   to break; to tear

- Rompí un vaso (/el juguete/los platos/el vidrio de la ventana/el papel).
  I broke a glass (/the toy/the dishes/the window/tore the paper).

- Los países rompieron las relaciones diplomáticas.
  The countries broke off diplomatic relations.

- Rompieron el compromiso.
  They broke the engagement.

- ¿Rompiste mi reloj? —No, no lo rompí.
  Did you break my watch? —No, I didn't break it.

- ¿A quién le rompiste las narices? —Le rompí la nariz a Juan.
  Whose nose did you smash? —I smashed Juan's nose.

- Yo quiero romperle la cara a Ricardo. Yo quiero romperle la cara.
  I want to smash Richard's face. I'd like to smash his face.

romper a + *inf*   to start (suddenly) to + *inf*

- Su hermana rompió a llorar (/reír)
  His sister suddenly burst into tears (/laughter) (or started crying (/laughing)).

- Rompió a llover temprano este año.
  It began to rain early this year.

romper con uno   to fall out with sb, break with sb

- Alejandra ha roto con su novio después de tres años de relación.
  Alexandra has broken off (or fallen out) with her fiancé after three years.

■ Rompieron con la tradición. Fueron en auto y no a caballo.
They broke with tradition. They went by car and not on horseback.

romperse   to break, fracture

■ Se rompió el vaso (/la rama/el radio).
The glass (/branch/radio) broke.

■ Me rompí el brazo (/la espalda/la pierna/la nariz/la cabeza).
I broke (or fractured) my arm (/back/leg/nose/skull).

■ Me rompí los sesos estudiando. (*fig*)
I busted my brains studying.

rozar algo (con)   to rub against/on sth, touch sth (with); to graze sth

■ ¡Ten cuidado!, tu abrigo roza la pared sucia (/la botella de aceite).
Be careful! Your coat is rubbing against (or touching) the dirty wall (/bottle of oil).

■ Mi mano la rozó.
My hand grazed her.

■ La bala le rozó la cabeza.
The bullet grazed her head.

■ Rozó la superficie con el codo (/la mano).
He touched the surface with his elbow (/hand).

■ Rocé la pared áspera con la yema de los dedos.
I (gently) rubbed the rough wall with my fingertips.

■ Ella me rozó con la mejilla.
She touched me gently with her cheek.

rozar en algo   to border on sth, touch on sth

■ Tu actitud roza en el ridículo.
Your attitude borders on the ridiculous.

■ Los argumentos sólo rozan en un punto.
The arguments only agree on one point.

rozarse con uno/algo   to associate *or* mix with sb/sth

■ Héctor sólo se roza con la aristocracia.
Hector only associates (or mixes) with aristocracy.

■ No me gusta rozarme con esa gente.
I don't like to mix with those people.

■ La niña no se roza con sus vecinas.
The girl does not socialize with her neighbors.

S

saber   to know; to taste

- Pablo sabe francés (/la lección/biología) muy bien.
  Paul knows French (/the lesson/biology) very well.

- Yo no sé mucho inglés.
  I am not very good at English.

- No sabemos dónde está mi hermano (/dónde está la Calle Real).
  We don't know where my brother is (/where Royal Street is).

- Esta comida sabe muy mal (/bien).
  This food tastes very bad (/good).

- ¿Supo Julia que le habías escrito? —No, no lo supo.
  Did Julia know that you had written her? —No, she didn't know it.

- ¿Sabes este poema? —Sí, claro. Lo sé de memoria.
  Do you know this poem? —Yes, of course. I know it by heart.

saber a algo   to taste like sth

- Los tamales saben a maíz fresco.
  The tamales taste like fresh corn.

- ¿A qué sabe? —Sabe a vinagre.
  What does it taste like? —It tastes like vinegar.

- Los helados saben a vainilla (/a miel de abeja).
  The ice cream tastes like vanilla (/honey).

saber + *inf*   to know how to + *inf*

- La gente de este país no sabe leer ni escribir.
  The people in this country don't know how to read and write.

- Enrique sabe hablar (/escribir) ruso.
  Henry knows how to speak (/write) Russian.

- ¿Sabes conducir (/escribir a máquina/pintar)?
  Do you know how to (or Can you) drive (/type/paint)?

saber de uno/algo   to know about/of sb/sth, be aware of sb/sth

- ¿Dónde está tu viejo amigo? —Hace dos años que no sé nada de él.
  Where is your friend? —It's been two years since I have heard from him.

- Alberto sabe de hoteles (/sitios) que son muy baratos.
  Albert knows of some hotels (/places) that are very reasonable.

- Luis sabe mucho de electrónica (/mecánica/comidas/flores).
  Louis knows a great deal about electronics (/mechanics/food/flowers).

sacar   to take (out), get (out), obtain; to pull out, extract

- El estudiante (/secretario) saca buenas fotografías.
  The student (/secretary) takes good pictures.

- ¡Saca la lengua!
  Stick your tongue out.

- La policía secreta le sacó al hombre la información que buscaba.
  The secret police got some important information from the man.

- ¿Dónde sacaste tu licencia de manejar? —La saqué en aquella oficina.
  Where did you get your driver's license? —I got it in that office.

- El dentista le sacó una muela a mi padre.
  The dentist pulled out my father's tooth.

- Pepe sacó muy buenas notas.
  Pepe got very good grades.

sacar a algo   to take (out) to sth

- Lo sacamos al parque.
  We are taking him out to the park.

- Sacaron el perrito al jardín.
  They took the puppy out to the yard.

- ¡Saquemos los muebles al patio!
  Let's take the furniture out to the yard.

sacar a + *inf*   to take (out) to + *inf*

- Lo sacamos a comer (/a ver una película).
  We are taking him out to eat (/to see a movie).

- Sacaron a María a bailar.
  They took Mary out to dance.

- La hemos sacado a jugar tenis (/correr/divertirse/tomar helados).
  We've taken her out to play tennis (/jog/enjoy herself/have ice cream).

sacar algo/uno de algo   to take out *or* get sb/sth from sth

- Lo sacan del colegio militar los domingos.
  They take him out of military school on Sundays.

- Sacó la idea de una novela que leyó en la escuela.
  He got the idea from a novel he read at school.

- Saqué mi dinero del banco.
  I took my money out of the bank.

- Saquemos su nombre de la lista.
  Let's take his name off the list.

- La mujer sacó el peine (/dinero) de la bolsa.
  The woman took the comb (/money) from her purse.

salir   to leave; to come out, appear, emerge; to date, go out

- Quiero salir ahora (/a las dos).
  I want to leave now (/at two o'clock).

- El tren salió anoche, a las ocho.
  The train left last night at eight.

- ¿Cuándo salió su última novela? —Hace dos años que salió.
  When did his last novel come out (or appear)? —It came out two years ago.

- ¿Cómo salió en el examen? —Salió muy bien.
  How did his exam go? —It was very good.

- Anita y Daniel salen juntos desde hace tres meses.
  Anita and Daniel have been dating (or going out together) for three months.

salir a + *inf*   to go out to + *inf*, leave to + *inf*

- ¿Cuándo salen a ver el desfile (/a comer con nosotros/a jugar en la playa)?
  When are you leaving to see the parade (/to eat with us/to play at the beach)?

- Salimos a terminar el trabajo (/limpiar el auto/vender frutas).
  We went out to finish the job (/clean the car/sell fruit).

salir a uno   to take after sb, be like sb

- Gloria (/La niña) salió a su madre.
  Gloria (/The child) is like her mother (or Gloria takes after her mother).

- Tomás salió a su padre.
  Thomas was exactly like his father (or Thomas took after his father).

salir con uno   to go (out) with sb, date sb; to leave with sb

- Felipe sale ahora con Lola.
  Phillip is dating (or is going with) Lola now.

- Salió con sus padres (/hijos/amigos).
  She left with her parents (/children/friends).

salir de algo   to leave sth; to come out of sth; to emerge from sth

- El avión salió del aeropuerto de San Francisco.
  The plane left the San Francisco airport.

- No sé a qué hora sale el tren de la estación (para Chicago).
  I don't know what time the train leaves the station (for Chicago).

- ¿A qué hora sales de casa? —Siempre salgo de casa a las siete.
  At what time do you leave the house? —I always leave the house at seven.
- Al salir del cine nos encontramos con Carolina.
  On leaving the cinema (or When we came out of the cinema) we met Carolyn.
- El enfermo salió del coma.
  The sick man emerged from a coma.
- A Rosalía no le salió el anillo del dedo.
  Rosalia couldn't take off the ring from her finger.

salirse de algo   to leave sth; to escape from sth

- El combustible (/agua) se sale del tanque.
  The fuel (/water) is escaping from the tank.
- Los pájaros se salieron de la jaula.
  The birds got out of the cage.
- Las naranjas se salían de la bolsa.
  The oranges fell out of the bag.

saltar (a, de, en, por)   to jump (to/into, from, on, out of), leap

- ¿Cuántos metros puedes saltar?
  How many meters can you jump?
- El niño (/sapito) saltó muy alto.
  The child (/frog) jumped (or leaped) very high.
- Las cabras pueden saltar en las rocas.
  The goats can jump on the rocks.
- ¡No salten en el césped!
  Don't jump on the grass!
- El nadador saltó al agua (/al río/a la piscina).
  The swimmer jumped into the water (/river/swimming pool).
- El paracaidista saltó al vacío.
  The parachutist jumped out into the void.
- El chico saltó del trampolín (/del puente/de la silla/de la cama).
  The boy jumped from the diving board (/bridge/chair/leaped out of bed).
- Los niños saltaron de alegría cuando vieron a su mamá.
  The children jumped with joy when they saw their mother.
- El orador (/profesor) saltó de un tema a otro.
  The speaker (/professor) jumped from one subject to another.
- Los paracaidistas saltaron del avión.
  The parachutists jumped from the plane.
- Salté por la ventana.
  I jumped (or leaped) out of a window.

saltàrse   to skip

- Sáltese esa página (/ese párrafo).
  Skip that page (paragraph).

sangrar   to bleed; to tap (*trees*)

- La herida sangraba mucho.
  The wound bled a lot.

- El toro sangró cuando le metieron la espada.
  The bull bled when they stuck the sword in him.

- Sangran el arce (/caucho) para sacar miel (/goma).
  They tap maple (/rubber) trees to get syrup (/rubber).

sangrar de/por algo   to bleed from sth

- Sangraba de (*or* por) la boca (/nariz/rodilla).
  He was bleeding from his mouth (/nose/knee).

- Está sangrando del (*or* por el) hígado (/los intestinos/la úlcera).
  He's bleeding from the liver (/intestines/ulcer).

satisfacer   to satisfy, please

- Les satisface su propuesta.
  Your proposal satisfies them.

- Sus notas los satisficieron plenamente.
  Her grades satisfied (or pleased) them completely.

satisfacerse con algo   to be satisfied with sth

- Me satisfago con poca comida (/poco dinero/mucho cariño).
  I am satisfied with a little food (/little money/lot of affection).

- Los obreros no se satisfacen con sueldos bajos.
  The workers aren't satisfied with low salaries.

- Yo no me satisfago con palabras (/promesas) solamente.
  I am not satisfied with words (/promises) only.

satisfacerse con + *inf*   to be satisfied *or* content to + *inf*

- Ellos se satisfacen con ayudar a la gente de ese país (/con leer novelas).
  They are content to help the people of that country (/to read novels).

- Se satisficieron con mirar las tiras cómicas.
  They were satisfied (or content) to see the comic strips.

secar (con)   to dry, wipe (with)

- Por favor, seca la mesa.
  Please, wipe (or dry) the table.

- Elena secó los platos con el trapo.
  Helen dried the plates with the cloth.
- Ella secaba la ropa en la secadora.
  She was drying the clothes in the dryer.
- La lavadora de platos también seca los platos.
  The dishwasher also dries dishes.

secarse   to dry (up), wipe

- Me secaré al sol después de nadar.
  I'll dry myself in the sun after the swim.
- La mujer se secó las lágrimas con el pañuelo.
  The lady wiped her tears with the handkerchief.
- La pintura se secó en la lata.
  The paint dried up in the can.
- Se le secó el cerebro. (*fig*)
  His brain dried up.

seducir (con)   to seduce (with); to charm, attract, fascinate (with)

- Don Juan seducía a las doncellas.
  Don Juan seduced maidens.
- Enrique seduce a todos con su simpatía (/dinero/fortuna/coche).
  Henry attracts everyone with his charm (/money/fortune/car).
- Hollywood seduce a muchos jóvenes.
  Hollywood seduces (or charms) many young people.
- Su propuesta me (/le) seduce.
  Your proposal fascinates (or intrigues) me (/him).
- El Mar Caribe seduce con sus playas a los turistas.
  The Caribbean Sea attracts (or seduces) tourists with its beaches.

seguir   to follow, pursue, continue

- ¡Sigue este camino hasta la calle Colón!
  Follow this road until you get to Columbus Street.
- No puedo seguir tus instrucciones.
  I can't follow your instructions.
- El muchacho siguió con la mirada a la joven.
  The boy followed (or pursued) the girl with his eyes.
- ¿Dónde sigue este artículo? —En la página 33.
  Where does this article continue? —On page 33.
- Seguimos por la orilla del mar (/un bosque).
  We followed along the sea shore (/side of a forest).

seguir + *adj*   to continue to be + *adj*, go on being + *adj*

- Ella sigue enferma (/enojada/cansada/contenta/sorprendida/enamorada).
  She's still ill (/angry/tired/happy/surprised/in love).

- Si el tiempo sigue mal, no iremos a la playa.
  If the weather stays (or continues to be) bad, we won't go to the beach.

- ¡No sigas tan pesimista (/fastidioso/insistente)!
  Don't continue to be (or go on being) such a pessimist (/so bothersome/so insistent).

seguir en algo   to be still in sth

- Mi padre sigue en su oficina (/trabajo/en Londres/en Madrid).
  My father is still in the office (/the same job/in London/in Madrid).

- Seguimos en problemas (/dificultades).
  We still have problems (/difficulties).

seguir + *ger*   to continue + *ger*, keep (on) + *ger*

- ¿Qué hace tu mamá ahora? —Ella sigue estudiando.
  What is your mother doing? —She's still studying.

- Pedro siguió leyendo (/nadando/comiendo).
  Peter continued reading (/swimming/eating).

seguir sin + *inf*   to be still not + *inf*, be still without sth

- Seguimos sin poder hablar con el director.
  We are still unable to talk to the director.

- El problema no es difícil, pero él sigue sin comprenderlo.
  The problem is not difficult, and yet he still doesn't understand it.

- Son las nueve y seguimos sin comer nada.
  It's nine o'clock, and we still haven't eaten.

- Mi tío sigue sin trabajar (/vender la casa).
  My uncle is still without a job (/has not yet sold the house).

semejarse a uno/a algo   to be like sb/sth, resemble sb/sth

- Esta figura se semeja a un elefante (/a una torre).
  This figure looks like an elephant (/a tower).

- La crisis económica actual se semeja a la de los años treinta.
  The current economic crisis resembles that of the thirties.

- Su conducta se semeja a la de su padre.
  His behavior is like his father's.

sentar (en)   to seat (on), sit; to suit, become; to fit

- Ellos lo sentaron en una silla.
  They seated him on a chair.

- Ese sombrero (/El amarillo/Ese vestido) te sienta muy bien.
  That hat (/Yellow/That dress) suits you very well.

- Te sienta mal esa actitud.
  That attitude is not becoming of you.

- Me sienta bien el pantalón, pero el abrigo me queda demasiado pequeño.
  The pants look good on me, but the coat is too small.

- La leche (/La comida picante) me sienta siempre mal.
  Milk (/Spicy food) always disagrees (or never sits well) with me.

sentarse (en) to sit (down) (on)

- Me senté en una silla (/en el sofá/en la alfombra/en el suelo).
  I sat down on a chair (/the sofa/the rug/the floor).

- Pepe se sentó enfrente (/detrás) de mí.
  Pepe sat (down) in front of (/behind) me.

sentarse a + *inf* to sit (down) to + *inf*

- Nos sentamos a comer uvas.
  We sat down to eat grapes.

- Debemos sentarnos juntos a discutir el problema.
  We must sit down together to discuss the problem.

- Quiero sentarme contigo a jugar una partida de ajedrez.
  I would like to sit down with you to play a game of chess.

sentir + *noun* (algo) to feel, sense (*N.B. This verb requires nominal complements in Spanish which are translated in certain contexts as adjectives in English; see also* **sentirse** *below.*)

- Yo siento hambre (/calor/frío/sed).
  I feel hungry (/warm/cold/thirsty).

- La madre ha sentido el dolor del hijo.
  The mother has felt (or sensed) the pain of her son.

- Sin sentir el frío, los muchachos siguieron jugando afuera.
  Without feeling the cold, the boys continued playing outside.

- ¡Lo siento (muchísimo)!
  I'm (very) sorry!

sentirse + *adj* to feel + *adj*

- Me siento alegre (/triste/feliz/deprimida/pesimista/obligada/enferma/mal/bien).
  I feel happy (/sad/happy/depressed/pessimistic/obligated/sick/bad/well).

- El niño siente calor, pero se siente bien.
  The child feels warm, but he feels well.

- Cecilia no se sentía feliz cuando trabajaba durante la noche.
  Cecilia wasn't happy when she was working at night.

- Sí, me siento hambriento.
  Yes, I feel famished.

separar   to separate

- Una pared roja separa las dos fábricas.
  A red wall separates the two factories.

- Los gemelos fueron separados cuando murieron los padres.
  The twins were separated when their parents died.

separar de uno/algo   to separate from sb/sth

- El trabajo (/Los viajes) lo separan de su familia.
  His work (/Traveling) keeps him away from his family.

- La receta dice: separar la clara de la yema.
  The recipe says: Separate the egg white from the yolk.

- Separa las papas grandes de las pequeñas.
  Separate the large potatoes from the small ones.

sepultar   to bury, entomb

- El derrumbe ha sepultado a los mineros.
  The landslide has buried the miners.

- La avalancha (de nieve) los sepultó.
  The avalanche (of snow) buried them.

- Ayer sepultaron a mi abuelo.
  Yesterday they buried my grandfather.

ser   to be

- Este señor es español (/inglés/simpático).
  This gentleman is Spanish (/English/very nice).

- ¿Quién es él? —Él es Ricardo.
  Who is he? —He is Richard.

- Son las dos (/Es la una).
  It is two (/one) o'clock.

- Era difícil aprender ruso.
  It was difficult to learn Russian.

- Es feliz (/feo).
  He is a happy (/an ugly) person.

ser de uno/algo   to be from sth, come from sth; to be (made) of sth; to belong to sb/sth; to be (written) by sb/sth

- ¿De dónde eres? —Soy de Francia (/Costa Rica/los Estados Unidos).
  Where are you from? —I'm from France (/Costa Rica/the United States).

- Esta cosa es de madera (/piedra/metal/plástico).
  This thing is made of wood (/stone/metal/plastic).

■ ¿De quién es este libro? —El libro es de la biblioteca.
Whose book is this? —The book belongs to the library.

■ ¿Quién escribió este libro? —Es de Cervantes.
Who wrote this book? —It was written by Cervantes.

■ Su hija se ha ido de la casa. ¿Qué será de ella?
Their daughter has run away from home. What will become of her?

■ Esa manera de hablar no es de una dama bien educada.
Such talk does not befit (or is not for) a well-bred lady.

ser de + *inf*   to be + *ptp*

■ Es de creer que el volcán hará erupción en un futuro cercano.
It may be assumed that the volcano will erupt again in the near future.

■ Es de esperar que así sea (/que el dinero llegue a tiempo).
It is to be hoped that it will be so (/that the money will arrive on time).

ser para uno/algo   to be for sb/sth

■ ¿De quién es esta carta? —Esta carta es para mí (/para tu padre).
For whom is this letter? —This letter is for me (/for your father).

■ El primer premio (/El trofeo/El dinero/La gloria) era para mi primo.
The first prize (/trophy/money/glory) went to my cousin.

■ Este cuchillo es para todo fin.
This knife is (good) for many purposes.

ser para + *inf*   to be for + *ger*

■ Esto es para comer (/beber/limpiar el auto).
This is for eating (/drinking/cleaning the car).

servir   to serve; to be of use *or* service

■ ¿Qué les sirvieron ustedes a los invitados? —Les servimos vino (/carne).
What did you serve the guests? —We served them wine (/meat).

■ Los camareros (/restaurantes) de la isla no sirven bien.
The waiters (/restaurants) on the island don't serve well.

■ El esclavo sirvió a su amo.
The slave served his master.

■ Los jóvenes no querían servir a la patria durante la guerra.
The young people did not want to serve the country in war.

■ Sírvase carne (/frutas/bebidas), por favor.
Help yourself to meat (/fruit/drinks), please.

■ ¿En qué puedo servirle? —¡Tráigame una cerveza!
In what way can I be of service to you? —Bring me a beer.

■ No se puede servir a Dios y al diablo. (*prov*)
You can't serve God and the devil at the same time.

- Esta cámara (/Esta máquina de escribir/Este cortacésped/Eso) no sirve.
  This camera (/This typewriter/This lawn mower/That) is no good.

servir de algo   to be used as sth

- Estas cajas sirven de mesa de noche.
  These boxes are used for nightstands.
- Este palo me sirve de bastón.
  I use this stick as a cane.
- Su casa también le sirve de oficina.
  He also uses his house as an office.

servir de uno   to serve as sb/sth

- Daniel sirvió de guía (/intérprete/director del departamento).
  Daniel served as a guide (/an interpreter/head of the department).

servir para uno/algo   to be good for sb/sth

- No sirve para nada que te pongas a llorar.
  It doesn't do any good for you to start crying.
- Él sólo sirve para soldado (/guerrillero/alboratador).
  He is only good as a soldier (/guerrilla/troublemaker).

servir para + *inf*   to be used to + *inf*, be used for + *ger*

- Esta máquina sirve para limpiar paredes.
  This machine is used to clean walls.
- Esta herramienta sirve para sacar y poner tornillos.
  This tool is used for driving in and taking out screws.

servirse de algo   to make use of sth, use sth

- Me serví de una piedra para abrir la puerta.
  I made use of a rock in order to open the door.
- La secretaria se sirvió de mi diccionario para poder traducir la carta.
  The secretary made use of my dictionary to translate the letter.
- Nos servimos de la influencia política de su familia para sacarlo del problema.
  We made use of his family's political influence to get him out of the problem.

significar   to mean

- ¿Qué significa esta palabra (/esta oración/este signo)?
  What does this word (/sentence/sign) mean?
- Este programa significará nuestro éxito.
  This program will mean our success.
- Lo que ese hombre dice no debe significar gran cosa en nuestra relación.
  What that man says should not mean much in our relationship.

simpatizar   to like

- Usted me simpatiza. Yo le simpatizo.
  I like you. He likes me.

simpatizar con uno   to get on well with sb, hit it off with sb

- Pedro simpatizó con usted.
  Peter hit it off with you.

- Roberto siempre simpatizaba con el candidato del partido perdedor.
  Robert always liked the losing party's candidate.

- Nos gusta simpatizar con todos.
  We like to get along well with everybody.

situar   to place, put, locate

- Nuestra casa está situada en un buen barrio.
  Our house is located in a nice neighborhood.

- Sitúan su nacimiento a principios del siglo XIII.
  They place his birth at the beginning of the 13th century.

- Este triunfo lo sitúa entre los mejores equipos de la liga.
  This victory places (or puts) it among the best teams in the league.

sobreponer (en)   to put on top (of), superimpose (on), add (to); to overcome

- Van a sobreponer otro piso en mi casa.
  They're going to put another floor on (or add another floor to) my house.

- Sobreponga estos libros en aquellas cajas.
  Put these books on top of those boxes.

- Sobrepusimos tejas en techo metálico.
  We put tiles on top of the metal roof.

sobreponerse a uno/a algo   to overcome sb/sth

- Ellos se sobrepusieron a todos los obstáculos que se presentaron en el negocio.
  They overcame all the obstacles that came up in their business.

- Le dijeron que tenía cáncer (/una enfermedad rara), pero se sobrepuso a la situación.
  They told him that he had cancer (/a rare disease), but he overcame the condition.

- El país (/pueblo) se sobrepuso a los problemas causados por el terremoto.
  The country (/people) overcame the problems caused by the earthquake.

- El personaje de la novela se sobrepuso a su rival (/estado nervioso).
  The character in the novel triumphed over his rival (/got over his nervous condition).

soler + *inf*   to be in the habit of + *ger*, be accustomed to + *ger*; to usually + *inf* (This is a defective verb; it lacks several tenses)

- Suelo pasar el sábado por el parque.
  I usually go to the park on Saturday.

- Pepe suele llegar tarde (/temprano).
  Pepe usually (or generally or often) arrives late (/early).

- No suelo beber alcohol (/cerveza/leche/vino) con las comidas.
  I usually don't drink alcohol (/beer/milk/wine) with meals.

- Los escandinavos suelen ser rubios.
  Scandinavians are usually blond.

- En este país suele hacer mucho frío durante el invierno.
  It is generally very cold in the winter in this country.

- El jefe suele trabajar muy tarde en su oficina.
  The boss frequently (or usually) works late in his office.

solicitar (sobre)   to ask for, request (about)

- Solicitó información sobre un plan de viajes.
  He asked for information about travel plans.

- Solicitó su retiro.
  He requested his retirement.

solicitar algo a uno   to ask sb for sth, request sth of sb

- Le solicité que llegara más temprano.
  I asked him to arrive earlier.

- Le solicitamos muy respetuosamente que aclarara sus palabras.
  We respectfully requested that he clarify his words.

- El gobierno solicita a todos comprensión.
  The government is asking everyone for understanding.

- Nos solicitó paciencia.
  He asked us to be patient.

someter   to subdue, put down; to submit

- El gobierno de ese país sometió a los rebeldes.
  The government of that country subdued (or put down) the rebels.

- Los incas sometieron a los chancas.
  The Incas subdued (or subjugated) the Chancas.

- Someteremos el informe a la aprobación (*or* consideración) del comité.
  We will submit the report for approval by the committee.

someterse a algo   to submit to sth

- Nos sometimos a su voluntad.
  We submitted to his will.

- Se sometió a las reglas del club.
  He followed the club's regulations.

- Ester fue sometida a un tratamiento contra la rabia.
  Esther submitted to (or underwent) a treatment for rabies.

sonar   to ring; to sound; to play, blow (*instrument*)

- Mi reloj sonó a las seis, pero yo no me levanté.
  My clock rang at six, but I didn't get up.
- Suenan las campanas de la iglesia.
  The bells of the church are chiming (or ringing).
- No me suena bien esa construcción.
  That construction does not sound right to me.
- En español la hache no suena; es muda.
  In Spanish the letter h is not pronounced; it is silent.
- Su nombre suena en los altos círculos sociales.
  Her name resounds (or is well-known) in high society.
- Ese nombre me suena. Lo he oído antes.
  That name rings a bell (or sounds familiar). I've heard it before.

sonreír   to smile at/on

- Me sonrió cuando la vi pasar.
  She smiled at me when I saw her go by.
- Le sonríe el porvenir (la vida/la fortuna).
  The future (/Life/Fortune) smiles on him.

soñar   to dream

- Usualmente no sueño por la noche.
  Usually I don't dream at night.
- Pablo siempre sueña despierto durante la clase.
  Paul always daydreams in class.
- Mi esposo soñaba que estaba despierto.
  My husband dreamed that he was awake.

soñar con uno/algo   to dream about/of sb/sth

- Soñé contigo (/con un televisor/con alguien) anoche.
  I dreamed about you (/a television set/someone) last night.
- Soñaba con un carro deportivo.
  He dreamed of (having) a sports car.
- ¡Sueña con los angelitos! (*fig*)
  Have sweet dreams.
- ¿Con qué soñaste anoche? —Soñé que estaba casada (/que me ahogaba).
  What did you dream last night? —I dreamed I was married (/was drowning).
- Es importante que los jóvenes sueñen con un futuro mejor.
  It is important that the young people dream of a better future.

soñar con + *inf*   to dream about/of + *ger*

- Sueño con ir a París. (*fig*)
  I dream of going to Paris.

- Soñaba con ser médico (/piloto), pero no pude estudiar. *(fig)*
  I used to dream of being (or becoming) a doctor (/pilot), but I could not study.

- Soñaba con trabajar en teatro. *(fig)*
  She used to dream about working in theater.

soplar   to blow

- El viento siempre sopla en las praderas.
  It's always windy on the prairies.

- El lobo sopló con fuerza y la casa del cerdito se derrumbó.
  The wolf blew hard, and the little pig's house fell down.

- Soplé el polvo que estaba en la mesa.
  I blew the dust which was on the table.

soplar a uno   to whisper to sb

- Como yo no sabía la respuesta, mi compañero me la soplaba.
  Since I didn't know the answer, my classmate whispered it to me.

- Le soplaron unos chismes antipáticos.
  They told (or whispered to) her some unpleasant gossip.

sorprender   to surprise, astonish, catch unaware

- Lo sorprendieron robando (/escapando/corriendo).
  They surprised (or caught) him stealing (/escaping/running).

- Me sorprende su actitud (/dolor/respuesta).
  His attitude (/pain/answer) surprises me.

- El ruido nos sorprendió.
  The noise took us by surprise (or caught us unaware).

sospechar   to suspect

- Sospecho que no se quieren como parece.
  I suspect that they do not love each other as they appear to.

- Su manera de hablar nos hace sospechar que lo sabe todo.
  The way he talks makes us suspect that he knows everything.

sospechar de uno/algo   to suspect sb/sth, be suspicious of sb/sth

- Los detectives sospechan del portero (/marido).
  The detectives are suspicious of the doorman (/the husband).

- Él sospecha de su esposa (/de ti/de él/de todos).
  He is suspicious of (or suspects) his wife (/you/him/everybody).

sostener   to hold up, support

- El cinturón le sostiene el pantalón.
  The belt holds (or keeps) his pants up.

- Sólo el ejército sostenía al dictador en el poder.
  Only the army kept the dictator in power.
- Él siempre sostiene sus principios.
  He always supports his principles.
- El padre la sostiene en la universidad.
  The father supports her at the university.

subir   to go up, climb; to raise

- Los precios han subido mucho.
  Prices have gone up a lot.
- Están subiendo la montaña.
  They are climbing the mountain.
- La deuda exterior ha subido tremendamente.
  The foreign debt has gone up (or risen) tremendously.
- Subió la cabeza y bajó los brazos.
  He raised his head and lowered his arms.
- El caudal del río ha subido por las fuertes lluvias.
  The level of the river has risen because of the heavy rains.

subir a algo   to climb (into/to) sth, go up to sth; to put sth in/on

- Mis amigos subieron las maletas al (*or* en el) autobús (/al coche/al tren).
  My friends put the suitcases on the bus (/car/train).
- Por favor, sube mi maletín al apartamento (/a mi habitación).
  Please carry my briefcase up to the apartment (/my room).
- Debemos subir en ascensor al quinto piso.
  We have to go up to the fifth floor in the elevator.
- Ellos subieron al árbol más alto (/al tejado).
  The children climbed the tallest tree (/on the roof).
- Subieron a la torre (/a la cima).
  They climbed the tower (/to the top).

subirse   to go up, climb

- Me subí al (*or* en el) techo de la casa (/a un árbol).
  I climbed on the roof of the house (/a tree).
- Se me subió la presión.
  My blood pressure went up.

suceder   (*impersonal*) to happen

- ¿Qué sucede? —Nada de particular.
  What's going on? —Nothing special.
- Lo que sucede es que no podemos hacerlo sin tu ayuda.
  The fact is that we cannot do it without your help.

- Sucederán muchas cosas extrañas.
  Many strange things will happen.
- Sucedió un accidente muy serio.
  A very serious accident happened (or occurred).

suceder a uno/en algo   to succeed to sb/sth, follow sb/sth

- Después de su muerte, su hija la sucedió en el trono.
  After her death, her daughter succeeded her to the throne.
- ¿Quién te sucedió en el puesto?
  Who succeeded you on the job?
- El rey Daniel sucedió en la lucha.
  King Daniel succeeded (or followed) his father in the struggle.
- El vice-presidente lo sucedió en la presidencia.
  The vice-president succeeded him in the presidency.
- El senador Pérez la sucederá en el ministerio.
  Senator Perez will succeed her in the ministry.

suceder con uno/algo   to happen to sb/sth

- Una cosa extraña sucedió con Pedro.
  A strange thing happened to Peter.
- Suceden con ellos tres desgracias.
  Three unfortunate events are happening to them.
- Sucederá con Luisa lo que con María.
  The same thing that happened to Louise will happen to Mary.

sufrir (de)   suffer (from)

- Hay minorías que han sufrido muchas persecuciones.
  There are minorities who have suffered many persecutions.
- Deben sufrir las consecuencias de los hechos.
  They have to suffer the consequences of their actions.
- Mi tío sufrió un ataque de asma (/de corazón).
  My uncle suffered an asthma (/a heart) attack.
- Sufre mucho de angina de pecho (/de jaquecas/de asma/de artritis).
  He suffers from angina pectoris (/migraine headaches/asthma/arthritis).
- Sufro de los nervios (/los pulmones/los ojos).
  I suffer from nerves (/lung disease/eye trouble).
- Mi esposa sufre todavía de su accidente.
  My wife is still suffering from her accident.

sugerir   suggest

- He sugerido tres buenas ideas.
  I have suggested three good ideas.

- Esa película me sugirió malos pensamientos.
  That film suggested bad thoughts to me.

- Yo le sugerí que no viniera.
  I suggested to him not to come.

sugerir + *inf*   to suggest + *ger*

- El médico sugiere operar la pierna (/sugiere hacer más ejercicio).
  The doctor suggests operating on the leg (/suggests doing more exercise).

- ¿Sugieres olvidarla después de tantos años de matrimonio?
  Are you suggesting that I forget her after so many years of marriage?

sugerir a uno/a algo   to suggest to sb/sth

- Sugerí al comité (/al gobierno/al presidente/al gabinete) que no lo hiciera.
  I suggested to the committee (/government/president/cabinet) not to do it.

- Sugería a mi esposa (/padre/hermano) que no lo hiciera.
  I was suggesting to my wife (/father/brother) not to do it.

sumir en algo   to sink *or* submerge in sth, plunge into sth

- Sumió la piedra (/la olla/los pies) en el agua.
  He sank (or submerged) the stone (/cooking pot/his feet) in the water.

- La muerte de su padre lo sumió en una depresión (/en un pesimismo). (*fig*)
  The death of his father plunged him into depression (/pessimism).

sumirse (en)   to become absorbed (in), dedicate oneself (to), be overwhelmed (by)

- El artista siempre se sumía en su obra cuando trabajaba. (*fig*)
  The artist always became absorbed in his work when he worked.

- Se sumió en el estudio (/la meditación/la desesperación).
  He dedicated himself entirely to his studies (/meditation/was overwhelmed by desperation).

suplir (con)   to supply; to substitute, replace (by)

- Él suplió los ingredientes con algunas otras cosas (/aceite/grasa animal).
  He replaced the ingredients with some other things (/oil/animal fat).

- Suplimos con ingenio lo que no teníamos.
  We supplied (or substituted) what we did not have with ingenuity.

suplir a/por uno/algo   to replace sb/sth, substitute for sb/sth

- El entrenador tiene que suplir al jugador lesionado.
  The coach has to replace the injured player.

- Vamos a suplir a la nueva mecanógrafa por otra más eficiente.
  We are going to replace the typist with a more efficient one.

- Te (/Le) supliremos por tu hermano.
  We'll substitute you (/him) for your brother.

suponer   to suppose, assume

- ¡Supongamos que vamos a ganar (/a hacerlo a tiempo)!
  Let's suppose that we are going to win (/to do it on time).

- No supongas nada. ¡Pregunta primero!
  Don't assume anything; ask first!

- Supongo que Teresa tiene veinte años.
  I suppose (or I would say) that Teresa is twenty years old.

surgir (de)   to arise, emerge (from)

- Surgió un problema. (*fig*)
  A problem arose.

- ¿Surgió el hombre de la nada?
  Did man emerge (or arise) from nothing?

- Los submarinos surgieron del fondo del mar.
  The submarines emerged from the bottom of the sea.

- El agua surgió de la fuente.
  The water emerged from the fountain.

suscribir (a)   to sign; to agree to, ratify; to subscribe (to)

- Te (/Le) suscribí a un nuevo periódico (/una revista).
  I subscribed to a new newspaper (/a magazine) for you (/him).

- No suscribimos esas ideas radicales.
  We don't subscribe to those radical ideas.

- Todos los representantes suscribieron el contrato.
  All the representatives signed (or agreed to or ratified) the contract.

suspender   to suspend; to fail

- El mago suspendió a la niña en el aire.
  The magician suspended the child in the air.

- Suspendió el año escolar.
  He failed the school year.

- Vamos a suspender el proyecto hasta nuevo aviso.
  We are going to put off (or suspend) the project until further notice.

suspender de algo   to suspend from sth; to hang from sth; to fail

- El entrenador lo suspendió del equipo.
  The coach suspended him from the team.

- La van a suspender del colegio.
  They are going to suspend her from school.

- Suspenden la maceta de una argolla.
  They hang the flower pot from a large ring.

- El jefe los suspendió del trabajo.
  The boss suspended them from work.

■ El trapecista la levantó de las manos.
The trapeze artist lifted her by her hands.

suspenderse (de)   to be suspended (from); to hang (from); to pull up

■ La reunión se suspendió.
The meeting was suspended.

■ El niño se suspendía de una rama.
The child was hanging from a branch.

■ La araña se suspende de un hilo.
The spider hangs from a web.

suspirar   to sigh

■ Cuando se está enamorado uno suspira con frecuencia.
When one is in love, one sighs frequently.

■ ¡Deja de suspirar!
Stop sighing!

suspirar de/por algo   to long for sth; to sigh for sth

■ Juan suspira de amor.
John is sighing with (or longs for) love!

■ Suspiro por la playa y el sol.
I long for the beach and the sun.

suspirar por + *inf*   to long to + *inf*

■ Supiro por vivir en un palacio (/por verte/por besarte).
I long to live in a palace (/to see you/to kiss you).

sustentarse con/de algo   to sustain oneself with sth, subsist on sth

■ Me sustento con poca comida (/con sólo vegetales/con poco dinero).
I subsist on little food (/only vegetables/little money).

■ Mi espíritu se sustenta de optimismo (/esperanzas/paz).
My spirit sustains itself on optimism (/hope/peace).

sustituir (por)   to substitute (for), replace (with)

■ El entrenador lo sustituyó porque jugaba mal.
The coach replaced him because he was playing poorly.

■ Queremos sustituir este juguete por otro.
We want to replace this toy with another.

■ La gente quiso sustituir el gobierno tiránico por uno democrático.
People wanted to replace the despotic government with a democratic one.

■ Sustituyó la camisa por el suéter.
She substituted the shirt for the sweater.

■ Voy a sustituir el café por el té.
I'm going to substitute coffee for tea.

- Lo sustituimos por otro empleado.
  We substituted him for another employee.

susurrar   to whisper

- Me susurró su nombre al oído.
  He whispered his name into my ear.
- "La fuente susurra sueños." (*poetic: from Antonio Machado*)
  The fountain whispers dreams.

T

taladrar (en)   to bore, drill (in), pierce

- Taladré dos agujeros en la madera (/el metal/la pared).
  I drilled two holes in the wood (/metal/wall).
- Esta música me (/le) taladra los oídos. (*fig*)
  This music is piercing my (/his) ears.

tallar (en)   to carve; to cut (*jewel*)

- El artista talló el cuerpo de un niño en madera (/piedra).
  The artist carved the body of a child in wood (/stone).
- El joyero talló el diamante para engarzarlo en el anillo.
  The jeweler cut the diamond to set it in a ring.

tapar (con)   to cover (with), cover up

- Tapé la olla.
  I covered the pan (cooking pot).
- Tapaba la caja con un libro (/el hoyo con cemento).
  I was covering the box with a book (/the hole with cement).
- Ella le tapó la cara al niño con un pañuelo.
  She covered the child's face with a handkerchief.

tardar   to take a long time, be long; to be late

- No voy a tardar mucho.
  I won't be too late.
- ¿Cuántos días tardará esta obra? —Tardará tres días.
  How many days will this work take? —It will take three days.
- El avión (de San José a Miami) tarda dos horas y media.
  The plane (from San José to Miami) takes two and a half hours.

tardar en + *inf*   to take (*time*) to + *inf*, be late (to delay) in + *inf*

- Carlos (/El taxi/El avión) tarda en llegar.
  Carl (/The taxi/The plane) is late in arriving.

- ¿Cuánto vas a tardar en escribirme? —No voy a tardar mucho.
  How long are you going to take to write me? —I am not going to delay too long.

- Sólo tardaré dos horas en pintar la mesa (/en hacer la obra).
  I will take only two hours to paint the table (/to do the work).

tasar (en)   to fix a price for, price (at); to value, appraise (at)

- Mañana van a venir a tasar la casa.
  Tomorrow they are going to come to appraise the house.

- Van a tasar los productos de exportación.
  They are going to fix (or regulate) the prices of products for export.

- Tasaremos la joya en su valor verdadero.
  We'll price the jewel at its true (or exact) value.

telefonear   to telephone, phone

- ¿Telefoneaste a Teresa? —Sí, le telefoneé anoche.
  Did you call Teresa? —Yes, I called her last night.

- Voy a telefonearle a mi mamá (/papá/familia).
  I am going to phone my mom (/dad/family).

- Voy a telefonearle un mensaje urgente.
  I am going to phone this urgent message to him.

telegrafiar   to telegraph, wire

- Mi papá me telegrafió un saludo por el día de mi cumpleaños.
  My dad wired me greetings for my birthday.

- Voy a telegrafiarle los resultados del partido.
  I am going to wire him the results of the game.

temblar (de)   to tremble, shake (with)

- Durante el terremoto todas las casas temblaban.
  All the houses were shaking in the earthquake.

- Temblaba de frío y de fiebre porque sufría un ataque de malaria.
  He trembled with cold and fever because he was experiencing a malaria attack.

- Yo temblé de miedo (/emoción/entusiasmo) cuando lo vi.
  I trembled with fright (/excitement/enthusiasm) when I saw him.

temer   to fear, be afraid of

- No le temo a nada; temo sólo a Dios (/a mi jefe).
  I don't fear anything; I only fear God (/my boss).

- ¡No temas, Rosita!
  Don't be afraid, Rose!

- Tememos que no nos pague (/que no vaya a llegar pronto).
  We are afraid he won't pay us (/he is not going to arrive soon).

temer por algo   to fear for, be afraid for

- La policía teme por la seguridad del testigo (/político).
  The police fear for the witness' (/politician's) safety.
- Tememos por su salud (/su estado emocional).
  We fear for his health (/his emotional state).

temerse   to be afraid

- Me temo que no voy a poder asistir a la fiesta.
  I'm afraid that I won't be able to attend the party.
- Se teme que volverá de nuevo.
  It's feared (or He fears) that it will return again.

tender (sobre)   to spread (over), spread out, hang out

- ¡Tienda la ropa para que se seque!
  Spread (or hang) out the clothes so they will dry.
- Mi madre tendió el mantel sobre la mesa.
  My mother spread the tablecloth over the table.

tender a algo   to tend toward sth, have a tendency towards sth

- El tiende a carpintero (/médico).
  He leans towards carpentry (/medicine).
- Mi hermana (/Su pronóstico) tiende al optimismo.
  My sister (/His prediction) has a tendency to be optimistic.

tender a + *inf*   to tend to + *inf*

- El alumno tiende a ser perezoso (/a dormir cuando se enoja).
  The student tends to be lazy (/tends to sleep when he's mad).

tenderse en algo   to lie down on sth, stretch out on sth

- Estábamos tan casados que nos tendimos en el césped.
  We were so tired we lay down on the grass.
- Me tendí en el piso.
  I stretched out on the floor.

tener   to have; to be + *adj (idiomatic)*

- Tengo mucho dinero (/dos coches/tres perros/dos libros).
  I have a lot of money (/two cars/three dogs/two books).
- Tengo mucha hambre (/mucha sed/mucho calor/mucho frío).
  I am very hungry (/thirsty/warm/cold).
- No tiene cuidado cuando lava los platos.
  He's not careful when he washes the dishes.

- No tiene miedo de nadie.
  He's not afraid of anybody.

- Él tiene razón (/vergüenza/suerte).
  He's right (/ashamed/lucky).

tener a uno por + *adj*   to think sb + *adj*, consider sb to be + *adj*

- Me (/Le) tiene por borracho (/tonto/pobre/bruto).
  He considers me (/him) to be a drunk (/a fool/poor/stupid).

- No quiero que me tenga por incumplido.
  I don't want you to think me unreliable.

tener que + *inf*   to have to + *inf*, must + *inf*

- Tengo que ir (/hablarle/comer) de todas maneras.
  I have to go (/speak to him/eat) in any case.

- Pablo ha tenido que comprarlo (/venderlo/pintarlo).
  Paul has had to buy it (/sell it/paint it).

tenerse por + *adj*   to consider oneself to be + *adj*, think oneself + *adj*

- Elena se tiene por muy bonita (/lista/elegante/popular).
  Helen considers herself pretty (/smart/elegant/popular).

- Se tiene por una persona muy importante.
  He considers himself to be very important.

tentar   to touch, feel; to tempt, lure

- Ella tentaba la pared en la oscuridad para encontrar el interruptor de la luz.
  She felt (or touched) the wall in the darkness in order to find the light switch.

- Mira, la idea (/la oferta) no me tienta nada.
  Look, the idea (/the offer) doesn't tempt me at all.

- La tentó el demonio (/el dinero/la envidia).
  The devil (/money/envy) tempted her.

tentar + *inf*   to try to + *inf*

- Tentó comer pero no pudo.
  He tried to eat but couldn't.

- Tenté pararme y me sentí débil.
  I tried to stand up, and I felt weak.

tentar a + *inf*   to tempt to + *inf*

- ¡Tiéntanos a hacerlo y vas a ver!
  Tempt us to do it, and you'll see!

- ¡No me tientes a hablar sobre lo que no quiero!
  Don't (try to) tempt me to talk about something I don't want to.

teñir (con, de, en)   to dye (with, in, of)

- Me voy a teñir el pelo.
  I am going to dye my hair.
- El cuero se tiñe con tintes.
  Leather is dyed (or stained) with dyes.
- Teñí mi suéter (/falda) de verde.
  I dyed my sweater (/skirt) green.
- Voy a teñir esta camisa blanca en verde.
  I'm going to dye this white shirt red.

terminar (en)   to conclude, end; to finish (in), complete

- La clase (/escuela/reunión) terminó temprano.
  The class (/school/meeting) ended (or finished) early.
- Voy a terminar mis estudios (/mi libro) en abril.
  I'm going to finish (or complete) my studies (/my book) in April.

termirar + *ger*   to finish (by) + *ger*, end up + *ger*

- Mi colega terminó yéndose a China.
  My colleague ended up going to China.
- Él terminó diciendo que no podían concluirlo (/comprarlo) a tiempo.
  He finished by saying that they were not able to finish (/buy) it on time.

terminar de + *inf*   to finish + *ger*

- No ha terminado de comer (/escribir/ayudarme).
  He hasn't finished eating (/writing/helping me).
- Cuando termine de bañarse (/de explicarlo) va a llamarte.
  When he finishes bathing (/discussing it), he's going to call you.

terminar en algo   to end in sth

- La discusión terminó en nada.
  The discussion resulted in nothing.
- La carretera termina en una curva.
  The highway ends in a curve.
- Creo que sus amores terminarán en tragedia.
  I think their love will end in tragedy.

tesar   to tauten, tighten (up)

- Tesaron los alambres eléctricos.
  They tautened the electric wires.
- Voy a tesar las cuerdas que sostienen la carpa.
  I'm going to tighten the ropes which hold the tent.

testificar   to testify, give evidence

- ¿Vas a testificar ante el juez?
  Are you going to testify before the judge?

- Testificaron contra (/por) el acusado.
  They testified against (/for) the accused.

tildar a uno de + *adj*   to brand sb as (being) + *adj*

- Me (/Le) tildaron de delicuente (/de vagabundo).
  They branded me (/him) as a criminal (/as a bum).

- Mi padre tildó a mi novia de ambiciosa.
  My father branded my girlfriend as being ambitious.

timar   to swindle sb (out of), cheat

- No tengo dinero porque me timaron.
  I don't have money because they swindled me.

- ¡Cuidado te timan con el viejo truco del cheque!
  Be careful! They will cheat you with the old check trick.

- Me timó con mucha habilidad.
  He swindled me with skill.

tirar   to throw (away); to hurl, fling; to sling; to spill; to shoot, fire

- Los alumnos tiraron los papeles.
  The students threw (or flung) the papers.

- El niño tiró la leche (/el agua).
  The child spilled the milk (/water).

- Tiraron un cañonazo (/un balazo).
  They fired a cannon (/a bullet).

- Desgraciadamente su hijo está tirando su fortuna (/dinero). (*fig*)
  Unfortunately, his son is throwing away his fortune (/money).

- No tires tu dinero, ¡ahórralo!
  Don't throw away your money; save it!

- Este televisor (/Esta fruta/Este abrigo) está para tirarlo.
  This television set (/fruit/coat) is ready to be thrown away.

- ¿Le tiraste un beso a tu novia? —Sí, le tiré un beso. (*fig*)
  Did you throw a kiss at your girlfriend? —Yes, I threw her a kiss.

- Me tiró un puñetazo.
  He threw a punch at me.

tirar a uno/a algo   to tend toward sb/sth; to take after sb/sth; to throw to sb/sth; to shoot at sb/sth, fire at/on sth

- Gloria tira más a su madre (/tía). (*fig*)
  Gloria takes more after her mother (/aunt).

- Esta camisa (/Este color) tira a amarillo. (*fig*)
  This shirt (/color) tends toward yellow.

- Mi tía tira a gorda (/tacaña/flaca). (*fig*)
  My aunt is (or tends to be) rather fat (/stingy/skinny).

- Le tiramos la moneda al mendigo.
  We threw the coin to the beggar.

- Los chicos tiraron la piedra a la ventana (/al hombre/a la puerta).
  The boys threw the rock at the window (/man/door).

- Tiramos los libros al suelo (/Los tiramos al suelo).
  We threw the books (/them) on the floor.

- Los cazadores tiraron (con rifles) a los animales.
  The hunters shot at the animals (with rifles).

tirar de algo   to pull sth, tug at sth

- El caballo tira del coche.
  The horse pulls the carriage.

- La locomotora tira de los vagones.
  The locomotive pulls the cars (or wagons).

- El niño tiraba de la falda de la madre.
  The child was tugging at his mother's skirt.

- Le tiró de las orejas.
  She pulled him by the ears.

tirarse a algo   to jump into sth, throw oneself into sth

- Los niños se tiraron al agua (/al río/a la piscina/al suelo).
  The children jumped (or threw themselves) into the water (/the river/the swimming pool/to the ground).

tirarse a + *inf*   to abandon oneself to + *inf*, dedicate oneself to + *ger*

- Me tiré a dormir.
  I abandoned myself to sleep.

- Los terroristas se tiraron a matar.
  The terrorists dedicated themselves to killing.

tirarse de algo   to throw oneself from sth

- Los chicos se tiraron del trampolín (/de la ventana/del techo).
  The boys jumped from the diving board (/window/roof).

- El suicida se tiró del risco (/puente/edificio).
  The suicidal person threw himself from the cliff (/bridge/building).

tirarse en algo   to jump on/with sth

- Estaba muy cansado y me tiré en la cama (/el sofá/el sillón/la hamaca).
  I was very tired, and I plopped myself down on the bed (/sofa/armchair/hammock).

■ Los soldados se tiraron en paracaídas (del avión).
The soldiers parachuted (from the airplane).

tirarse sobre uno/algo   to jump on sb/sth

■ El perro se tiró sobre el ladrón (/gato/cartero).
The dog jumped on the thief (/cat/mailman).

■ Yo me tiré sobre la carga del camión (/las frazadas/los sacos de lana).
I jumped on top of the truck's load (/blankets/bundles of wool).

tocar   to touch, feel; to play (*music*)

■ Anita le tocó la mano (/la camisa/el hombro).
Anita touched him on the (or felt his) hand (/shirt/shoulder).

■ La silla toca la pared.
The chair touches the wall.

■ El profesor no quiso discutir el asunto. Tocó el tema brevemente.
The professor didn't want to discuss the matter. He touched on the idea only briefly.

■ ¿Quién toca a la puerta?
Who's knocking on the door?

■ ¿Cuál instrumento tocas? —Toco la guitarra (/el piano).
Which instrument do you play? —I play the guitar (/piano).

tocar a uno (+ *inf*)   to be one's turn (to + *inf*); to be up to (one's duty) to + *inf*

■ ¿A quién le toca? ¿Me toca a mí? —Sí, creo que (a ti) te toca.
Whose turn is it? Is it my turn? —Yes, I think it is your turn.

■ ¿A quién le toca pagar esta vez las comidas? —A usted le toca.
Whose turn is it to pay this time for the meals? —It is your turn.

■ Me toca trabajar (/estar de guardia/vigilar) esta noche.
It's my turn to work (/to be on duty/to watch) tonight.

■ A él le toca limpiar la casa (/fregar los platos).
It's his turn to clean the house (/wash the dishes).

■ A mí me toca decirle que su abuelo tuvo un accidente.
It's up to me to tell her that her grandfather had an accident.

■ No le tocaba a él (/a Ricardo) hacer este trabajo.
It was not up to him (/Richard) to do this job.

■ Le toca a usted reprenderle por lo que pasó.
It is up to you (or your duty) to reprimand him for what happened.

tocarle a uno   to fall to sb *or* be sb's lot

■ No me tocó ni un centavo de la herencia de mi padre.
Not a penny of my father's inheritance fell to me.

■ La finca les tocó a los tres hijos.
The farm was divided among the three sons.

tolerar   to tolerate, allow; to bear, endure

- Estos pueblos no toleran a nadie (/a extranjeros/las ideas diferentes).
  These towns don't tolerate anyone (/foreigners/different ideas).
- No tolero que mi hijo se comporte así.
  I won't allow my son to behave like that.
- Nosotros no le podemos tolerar tal abuso.
  We can't allow him such abuse (or an imposition).
- Mi estómago no tolera la leche.
  My stomach doesn't tolerate milk.
- No tolera el dolor físico.
  He can't bear (or endure) physical pain.

tomar   to take; to get; to make (*decision*)

- ¿A qué hora vas a tomar el tren (/autobús) a la ciudad?
  What time are you going to take the train (/bus) to the city?
- Tienes que tomar este camino (/esta carretera) para ir al pueblo.
  You have to take this road (/highway) to go to town.
- Mi hermano va a tomar un baño del sol.
  My brother is going to sun himself.
- Ella necesitaba tomar aire (/sol).
  She needed to get air (/sun herself).
- ¿Qué decisión ha tomado él?
  What decision has he made?
- ¿Le has tomado la temperatura a la niña?
  Have you taken the child's temperature?
- El sastre le tomó las medidas para hacerle una chaqueta.
  The tailor took his measurements to make him a jacket.
- Tomaron las armas (/la pluma) contra el tirano.
  They took up arms (/the pen) against the tyrant.
- Ayer tomamos el desayuno (/el té/el café) más tarde.
  Yesterday we had our breakfast (/tea/coffee) later.

tomar por uno   to take for sb

- Me ha tomado por ladrón.
  He has taken me for a thief.
- Lo ha tomado por su hermano.
  He has mistaken him for his brother.
- ¿Por quién me toma usted? Soy la persona más importante de aquí.
  What (or who) do you take me for? I am the most important person here.

tomarse por uno   to think oneself to be sb, take oneself for sb

- ¿Por quién se toma el director (/ese hombre)?
  Who does that director (/that man) think he is?

■ Se toma por una persona muy importante (/por la reina Isabel).
   She thinks she is a very important person (/she is Queen Elizabeth).

topar con (algo)   to run across/into; to butt

■ Buscaba petróleo y toparon con unas ruinas antiguas.
   They were looking for oil, and they ran across some ancient ruins.

■ Como topamos con tantos obstáculos, no continuamos la obra. (*fig*)
   Since we ran into so many obstacles, we didn't finish the job.

■ Cuando caminaba topó con la pared.
   When he was walking, he ran into a wall.

toparse (con uno)   to meet (sb), run across/into sb

■ En la calle me topé con Luis.
   I ran into Louis in the street.

■ Anoche se toparon en la plaza.
   They ran across each other (or *met*) *last night in the square.*

toser   to cough

■ Ella tosía mucho cuando tomaba leche.
   She coughed a lot when she drank milk.

■ Ella tosió en mi cara (/tosió toda la noche).
   She coughed in my face (/coughed all night).

■ Cuando tosas, ¡cúbrete la boca!
   When you cough, cover your mouth!

trabajar   to work

■ ¿Dónde trabajas? —Trabajo en una tienda (/una obra).
   Where do you work? —I work in a store (/on a construction site).

■ Pedro trabajaba como un esclavo (/una bestia/un mulo).
   Peter worked like a slave (/an animal/mule).

■ ¡No trabajes tanto!
   Don't work so hard.

trabajar por + *inf*   to strive to + *inf*, work for the sake of + *ger*

■ Ella trabaja por distinguirse (*or* sobresalir) entre sus colegas.
   She works for the purpose of distinguishing herself among her colleagues.

■ Ella trabaja por ayudar a su gente.
   She works for the sake of helping (or *strives to help*) *her people.*

trabar   to join, unite, link

■ El carpintero trabó una viga con otra.
   The carpenter joined one beam to another.

- El fontanero trabó dos cañerías.
  The plumber joined (or linked) two pipes.
- Los dos hombres trabaron amistad.
  The two men became friends (or united in friendship).

traducir (a, de)   to translate (into, from)

- ¿Quién tradujo la oración? —Pepe la tradujo.
  Who translated the sentence? —Pepe translated it.
- Los misioneros tradujeron el libro (/la Biblia/el ensayo) del latín al español.
  The missionaries translated the book (/Bible/essay) from Latin to Spanish.

traducirse en algo   to result in sth

- Ojalá que los esfuerzos de los trabajadores se traduzcan en mejoras salariales.
  It is hoped that the workers' efforts will result in better salaries.
- El trabajo de los hombres se ha traducido en riqueza.
  The men's work has resulted in wealth.

traer   to bring, get, fetch; to carry, have; to wear

- Le traje un regalo (/una camisa/buenas noticias).
  I brought him a gift (/a shirt/good news).
- ¡Tráigaselo (/Tráigamelo)!
  Bring it to (or Get it for) him (/me)!
- Esta biografía no trae nada importante (/nada sobre su vida íntima).
  This biography doesn't have anything important (/about his intimate life).
- Su llegada (/El regalo) me trajó mala suerte (/felicidades/disgustos).
  His arrival (/The gift) brought me bad luck (/happiness/misfortunes).
- ¿Qué trae Carolina hoy? —Trae un vestido nuevo.
  What is Carolyn wearing? —She's wearing a new dress.

traficar (con, en)   to trade, deal (with in); to traffic

- Ella trafica en drogas (/en lana).
  She traffics (or deals) in drugs (/wool).
- Ellos trafican con su crédito.
  They trade with their credit.

transferir (a, de)   to transfer (to, from)

- El estudiante transfirió su matrícula (/cuenta) a otra universidad (/a otro banco).
  The student transferred his registration (/account) to another university (/bank).
- Me van a transferir de Chile a Guatemala.
  They are going to transfer me from Chile to Guatemala.
- Transfirieron de esta ciudad (/compañía) al Sr. Rodríguez.
  Mr. Rodriguez was transferred from this city (/company).

transigir (con, en cuanto a)   to compromise (with, on/about)

- Los diputados no quisieron transigir en cuanto al presupuesto.
  The congressmen did not want to compromise on the budget.

- Yo no puedo transigir con gente que no cede.
  I cannot compromise with people that do not yield.

- ¡Transijamos para no litigar más!
  Let's compromise in order to stop litigating.

transigir en + *inf*   to agree to + *inf*

- Transigimos en trabajar dos horas más (/en cancelar la deuda vieja).
  We agreed to work two more hours (/to cancelling the old debt).

- Ella transigió en cobrarles sólo la mitad.
  She agreed to charge them only half the price.

transformar en uno/algo   to transform into sb/sth

- Transformamon nuestro garaje en un apartamento.
  They transformed our garage into an apartment.

- Transformaron esta nación atrasada en una potencia industrial.
  They transformed this backward nation into an industrial power.

- El mago transformó un huevo (/a la mujer) en un conejo.
  The magician transformed an egg (/the woman) into a rabbit.

transformarse en uno/algo   to be transformed into sb/sth, change

- El oso se transformó en una bella princesa.
  The bear was transformed into a beautiful princess.

- Ese imperio se transformó en una república.
  That empire was transformed into (or became) a republic.

- Ella se ha transformado. ¡Es tan simpática ahora!
  She has changed. She is so nice now!

transitar por algo   to travel on, go along

- ¡Transitemos silenciosamente por el camino del hospital!
  Let's go quietly along the hospital road.

- Los peatones transitan por la vereda.
  Pedestrians travel (or walk) on the sidewalks.

- Los autos transitan por las carreteras.
  Cars travel on the roads.

transmitir (a)   to transmit (to); to broadcast

- Este cable transmite la electricidad (/Este cable la transmite).
  The cable transmits electricity (/it).

■   Transmitieron los juegos olímpicos (/las señales de radio) a todo el mundo.
They transmitted (or broadcasted) the Olympic games (/radio signals) to the entire world.

■   El mosquito transmite el paludismo.
Mosquitoes transmit malaria.

■   Esta estación de radio transmite sólo noticias.
This radio station only broadcasts news.

transpirar   to perspire

■   Le transpiran las palmas de las manos cuando viaja en avión.
The palms of his hands perspire when he travels by plane.

■   Después de correr, ellos transpiraban mucho.
After running, they were perspiring a lot.

trascender   to smell (of); to emit

■   El bosque trasciende olor a pino.
The forest emits a pine smell (or smells of pine).

■   El rosal trasciende un perfume agradable.
The rose bush emits a pleasant smell.

trascender a uno/a algo   to reach sb/sth; to have an effect on sb/sth

■   Las aventuras del Quijote trascienden a toda la literatura.
The adventures of Don Quixote have an effect on all literature.

■   La influencia del estadista ha trascendido a todos los países (/todo el mundo).
The influence of the statesman has reached (or had an effect on) every country (/everyone).

■   Las ideas del Marxismo han trascendido a varias generaciones.
The ideas of Marxism have reached (or had an effect on) several generations.

traslucirse (de, en)   to be transparent, shine (through)

■   En su cara se traslucía el odio. (*fig*)
Hatred was transparent in his expression.

■   La amargura se traslucía en la expresión de su rostro. (*fig*)
Her bitterness was transparent (or shown) in the expressions of her face.

■   Cierta inseguridad se traslucía de sus ojos. (*fig*)
A certain insecurity shone through her eyes.

trasnochar (en)   to not sleep on, stay up; to spend the night (in)

■   Siempre que tiene examen, trasnocha.
Every time he has an exam, he stays up all night.

■   Trasnochamos en un pueblito pintoresco de la sierra.
We spent the night in a picturesque little mountain town.

■ Trasnochamos porque había una fiesta en casa de los vecinos.
We didn't sleep (or We sat up all night) because there was a party at the neighbor's house.

traspasar   to pierce, penetrate, go through

■ Las balas le traspasaron el cuerpo (/corazón).
The bullets pierced his body (/heart).

■ El agua ha traspasado el techo (/la alfombra).
The water has seeped (or gone) through the roof (/rug).

■ Los exploradores pudieron traspasar el río.
The explorers were able to go across the river.

■ Ese grito me traspasó el oído.
This noise went through my ear.

■ Lo que ha pasado traspasa los límites de lo tolerable.
What has happened surpasses the limits of tolerance.

tratar   to treat, handle

■ ¿Cómo tratan a tu abuelo en ese hospital? —Lo tratan muy bien.
How are they treating your grandfather in that hospital. —They treat him well.

■ Tratamos el asunto (/problema) con cuidado.
We handled the subject (/problem) carefully.

■ Tratamos el metal con ácido nítrico.
We treat this metal with nitric acid.

■ Trataron al criado (/al chico) como a un perro.
They treated the servant (/boy) like a dog.

■ Siempre lo tratan con naturalidad (/cariño/amor).
They always treat him with simplicity (/affection/love).

tratar a uno   to treat sb; to deal with sb

■ Le tratamos (a Juan) desde que tenía 2 años.
We have been dealing with (or known) him (John) for 2 years.

■ Tratamos a Juan desde que era niño.
We have treated (or dealt with) John since he was a child.

■ Hemos tratado a los muchachos desde hace mucho tiempo.
We have dealt with the boys for a long time.

tratar con uno/algo   to associate with sb/sth, deal with sb/sth

■ El lexicógrafo trata con diccionarios.
The lexicographer deals with dictionaries.

■ ¿Con qué trata un geólogo? —Trata con rocas.
What does a geologist deal with? —He deals with rocks.

■ Yo no puedo tratar con personas mal educadas.
I can't have dealings (or deal) with ill-mannered people.

■   Estoy cansado. No quiero tratar ya con este tema (/problema/asunto).
I'm tired. I don't want to have anything more to do with this subject (/problem/matter).

tratar de + *inf*   to try to + *in*

■   Trató de cumplir el trabajo (/hacerlo/nadar/hablarle).
He tried to complete the work (/do it/swim/talk to him).

■   Trató de correr cinco kilómetros (/conducir con cuidado).
He tried to run five kilometers (/to drive carefully).

tratar de/sobre algo   to deal with sth, be about sth; to talk about sth

■   ¿De qué trata este ensayo? —Trata de (or sobre) las leyendas griegas.
What is this essay about? —It is about the Greek legends.

■   Se reúnen hoy para tratar de (*or* sobre) la huelga de mineros.
They're meeting today to talk about the miners' strike.

■   La conferencia trató del (*or* sobre el) origen del universo.
The conference dealt with the origins of the universe.

tratar en algo   to deal in sth (*commercial*)

■   ¿En qué trata el comerciante? —Trata en arroz (/frutas/coches/telas).
What does the merchant deal in? —He deals in rice (/fruits/cars/cloth).

tratar(se) de uno/algo   to be a question of sth; to deal with sth; to call by sth

■   ¿De qué se trata el artículo? —Se trata de la nueva biblioteca.
What does the article deal with? —It's about the new library.

■   En la oficina (/universidad) nos tratamos de usted (/a veces de tú).
At the office (/university) we are on "usted" (/sometimes on "tú") terms (or on a first name basis).

■   Si usted me permite, lo voy a tratar de tú.
If you'll permit me, I will call you by your first name.

■   La novela se trata de la vida de una mujer del siglo XVIII.
The novel deals with the life of a woman in the 18th century.

■   Si se trata de dinero, yo no puedo ayudar.
If it is a question of money, I can't help.

tratarse de + *inf*   to be a question of + *ger*

■   Se trata de conseguir una beca.
It's a question of obtaining a scholarship.

■   Se trataba de tomar una decisión inteligente.
It was a question of making an intelligent decision.

trepar (a, por)   to climb (up); to climb *or* creep (up) (*botanical*)

■   Los pasajeros treparon al avión a las dos.
The passengers climbed into the plane at two.

- Los niños treparon a un árbol muy alto.
  The children climbed a very tall tree.

- La hiedra trepa por las paredes (/los árboles).
  The ivy creeps up walls (/the trees).

- Es difícil trepar por este lado de la montaña.
  It is difficult to climb (or scale) this side of the mountain.

trinchar   to carve, slice, cut up

- Trinchamos el asado para servirlo.
  We cut (or carved) the roast in order to serve it.

- Ella trincha el lomito para que lo coma el niño.
  She cut (or sliced) up the tenderloin so that the child could eat it.

triunfar   to triumph

- No es fácil triunfar en la vida (/en los negocios).
  It's not easy to succeed in life (/business).

- Los soldados triunfaron en la guerra.
  The soldiers won the war.

- Triunfaron en los juegos olímpicos.
  They triumphed in the Olympic games.

trocar (por)   to exchange (for); to change

- Trocamos mis libros por dinero.
  We exchanged my books for money.

- Ella y yo trocamos el asiento en el avión.
  She and I changed seats in the airplane.

trocarse (en)   to change (into)

- Ellos se trocaron en aventureros.
  They changed into (or became) adventurers.

- Se me trocó la suerte y gané la lotería.
  Luck changed for me, and I won the lottery.

tronar   to roar, thunder

- Tronaron los cañones (/fusiles/cohetes).
  The cannons (/rifles/firecrackers) thundered (or roared).

- Está tronando. Va a llover.
  It is thundering. It's going to rain.

- Tronó su voz en el discurso.
  Her voice thundered during the speech.

tropezar (en)   to trip, stumble (on)

- Pepe tropezó al entrar en la casa.
  Pepe tripped (or stumbled) coming into the house.

- Tropecé en una piedra y me rompí la rodilla.
  I tripped on a rock and broke my knee.

tropezar con uno/algo   to run into sb sth (unexpectedly); to run across sth

- Tropecé con la pared y se me rompieron los anteojos.
  I ran into the wall, and I broke my glasses.

- Tropezamos con Juan.
  We ran into Juan unexpectedly.

- Tropecé con (*or* contra) muchos obstáculos, por lo tanto no pude terminar mi carrera.
  I ran into so many obstacles; therefore, I could not finish my career.

tropezarse   to run into *or* meet each other

- Nos tropezamos con la secretaria en el restaurante.
  We met (or ran into) the secretary in the restaurant.

- Me tropecé con un fajo de billetes.
  I stumbled across a bundle of bills.

tumbar   to knock down, knock over

- Tumbaron el poste (/la torre/el edificio) de la esquina.
  They knocked down the post (/tower/building) on the corner.

- Es un olor que tumba. (*fig*)
  It is a smell which knocks you over.

- Tumbamos al candidato del partido conservador.
  We knocked down the conservative party's candidate.

tumbarse   to lie down, fall down

- Se tumbó a dormir.
  He lay down to sleep.

- Se tumbó la torre de la iglesia.
  The tower of the church fell down.

turnar   to take turns, work in shifts

- Vamos a turnar al personal de la fábrica.
  The personnel of the factory will work in turns (or shifts).

- Turnamos las horas de servicio entre mañanas y tardes.
  Hours of service alternate between mornings and afternoons.

turnarse   to take turns

- Ellos se turnan para dormir porque sólo hay una cama.
  They take turns sleeping as there is only one bed.
- Ellas se turnan para lavar los platos (/para usar el libro).
  They take turns washing the dishes (/using the book).

U

unir   to join, unite; to combine

- Uniremos nuestros recursos para comprar la casa.
  We'll combine (or join) our resources to buy the house.
- Irene une en su personalidad la bondad y la firmeza.
  Irene combines within herself kindness and firmness.
- Unió dos partes del juguete con un pegamento especial.
  He joined the two toy pieces with a special glue.
- El presidente unirá el país.
  The president will unite the country.
- El sacerdote unió a la pareja en matrimonio.
  The priest united the couple in matrimony.

unirse (en)   to join together, be united (in)

- Nuestras familias se unieron por (*or* en) un matrimonio.
  Our families were united by (or in) a marriage.
- Las dos compañías se unirán.
  The two companies will merge.
- Nos unimos en una fraternidad (/comunidad/hermandad).
  We became united in a fraternity (/community/brotherhood).
- Los dos partidos van a unirse para obtener más fuerza política.
  The two parties are going to join together in order to have more political power.

unirse a algo   to join sth

- Me uní a un grupo de turistas.
  I joined a group of tourists.
- ¿Te uniste al partido político?
  Did you join the political party?

unirse con uno/algo   to unite with sb/sth

- Este país se unió con el otro para formar una confederación.
  This country joined with another to form a confederation.

- Estos obreros se unieron con otros para formar un sindicato.
  These workers joined with others to establish a union.

ungir   to annoint

- El sacerdote ungió al enfermo.
  The priest annointed the sick person.

- Mi tío fue ungido por el cura.
  My uncle was annointed by the priest.

urgir   to urge; to be urgent

- Nos urge hablar con el presidente.
  It's very urgent that we speak with the president.

- Tenemos que urgir al secretario con el trabajo.
  We must press the secretary for the work.

- Me urge tener el libro pronto.
  I need to have this book soon.

usar   to use, make use of; to wear

- Debo usar la computadora hoy.
  I have to use the computer today.

- Ella no puede usar sal en sus comidas.
  She can't use salt in her foods.

- A Rosalía le gusta usar camisas de seda (/pantalones de lana).
  Rose likes to wear silk shirts (/wool pants).

usar de algo   to use, make use of

- La mamá usó de toda su imaginación para convencerlo.
  The mother used all her imagination to convince him.

- Usó de buenas palabras para decirle que no.
  He used nice words to tell him no.

- Él usó de mañas para engañarla.
  He used tricks to deceive her.

usarse   to be used

- ¿Cómo se usa esta palabra? —Esa palabra ya no se usa en español.
  How is this word used? —That word is no longer used in Spanish.

- Hay dichos que ya no se usan.
  There are proverbs which are no longer used.

V

vaciar   to empty (out); to drain, pour away; to cast (*statue*)

- Voy a vaciar el contenido de este recipiente.
  I'm going to empty (or drain) the contents of this receptacle.

- El río más grande de mi país se vació.
  The biggest river in my country drained itself (or dried) up.

- Vaciamos la botella (/jarra/lata).
  We emptied the bottle (/jug/pitcher).

- Hemos vaciado una estatua en yeso (/en bronce).
  We have cast the statue in plaster (/in copper).

vacilar (entre)   to vacillate, be unsteady, sway; to hesitate, waver (between)

- El edificio vaciló, pero no se cayó.
  The building swayed but did not collapse.

- Lola vaciló un momento antes de contestarle. (*fig*)
  Lola hesitated a moment before answering him.

- A menudo vacilamos entre lo inconveniente y lo correcto. (*fig*)
  Often we waver between what is correct and what's inappropriate.

- En esa situación vacilábamos entre la esperanza y el temor. (*fig*)
  In that situation we vacillated between hope and fear.

vacilar en + *inf*   to hesitate to + *inf*, hesitate in + *ger*

- No vacilaré en comunicarte la noticia (/en aceptar su regalo). (*fig*)
  I'll not hesitate in letting you know the news (/to accept his gift).

- Vaciló en dárselo (/en comprar la propiedad que te gusta). (*fig*)
  He hesitated in giving it to him (/to buy the property that you like).

valer   to cost; to be worth

- El kilo de carne vale mil pesos.
  A kilogram of beef is worth (or costs) one thousand pesos.

- Tu amistad (/Esta moneda/Este libro) vale muchísimo.
  Your friendship (/This coin/This book) is worth a great deal.

- La primera novela del autor vale más que la segunda.
  The author's first novel is better than the second one.

valer a algo   to cost per sth

- ¿Cuánto cuesta la carne? —La libra (/El kilo/La carga) vale (a) cuarenta.
  How much is the meat? —Forty per pound (/kilo/load).
- ¿Cuánto vale la tierra? —Vale a 100 la hectárea (/el lote).
  How much is the land worth? —One hundred per hectare (/lot).

valer por algo   to be worthy of sth, be worthy (because of) sth

- Tu bella actitud vale por mil besos.
  Your great attitude is worth (or worthy of) a thousand kisses.
- La bandera de un país vale por lo que representa.
  The flag of a country is respected for (or worthy of) what it represents.
- Ese gesto vale por un discurso.
  That action is worth a speech.
- Hay un refrán que dice: "Hombre prevenido vale por dos."
  There is a proverb that says, "a prepared man is worth two."

valerse de uno/algo   to use sb/sth, take advantage of sb/sth

- El hombre se valió de su esposa para cometer la fechoría.
  The man used his wife to commit the crime.
- ¡No te valgas de mí para lograr tus propósitos!
  Don't use me to achieve your aims!
- El político se valió de su puesto para enriquecerse.
  The politician took advantage of (or used) his position to get rich.

variar de algo   to change sth

- Nosotros hemos variado de opinión. No votaremos por ti.
  We've changed our mind. We are not going to vote for you.
- Todos los años vamos a variar de jefe.
  We are going to change bosses every year.
- Yo he variado de gustos.
  I have changed my tastes.

variar en algo   to vary in regard to sth

- Las opiniones de los ministros varían en la política exterior.
  The opinions of the ministers vary in (or in regard to) foreign policy.
- Las opiniones legales de los jueces varían en el contenido.
  The legal opinions of the judges vary in their content.

vedar   to prohibit, forbid, ban

- Cada año vedan la cacería de patos.
  Every year they ban duck hunting.
- Una ley del congreso ha vedado la pornografía.
  A law from Congress has prohibited pornography.

- La autoridad vedó el paso por el sendero.
  The authorities closed the path.

velar por uno/algo   to keep watch *or* vigil over sb/sth; to look after sb/sth

- Mi padre vela por su familia (/por nuestros intereses económicos).
  My father looks after his family (/our economic interests).
- El sacerdote de mi parroquia vela por mi salud espiritual.
  The priest of my parish keeps watch over my spiritual health.

vencer   to defeat, beat; to conquer; to come *or* fall due

- En la película los buenos vencieron y los malos perdieron.
  In the movie the good guys won out, and the bad guys lost.
- Para progresar hay que vencer muchos obstáculos.
  To advance (or succeed), you have to conquer (or overcome) many obstacles.
- La cuenta del teléfono vence el quince.
  The telephone bill falls due the 15th.
- Los venció en el campo del honor (/en el campo intelectual).
  He defeated them in the field of honor (/intellectual arena).

vencer a uno/a algo   to defeat sb/sth

- El luchador venció a su contricante dos veces.
  The fighter defeated his opponent twice.
- El pueblo no pudo vencer al ejército del tirano.
  The people could not defeat (or beat down) the tyrant's army.
- El caballero venció a su adversario y se casó con la princesa.
  The knight defeated his enemy and married the princess.

vencer con algo   to beat with sth, defeat with sth

- Nos vencieron con armas modernas (/con argumentos de peso).
  They defeated us with modern arms (/with weighty arguments).
- El ejército fue vencido con cañones y bombas.
  The army was defeated with cannons and bombs.

vender   to sell; to market

- Los vecinos venderán la casa y el auto.
  The neighbors will sell the house and the car.
- Cuando era pequeño, vendía periódicos.
  When I was young, I used to sell newspapers.
- Gerardo le vendió la bicicleta a Tomás.
  Gerard sold the bicycle to Thomas.

vender a algo   to sell at sth, sell (on the basis of) sth

- ¿Vendimos la finca a buen precio? —Sí, la vendimos a buen precio.
  Did we sell the farm at a good price? —Yes, we sold it at a good price.

- Mi tío, el comerciante, vendía al por mayor (/al contado/a crédito/al por menor).
  My uncle, the merchant, used to sell wholesale (/on a cash basis/on credit/retail).

venderse (por)   to sell oneself, be sold (for)

- Ese coche se vende solo.
  That car will sell itself.
- El espía se vendió al mejor postor.
  The spy sold himself (or *was sold*) *to the highest bidder.*
- Dicen que el jugador de fútbol se vendió, por eso el equipo ha perdido.
  They say the football player sold out; that's why the team lost.
- Las papas se venden a 20 pesos el kilo.
  Potatoes are sold for 20 pesos a kilo.
- Ella se vendió por dinero (/amor).
  She sold herself for money (/love).
- Vendí la casa por lo que me ofrecieron.
  I sold the house for what they offered me.

venir (a, de)   to come (to, from); to arrive

- Esta noche vendrá mi primo (de Las Vegas).
  Tonight my cousin will arrive (from Las Vegas).
- Me viene a la memoria una canción muy bonita.
  A beautiful song comes to mind.
- Ya vienen las lluvias.
  The rain is on the way.

venir a + *inf*   to come to + *inf*

- No creemos que ella venga a hablar sobre agricultura.
  We don't think she is coming to talk about agriculture.
- Rogelio sólo vino a trastornar nuestras vidas.
  Roger only came to disrupt our lives.

venir de algo   to come from sth, originate from sth

- Laura viene de Guatemala (/de España/de una familia aristócrata).
  Laura comes from Guatemala (/Spain/a very aristocratic family).
- La luz del día viene del sol.
  The light of day comes from the sun.
- La palabra "familia" viene del latín.
  The word "family" comes from Latin.

ventear   to sniff, air out

- Hay que ventear la ropa porque huele mal.
  It's necessary to air out the clothing because it smells bad.
- No me gustaría que ventearas las cosas que te he contado. (*fig*)
  I do not want you to repeat the things I've told you.

- ¡No se muevan! El perro está venteando la liebre.
  Don't move! The dog is catching the scent of a hare.

ver   to see, watch; to see, understand (*fig*)

- Nos gustaría que usted viera la película que vimos anoche.
  We would like you to see (or watch) the movie we saw last night.
- Es posible que usted no la vea más.
  It's possible that you'll never see her again.
- No veo por qué usted no puede trabajar.
  I don't see (or understand) why you cannot work.

ver a uno + *inf*   to see sb + *ger*

- Sí, yo lo veo estudiar (/trabajar/leer/comer).
  Yes, I see him studying (/working/reading/eating).
- Mi mamá me ve lavar (/limpiar/planchar) la ropa.
  My mom sees me washing (/cleaning/ironing) the clothes.

verse (con, en)   to see oneself *or* each other (with, as)

- Luis se ve todos los días con María.
  Louis and Mary see each other every day.
- En los sueños me veo volando.
  In my dreams I see myself flying.
- El paisaje se ve muy bien desde aquí.
  We can see the landscape very well from here.

verter a algo   to translate into sth (*language*)

- La editorial verterá tu obra al español.
  The publishing house will translate your work into Spanish.

verter en algo   to pour (into) sth; to spill

- ¡Qué vergüenza!, vertí el café caliente en la mesa.
  How embarrassing! I spilled the hot coffee on the table.
- Voy a verter el refresco en el vaso.
  I am going to pour the refreshment into the glass.
- El niño ha vertido la leche en el (*or* al) suelo.
  The boy has spilled the milk on the floor.

vestir (de)   to dress (in); cover, drape (in, with)

- Ella viste elegantemente.
  She dresses elegantly.
- El sospechoso viste traje azul.
  The suspect is dressed (or draped or covered) in blue.
- Un sastre muy viejo viste a la familia real.
  An old tailor dresses the royal family.

vestirse (con, de)   to get dressed, dress (with, in)

- Voy a vestirme. ¡Espere un momentito!
  I am going to get dressed. Wait a minute!
- Se viste pobremente.
  She dresses poorly.
- ¡Vístase con delicadeza y elegancia (/con decoro)!
  Dress (yourself) with refinement and elegance (/with decorum)!
- El pordiosero se viste con andrajos para provocar lástima.
  The beggar dresses himself in rags to provoke sympathy.
- Las viudas se visten de negro.
  Widows dress in black.
- A Raquel le gusta vestirse de payaso.
  Rachel likes to dress herself as a clown.
- La montaña se vistió de blanco. (*poetic*)
  The mountain was covered (liter. *dressed itself) in white.*

viajar (a, por)   to travel (to, through)

- ¿Por qué viaja tanto el presidente?
  Why does the president travel so much?
- Ellos van a viajar al Polo Norte (/al país de las maravillas).
  They are going to travel to the North Pole (/to Wonderland).
- Mi hermano, Oscar, ha viajado por Italia (/Europa/China).
  My brother, Oscar, has traveled through Italy (/Europe/China).

viajar en/por algo   to travel in, on/by sth

- Viajaremos por tren (/avión/mar/tierra).
  We'll travel by train (/plane/sea/land).
- Viajaremos en autobús (/auto/heliocóptero).
  We'll travel on a bus (/in a car/in a helicopter).

vigilar   to watch, watch over, look after

- ¡Vigila mi casa mientras estoy fuera!
  Watch (over or Look after) my house while I'm gone.
- Vigilaremos lo que hacen los muchachos.
  We'll watch what the boys do.
- Los científicos vigilan el volcán día y noche.
  The scientists watch the volcano night and day.
- El centinela vigilaba la entrada del cuartel.
  The sentinel was guarding (or *watching) the entrance to the fort.*

vigilar a uno   to watch sb, keep an eye on sb

- La madre vigila a los niños mientras juegan.
  The mother watches the children while they play.

- El guardia vigila a los prisioneros.
  The guard watches the prisoners.

- Es conveniente que vigiles a tus empleados.
  It's in your best interest to keep an eye on your employees.

virar (a, de, hacia)   to veer, turn, change (to, from, towards)

- Viramos a la derecha (/a la izquierda).
  We veered (or turned) right (/left).

- El gobierno viró de política económica (/de dirección).
  The government changed its economic policy (/its direction).

- El automóvil viró hacia el sur (/el norte/la playa/la plaza).
  The auto veered south (/north/towards the beach/towards the plaza).

visitar   to visit; to call on, go and see

- Visitaremos San José de Costa Rica el próximo mes.
  We'll visit San José, Costa Rica next month.

- Voy a visitar a mis suegros porque cumplen años de casados.
  I am going to visit (or call on) my in-laws because they are having a wedding anniversary.

- Los martes el grupo visitaba museos (*or* teatros).
  On Tuesdays the group would visit museums (or would go to the theater).

vivir (en)   to live (at, in, on)

- ¿Dónde vives? —Vivo en la Calle Tano (/en esta ciudad).
  Where do you live? —I live on Tano Street (/in this city).

- Si respiramos es porque vivimos.
  We breathe because we are alive.

- El pajarito aún vive.
  The little bird still is living.

- Viven muy bien en ese pueblo.
  They live very well in that town.

vivir a algo   to live (*certain ways*), live a distance

- Ella vive a su gusto en este país.
  She lives the way she wants to in this country.

- Los gemelos viven a su manera.
  The twins live their own way.

- Pepe vive a pocos kilómetros (de aquí).
  Pepe lives a few kilometers away (from here).

vivir de algo   to live from sth

- Tu madre vivía de sus rentas.
  Your mother lived from (or off) her investments.

- El viejo vive de las limosnas que recibe los domingos.
  The old man lives off the charity he receives on Sundays.
- Muchos novelistas viven de la literatura.
  Many novelists (or authors) live off their work.

vivir en algo   to live in sth

- En esta isla, viven en paz (/en la opulencia).
  In this island they live in peace (/in opulence).
- Es difícil vivir en santidad.
  It's difficult to be saintly.

vivir por algo   to live for/by sth

- El enfermo vivía por milagro.
  The sick man was alive by a miracle (or It's a miracle that the sick man was alive).
- Esa mujer vive por sus hijos.
  That woman lives (only) for her children.

volar (a/hacia, sobre)   to fly (away) (to, over)

- Las avestruces no vuelan.
  Ostriches don't fly.
- El viento entró por la ventana y todas las cosas volaron.
  The wind came in the window, and everything blew away.
- Los patos (/Las golondrinas) vuelan al (*or* hacia el) sur.
  Ducks (/swallows) fly south.
- Nosotros volaremos a (*or* hacia) Colombia.
  We'll fly to Colombia.
- El avión voló sobre los Andes.
  The plane flew over the Andes.
- El platillo volador voló sobre la selva y después desapareció.
  The flying saucer flew over the jungle, and then it disappeared.

volcar   to turn over; to upset

- Volcamos el barril para lavarlo.
  We turned over the barrel in order to wash it.
- Volcó la carretilla y se cayeron los ladrillos.
  The wheelbarrow turned over, and all the bricks fell out.
- Ha estado tres días en cama porque la gripe la volcó. (*fig*)
  She has been in bed for three days because the flu upset her (or knocked her out).

volcarse   to tip over, overturn

- Juan se ha volcado, ahora es de mi partido. (*fig*)
  John has gone (or switched) over, and now he is a member of my political party.

■ El autobús se volcó, dichosamente no hubo heridos.
The bus overturned; fortunately, there were no casualties.

■ Se volcó la copa y el vino se derramó.
The glass tipped over and the wine spilled.

voltear   to turn over, roll over

■ El médico forense volteó el cadáver para examinarlo mejor.
The coroner turned (or rolled) the cadaver over to examine it better.

■ Voltea la máquina de escribir para limpiarla.
Turn over the typewriter in order to clean it.

■ Volteó el cubo para que corriera el agua.
He turned the bucket over so that the water would run out.

voltearse   to turn around, turn

■ Ellos se voltearon para mirar el paisaje.
They turned to see (or look at) the landscape.

■ Voltéese, que le voy a tomar una foto.
Turn around; I am going to take your picture.

■ El niño se volteó en la cuna.
The child turned around in his crib.

volver (a, de)   to return (to, from), go back to; turn over

■ ¡No te preocupes!, volveré temprano.
Don't worry. I'll be back soon.

■ El cocinero volvió la carne (/la volvió).
The cook turned the meat (/it) over.

■ Los invitados volvieron al (/del) comedor.
The guests returned to (/from) the dining room.

■ Después de la fiesta volvimos al hotel.
After the party we returned (or went back) to the hotel.

■ Por favor, vuelvan a sus asientos.
Please return to your seats.

volver a + *inf*   to do something again

■ Elena ha vuelto a fumar.
Helen has started smoking again.

■ No quiero que vuelvan a insultarme.
I don't want you to insult me again.

■ Volvimos a perder contra el mismo equipo.
We lost again to the same team.

volver a/para + *inf*   to return to + *inf*

■ Volvió a (*or* para) terminar lo que había dejado inconcluso.
He returned to finish what he had left undone.

■ Volvió a (*or* para) recoger las flores que había olvidado.
He returned to pick up the flowers that he had forgotten.

volverse   to turn around, turn; to become

■ ¡Vuélvete y muéstrame la cara!
Turn around, and show me your face!

■ Ricardo se volvió contra su propia familia.
Richard turned against his own family.

■ José no creía que Esteban se había vuelto loco.
Joseph didn't believe that Steven had gone (or become) crazy.

votar (por, contra)   to vote (for, against)

■ Esperamos que todos los diputados hayan votado.
We hope that all the congressmen have voted.

■ Toda mi familia votará el próximo domingo, porque es un deber ciudadano.
All my family will vote next Sunday because it's a civic responsiblity.

■ Esta vez no votaré por nadie.
This time I will not vote for anyone.

■ Ellos votaron por (/contra) el mejor candidato.
They voted for (/against) the best candidate.

■ Dudo que usted vote por mi partido.
I doubt you'll vote for my party.

Y

yacer (en)   to lie (in)

■ Aquí yace una persona honesta.
Here lies an honest person.

■ ¿Quién yace en esta tumba?
Who lies in this grave?

■ Cuando llegó la ambulancia, los heridos yacían en el pavimento.
When the ambulance arrived, the injured were lying on the pavement.

yuxtaponer   to juxtapose

■ ¡No yuxtapongas una oración en presente a otra en pretérito!
Do not juxtapose (or use) a present with a preterite sentence.

- Si yuxtapones tus ideas a las mías, realizaremos una gran obra.
  If you juxtapose (or put) your ideas with mine, we'll create a great work.

- Vamos a yuxtaponer esas varillas de hierro a la columna para fortalecerla.
  We are going to juxtapose those steel rods to the column to strengthen it.

Z

zafar   to loosen, untie

- ¡Zafa el piñón cuidadosamente!
  Loosen the pinion carefully.

- ¡Zafemos los tornillos y las tuercas!
  Let's loosen the nuts and bolts.

- La costurera zafó la correa de la máquina.
  The seamstress loosened (or untied) the belt on the sewing machine.

zafarse   to get loose, get away

- La correa se ha zafado de la rueda.
  The belt got loose from the wheel.

- El carterista se zafó.
  The pickpocket got away.

- ¡Zafémonos ahora que no nos ven!
  Let's get away before they see us!

zaherir   to criticize sharply, attack, reproach

- Te recomiendo que no zahieras a tus compañeros.
  I suggest that you don't attack (or reproach) your colleagues.

- Me siento mal porque el jefe me (/lo) ha zaherido.
  I feel bad because my boss has criticized me (/him).

zambullir (en)   to dip, plunge (in, into)

- El cocinero zambulló la liebre en la olla.
  The cook dipped (or plunged) the rabbit into the pot.

- El instructor zambulle a sus discípulos en la piscina.
  The instructor ducks the students into the pool.

zambullirse **(en)** to dive (in, into)

- Las chicas se zambulleron como sirenas.
  The girls dove (in) like mermaids.

- Cuando éramos jóvenes nos zambullíamos en el río.
  When we were young, we used to dive in the river.

- Tú no sabes nadar, así es que no te zambullas en el mar.
  You don't know how to swim, so don't dive in the ocean.

zampar (en) to put away hurriedly (in)

- El niño zampó el dinero en la alcancía.
  The child stuck his money (hastily) in the piggy bank.

- El abogado zampó los libros (/los zampó) en la gaveta y salió de prisa.
  The lawyer shoved the books (/them) in the cabinet and left in a hurry.

zamparse (en) to bump *or* crash (into); to wolf (down)

- El borracho se zampó en la cocina.
  The drunk crashed (or staggered) into the kitchen.

- Los delicuentes se zamparon en un callejón para ocultarse.
  The delinquents ducked into an alley to hide.

- Estoy que reviento. Me zampé un kilo de fresas.
  I am about to pop. I wolfed down (or devoured) a kilo of strawberries.

- No puedo creer que usted se haya zampado una botella de ron. *(fig)*
  I can't believe you killed off a bottle of rum.

zumbar to buzz, hum

- Este televisor zumba demasiado. Hay que arreglarlo.
  This TV set hums too much. It needs to be fixed.

- Algunos insectos zumban al volar.
  Some insects buzz (or make a buzzing sound) when they fly.

- Cada vez que Rosa nada, le zumban los oídos.
  Every time Rose swims, her ears ring.

zurcir to darn, mend, sew up; *(fig)* to concoct

- La costurera le ha surcido toda la ropa.
  The seamstress has mended all her clothes.

- ¿Podría usted zurcir estas medias?
  Could you darn (or sew up) these socks?

- Te recomiendo que dejes de zurcir mentiras. *(fig)*
  I suggest that you stop fabricating stories.

Appendix
Verbal and Prepositional Reference

Prepositions

Common Simple Prepositions

a	to, at, by, into
ante	before, in the presence of, in the face of
bajo	under
con	with
contra	against, opposite, facing
de	of, from
desde	from, since, after
durante	during
en	in, into, on, upon, at
entre	among, amongst, in the midst of
hacia	towards, in the direction of, about, near
hasta	as far as, up to, down to, till, until
para	for, intended for
por	for, in order to, out of, because of, from
según	according to, in accordance with, in line with
sin	without, apart from, not including
so	under
sobre	on, upon, on top of, over, above
tras	behind, after

Common Prepositional Phrases

acerca de	about
además de	in addition to, besides
alrededor de	around, about
antes de	before, previous to
a pesar de	in spite of
arriba de	above; higher than
cerca de	about
con rumbo	in the direction of
debajo de	under, below, beneath
de entre	out of, from among
delante de	in front of
dentro de	in, inside, within
desde abajo	from below
desde arriba	from (up) above
desde lejos	from afar
después de	after

(continued)

detrás de	behind, back of
encima de	above, over, on, on top of
en contra de	against
en cuanto a	as far as
en lugar de	in place of, instead of
en medio de	in the middle of
en vez de	instead of
encima de	on top of, upon
enfrente de	opposite
frente a	in front of
fuera de	outside of
hacia abajo	down, downwards
hacia arriba	up, upwards
junto a	next to
lejos de	far from
por encima de	over
por valor de	worth
tras de	besides, in addition to, after

Many compound prepositions, such as the ones presented above, are considered prepositional because of the preposition **de, desde, hacia,** and **a,** which are included in the phrases. Without these prepositions, most of them are adverbs; for example: **cerca,** near, nearby; **cerca de** near; **después,** afterwards, later; **después de** after; **encima,** over, at the top, overhead; **encima de** above, over, etc.

Personal A

The preposition **a** always precedes a direct object in Spanish when the direct object is a definite person, a group of people, or a personified object. It is called the personal **a** and is never translated in English (*veo a Carlos; ¿a quién llamas?; no conozco a ninguno aquí; llamamos un médico; llamamos al médico; necesitamos a este alumno aquí; necesitamos una persona que dibuje bien*).

The personal **a** is placed before names of towns and countries which are not preceded by the definite article (*quiero visitar a Costa Rica/a Chicago*). Many speakers, however, often disregard this rule. It is also used with pets (*Elena busca a su pájaro*).

The personal **a** occurs before the direct object of a verb which usually has a person for its object (*amo a mi país*). The personal **a** is not used, however, after the verb **tener** (*tengo dos hermanos*).

Verb Tenses and Moods in Spanish

The following table shows the tenses and moods in Spanish. On the left the simple tenses are given. A verb tense is referred to as simple if it consists of one verb, and compound if it contains more than one. As can be noted, the auxiliary **haber** is used to form the compound tenses of all Spanish verbs. The past participle remains invariable throughout the conjugation. In addition to the seven compound tenses, there are two other compound tenses which are called progressive tenses. The progressive tense is formed by the appropriate tense of the auxiliary verb **estar** along with the present participle. Other auxiliary verbs such as **seguir, ir,** or **andar** may occasionally replace **estar** in certain situations. The verb **ser,** like the English verb *to be,* is used to form the passive voice in Spanish (The passive voice is not given below; see p. 308).

SIMPLE TENSES	COMPOUND TENSES

Present Indicative
Presente de indicativo
hablo = I speak, I do speak,
  I am speaking

Present perfect Indicative
Perfecto de indicativo
he hablado = I have spoken*

Imperfect Indicative
Imperfecto de indicativo
hablaba = I was speaking *or*
  I spoke *or* I used to speak

Pluperfect *or* Past perfect Indicative
Pluscuamperfecto de indicativo
había hablado = I had spoken*

Preterit
Pretérito
hablé = I spoke *or* I did speak

Preterit Perfect *or* Past anterior
Pretérito anterior *or* Pretérito perfecto
hube hablado = I had spoken**

Future
Futuro
hablaré = I will (*or* shall) speak

Future Perfect *or* Future anterior
Futuro perfecto
habré hablado = I shall (*or* will) have spoken

Conditional
Condicional simple
hablaría = I would speak

Conditional Perfect
Condicional compuesto
habría hablado = I would have spoken

Present Subjunctive
Presente de subjuntivo
hable = (that) I (may) speak

Present Perfect *or* Past Subjunctive
Perfecto de Subjuntivo
haya hablado = I have spoken*

Imperfect Subjunctive
Imperfecto de Subjuntivo
hablara or *hablase* = (that) I
  (might) speak

Pluperfect *or* Past Perfect Subjunctive
Pluscuamperfecto de subjuntivo
hubiera hablado = I had spoken*

Present Progressive
Presente progresivo
estoy hablando = I am speaking

Imperfect Progressive
Imperfecto progresivo
estaba hablando = I was speaking

* Note that the Spanish present and past perfect indicative and subjunctive are translated the same in English, although their use in Spanish differs greatly.

** Preterit perfect indicative and pluperfect indicative are translated the same in English. In general, the former is used in spoken Spanish, while the preterit perfect is used in formal writing.

The Indicative

1. **The present tense** in Spanish corresponds to the simple present (*hablo,* I speak), the progressive tense (*piensa,* he's thinking) and the emphatic form with *do* (*no hablo ahora, pero cuando hablo...,* I don't speak now but when I do (speak)...).

2. **The preterit and imperfect** in Spanish both correspond to the English simple past or preterit, but they have different uses and are not interchangeable. Preterit in Spanish expresses an action that was completed at some time in the past. The imperfect expresses an action or a state of being that was going on in the past

and its completion is not indicated (*estudiaba cuando Juan llegó,* I was studying when Juan arrived).

3.   **The future** tense in Spanish and English is used to express future action (*llegaré a la una,* I will arrive at one).

4.   **The conditional** is used in English and Spanish to express what would happen if it were not for some other circumstance (*yo lo compraría pero no tengo dinero,* I would buy it but I don't have money; *¿por qué no irías en tren?,* why wouldn't you go by train?).

5.   **The present perfect** tense in English and Spanish is used to express a past action without reference to a particular time and represents a past action that continues into the present or close to the present (*he comido,* I have eaten).

6.   **The pluperfect indicative** is used in English and Spanish to express an action which happened and was completed in the past (*había hablado,* he had spoken).

7.   **The preterit perfect indicative** is not often used in Spanish. It is used as a very literary tense and is translated into English like the pluperfect indicative (*hubo hablado,* he had spoken). Commonly, the pluperfect indicative is used in spoken Spanish in place of the preterit perfect.

8.   **The future perfect** tense in English and Spanish is used to express a future action that will be completed prior to another future action (*ellos ya habrán vuelto de los Estados Unidos,* they will have returned from the United States).

9.   **The conditional perfect** tense is used in English and Spanish to express an action that would have taken place had something else not interfered (*habríamos comido pero no teníamos hambre,* we would have eaten but we weren't hungry).

The Subjunctive

The indicative is used to express the fact that an action has taken, is taking, or will take place. When the statement is a fact or when it implies a probability, the indicative mood is used. The *subjunctive,* however, by definition implies *subjectivity.* The subjunctive mood is, therefore, used to express when a certain action has not or may not take place, because it is a supposition, desire, or conjecture, rather than a fact. When a statement is contrary to fact or when it implies a possibility rather than a probability, the subjunctive mood is used. Because of the indefinite nature of the subjunctive, it is almost always found in dependent or subordinate clauses.

Most English verbs (with the exception of the verb *to be*) do not have a special form for the subjunctive. Thus, while one uses structures that denote subjunctive in English, subjunctive forms are seldom used. Subjunctive is, however, extensively used in Spanish. Thus, since there are no specific forms of subjuntive in English, the subjunctive and indicative in Spanish are almost always rendered as one form, indicative, in English.

1.   *The present subjunctive* of all verbs is formed from the first person singular of the present indicative. The personal ending **-o** is dropped and the personal endings of the subjunctive are added to this root. In the table for the conjugation of the regular verbs (see the appropriate table, p. 310), you will note that the personal endings of the present subjunctive are the reverse of those used for the indicative. The vowel **e** is used for **-ar** verbs and the vowel **a** is used for **-er** and **-ir** verbs.

There is strict correspondence in Spanish between the tense of the subjunctive used in the subordinate clause and that of the main verb. The present or perfect subjunctive is used after a verb in the present, future, or future perfect.

The present subjunctive is most commonly used:

a.   *With impersonal expressions* that denote an element of subjectivity (*es necesario que tú lo hagas,* it's necessary that you do it; *es posible que él vuelva pronto,* it is possible that he'll return right away).

b.   *With expressions of doubt or uncertainty.* The subjunctive is used when a clause is introduced with a statement of doubt or uncertainty (*dudo que Juan lo prepare,* I doubt that Juan will prepare it).

c.   *With a relative pronoun* with a negative or indefinite antecedent (*haré lo que pueda,* I'll do what I can; *necesito un abogado que hable español,* I need a lawyer who speaks Spanish).

d.   *After certain conjunctions of time* such as *antes (de) que, cuando, en cuanto, tan pronto como, luego que, hasta que, después de que (yo volveré antes de que tú vayas a Perú,* I'll return before you go to Peru).

e.   *After por . . . que, (por mucho que Juan reciba, nunca estará satisfecho,* however much Juan gets, he'll never be satisfied.

f.   *With commands:* (see the appropriate section for commands, pp. 307–8).

2.   *The imperfect subjunctive* is used under the same conditions under which the subjunctive is used in general but the verb in the main clause is in the imperfect, preterit, or conditional (*ella quería que yo viniera con mi esposa,* she wanted me to come with my wife; *el hombre mandó que ellos lo vendieran,* the man ordered that they sell it; *mi amigo te aconsejaría que no salieras,* my friend would advise you not to leave).

The imperfect subjunctive is formed from the root of the third person plural of the preterit. For all verbs the root is obtained by dropping the **-ron** ending of the third person plural of the preterit. The following endings are added to this root: **-ara, -aras, -ara, -áramos, -arais, -aran** to **-ar** verbs and **-iera, -ieras, -iera, -iéramos, -ierais, -ieran** to **-er** and **-ir** verbs (for examples, see the appropriate section for the conjugation of regular verbs, p. 310).

3.   *The present perfect subjunctive* is used under the same conditions in which the subjunctive is required but the verb of the main clause is in the present or future (*espero que Pepe haya pasado un buen día,* I hope that Pepe has had a good day; *no creerá que tú lo hayas terminado,* he won't believe that you have finished it).

The present perfect subjunctive is formed by using the present subjunctive of **haber** as the auxiliary verb and the past participle (for examples, see the appropriate section for the conjugation of the regular verbs, p. 311).

4.   *The pluperfect subjunctive* is used in clauses which require the subjunctive and the main verb in the past tense (*no creyó que yo hubiera tenido tanta suerte,* he didn't believe that I had had such luck).

The pluperfect subjunctive is formed by using the imperfect subjunctive of **haber** as the helping verb plus the past participle (for examples, see the appropriate section for the conjugation of the regular verbs, p. 311).

Imperative

1.   *The formal commands* (**usted, ustedes**) are formed by using the subjunctive form of the verb. The first person singular of the present indicative serves as the root for the formation of the formal commands. The opposite conjugational endings are added to form the formal commands: **-ar** verbs have the vowel **-e,** and **-er** and **-ir** verbs have the vowel **-a** (*hable usted/hablen ustedes; coma usted/coman ustedes; viva usted/vivan ustedes; duerma usted/duerman ustedes; ponga usted/pongan ustedes; oiga usted/oigan ustedes*). The same form of the verb is also used for the formal negative commands (*no hable usted/no hablen ustedes*).

2.   *The familiar affirmative* (**tú**) *command* is always the same as the third person singular indicative form of the verb (*habla/piensa/come/vuelve/sirve/escribe*).

a.   When an affirmative **tú** command is used with a direct or indirect object pronoun, the pronoun is attached to the verb (*dime,* tell me; *házlo,* do it). If a command form has more than one syllable, a written accent is placed over the stressed syllable when an object pronoun is added *(ayúdame,* help me; *cómpranos el libro,* buy us the book; *lávate la cara,* wash your face).

b.   The affirmative familiar plural (**vosotros, vosotras**) command is formed by dropping the final **r** of the infinitive and adding **d** *(hablad/comed/venid/id).*

c.   Negative commands: Similar to the formal commands, in all the negative informal commands the subjunctive form of the verb is used *(no hables/no pienses/no comas/no vuelvas/no sirvas/no vengas/no pongas/no pidas/no vayas/no des/no seas/no estés; no habléis/no penséis/no comáis/no volváis/. . .).*

3.   *The inclusive command* or the idea *let's,* is expressed by the first person plural form of the subjunctive *(escribamos,* let's write; *comamos a las dos,* let's eat at two; *cantemos la canción,* let's sing the song).

Summary of Direct Commands

Informal
(tú/vosotros forms)

Affirmative	canta (tú)	aprende (tú)	vive (tú)
	cantad	aprended	vivid
Negative	no cantes	no aprendas	no vivas
	no cantéis	no aprendáis	no viváis
Formal	(no) cante Ud.	(no) aprenda Ud.	(no) viva Ud.
	(no) canten Uds.	(no) aprendan Uds.	(no) vivan Uds.

The Passive Voice

The passive voice is used less commonly in Spanish than in English. When the agent is expressed the Spanish speakers often prefer to use an active construction.

1.   *With ser:* The passive voice is formed with the auxiliary verb **ser** and the past participle of the verb which agrees in number and gender with the subject. The agent is introduced by **por** *(el libro fue escrito por Thomas Mann,* the book was written by Thomas Mann; *la comida fue preparada por la mamá,* the food was prepared by the mother; *las casas fueron destruidas por el incendio,* the houses were destroyed by the fire).

2.   *With se:* A common way to express the passive in Spanish is to use the reflexive form of the verb, i.e., the reflexive pronoun **se** with the third person singular or plural of the verb *(se venden vestidos en esta tienda,* clothes are sold in this shop; *¿cómo se dice "watch" en español?,* how does one say "watch" in Spanish?; *la cena se sirve a las ocho,* the supper is served at eight o'clock; *aquí se habla español,* spanish is spoken here; *¿ a qué hora se cierra la tienda?,* at what time is the shop being closed?).

Special Uses of the Infinitive

1.   *After a Preposition:* In Spanish the infinitive is always used after a preposition. Note that in English the present participle is used instead. *Yo salí sin terminar,* I left without finishing; *María me habló antes empezar,* Maria spoke to me before starting; *al oír el anuncio, ella se puso a llorar,* on hearing the announcement she began to cry. (Note that the gerund, or verbal noun, in English is the present

present participle of a verb used as a noun. The term gerund is thus used to represent like structures throughout this book.)

2.   *As a Noun:* The infinitive either alone or with the definite article **el** can function as a noun in Spanish. On the other hand, in English the present participle rather than the infinitve is used as the verbal noun: *el hablar de este político me molesta,* talking of this politician bothers me; *el cantar de ella me encanta,* I enjoy her singing; *comió la comida en un abrir y cerrar de ojos,* he ate the food in the twinkling of an eye.

3.   A *before certain infinitives:* The preposition **a** must precede the infinitive used after verbs of motion (*voy a comer,* I'm going to eat), beginning (*empecé a cantar,* I began to sing), inviting (*nos invitaron a comer,* they invited us to eat), and committing, in their reflexive forms (*me decidí a hacerlo,* I decided to do it; *se negó a participar,* he refused to participate).

4.   **Sin** *before an infinitive:* **sin** followed by an infinitive portrays a negative idea: *salió sin hablar/comer,* he left without saying/eating anything.

Complete Conjugation of Regular Verbs
Simple Tenses

INDICATIVE			
Present	**cantar**	**aprender**	**vivir**
	canto	aprendo	vivo
	cantas	aprendes	vives
	canta	aprende	vive
	cantamos	aprendemos	vivimos
	cantáis	aprendéis	vivís
	cantan	aprenden	viven
Imperfect	cantaba	aprendía	vivía
	cantabas	aprendías	vivías
	cantaba	aprendía	vivía
	cantábamos	aprendíamos	vivíamos
	cantabais	aprendíais	vivíais
	cantaban	aprendían	vivían
Preterit	canté	aprendí	viví
	cantaste	aprendiste	viviste
	cantó	aprendió	vivió
	cantamos	aprendimos	vivimos
	cantasteis	aprendisteis	vivisteis
	cantaron	aprendieron	vivieron
Future	cantaré	aprenderé	viviré
	cantarás	aprenderás	vivirás
	cantará	aprenderá	vivirá
	cantaremos	aprenderemos	viviremos
	cantaréis	aprenderéis	viviréis
	cantarán	aprenderán	vivirán

(continued)

Conditional	cantaría	aprendería	viviría
	cantarías	aprendería	viviría
	cantaría	aprendería	viviría
	cantaríamos	aprenderíamos	viviríamos
	cantaríais	aprenderíais	viviríais
	cantarían	aprenderían	vivirían

SUBJUNCTIVE

Present	cante	aprenda	viva
	cantes	aprendas	vivas
	cante	aprenda	viva
	cantemos	aprendamos	vivamos
	cantéis	aprendáis	viváis
	canten	aprendan	vivan
Imperfect	cantara	aprendiera	viviera
	cantaras	aprendieras	vivieras
	cantara	aprendiera	viviera
	cantáramos	aprendiéramos	viviéramos
	cantarais	aprendierais	vivierais
	cantaran	aprendieran	vivieran

Compound Tenses

INDICATIVE

Present Perfect	he has ha hemos habéis han	cantado	aprendido	vivido
Pluperfect	había habías había habíamos habías habían	cantado	aprendido	vivido
Preterit Perfect	hube hubiste hubo hubimos hubisteis hubieron	cantado	aprendido	vivido

Future	habré			
Perfect	habrás			
	habrá			
		cantado	aprendido	vivido
	habremos			
	habréis			
	habrán			
Conditional	habría			
Perfect	habrías			
	habría			
		cantado	aprendido	vivido
	habríamos			
	habríais			
	habrían			

SUBJUNCTIVE

Present	haya			
Perfect	hayas			
	haya			
		cantado	aprendido	vivido
	hayamos			
	hayáis			
	hayan			
Pluperfect	hubiera			
	hubieras			
	hubiera			
		cantado	aprendido	vivido
	hubiéramos			
	hubierais			
	hubieran			

Progressive Tenses

Present	estoy			
	estás			
	está			
		cantando	aprendiendo	viviendo
	estamos			
	estáis			
	están			
Imperfect	estaba			
	estabas			
	estaba			
		cantando	aprendiendo	viviendo
	estábamos			
	estabais			
	estaban			

Stem-Changing Verbs

	First Class			
	e → ie	o → ue	e → ie	o → ue
Infinitive	**pensar** *to think*	**contar** *to tell*	**entender** *to understand*	**colgar** *to hang*
Present Participle	pensando	contando	entendiendo	colgando
Past Participle	pensado	contado	entendido	colgado
		Indicative		
Present	pienso piensas piensa	cuento cuentas cuenta	entiendo entiendes entiende	cuelgo cuelgas cuelga
	pensamos pensáis piensan	contamos contáis cuentan	entendemos entendéis entienden	colgamos colgáis cuelgan
		Subjunctive		
Present	piense pienses piense	cuente cuentes cuente	entienda entiendas entienda	cuelgue cuelgues cuelgue
	pensemos penséis piensen	contemos contéis cuente	entendamos entendáis entiendan	colguemos colguéis cuelguen

	Second Class		Third Class
	e → ie, i	o → ue, u	e → i, i
Infinitive	**sentir** *to feel*	**dormir** *to sleep*	**repetir** *to repeat*
Present Participle	sintiendo	durmiendo	repitiendo
Past Participle	sentido	dormido	repetido
	Indicative		
Present	siento sientes siente	duermo duermes duerme	repito repites repite
	sentimos sentís sienten	dormimos dormís duermen	repetimos repetís repiten

Preterit	sentí	dormí	repetí
	sentiste	dormiste	repetiste
	sintió	durmió	repitió
	sentimos	dormimos	repetimos
	sentisteis	dormisteis	repetisteis
	sintieron	durmieron	repitieron

Subjunctive

Present	sienta	duerma	repita
	sientas	duermas	repitas
	sienta	duerma	repita
	sintamos	durmamos	repitamos
	sintáis	durmáis	repitáis
	sientan	duerman	repitan
Imperfect	sintiera	durmiera	repitiera
	sintieras	durmieras	repitieras
	sintiera	durmiera	repitiera
	sintiéramos	durmiéramos	repitiéramos
	sintierais	durmierais	repitierais
	sintieran	durmieran	repitieran

Conjugation of Some Irregular Verbs

This section includes a list of common irregular verbs. The present and the past participles are given after each infinitive. For the most part, the list includes only the conjugation of tenses that are irregular and does not include tenses that are predictable, such as the compound tenses and the present and imperfect subjunctive.

	andar	*to walk, go*			**andando**	**andado**
Preterit	anduve	anduviste	anduvo	anduvimos	aduvisteis	anduvieron
	caber	*to fit*			**cabiendo**	**cabido**
Present	quepo	cabes	cabe	cabemos	cabéis	caben
Preterit	cupe	cupiste	cupo	cupimos	cupisteis	cupieron
Future	cabré	cabrás	cabrá	cabremos	cabréis	cabrán
Conditional	cabría	cabrías	cabría	cabríamos	cabríais	cabrían
	caer	*to fall*			**cayendo**	**caído**
Present	caigo	caes	cae	caemos	caéis	caen
Preterit	caí	caíste	cayó	caímos	caísteis	cayeron
	conocer	*to know*			**conociendo**	**conocido**
Present	conozco	conoces	conoce	conocemos	conocéis	conocen
	dar	*to give*			**dando**	**dado**
Present	doy	das	da	damos	dais	dan
Preterit	di	diste	dio	dimos	disteis	dieron
Present Subj.	de	des	dé	demos	deis	den

(continued)

	decir	*to say, tell*			**diciendo**	**dicho**
Present	digo	dices	dice	decimos	decís	dicen
Preterit	dije	dijiste	dijo	dijimos	dijisteis	dijeron
Future	diré	dirás	dirá	diremos	diréis	dirán
Conditional ·	diría	dirías	diría	diríamos	diríais	dirían
Imperative (tú)	di	no digas				
	estar	*to be*			**estando**	**estado**
Present	estoy	estás	está	estamos	estáis	están
Preterit	estuve	estuviste	estuvo	estuvimos	estuvisteis	estuvieron
Present Subj.	esté	estés	esté	estemos	estéis	estén
	haber	*to have*			**habiendo**	**habido**
Present	he	has	ha	hemos	habéis	han
Preterit	hube	hubiste	hubo	hubimos	hubisteis	hubieron
Future	habré	habrás	habrá	habremos	habréis	habrán
Conditional	habría	habrías	habría	habríamos	habríais	habrían
Present Subj.	haya	hayas	haya	hayamos	hayáis	hayan
	hacer	*to do, make*			**haciendo**	**hecho**
Present	hago	haces	hace	hacemos	hacéis	hacen
Preterit	hice	hiciste	hizo	hicimos	hicisteis	hicieron
Future	haré	harás	hará	haremos	haréis	harán
Conditional	haría	harías	haría	haríamos	haríais	harían
Imperative (tú)	haz	no hagas				
	incluir	*to include*			**incluyendo**	**incluido**
Present	incluyo	incluyes	incluye	incluimos	incluís	incluyen
Preterit	incluí	incluiste	incluyó	incluimos	incluisteis	inclyeron
Imperative (tú)	incluye	no incluyas				
	ir	*to go*			**yendo**	**ido**
Present	voy	vas	va	vamos	vais	van
Preterit	fui	fuiste	fue	fuimos	fuisteis	fueron
Imperfect	iba	ibas	iba	íbamos	ibais	iban
Present Subj.	vaya	vayas	vaya	vayamos	vayáis	vayan
Imperative (tú)	ve	no vayas				
	oír	*to hear*			**oyendo**	**oído**
Present	oigo	oyes	oye	oímos	oís	oyen
Preterit	oí	oíste	oyó	oímos	oísteis	oyeron
	poder	*to be able*			**pudiendo**	**podido**
Present	puedo	puedes	puede	podemos	podéis	pueden
Preterit	pude	pudiste	pudo	pudimos	pudisteis	pudieron
Future	podré	podrás	podrá	podremos	podréis	podrán
Conditional	podría	podrías	podría	podríamos	podríais	podrían
	poner	*to put, place*			**poniendo**	**puesto**
Present	pongo	pones	pone	ponemos	ponéis	ponen
Preterit	puse	pusiste	puso	pusimos	pusisteis	pusieron
Future	pondré	pondrás	pondrá	pondremos	pondréis	pondrán
Conditional	pondría	pondrías	pondría	pondríamos	pondríais	pondrían
Imperative (tú)	pon	no pongas				

	querer	*to want*			**queriendo**	**querido**
Present	quiero	quieres	quiere	queremos	queréis	quieren
Preterit	quise	quisiste	quiso	quisimos	quisisteis	quisieron
Future	querré	querrás	querrá	querremos	querréis	querrán
Conditional	querría	querrías	querría	querríamos	querríais	querrían

	saber	*to know*			**sabiendo**	**sabido**
Present	sé	sabes	sabe	sabemos	sabéis	saben
Preterit	supe	supiste	supo	supimos	supisteis	supieron
Future	sabré	sabrás	sabrá	sabremos	sabréis	sabrán
Conditional	sabría	sabrías	sabría	sabríamos	sabríais	sabrían
Present Subj.	sepa	sepas	sepa	sepamos	sepáis	sepan

	salir	*to leave*			**saliendo**	**salido**
Present	salgo	sales	sale	salimos	salís	salen
Future	saldré	saldrás	saldrá	saldremos	saldréis	saldrán
Conditional	saldría	saldrías	saldría	saldríamos	saldríais	saldrían
Imperative (tú)	sal	no salgas				

	ser	*to be*			**siendo**	**sido**
Present	soy	eres	es	somos	sois	son
Preterit	fui	fuiste	fue	fuimos	fuisteis	fueron
Imperfect	era	eras	era	éramos	erais	eran
Present Subj.	sea	seas	sea	seamos	seáis	sean
Imperative (tú)	sé	no seas				

	tener	*to have*			**teniendo**	**tenido**
Present	tengo	tienes	tiene	tenemos	tenéis	tienen
Preterit	tuve	tuviste	tuvo	tuvimos	tuvisteis	tuvieron
Future	tendré	tendrás	tendrá	tendremos	tendréis	tendrán
Conditional	tendría	tendrías	tendría	tendríamos	tendríais	tendrían
Imperative (tú)	ten	no tengas				

	traer	*to bring*			**trayendo**	**traído**
Present	traigo	traes	trae	traemos	traéis	traen
Preterit	traje	trajiste	trajo	trajimos	trajisteis	trajeron

	valer	*to be worth*			**valiendo**	**valido**
Present	valgo	vales	vale	valemos	valéis	valen
Future	valdré	valdrás	valdrá	valdremos	valdréis	valdrán
Conditional	valdría	valdrías	valdría	valdríamos	valdríais	valdrían
Imperative (tú)	val	no valgas				

	venir	*to come*			**viniendo**	**venido**
Present	vengo	vienes	viene	venimos	venís	vienen
Preterit	vine	viniste	vino	vinimos	vinisteis	vinieron
Future	vendré	vendrás	vendrá	vendremos	vendréis	vendrán
Conditional	vendría	vendrías	vendría	vendríamos	vendríais	vendrían
Imperative (tú)	ven	no vengas				

	ver	*to see*			**viendo**	**visto**
Present	veo	ves	ve	vemos	veis	ven
Preterit	vi	viste	vio	vimos	visteis	vieron
Imperfect	veía	veías	veía	veíamos	veíais	veían

Principal Parts of Some Common Verbs

Infinitive	Present Indicative	Preterit	Present Participle	Past Participle	Meaning
abrir	abro	abrí	abriendo	abierto	to open
agorar	agüero	agoré	agorando	agorado	to predict
andar	ando	anduve	andando	andado	to walk, go
averiguar	averiguo	averigüé	averiguando	averiguado	to investigate
caber	quepo	cupe	cabiendo	cabido	to fit
caer	caigo	caí	cayendo	caído	to fall
cerrar	cierro	cerré	cerrando	cerrado	to close
coger	cojo	cogí	cogiendo	cogido	to seize, grasp
conocer	conozco	conocí	conociendo	conocido	to know
conseguir	consigo	conseguí	consiguiendo	conseguido	to get, obtain
construir	construyo	construí	construyendo	construido	to build
contar	cuento	conté	contando	contado	to count; to tell
corregir	corrijo	corregí	corrigiendo	corregido	to correct
creer	creo	creí	creyendo	creído	to think
cruzar	cruzo	crucé	cruzando	cruzado	to cross
cubrir	cubro	cubrí	cubriendo	cubierto	to cover
dar	doy	di	dando	dado	to give
decir	digo	dije	diciendo	dicho	to say, tell
delinquir	delinco	delinquí	delinquiendo	delinquido	to be guilty
descubrir	descubro	descubrí	descubriendo	descubierto	to discover
deshacer	deshago	deshice	deshaciendo	deshecho	to undo, destroy
despedirse	me despido	me despedí	despidiéndose	despedido	to say goodbye to
destruir	destruyo	destruí	destruyendo	destruido	to destroy
devolver	devuelvo	devolví	devolviendo	devuelto	to return
dirigir	dirijo	dirigí	dirigiendo	dirigido	to direct
distinguir	distingo	distinguí	distinguiendo	distinguido	to distinguish
divertirse	me divierto	me divertí	divirtiéndose	divertido	to have a good time
dormir	duermo	dormí	durmiendo	dormido	to sleep
enviar	envío	envié	enviando	enviado	to send
erguir	yergo/irgo	erguí	irguiendo	erguido	to erect
errar	yerro	erré	errando	errado	to err; to miss
escribir	escribo	escribí	escribiendo	escrito	to write
esparcir	esparzo	esparcí	esparciendo	esparcido	to scatter, spread
estar	estoy	estuve	estando	estado	to be
gruñir	gruño	gruñí	gruñendo	gruñido	to grunt; to snarl
haber	he	hube	habiendo	habido	to have
hacer	hago	hice	haciendo	hecho	to do
huir	huyo	huí	huyendo	huido	to escape, flee
ir	voy	fui	yendo	ido	to go
irse	me voy	me fui	yéndose	ido	to go away

Infinitive	Present Indicative	Preterit	Present Participle	Past Participle	Meaning
jugar	juego	jugué	jugando	jugado	to play
leer	leo	leí	leyendo	leído	to read
lucir	luzco	lucí	luciendo	lucido	to illuminate
mentir	miento	mentí	mintiendo	mentido	to lie, tell a lie
morir	muero	morí	muriendo	muerto	to die
mover	muevo	moví	moviendo	movido	to move
oír	oigo	oí	oyendo	oído	to hear
oler	huelo	olí	oliendo	olido	to smell
pagar	pago	pagué	pagando	pagado	to pay
pedir	pido	pedí	pidiendo	pedido	to ask for, request
perder	pierdo	perdí	perdiendo	perdido	to lose
picar	pico	piqué	picando	picado	to prick, sting
poder	puedo	pude	pudiendo	podido	to be able, can
poner	pongo	puse	poniendo	puesto	to put, place
querer	quiero	quise	queriendo	querido	to want, wish
reducir	reduzco	reduje	reduciendo	reducido	to reduce
reír	río	reí	riendo	reído	to laugh
repetir	repito	repetí	repitiendo	repetido	to repeat
resolver	resuelvo	resolví	resolviendo	resuelto	to resolve
romper	rompo	rompí	rompiendo	roto	to break, tear
saber	sé	supe	sabiendo	sabido	to know
salir	salgo	salí	saliendo	salido	to leave
seguir	sigo	seguí	siguiendo	seguido	to follow, pursue
sentir	siento	sentí	sintiendo	sentido	to feel (sorry)
ser	soy	fui	siendo	sido	to be
servir	sirvo	serví	sirviendo	servido	to serve
situar	sitúo	situé	situando	situado	to put, place
tener	tengo	tuve	teniendo	tenido	to have
traer	traigo	traje	trayendo	traído	to bring
valer	valgo	valí	valiendo	valido	to be worth
vencer	venzo	vencí	venciendo	vencido	to conquer, defeat
venir	vengo	vine	viniendo	venido	to come
ver	veo	vi	viendo	visto	to see
vestir	visto	vestí	vistiendo	vestido	to put on, wear
volver	vuelvo	volví	volviendo	vuelto	to return, go back

Glossary

abandon   abandonar; dejar; desertar
  abandon oneself   abandonarse; tirarse
abbreviate   abreviar
abdicate   abdicar
be **able to**   poder
be **absent**   faltar
absolve   absolver
absorb   absorber
abstain   abstener(se)
abuse   abusar
accede, agree   acceder
accelerate   acelerar
accept   aceptar; admitir
acclaim   aclamar
accommodate   acomodar
accompany   acompañar
accuse   acusar; culpar
accustom   acostumbrar
  be **accustomed**   soler
  become **accustomed**   familiarizar(se)
ache, pain   doler
achieve   lograr
get **acquainted**   relacionarse
acquit   absolver
act, behave   manejarse
  act as   estar de
adapt   adaptar
  adapt oneself   adaptarse
add   añadir
  add, join   agregar
adhere, stick   adherir(se)
be **adjacent**   colindar; lindar
adjoin   colindar; lindar
adjust, fit   ajustar; adaptar
admire   admirar(se)
admit   admitir
  admit (*medical*)   internar
adopt   adoptar
adore   adorar
adorn   adornar
advance   adelantar; anticipar; avanzar
take **advantage of**   abusar de; aprovechar(se); valerse de
advise   aconsejar; prevenir; recomendar
affect   afectar
be **afraid**   espantarse; temer(se)

aggravate   agravar
agitate   agitar(se)
ago (*time*)   hacer
agree   acordar; acceder; aceptar; avenirse; comprometerse; conformar; consentir; convenir; quedar en; transigir
  agree with/against   ir con/contra
  be in **agreement**   avenirse
be **ahead**   llevar
  get **ahead**   adelantarse
aid   ayudar
aim   apuntar
air out   ventear
alert   advertir
be **alike**   asemejarse
allow, let   consentir; dejar; permitir; tolerar
alloy   ligar
allude   aludir
alter   mudar
alternate   alternar
be **amazed**   admirarse; asombrarse; espantarse
amount to   ascender a; importar
amuse   divertir
  amuse oneself   entretenerse
anger   enojar; indignar
  get **angry**   calentarse; enfadarse; enojarse
announce   anunciar
annoy   disgustar; enfadar(se)
  be **annoyed**   enojarse
  get **annoyed**   molestarse
anoint   ungir
answer   contestar; responder
anticipate   anticipar
apologize   disculparse; excusarse
appeal   apelar; interesar
appear   aparecer; asomar(se); presentarse
  appear, look like   parecer
applaud   aplaudir
apply   aplicar
appraise   tasar
approach   acercar(se)
appropriate   adueñarse de; apropiarse (de)
argue   discutir; reñir
arise   surgir
arouse   excitar
arrange   acomodar; arreglar; disponer; ordenar
  come to an **arrangement**   entenderse
arrive   llegar
ascend, climb   ascender
be **ashamed**   abochornarse; avergonzarse

set **aside**   apartar
ask   preguntar
  ask for   pedir; rogar; solicitar
fall **asleep**   cabecear; dormirse
aspire   aspirar
assemble   reunir
assess   tasar
assign   destinar
assist   asistir
associate   asociar; tratar
  associate, mix   rozarse
assume   suponer; cargar con
assure   asegurar
be **astonished**   admirarse
become **attached**   apegarse
attack   acometer; atacar
attain   lograr
attempt   intentar
attend   asistir; atender; concurrir
  attend to, look after   ocuparse
  attend to, respond   acudir a
pay **attention**   fijarse; reparar
attract   seducir
avoid   ceder; guardar(se); huir; rehuir
await   esperar
keep **awake**   desvelar(se)
  awaken   despertar
make one **aware**   enterar

ban   prohibir; vedar
baptize   bautizar
bargain over   regatear
base oneself   fundamentarse
bathe   bañar; bañarse
be   encontrarse; estar; hacer; hallarse; ser
  be about   estar para
  be almost   ir para
  be at, sell at   estar a
  be (out, away)   estar de
  be getting on for   ir para
  be, remain   quedar
bear   tolerar
  bear, stand   resistir
beat   vencer
  beat, churn   batir
become   hacerse; ir para; llegar; meterse a; volverse
beg   rogar
begin   comenzar; empezar; ponerse; principiar
behave, conduct   conducirse

believe (oneself) creer(se)
belong pertenecer
bend down encorvarse; inclinarse
bet apostar
get **better** mejorar
be **between** mediar
bind ligar
  bind oneself obligarse
bite morder
  bite (*insects*) picar
blame acusar; culpar
bleed sangrar
bless bendecir
blind cegar(se)
block impedir
blow soplar
boast glorificarse
boil hervir
  boil, bubble bullir
border limitar; lindar
bore aburrir
  be *or* become **bored** aburrirse
  bore, drill taladrar
be **born** nacer
bother fregar; molestar(se)
bow to inclinarse
brand marcar
  brand as tildar de
break quebrar; romper(se)
  break into forzar
breakfast desayunar
  have **breakfast** desayunarse
breathe in aspirar
bring traer
  bring closer/over acercar
broadcast transmitir
build construir; fabricar; hacer
bump zampar
bundle up abrigarse
burn freír
  burn (oneself) quemar(se)
  burn (up) abrasar(se)
burst romper
bury sepultar
busy oneself ocuparse
be **busy** with estar en
butt topar
buy comprar
buzz zumbar

cackle   cacarear
call   llamar
  call for   convocar
camp   acampar
can   poder
care, worry   preocupar(se)
  take **care of**   atender; cuidar, mirar por; occuparse
  take great **care**   desvelarse
  take **care of oneself**   tratarse
be **careful not to**   guardar(se)
carry   traer
  carry (off)   llevar(se)
  carry forward   llevar adelante
  carry out   llevar a cabo
  carry out *or* **fulfill**   cumplir
carve   trinchar
cast   vaciar; tirar
catch, seize   agarrar(se)
  catch fire   abrasarse
  catch in a net   enredar
  catch on   aclararse
  catch up   alcanzar
  get **caught** in   enredarse
be the **cause of**   estar en
cease   cesar
change   cambiar; convertir(se); mudar(se); transformar(se); trocar; variar; virar
take **charge**   encargarse
charge with   acusar de
charm   seducir
chat   charlar, platicar
chatter   charlar
cheat   engañar; timar
cheer (up)   alegrar(se); animar
chew (up)   comerse
be **chilled**   pasmarse
choose   elegir; escoger; optar
claim   reclamar
clarify   aclarar; explicarse
clash   chocar
clean (oneself)   limpiar(se)
cleanse   limpiar(se)
clear (up)   absolver; aclarar; constar
climb   escalar; trepar; ascender
  climb (up)   subir(se)
cling to   abrazarse de
close (oneself)   cerrar(se)
clothe   vestir
clutch   abrazarse de
collaborate   colaborar
collect   colegir; recoger

collide   chocar
comb   peinarse
combine   combinar; juntar; reunir; unir(se)
come   llegar; venir
  come from   arrancar de (*fig*), proceder de
  come from, arise   provenir de
  come/go to   acudir a
  come together   juntarse
  come under   acogerse
comfort   animar
command   mandar
comment on   comentar
commit   cometer; compremeter
  commit an outrage   atentar
  commit oneself to   comprometerse a
  commit suicide   matarse
  make a **commitment**   comprometerse
communicate   comunicar
compare   comparar; contraponer
compensate   compensar
compete   competir; contender; optar
complain   lamentarse; quejarse
complete   cumplir; terminar
compose   componer
comprise   incluir
compromise   compremeter; transigir
conceal   ocultar
concentrate   concentrar
concern   interesar
  concern oneself   ocuparse; preocuparse
conclude   concluir; terminar
concoct (*fig*)   zurcir
condemn   condenar
conduct, behave   conducir(se)
confess   acusarse de; confesar
confide in   abrir a/con; fiar
  be **confided in**   fiar
conform to   conformarse con
confound   enredar
confront   enfrentarse
confuse   confundir; enredar
  get **confused**   confundirse
congratulate   felicitar
connect   comunicar; relacionar
consent   consentir
consider   creer; dar por/como
  consider oneself   tenerse
  be **considered as**   pasar por
consist   consistir
  consist of   constar de; componerse

construct construir
consult consultar
contain incluir
contaminate infectar
contend contender
  contend (with) bregar
be **content** satisfacer
continue continuar; proseguir; seguir
contract encoger(se)
contrast contrastar
contravene contravenir
contribute contribuir
convalesce convalecer
be **convenient** convenir
converge converger
converse conversar
convert convertir
convict condenar
convince convencer(se)
cook cocer; cocinar; hervir
cooperate colaborar
correct corregir
correspond corresponder
cost costar; importar; valer
cough toser
count contar
act **counter to** contravenir
court enamorar
cover cubrir; forrar; llenar
  cover (up) tapar
crash chocar
create, make hacer
creep trepar
cringe encogerse
criticize zaherir
cross atravesar; cruzar
  cross out borrar
cry llorar
  cry out, shout gritar
cure (oneself) curar(se)
curse maldecir
cut (up) cortar; trinchar

be **damned** condenarse
damp(en) mojar
dance bailar
dare osar
  dare to atreverse a
darn zurcir
dash, run off dispararse

date (from)   datar (de)
  date *or* **go out**   salir
deal   traficar; tratar
  deal, trade   comerciar
  deal with   haberse
be **deceitful**   engañar
deceive   burlar; engañar
decide   decidir(se); determinarse
  decide, agree on   acordar
  decide between   optar entre
decorate   adornar
dedicate   dedicar
  apply oneself   aplicarse
deem   juzgar; creer
defeat   vencer
defend (oneself)   defender(se)
delay   entretener; tardar
deliver   entregar
demolish   abatir
demonstrate   demostrar
deny   negar; privar
depend   atenerse; depender
deposit   ingresar
be **depressed**   abatirse
deprive   privar
derive   derivar; descender
  be **derived**   derivarse
descend   bajar; descender
describe   describir
desert   desertar
deserve   merecer
desire   desear
  desire, die for   deshacerse por
desist   desistir
despair   desesperar
destine   destinar
destroy   destruir
detain   detener; entretener
determine   determinar
  be **determined**   empeñarse
detest, hate   maldecir
deviate   desviar
devote (oneself)   dedicar(se); entregarse
  be **devoted**   aplicarse
die   morir(se); perecer
  die for, desire   deshacerse por
  die of, burn with   abrasarse de
  be **dying to**   morirse por
be **different**   diferenciarse
differentiate   diferenciarse

dip   zambullir
direct   dirigir
disappear   borrarse; perderse
discover   hallar
discuss   discutir; consultar
dismantle   abatir(se)
dispense   dispensar
display   exponer; mostrar
displease   disgustar
dispose   disponer(se)
dissuade   disuadir
distinguish   reconocer
   be **distinguished**   distinguir(se)
distribute   repartir
dive   bucear
   skin dive   bucear; zambullirse
divert   desviar
divide   compartir; partir; repartir
divorce   divorciar
   get a **divorce**   divorciarse
do   hacer
   do without   prescindir
double   doblar
doubt   dudar
drain   escurrir; vaciar
draw in   retraer
   draw near to   acercarse
dream   soñar
drench   empapar
dress   vestir
   get **dressed**   vestirse
drill, bore   taladrar
drink   beber
   drink, toast   brindar
   drink up   apurar
drive   conducir; manejar; ir
drown   ahogar(se)
drop   caer(se)
dry   secar(se)
   dry up   abrasarse
be **due**   vencer
dye   teñir

earn   ganar(se)
eat   comer
   eat breakfast   desayunar(se)
   eat lunch   almorzar
   eat up   comerse
have an **effect**   trascender

elevate   elevar
embark   embarcar
feel **embarrassed**   abochornarse
embrace   abrazar
emerge   surgir
emit   trascender
emphasize   enfatizar
empty (out)   vaciar
be **enchanted with**   prendarse de
encourage   animar
enclose   encerrar
end, end up   parar
  come to an **end**   acabar
  end up   concluir; terminar
  end with   acabar con
endanger   atentar
endure   tolerar
make an **enemy**   enemistar(se)
engrave   tallar
engulf   hundir
enjoy (oneself)   disfrutar; divertirse; gozar
enlighten   alumbrar
enliven, liven up   animar
be **enough, reach**   alcanzar; llegar
entail   suponer; traducirse (*fig*)
become **entangled**   enredarse
enter   entrar; ingresar
entertain   divertir; entretener
entrust   confiarse; encargar; fiar
equal   igualar
  be **equal**   igualarse
erase, rub out   borrar
escape   escapar; salir
espress (oneself)   expresar(se)
establish   constituir; formar
  be **established**   constar
estimate   estimar
exact, levy   exigir
exceed   llevar; rebasar
excel   lucirse
exchange   cambiar(se); canjear; trocar
excite   excitar
  get **excited**   excitarse
exclude   excluir
excuse   disculpar; dispensar; excusar; perdonar
exercise   ejercer; practicar
expect   aguardar; esperar(se)
  be **expected**   estimar
expel   expulsar

be an **expert on**   entender
explain (oneself)   explicar(se)
expose (oneself)   exponer(se)
export   exportar
extend   extenderse
extinguish   apagar

face   enfrentar(se)
fade   borrarse
fail *(business)*   quebrar
fall   caer
  fall back   recaer
  fall down   caerse; tumbar(se)
  fall ill   enfermar
  fall in love   enamorarse de; prendarse
  fall into   incurrir en
  fall on/in/upon   incidir en
  fall out   indisponer(se); romper con
  fall short   faltar
familiarize oneself   familiarizarse
fascinate   seducir
fasten   fijar
be in **favor of**   estar por
fear   temer
feel   sentir(se); tentar; tocar
feign   pretend
fetch   traer
fight   batallar; batirse; combatir; luchar
fill (up)   llenar(se)
  fill to the brim   colmar
  be **filled with**   caber de
filter   colar; filtrar
find   encontrar
  find guilty   condenar
  find (oneself)   hallar(se)
  find oneself   encontrarse
  find out   averiguar, enterarse
finish   instruirse; terminar
  just **finish, finish**   acabar
catch **fire**   incendiarse
  fire, shoot   disparar
  be **fired**   despedir de
  set on **fire**   incendiar
  set **fire to**   encender
fit   caber
  fit, suit   sentar
fix   arreglar(se); componer; fijar
flee   huir

fling   tirar
flow with   manar
fly   volar
focus   fijar
fold, bend   doblar
follow   seguir
get **fond of**   aficionarse
fool oneself   engañarse
forbid   privar; prohibir; vedar
force   obligar
   force (upon)   forzar
forget   olvidar(se)
form   formar(se)
found   fundar
free   librar
  free from   liberar
freeze   helar; pasmar
frighten   asustar; espantar
fry   freír(se)
fulfill   cumplir; llenar
function   funcionar
make **fun**   bromear
furnish   amueblar
fuse together   fundir(se)

gain   ganar(se)
gamble (away)   jugarse
gather (up)   colegir; recoger
gaze at   mirar
get   conseguir; ganar(se); lograr; obtener; tomar; traer;
  get (hold of)   hacer con
  get away   escaparse; zafarse
  get by   pasar con
  get halfway   mediar
  get into (sth)   echarse
  get into, enter into   entrar; meterse en (*fig*)
  get off   bajar de
  get on, ride   montar
  get on well   simpatizar
  get on well with   avenirse con
  get out of   escaparse de
  get to   ponerse a/en
  get together   reunirse
  get up   levantarse
give   dar
  give, present   regalar
  give back   regresar
  give off   despedir

give oneself   darse
give up   desesperar; desprenderse; renunciar
be **glad**   alegrarse
glorify   glorificar
glue   pegar
go   ir
  go (along)   andar
  go about (sth)   ir sobre (algo)
  go after   ir sobre; tras
  go against   ir contra
  go along   transitar
  go away   irse, marchar(se), egresar; alejarse
  go back   remontarse
  go by   pasar por
  go down to   bajar a; descender a
  go for/by   ir de/en
  go forward   adelantarse
  go into (deeply)   internarse en
  go into, get into   meterse en
  go off   dispararse
  go on   continuar
  go out   salir
  go to bed   acostarse
  go up, climb   subir
  go with   acompañar
have a **good time**   divertirse
  be **good for**   servir para
say **goodbye**   despedir(se)
govern   gobernar
  govern, rule   regir
grab   agarrar
graduate   recibirse
grasp, seize   coger
  grasp, hold   agarrar
gratify   placer
gravitate   gravitar
graze   rozar
greet, receive   acoger
grieve (over)   apenar
grow   crecer
grumble   quejarse
guard (sports)   marcar
guess   adivinar
guide   guiar
  be **guided**   guiarse

be in the **habit of**   acostumbrar; soler
  get into the **habit of**   dar en

haggle over   regatear
hand   dar; entregar
  hand over   pasar
handle   manejar; tratar
hang   colgar; suspender; tender
  hang oneself   colgarse
happen   ocurrir; pasar; suceder
be **happy**   alegrarse; contentar
harm oneself   lacrarse
hasten   apresurar
hate   aborrecer; maldecir
have   haber; tener; disponer de
  have, carry   llevar
  have just   acabar de
  have to, must   deber; tener que
head   cabecear
  head for   dirigirse
hear   escuchar; oír
heat   calentar
  heat up   abochornar
help   ayudar
hesitate   vacilar; dudar
hide   ocultar(se)
hit   dar (de)
  hit on/upon   acertar con
  hit oneself (*fig*)   darse; pegar
hold   agarrar
  hold (up)   detener
  take **hold of**   coger
  hold on   quedarse
  hold up   mantener; sostener
honor   honrar
  be **honored**   honrar
hope (for)   esperar
get **hot**   acalorarse
hug   abrazarse
hum   zumbar
hurl   botar; tirar
hurry   afanar; apresurar; apurar; acelerarse
hurt   doler; herir; lastimar; resentirse

ignite   encender
ignore   ignorar
make **ill**   enfermar
illuminate   alumbrar; lucir
impede   impedir
implicate   comprometer
import   importar

be **important**   importar
impose   imponer
impregnate   impregnar
improve   mejorar
incline, bend   inclinar
be half **inclined to**   estar por
  inclined towards   derivar hacia
include   incluir
  be **included**   constar
increase   añadir; crecer
incur   incurrir
indicate   indicar
indict oneself   condenarse
get **indignant**   indignarse
induce   inclinar; inducir
become **infected**   infectarse
infer, gather   colegir
influence   influir
inform   avisar; enterar; informar
  inform oneself   imponerse; informarse
  gather **information**   informarse
inhabit   habitar
inherit   heredar
inject   inyectar
injure   herir; lacrar
  injure (oneself)   lastimar(se)
inquire   interesarse; preguntar
insert   meter en
insist   insistir
inspire   inspirar
  be **inspired**   inspirarse
instruct   enseñar; instruir
intend   intentar; pensar
interest   interesar
  be **interested**   interesarse
interfere   atravesarse; interferir(se)
intervene   intervenir
have an **interview**   entrevistar
introduce   introducir
invigorate   esforzar
invite   convidar; invitar
involve sb in sth   meter a uno en algo
  get **involved**   comprometerse; enredarse; envolverse
irritate   enfadar(se)
itch   picar

join   ingresar; juntar; trabar; unir(se)
joke   bromear
judge   juzgar

jump   brincar; lanzarse; saltar; tirarse
juxtapose   yuxtaponer

keep   guardar; mantenerse
  keep, protect   guardar
  keep away   apartarse
  keep watch   velar
kick   dar de
kid, crack jokes   bromear
kill (oneself)   matar(se)
kiss   besar(se)
knock down   abatir; tumbar
know   conocer; saber

lack   carecer
be **lacking**   faltar
lament   lamentar(se)
laugh   reír(se)
launch   lanzar(se)
lay out   disponer
lead   guiar
  lead by   llevar
  lead to   conducir a
lean   apoyar(se); ladearse
  lean, rest on   descansar
  lean back   reclinar(se)
learn   aprender; instruirse
leave   abandonar; dejar; irse; marcharse; salir
be **left**   quedar
lend (oneself)   prestar(se)
let, allow   dejar
  let oneself be   dejarse
liberate   liberar
lie   yacer
  lie down   acostarse, tenderse, tumbarse
lie, tell a lie   mentir
lift (up), raise   alzar; levantar
light   encender
  light up   lucir
lighten   aclarar
  lighten, relieve   aliviar(se)
like   gustar; simpatizar
  be **like** *or* **take after**   salir (a)
be **like**   semejarse
limit (oneself)   limitar(se)
line (with)   forrar
link   trabar; comunicar
listen   oír
  listen (to)   escuchar

live vivir
  live in, inhabit habitar
load cargar; embarcar
  be **loaded** caerse
locate situar
lock cerrar
  lock in/up encerrar
  lock oneself encerrarse
lodge acomodar; fijarse
be **long** tardar
long for suspirar
look (at) mirar
  look, appear parecer
  look after cuidar; mirar por; valer por; vigilar
  look alike parecerse
  look at oneself mirarse
  look for buscar
  look on/out on dar a
  look up mirarse
loosen zafar
  get **loose** zafarse
lose perder
  get **lost** perderse
  lose hope desesperarse
love amar; querer
  inspire love enamorar
lower (oneself) bajarse; rebajar(se)
lunch, have lunch almorzar

maintain mantener
make fabricar; hacer; provocar
  make do pasar con
  make up componer; pintarse
manage acertar; alcanzar; lograr; manejar(se); regir
manifest manifestar(se)
manufacture fabricar
march marchar(se)
mark marcar
marry casar
  get **married** casarse
matter, count contar
mean significar
measure medir
  measure up to medirse con
meet concurrir; conocer; dar con; encontrarse; juntarse; tropezarse
mend zurcir
mention mencionar
merit merecer
be in the **middle** mediar
mingle mezclar

misinterpret   equivocar
miss   faltar; perder
  miss, yearn for   extrañar
  be **missing**   faltar
mistake   confundir; equivocar
  (make a) **mistake**   equivocarse
misunderstand   equivocar
mix   alternar; combinar; revolver
  mix (up)   mezclar
  mix, associate   rozarse
  mix with   alternar con
  get **mixed up**   mezclarse; enredarse
moisten   mojar
mold   plasmar
mop   fregar
motivate   motivar
mount   montar
move   ir; marchar(se); mover(se); provocar
  move, stir   bullir
  move away   retirar(se)
  move away, remove   alejar
  move forward   adelantar
murmur   murmurar
must   deber (de); tener que
mutter   murmurar

name   llamar
narrow   estrechar
navigate   navegar
be **necessary** to   haber que
need   necesitar
  still **need to**   faltar por
net   enredar
nibble   picotear
have a **night** out   trasnochar
nod   cabecear
take **note** of   percatarse
notice   advertir; fijarse; percatarse

be **obedient**   obedecer
obey   obedecer
observe   advertir; observar
obtain   conseguir; lograr; obtener
occupy   ocupar
occur (to oneself)   ocurrir(se)
be **offended**   picarse; resentirse
offer   ofrecer
open (up)   abrir
  open out   abrirse
operate   manejar; funcionar

oppose   contraponer; oponerse
  be **opposed**   oponerse
order   mandar; ordenar
orient   orientar
be **orientated**   orientarse
originate   proceder
ought to   deber
overcome   sobreponerse
  overcome, be filled   acometer
overlook   dar a
oversee   velar
overwhelm   sumirse
owe   adeudar(se); deber
own, have   disponer

pain, ache   doler
paint   pintar
pamper, spoil   consentir
be **parched**   abrasarse
pardon   perdonar
part with   desprender(se) (de)
pass   pasar
  pass (off)   pasarse
paste   pegar
pawn   empeñar
pay   pagar
  pay attention   fijarse
peck   picar
penetrate   traspasar; internarse
permit   permitir; consentir
persist   persistir; empeñarse
perspire   transpirar
persuade   decidir
phone   telefonear
pick   picotear
  pick (out)   escoger
  pick a quarrel   meterse
  pick up   recoger
  pick up, lift   alzar
pierce   traspasar
pity   compadecer
place   situar; introducir
  place, put   colocar
  place (oneself)   poner(se); colocarse
  take **place early**   anticiparse
  place, put   meter en
plan   planear
plant   plantar
play   jugar; pulsar; tocar
plead with   rogar

please   gustar; placer; satisfacer
  please, be pleasant to   complacer
  please, be pleasing   agradar; gustar
  be **pleased**   contentar
pledge   empeñar
plunge   zambullir; sumir(se)
take **possession** of   adueñarse; apoderarse de
pounce   abatirse
pour (out)   manar; verter
practice   ejercer; practicar
pray   orar; rezar
preach   predicar
predict   pronosticar
prefer   inclinarse; preferir
preoccupy   preocupar
prepare   disponerse; hacer; prevenir
  prepare (oneself)   preparar(se)
present (oneself)   presentar(se)
present, give   regalar
press dry   escurrir
put **pressure**   influir
pretend   fingir
prevail   imponerse
prevent   impedir; privar
be **priced**   estar a
print   imprimir
be **probably**   haber de
proceed to, go in   pasar a
produce   dar
prohibit   prohibir; vedar
promise   prometer
promote   ascender; elevar
pronounce   pronunciar
prophesy   adivinar
propose   proponer
protect (oneself)   abrigar; amparar; cuidarse; defender; proteger(se)
  protect, watch over   guardar
protest   protestar
provide (oneself)   proveer(se)
provoke   meterse; provocar
pull   tirar
pulsate   pulsar
purchase   comprar
pursue   seguir
push   empujar
put   poner
  put, place   meter en
  put away hurriedly   zampar
  put down   someter
  put on shoes   calzar

put on top   sobreponer
put out   apagar
put to bed   acostar

quarrel   reñir
quench   apagarse
question   preguntar
  be a **question of**   tratarse de
  question, doubt   dudar en
quicken   apurar; apresurar
be *or* keep **quiet**   callar(se)
quit   dejar de

rain   llover
raise, lift   elevar; levantar; subir
rape, ravish   forzar
reach   alcanzar; llegar; ponerse a/en; trascender
read   leer
get **ready (to)**   aprestarse; disponerse
rebel   rebelarse
recall   acordarse; recordar
receive   recibir
  receive, greet   acoger
reciprocate   corresponder
recognize   reconocer
recommend   recomendar
recount   referir
recover   convalecer; curarse
rectify   enderezar(se)
recuperate   convalecer
reduce   rebajar
refer   remitirse; referir(se)
reflect   reflejar
refrain   abstener(se)
take **refuge**   acogerse
refuse   negar; oponerse; rehusar; resistirse
have **regard** for   estimar
  regard, consider   dar por/como
regret   arrenpentirse; dolerse; lamentar
relapse   recaer
relate   relacionar
release   liberar
relieve   aliviar(se); relevar(se)
relinquish   abdicar de
rely   atenerse
remain   estar sin
  remain, stay   quedar(se)
remember   acordarse de
remind (oneself)   recordar

remove (oneself)   quitar(se)
  remove, move away   alejar
renounce   abdicar; renunciar
rent   alquilar
repair   reparar
repeat   repetir
repent   arrepentirse; dolerse
replace   relevar; suplir
reply   contestar; responder
report   informar
reproach   zaherir
request   pedir; solicitar
require   obligar
rescue   librar
resemble   parecerse
resent   resentirse
resign   renunciar
resign oneself   conformarse; resignarse
resist   resistir
resolve   resolver(se)
resort   acudir
respect oneself   estimarse
respond   acudir; responder
be **responsible (for)**   responder (de, por)
rest   descansar
restrict   limitar
result   resultar; traducirse (*fig*)
retract   retraer
return   devolver; regresar; volver
reveal   manifestar
reveal, register   acusar
revolt   rebelarse
revolve   girar
get **rid of**   deshacerse de
ride   cabalgar; ir; montar
get **right**   acertar
ring   sonar
rise   crecer; elevarse; levantarse
run the **risk** of   exponerse
roar   tronar
roll over   voltear
root (out, up)   arrancar
rotate, twist   girar
rub (on)   rozar
ruin   deshacer
rule, govern   gobernar; regir
rummage about   revolver
run   correr
  run *or* **manage**   regir

run across   encontrarse con, toparse
run away   escaparse; huir
run into   dar con; pegar
run into/across   tropezar con
run off   dispararse
run out of   acabarse
rush   abalanzarse; apurarse

become **sad**   apenar
sail   navegar; embarcarse
satisfy   satisfacer
  satiate   hartar
  be satisfied   hartarse; satisfacerse
save   librar
  save, avoid   ahorrarse
  save, economize   ahorrar(se)
say   decir
  say goodbye   despedir
scare   asustar
  be **scared**   espantarse
scatter, spread   esparcir
score   marcar
scream, shout   gritar
seal (*with wax*)   lacrar
seat   sentar
secure   asegurar(se); fijar
seduce   seducir
see (oneself)   ver(se)
  see off   despedir
seek protection   ampararse
seem, appear   parecer
seep   traspasar
seethe   hervir
seize, grasp   coger
select   escoger; elegir
sell   vender
  sell on credit   fiar
  sell oneself   venderse
  be **sold**   venderse
send   enviar; mandar; remitir
sense, feel   oler
sentence   condenar
separate   separar; apartar; desprender
serve   servir
be of **service**   servir
set   figar; poner
  set against   indisponer
  set aside   apartar, destinarse
  set off, leave   partir

set on fire quemarse
set up fire disponer; fundamentar; fundar
settle fijarse
sew up zurcir
shake temblar
  shake, stir agitar
shape formar(se); plasmar
  shape, put together conformar
share, divide compartir
shave afeitar(se)
shelter abrigar
  shelter, harbor acoger
shine dar; lucir; traslucirse
shoot tirar
  shoot, fire disparar
  shoot down abatir
shout, yell gritar
show asomar; enseñar; manifestar(se); mostrar(se); presentar
  show, reveal acusar
  show (off) demostrar
  show up aparecer
shoot tirar
show exponer
shrink encoger(se)
  shrink from rehuir
shrivel up encoger
shrug encogerse
shut, close cerrar(se)
  shut in encerrar
get **sick** enfermarse
sign firmar; suscribir
  sign for suspirar
be **silent** callarse
be **similar** asemejarse
sing cantar
sink hundir(se); sumir(se)
sit (down) sentar(se)
be **situated** encontrarse
skip saltarse
slaughter matar
slay matar
sleep dormir; trasnochar
  fall **sleep** adormecer(se)
  put to **sleep** adormecer
  get **sleepy** admormecerse
slice trinchar
slide deslizar(se)
sling tirar
slip escurrirse

smash   quebrar
smell   oler(se); trascender
smile   sonreír; reír
smoke   fumar(se)
snatch away   arrancar
sneak in   colarse en
sniff   ventear
snow   nevar
soak   empapar
solve   resolver
be **sorry, apologize**   disculparse
  be **sorry about**   lamentar
  be **sorry for**   dolerse por
  feel **sorry**   compadecer
sound   sonar
sound   sonar
speak   hablar
  be **spoken**   hablarse
speed (up)   acelerar
spend (*money*)   gastar
  spend (*time*)   llevar
  spend the night   trasnochar
spill   tirar; verter
spin, rotate   girar
split   partir
  split, crack   partirse
spoil   consentir; deshacer
spread   extender; tender
  spread, scatter   esparcir
spring   abalanzarse
  spring from   manar de
squeeze   estrecharse
stagger   zamparse
stammer   balbucear
stand up   levantarse
  place, **stand**   colocar(se)
  stand on   pisar
  stand out   distinguirse
start   comenzar; empezar; meterse; romper
startle   asustar
stay, remain   quedar
  stay up   trasnochar
steal   robar; timar
stick   adherir(se); pegar
be **still**   seguir
stir, beat   batir
  stir, shake   agitar
stop   cesar; dejar de; desistir; detener(se); parar
straighten (up)   enderezar(se)
strain (off)   colar; esforzar

find **strange**   extrañar
strengthen   esforzar; fortalecer
stress   enfatizar
strike   dar (de); pegar
strip   desnudar; despojar
strive   afanarse; trabajar
struggle   batallar; combatir; esforzarse; luchar; matarse
study   estudiar
subdue   someter
submerge   sumir
submit   someter
subscribe   suscribir
substitute   suplir; sustituir
succeed   alcanzar; suceder
suffer   sufrir; resentirse; padecer
suggest   proponer; sugerir
suit   convenir
  be **suitable**   convenir
summon   convocar
sunbathe   broncearse
supply   suplir
support   apoyar(se); sostener
  support (oneself)   mantener(se)
suppose   poner; suponer
  be **supposed to**   haber de, deber de
surpass   rebasar
surprise   sorprender
  be **surprised**   extrañarse
  find **surprising**   extrañar
surrender   rendirse; entregarse
survey   medir
suspect   sospechar
suspend   suspender
sustain (oneself)   sustentar(se)
swarm   hervir
sway   vacilar
swear   jurar
  swear, curse   maldecir
sweep   barrer
swim   nadar
  swim, bathe   bañarse
swindle   engañar; timar
swoop on   abatirse sobre

take   llevar; sacar; tomar
  take after   tirar
  take away   llevarse, quitar
  take in   acoger
  take into one's head   dar por
  take it upon oneself   meterse a

take (out)   sacar
take part   intervenir
take (*time*)   tardar
take to   dar en
talk   charlar; conversar; hablar; platicar
tan   broncearse
tangle (up)   enredar
tap (*trees*)   sangrar
taste   probar; saber
teach   enseñar; instruir(se)
tear   romper
  tear off (away)   arrancar
tease   meterse con
telegraph, wire   telegrafiar
telephone   telefonear
tell   contar; decir
tempt   tentar; provocar
tend   tirar; tender
have a tendency   tender
testify   testificar
thank, be thankful   agradecer
there is/are, etc.   hay/había, etc.
thin down   aclarar
think   creer; pensar
  think of oneself as   tomarse por
threaten   amenazar
throw   echar
  throw (away)   botar
  throw (oneself)   arrojar(se); lanzar(se); tirar(se)
thunder   tronar
tie, bind   ligar
tilt   ladear
tip   ladear
  tip over   volcarse
tire   cansar; fatigar
  tire (of)   hastiarse (de)
  get **tired**   cansarse; fatigarse, hartarse
toast, drink   brindar
get **together**   reunirse
  put **together**   asociar
tolerate   tolerar
touch   pegar; rozar; tentar; tocar
  get in touch with   comunicarse (con)
toy with   jugar
trade   comerciar; traficar
be **trained**   formarse
transfer   transferir
transform   transformar
  transform oneself   convertir(se)
translate   poner; traducir; verter

transmit   transmitir
transparent   traslucirse
travel   ir; transitar; viajar
tread on   pisar
treat   tratar
  treat (oneself)   regalar(se)
tremble   temblar
trick   burlar; engañar
trip, stumble   tropezar
triumph   imponerse; triunfar
trust   confiar; fiarse
try   intentar; pretender
  try (on)   probar
  try to   tratar de
tug at   tirar de
turn   doblar; virar; volver
  turn *(age)*   cumplir
  turn (around)   girar
  be one's **turn**   tocar a uno
  turn around   revolverse
  turn off   apagar
  turn on   encender
  turn out   quedar, resultar
  turn over   volcar, voltear
  take **turns**   turnar(se)

be **unaware of**   ignorar
understand   entender
undertake   encargarse de
undo   deshacer
undress   desnudarse; despojarse de
unite   combinar; fundir; juntar; unir(se)
  be **united**   unirse
unmake   deshacer
unveil   desvelar(se)
upholster   forrar
(get) **upset**   disgustar(se); enojar(se); volcar
urge   urgir
be **urgent**   urgir
usually + *inf*   acostumbrar + *inf*
use   usar
  be of **use**   servir
  be **used**   usarse
  be **used as**   servir
  get **used to**   acostumbrar(se); aficionarse
  make **use of**   servirse
  make good **use of**   aprovechar(se)

vacillate   vacilar
vary   variar

veer   virar
violate   contravenir
visit   visitar
vote   votar
vouch for   responder

wait (for)   esperar
  wait for   aguardar
wake (up)   despertar(se)
walk   andar; pasear
want   desear; querer
warm up (*fig*)   acalorarse
warn   advertir; avisar; prevenir
wash (oneself)   lavar(se)
  wash *(dishes)*   fregar
watch   mirar; ver
  watch (*vigil over*)   vigilar; guardar
waver   vacilar
be **weakened**   resentirse
wear   calzar; llevar; traer; usar
(get) **weary**   fatigar(se)
weep   llorar
welcome   recibir
wet   mojar
whisper   murmurar; susurrar
win   ganar(se)
wink   guiñar
wipe   secar
  wipe (off) (oneself)   limpiar(se)
wish   desear
withdraw   retraerse
wobble   vacilar
work   funcionar; trabajar
  work as   andar en; hacer de
  get **worked up**   acalorarse
worry   preocupar(se); apurarse
worship   adorar
be **worth**   merecer; valer
  be **worthy of**   valer por
wound   herir
wrap   envolver
wring out   escurrir
write   escribir
be **wrong**   equivocarse

yawn   bostezar
yearn for   extrañar
yell   gritar
yield   ceder; rendirse